SCHOOLWIDE AND CLASSROOM MANAGEMENT

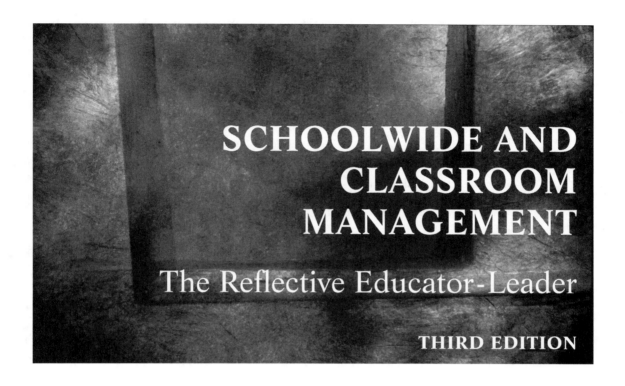

SCHOOLWIDE AND CLASSROOM MANAGEMENT

The Reflective Educator-Leader

THIRD EDITION

LEN A. FROYEN
University of Northern Iowa

ANNETTE M. IVERSON
University of Northern Iowa

Merrill
an imprint of Prentice Hall
Upper Saddle River, New Jersey   Columbus, Ohio

Library of Congress Cataloging-in-Publication Data

Froyen, Len A.
    Schoolwide and classroom management : the reflective educator-leader / Len A. Froyen,
    Annette M. Iverson. — 3rd ed.
       p.   cm.
    Rev. ed. of: Classroom management. c1988.
    Includes bibliographical references (p.) and index.
    ISBN 0-13-573205-0
    1. Classroom management.   I. Iverson, Annette M.
  II. Froyen, Len A.   Classroom management.   III. Title.
  LB3013.F783   1999
  371.102′4—dc21
                                                 98-19226
                                                  CIP

Editor: Debra A. Stollenwerk
Production Editor: Mary Harlan
Design Coordinator: Diane C. Lorenzo
Text Designer: Kip Shaw
Cover Designer: Linda Fares
Production Manager: Pamela D. Bennett
Electronic Text Management: Marilyn Wilson Phelps, Karen L. Bretz, Tracey B. Ward
Illustrations: Kurt Wendling
Director of Marketing: Kevin Flanagan
Marketing Manager: Suzanne Stanton
Marketing Coordinator: Krista Groshong

This book was set in Life by Prentice Hall and was printed and bound by R. R. Donnelley &
Sons Company. The cover was printed by Phoenix Color Corp.

 © 1999 by Prentice-Hall, Inc.
Simon & Schuster/A Viacom Company
Upper Saddle River, New Jersey 07458

Earlier editions, entitled *Classroom Management: The Reflective Teacher-Leader,* © 1993 by
Macmillan Publishing Company, and *Classroom Management: Empowering Teacher-Leaders,*
© 1988 by Merrill Publishing Company.

Photo credits: All photos supplied by the author.

Printed in the United States of America

10 9 8 7 6 5 4 3 2 1

ISBN: 0-13-573205-0

Prentice-Hall International (UK) Limited, *London*
Prentice-Hall of Australia Pty. Limited, *Sydney*
Prentice-Hall of Canada, Inc., *Toronto*
Prentice-Hall Hispanoamericana, S. A., *Mexico*
Prentice-Hall of India Private Limited, *New Delhi*
Prentice-Hall of Japan, Inc., *Tokyo*
Simon & Schuster Asia Pte. Ltd., *Singapore*
Editora Prentice-Hall do Brasil, Ltda., *Rio de Janeiro*

To our spouses who taught us and loved us.

To all students and the educators who taught them and loved them.

Preface

The title of the third edition, *Schoolwide and Classroom Management: The Reflective Educator-Leader*, reflects our commitment to an ecological/systems approach to effective classroom management. The ecological approach assumes that all employees across the school building, not only teachers, need to contribute to successful schoolwide and classroom management. Accordingly, this book is written for anyone who is responsible for managing the learning environments of children and youth.

New to This Edition

Although some portions of the second edition have been deleted, we retained Len's model of classroom management that cast the vast number of management tasks into the domains of content (instructional), conduct (behavioral), and covenant (relational) management. The first six chapters contain many new additions. The remaining chapters have minor changes.

Kagan's (1992) meta-analytic review of forty learning-to-teach studies provided the impetus for many of the changes in this edition. Her review culminated in a model of professional growth that concurred with and refined earlier models (Berliner, 1988; Fuller, 1969). One of Kagan's major refinements advised teacher-educators to help novices reflect on their own beliefs and behaviors rather than on the moral and ethical implications of classroom practices.

Kagan suggested that preservice education programs generally fail to address adequately any of the three developmental tasks of novices. One of the three tasks is to develop standard, procedural routines that integrate classroom management and instruction.

Accordingly, we have eliminated parts of the previous edition that were more theoretical in nature and have added text rich in standard procedures and routines. In fact, we go so far as to include scripts for novices that suggest what to say when they are teaching procedures. We have included some of our students' own scripts in the text.

Organization of the Text

Chapter 1 now has an emphasis on readers examining their own beliefs and behaviors. Chapters 2, 3, 4, and 5 are largely ones of procedures. We rely on the work of Sprick, Sprick, and Garrison (1993) for some of the basics of our procedural training. Chapter 2 content reflects our intent to prepare readers to think about management from a systems-level perspective early in the course. We equip readers in the how-to's of developing positive schoolwide discipline policies. A particular strength of the chapter is the clarification of how, when, and why to use out-of-class consequences that positively affect youth.

In Chapter 3, readers learn how to preplan content, conduct, and covenant management of classrooms, particularly in readiness for the first two weeks of school. They learn how to implement the basic classroom management plan and manage classroom crises that involve physically dangerous behavior.

Chapter 4, with an emphasis on developing effective communication, promotes readers' insight into their beliefs and behaviors and provides a foundation for preventing and remediating management difficulties. Special attention is devoted to communication styles of ethnic minority youth.

Chapter 5 includes procedures and scripts for content or instructional management with specific how-to's of cooperative learning. We included a section on common behavior problems that disrupt instruction and the strategies to resolve the problems: off-task, talking without permission, poor listening and not following directions, not bringing materials to class, late or incomplete assignments, tardiness, failure to be motivated, cheating, and test anxiety.

Chapter 6 offers guidelines for managing the chronic and more severe student behavior problems that do not respond to the basic classroom management plan. Such student behavior is often impacted by systems-level variables and teachers need systems-level assistance to devise effective interventions. We offer information on how and when to access the student assistance team.

The remaining chapters in the book are similar to the content of the second edition: covenant management, management style and power, home–school partnerships, legal and ethical issues, and educator stress. The appendixes include an updated, refined version of an observation checklist for content or instructional management.

ACKNOWLEDGMENTS

A number of people have been generous with their time and energy during the rewriting process. Several practitioners critiqued early drafts of this edition. Gina Iverson, collaborative special and regular education teacher; Steve Iverson, school psychologist and educational administrator; Sue Jorgensen, teacher and educational consultant; and Vickie Robinson, teacher and high school principal, provided kind and quality comments that assisted us in clearly communicating management practices. Jodi Bronson, graduate assistant, was cheerful and tireless in her accurate presentation of references.

We especially thank those who reviewed the manuscript:

Sue R. Abegglen, Culver–Stockton College

William M. Bechtol, Southwest Texas State University

Charollene M. Coates, Chadron State College

Rey A. Gomez, Arizona State University

Dorothy Mandelbaum, Rutgers, Camden

Jane McCarthy, University of Nevada, Las Vegas

Leonard L. Mitchell, Evangel College

Annette Iverson would like to acknowledge the good will of Len Froyen in inviting her to write the third edition. His constant trust in her revisions made the new partnership sweet and easy. She would also like to acknowledge parents, children, and teachers with whom she has worked for twenty years; they provided the context for this writing. Her husband, Loren, provided word processing expertise, patience, and encouragement without fail.

REFERENCES

Berliner, D. C. (1988). Implications of studies on expertise in pedagogy for teacher education and evaluation. In *New directions for teacher assessment: Proceedings of the 1988 ETS Invitational Conference* (pp. 39–68). Princeton, NJ: Educational Testing Service.

Fuller, F. F. (1969). Concerns of teachers: A developmental conceptualization. *American Educational Research Journal, 6,* 207–226.

Kagan, D. M. (1992). Professional growth among preservice and beginning teachers. *Review of Educational Research, 62,* 129–169.

Sprick, R., Sprick, M., & Garrison, M. (1993). *Interventions: Collaborative planning for students at risk.* Longmont, CO: Sopris West.

Brief Contents

Contents

PART III

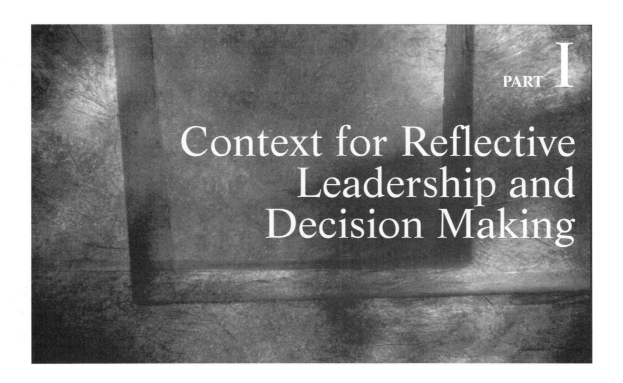

PART I

Context for Reflective Leadership and Decision Making

CHAPTER 1
Foundations of Management: Beliefs and Realities

CHAPTER 2
Foundations of Management: Schoolwide Discipline

CHAPTER 3
Foundations of Management: Basic Classroom Management Plan

CHAPTER 4
Foundations of Management: Communication Skills

Foundations of Management: Beliefs and Realities

An understanding of the material in this chapter will help you do the following:

❑ Define schoolwide and classroom management.
❑ Cite the importance of schoolwide discipline to effective classroom management.
❑ Discuss the impact of classroom management on academic achievement and social-emotional development of children and adolescents.
❑ Compare major philosophical positions and theoretical models as to how they shape management practices.
❑ Develop awareness of personal assumptions about human nature.
❑ Appreciate alternative explanations of human nature.
❑ Suggest ways to identify educators' assumptions about human nature based on their actions.
❑ Summarize the importance of an eclectic approach to management.
❑ Memorize an explicit problem-solving process to apply to later chapter problems.
❑ Set personal goals to participate in active learning of management skills.

Jerad was a seventh-grade male student who was upset and did not want to stay in his classroom. The seventh-grade teacher, Mr. Fix, grabbed Jerad as he tried to run from the room. Mr. Fix held Jerad underneath his arm because Jerad was unruly. The teacher was trying to keep him "in line," keep other students safe, and keep Jerad himself safe. Jerad was then taken to the vice principal, Ms. Bose, to telephone his mother and explain what he had done.

Jerad's mother, Ms. Barthel, understood her son to say that Mr. Fix had put his hands around Jerad's neck to restrain him and she immediately came to school with a male friend. Once at school, Ms. Barthel's meeting with Ms. Bose was not private but very public. Students, secretaries, teachers, administrators, and others were on the scene to witness all events.

Ms. Barthel believed that no one was listening to her son's complaints and that she was not being listened to either. When she decided that Ms. Bose was taking the teacher's side, she punched her. Then Ms. Barthel began throwing vases. She later told the press that these actions were precipitated by her fear of a teacher in the group who had a pair of scissors. Hair pulling was also reported. Ms. Barthel and her male friend exited the building. Several school personnel sustained minor injuries and one required medical attention at a local hospital.

The above scenario is based on a mid-1990s newspaper report of a disciplinary action in a middle school class in the Midwest, with names changed to protect identities. The local newspaper quoted the school spokesman as stating that the student's mother started the fight and that, in fact, the student was treated according to school policy. The insinuation was that school personnel believed they were in the right and had done nothing to cause the problems. The same newspaper quoted Ms. Barthel as stating that she was angry with the school before her son phoned home because older students had beaten up on him a few days previously. She shared that she was also angry because school officials had Jerad phone her. She believed that the call home was the responsibility of school officials. She expressed sorrow that the confrontation occurred and hope that matters could be resolved (Iverson, 1996).

Administrators, guidance counselors, school psychologists, social workers, and teachers hope situations like the one above never happen in their school buildings. Realistically, a whole host of management problems will present themselves, some less complex than this and some more complex.

To prepare to resolve these situations successfully, you must believe that schoolwide and classroom management skills are important to develop. A next step is to examine critically your personal beliefs about why children do the things they do and how they get to be the way they are. When you have some awareness of your own beliefs, it will be helpful to compare them to major theories of human development. From each theory base, management strategies have been developed. The strategies differ from each other but the intended outcomes are similar. You will be able to determine which theory or theories best match your beliefs about the nature of children and adolescents and, subsequently, which management strategies you will be most comfortable implementing.

Declarative, procedural, and conditional knowledge (Woolfolk, 1995) necessary for managing behavior like that of Jerad's is presented in this text. *Declarative knowledge* about schoolwide and classroom management is verbal information or facts, beliefs, theories, and opinions. Educators rich in declarative knowledge would have various beliefs or theories about why Jerad wanted to leave the classroom when upset. *Procedural knowledge* is knowing how to do something. When faced with a student like Jerad who wanted to leave the classroom because he was feeling upset, educators with procedural knowledge would know how to manage the situation in a variety of ways that would prevent escalating Jerad's behavior. *Conditional knowledge* is knowing when and why to apply declarative and procedural knowledge. Expert educators typically have more conditional knowledge than novices and are able to select from a menu of all possible procedures the one that is most likely to help Jerad make good choices when he is upset.

You also will learn to decrease the frequency of occurrences like Jerad's through preventive strategies, commonly referred to as *primary prevention programming.* Two additional levels of programming strategies that you will build skills in are *maintenance programming,* or short-term intervention strategies, and *corrective programming,* or long-term remediation/rehabilitation strategies. Corrective programming typically requires building-level assistance and specialized strategies provided by support personnel in collaboration with classroom teachers. You will learn when corrective programming is necessary and how to access special assistance.

Our beliefs are that strategies from across all the major theoretical models can be effective in different management situations. In this chapter and throughout the text, we will encourage you not only to develop awareness of your preferred theory and subsequent strategies, but also to remain flexible in adopting strategies from other theoretical orientations.

IMPORTANCE OF MANAGEMENT

Management in school buildings and classrooms involves more than just disciplining students. It is a process of facilitating positive student achievement and behavior with the ultimate goal of student self-control (McCaslin & Good, 1992). The importance of management in schools is illustrated in studies of academic achievement, teacher efficacy, and social factors influencing teacher and student behavior.

Schoolwide and classroom management is getting more attention in the research literature than ever before. For example, a meta-analytic investigation of variables that contributed to school learning showed that effective classroom management was more important than student demographics, home support, school policy, curriculum design, classroom instruction, and motivation (Wang, Haertal, & Walberg, 1993).

Bridges (1986) found that teacher incompetence probably could be defined as chronic failure to maintain classroom discipline. A high sense of teacher competency or efficacy is linked to learning gains in basic skills (Good & Brophy, 1984). Some researchers have reported that teachers' feelings of competence or efficacy are enhanced by formal planning (Charles, 1992; Unruh, 1994). It would seem, then, that teachers need to plan classroom management just like they plan lessons in order to feel competent. Kagan's findings (1992) support this position. She concluded that novices need standardized classroom procedures that reflect an integration of management and instruction before they have a sense of self as teacher and can focus on students' learning behaviors.

Management in schools is also important because of social factors (Hyman, 1997). In the past, society was less pluralistic and management was easier. Whole communities tended to agree on expectations for behavior and that the teacher was in charge of the class. She was free to teach what she wanted and discipline children as she deemed fit. At times discipline consisted of corporal punishment and few parents objected. Since the 1980s, parents and communities have questioned the authoritarian discipline approach (Dornbusch & Ritter, 1992). Now teachers must consider the wishes of diverse students and parents, not to mention legal issues, in managing their classrooms.

Contemporary sociological problems of students stem from a host of interacting variables: changes in the family structure that result in reduced adult supervision, the effects of TV modeling with reduced adult feedback due to inadequate levels of supervision, U.S. economic changes and their impact on education, and discrepancies between the needs of children at the schoolhouse door and the processes and programs that determine what goes on in school buildings (Batsche, 1996). Sociological changes can lead to student problems, as evidenced by the following examples. Justin is fourteen years old. He has two probation officers but is able to stay in school with support. Darian is twelve years old. He attacks children who call him names. Karl is five years old. He stomps on, pushes down, spits on, scratches, bites, and hits other children in his kindergarten room. Gabrielle is five years old. She is noncompliant with directions and pushes desks around.

When a classroom population ranges from twenty to forty students from disparate backgrounds, peaceable and productive learning environments depend on the management of explicit standards and expectations to which all adhere. Schools need to set up management structures that promote prosocial behaviors and educators must be prepared to teach replacement behaviors that are prosocial. A major flaw in school management has been that of erasing negative behaviors without teaching prosocial replacement behaviors (Batsche, 1996).

Given this evidence of the importance of management, it is appropriate for preservice teachers to be more concerned about their management skills than other skills during their first few years of teaching (Veenman, 1984). Recall the case of Jerad, who started to leave the classroom without permission. Because it was not managed well (e.g., in a way that was sensitive to parent wishes), it became a teacher's and administrator's worst nightmare. If managed according to strategies you will learn in this text, there would not have been a conflagration. It would never have been newsworthy enough to end up in the local paper.

Interestingly, university students reported that the knowledge gained in university courses did not provide them with practical classroom management procedures (Chamberlin & Vallance, 1991) for resolving problems like Jerad's. Likewise, Tucker, Plax, and Kearney (1985) found that inexperienced teachers had a meager repertoire of classroom management strategies, regardless of the misbehavior described in students. Thus, it would seem that teachers may have declarative knowledge but not the procedural and conditional knowledge that is so necessary in managing potential discipline problems.

SCHOOLWIDE AND CLASSROOM MANAGEMENT APPROACHES

Now that the importance of schoolwide and classroom management has been reviewed, let us briefly consider the range of expert approaches to schoolwide and classroom management. Approaches typically include introduction to models and a parallel component of reflection on the moral and ethical implications of classroom practices. Some educators learn a single model of management and implement it in every situation (e.g., the Canter model of assertive discipline; Canter & Canter, 1992). Educators may learn a multitude of theoretical models and pick and choose strands that appeal to them in developing classroom management plans (Charles, 1996). There are also atheoretical approaches to systems of classroom management planning in which educators may select from a variety of strategies and techniques without considering models (Lee, 1994).

In this text, you will be introduced to a rich menu of strategies that good managers use in the first two weeks of school and throughout the semester or year. The first weeks of school are emphasized because of the importance of getting off to a good start (Emmer, Evertson, Clements, & Worsham, 1994). To organize vast amounts of information about what good managers do, we categorize strategies according to one of three basic management functions: (1) content or instructional management, (2) conduct or behavior management, and (3) covenant or relationship management.

You will have the opportunity to develop basic management skills that meet the diverse instructional and social-emotional needs of approximately 96 percent of students (Batsche, 1996). A remaining small percentage of students will not be successful in meeting the expectations of a basic group management plan. It is at these times that educators must be competent in the use of an ecological and developmental approach to problem-solving that results in flexible intervention planning. A number of interventions that can be used to assist students with special needs are described in upcoming chapters. It is important to have many intervention approaches in your repertoire.

It is equally important to reflect on the different approaches in terms of how they match your beliefs. In the next section, you will review the type of reflection Kagan (1992) recommends for novice and preservice teachers. This is followed by an opportunity to reflect on your own beliefs about the basic nature of people.

Reflection on Management Beliefs

Kagan (1992) examined forty studies of professional growth among preservice and beginning teachers. Three studies focused on the impact of preexisting beliefs on new learning early in teacher education programs (Calderhead & Robson, 1991;

McDaniel, 1991; Weinstein, 1990). All studies documented that (1) content of course work was filtered through preexisting beliefs and prior experience and (2) prior beliefs were stable and inflexible.

Six studies focused on novices' changes in their knowledge of teaching as they progressed through the college curriculum (Aitken & Mildon, 1991; Florio-Ruane & Lensmire, 1990; Gore & Zeichner, 1991; McLaughlin, 1991; Pigge & Marso, 1989; Shapiro, 1991). The results of the six studies suggested that, for change to occur, prior beliefs had to be reconstructed. Based on these findings, Kagan (1992) recommended that novices be required to examine their prior experiences in classrooms and with authority figures. Ultimately, the examination should include comparisons to the experiences of peers in order to undo tendencies to believe that everyone's experiences are the same. In turn, this should help reduce the tendency for educators to assume that all learners learn in the same way the educators themselves do.

Educators need to explore their personal philosophies and beliefs about why people do the things they do and how they get to be the way they are. Your deeply held beliefs about human nature will subsequently influence your management of human behavior. For example, you may believe that Jerad and other seventh-grade students are basically bad kids. You may support this by describing them as generally rebellious, disrespectful preadolescents who got to be that way because they had overindulgent parents who did not teach them respect for authority. These beliefs will influence your management style. More than likely, you will rely on high control and punishment techniques to keep students like Jerad in line. That sounds very similar to what Mr. Fix did. Could it be that he held the beliefs just described? Recognition of your beliefs, a willingness to modify dogmatic beliefs, and appreciation for the diversity of beliefs held by others are necessary precursors to becoming flexible managers who use alternate strategies.

As you consider alternate strategies, be cognizant of the relationship between your prior learning/beliefs and management. Once again, think about the episode with Jerad and his mother. What approach seemed to be used by the teacher? By the administrator? What do you think each of the two believed about children and about discipline? Imagine that you were the teacher or the administrator in this situation. What would you have done when Jerad either ran out of the room or when he appeared at your administrative office? Before you respond, you should begin with reflection on your deeply held beliefs about why children do what they do and how they get to be the way they are. Deeply held beliefs often operate outside of your immediate awareness. You will have to pay deliberate attention to them over a period of time in order to become familiar with them.

ASSUMPTIONS/BELIEFS THAT AFFECT MANAGEMENT

The challenges of learning about good management vary. One challenge is that the effect of past learning on present learning is not always positive and may present barriers (Woolfolk, 1995). For example, if you currently rely on some ineffective management strategies, it may be difficult to learn more effective replacement strategies. Prior knowledge, beliefs, and attitudes can have an inhibitory effect on new learning.

Another challenge is that classroom realities often do not match novices' images of students. For example, novice teachers often believe that students will respond to innovative instruction with excitement and interest (Kagan, 1992). In actuality, most novices are faced with students who are not very motivated and often misbehave. Therefore, Kagan recommended that university course work promote not only preservice teachers' insights into their personal beliefs, but also prepare them for the reality of classrooms.

People may be unaware of their basic beliefs and how those beliefs influence their choice of actions. Nevertheless, all people hold beliefs or philosophies that influence their thinking and actions. Educators can challenge themselves to become aware of their own basic philosophies, to examine personal philosophies in terms of strengths and weaknesses, to explore different beliefs and philosophies, and to select from the various positions what work best in different situations. Educators can challenge themselves to do more planning and be more flexible in their management as opposed to being rigidly influenced by personal beliefs that are near and dear to their hearts.

As an educator or future educator, you will be asked to examine critically your management beliefs because they are influential in your thinking about appropriate ways to behave. Your first step will be to investigate diverse beliefs about the nature of human beings. You will examine basic assumptions that can be traced from philosophy to the arts and literature and from the arts and literature to the behavioral sciences. These disciplines shape and influence individuals and, ultimately, cultures. True education means thinking by associating across the various disciplines versus being highly qualified in just one field, as a technician might be. Although the discussion of the above disciplines will be brief, it should prove helpful in understanding why various educators manage the way they do.

Assumptions About the Nature of Human Beings

The beliefs and assumptions that individuals hold about the nature of people have been subtly or not so subtly influenced by their cultural milieus. In the words of Schaeffer (1982), "There is a flow to history and culture. This flow is rooted and has its wellspring in the thoughts of people" (p. 83). Schaeffer offers the following additional observations. What people are in their thought world determines how they act. This is true of people's value systems, creativity, corporate actions, political decisions, and personal lives. Entire cultural milieus have been shaped by people's thought worlds in philosophy, art, music, drama, literature, religion, and other forms of conveying knowledge. People's thought worlds flow through their fingers and from their tongues. It is just as true for the school building principal and the classroom teacher as it was true of "Michelangelo's chisel and the dictator's sword" (Schaeffer, 1982, p. 83).

The beliefs and thoughts that we hold about why other people do the things they do and how they get to be the way they are have a great influence on how we understand and interact with the people around us. In the Western world, there are four predominant sets of beliefs or assumptions about the nature of human beings. These assumptions are set forth in the psychological theories of the behavioral sciences but have historical roots in philosophy, art, music, the general culture, and theology. The culture that you have been exposed to has influenced your set of beliefs. Of the sets of beliefs that will be described, one will best match your assumptions about why people do the things they do and why you interact with them in the way that you do.

Descriptions follow of four philosophical positions or worldviews about the nature of human beings. The order of the listings should not be understood as an inference of one position being more true than another. It simply reflects the variety of philosophical and theoretical positions that ultimately impact what is written in textbooks as "knowledge" or "truth," taught to university students, and lived out in schools for children and adolescents. The extent to which these views appear to match your beliefs will influence your commitment to corresponding ways of intervening in schoolwide and classroom management problems.

You can examine your beliefs against the backdrop of several theoretical positions: (a) humanism, (b) behaviorism, (c) psychoanalytic thought, and (d) interactionism. Most people lean toward one view more than another, but, practically speaking, most of us borrow from each view to deal with the complexities of life. Do not be surprised if you find something appealing and convincing about each of these views of human nature.

Humanism

A contemporary position presupposes that humans are born "good" or with a natural inclination toward positive behaviors and that they must learn or acquire negative behaviors in order to exhibit negative behaviors. In positive, supportive, nurturing environments, humans are able to realize their own positive potential. A metaphor is that of a rose bud's potential to unfold in an optimal environment and make a beautiful, full rose. No one has to help the rose unfold perfectly. It will accomplish that on its own as long as the weather is supportive and aphids do not invade. Likewise, it is presupposed that human beings do not need someone to help them optimally grow. They will accomplish it on their own as long as the environment is supportive (e.g., provides freedom to explore and adequate materials).

It is from this presupposition that Rogerian theory developed in the behavioral sciences and Gordon's teacher effectiveness training (1974) and Raths, Harmin, and Simon's values clarification (1966) approaches developed in education. This presupposition has produced humanistic education, a pervasive theoretical model of the day. Educators who hold this view see their primary task as creating an optimally positive environment in which they do not interfere with or intrude in students' academic or social growth and development but, instead, allow them to unfold, search, explore, grow, and develop according to their own inner directedness. These beliefs are the foundation of constructivist education, whole language curriculum approaches, and a number of discipline techniques focused on relationship building, listening, and giving students freedom to solve their own problems. Schoolwide discipline and classroom management techniques that stem from the assumptions underlying humanism are clearly distinguishable from techniques stemming from other assumptions.

Educators who ascribe to humanistic assumptions might have dealt with Jerad in the following manner. He would know that there was a special place in the building for "cooling down" and he would be allowed to make his own choice to leave the room and go there. After Jerad was calm, he would have the opportunity to talk with a peer or adult about his feelings. An adult would listen to him and support him when he was ready to explore solutions. He would not have been grabbed around the neck and he would not have been sent to the office to call his mother.

Behaviorism

A second position is based on the presupposition that humans are born with no predisposition toward positive or negative behaviors (i.e., neither "good" nor "bad"). What human beings become is a direct result of their environment and their biology (e.g., genetic influences, physiological influences). In other words, they are the product of all positive and negative environmental influences that shaped them. They do not add anything from themselves. This is the "man is a machine" belief and it is from these assumptions that Skinner's behavioral theory developed. Canter and Canter's (1976) model of assertive discipline developed in education.

Educators who hold such assumptions see their primary task as controlling, shaping, and directing students to go in a particular, desired direction. For example, educators will direct all learning and tell students precisely what to do in every project without student input or negotiation. Educators will provide solutions to problems with peers on the playground and in the hallways, cafeteria, and bus line. They will tell students when to go to the rest room, get a drink, and sharpen a pencil.

Behavioral theory and its applications are the antithesis of humanistic theory and its applications. Given the antithesis, it is not surprising that people who hold humanistic beliefs may be completely opposed to behavioral applications in education and vice versa. Accordingly, classroom management textbooks that promote humanistic theories often warn against the harmful effects of behavior management and other behavioral applications. Classroom management techniques that stem from the presupposition that humans are born blank slates are clearly distinguishable from techniques stemming from the other presuppositions.

Educators who ascribe to the behaviorist assumptions might have dealt with Jerad in the following manner. He would know that there was a special place in the building for "cooling down." He would also know that he would need to make up time in his classroom for time spent in the "cooling down" room. The teacher would either tell him to go to the special room or give him a choice of calming in the regular class or the special room. After Jerad was calm, a number of consequences could potentially occur. For example, he might have to call his mother or make up time in the regular classroom. If the problem was a persistent one, behavior management plans might be generated (e.g., goal setting and behavioral contracting, structured reinforcement plan). He would not have been grabbed around the neck.

Psychoanalytic Thought

A third position presupposes that humans are born with a natural inclination to serve their own needs to the utter disregard of the needs of others. In this world-view, human beings can acquire healthy self- and other-centered behaviors. However, this occurs only when adults, particularly parents, assist their children in developing an adequate sense of self and a social conscience. It is from this third position that psychoanalytic theory and its applications developed. Religious groups that believe in the concept of original sin tend to support the presupposition that, from birth on, humans strive to meet their own needs before the needs of others and even to the detriment of others.

The implications for education are that parents are responsible for the prosocial development of their children. The role of the school is simply to teach academics. Educators hold expectations for appropriate social behavior and often give marks for deportment. However, social skills are not taught explicitly because parents are supposed to do this. This phenomenon has been referred to as the "hidden" curriculum. When students have academic or social-emotional difficulties, it is believed that the problems come from within the bad ("ill") child or, sometimes, the bad ("ill") family. Diagnosis and prescription are dominant approaches to intervention. This model also is referred to as the *medical model*. In this model, educators often tell guardians to seek professional help outside of the school, particularly through medical and mental health facilities. Character education programs also stemmed from this model. Once again, classroom management techniques that developed from the set of presuppositions that humans are born with the predisposition to meet their own needs are clearly distinguishable from techniques stemming from the other presuppositions.

Educators who ascribe to this theory might have dealt with Jerad in the following manner. He would be sent to the office and his mother contacted by an adult. The mother would be asked to work on the problem. The mother might be referred to the school counselor, school psychologist, or some community mental health center. Jerad might be referred for special education services. In sum, the problem would be dealt with as a "within" child or "within" family deficit that needed "fixing." Jerad would not have been grabbed around the neck.

Interactionism

The fourth, and final, position is actually an integration of the first three positions. The presupposition is that human beings are born with their own inherent potential for "good" and for "bad" versus being born a blank slate or like a machine that contributes nothing to their own development. Interactionism is like humanism in that value is placed on the inner unfolding or development of the self. It is different from humanism in that it presupposes that direct adult leadership is critical to a child's optimal development. The amount of direct adult leadership varies according to the developmental needs of children in any given learning situation.

It is like the second (behavioral) position in that value is placed on the management of environmental influences. It is different from behavioral theory in that it does not characterize the individual as relying totally on the environment to shape learning.

It is like position three (psychoanalytic thought) in recognizing that children sometimes do try to meet their own needs above all else. It is different from the beliefs of position three that interventions are directed solely at deficits within children.

The fourth position actually values something from each of the other positions and is eclectic in nature. Those who ascribe to this interactive model believe that human behavior is too complex to be understood from any single theoretical position that considers only the contributions of the individual or the environment (Dreikurs, 1968; Glasser, 1969).

Assumptions of every model are rebuttable; they cannot be proven to be true. Therefore, it seems wise to select interventions from the model or models that best meet the needs of students. Students have differing views of themselves and the world about them, also. Meeting them on their terms is likely to strike a responsive chord and produce behavior that is considered more appropriate in the school setting. The selection from every model also enables educators to develop the best interventions from seemingly competing and disparate viewpoints.

Educators who ascribe to the interactionist model see their primary task as managing the ecology in a way that matches the developmental needs of the child. They change the environment, including instruction and their own behavior, in order to assist children in learning, rather than assuming that children are "ill." Of course, they also consider the contribution of the individual to growth and development but it is only one factor among many.

Cognitive behavioral and Adlerian theory reflect the presuppositions of the interactive position and provide educators with schoolwide and classroom management techniques from each of the four major belief systems.

Educators who ascribe to the interactionist model might have dealt with Jerad in the following manner. He would know that there was a special place in the building for "cooling down" and he would be allowed to make his own choice to leave the room and go there. He would also know that he would need to make up time in his classroom for time spent in the "cooling down" room. The teacher would either tell him to go to the special room or give him a choice of calming in the regular class or the special room.

After Jerad was calm, a number of consequences could potentially occur in the interactionist model but there definitely would be an educational component. For example, Jerad might have to call his mother or make up time in the regular classroom. If the problem was a persistent one, behavior management plans might be generated (e.g., goal setting and behavioral contracting, structured reinforcement plan). Paired with behavior management plans would be skill building in problem solving, conflict resolution, or anger control. The school would not take the position that they did nothing to contribute to the problems. Jerad would not have been grabbed around the neck.

The interactionist model will be supported throughout the text. At the outset, you should understand and realize the implications of this choice because they are very great. Implementing the model requires reflection and flexibility versus rigidity in thinking and doing. Readers will need to examine their belief systems carefully to ascertain which one of the models reflects the foundation of their natural management style. Then they will need to open up their belief systems to critical examination and be willing to "try on" competing management styles. Learning to integrate these styles and maximize flexibility is a major aim of this text. Novice teachers often rely too heavily on the repetitive use of techniques that do not work. They use few or poorly chosen strategies because they know too little about how their beliefs affect their management strategies.

The importance of this discussion is that what educators believe greatly influences their management of children and adolescents in schools. It is important to reiterate that what people *say* they believe may be the acceptable or politically correct thing to say. Students do this in our classrooms, particularly when they believe that they should be humanistic. However, it may not be what they really believe. When push comes to shove, that is, when educators are dealing with a frustrating problem that seems to require immediate action, they will act automatically to manage the problem. Actions during moments of automaticity reflect their most basic beliefs about the nature of human beings. Everyone's beliefs are accepted and acceptable. What is important is recognizing how one's beliefs can interfere with effective management in some situations.

Truth of Assumptions

It is important to point out that beliefs or assumptions with roots in philosophy cannot be known to be absolutely true. On the basis of certain sets of assumptions that are not necessarily true, theories of human behavior are developed. Researchers gather data that either directly support or do not support theories and, thus, indirectly support their underlying assumptions. Replications of research findings result in principles that are considered to be true. However, principles that are considered to be true do not make the original set of assumptions true. If the assumptions are not true, then it logically follows that the principles are not universally true but only sometimes true.

To better understand the previous discussion, consider an example of how behavioral principles that are purported to be true on the basis of replicated research findings are affected by underlying assumptions that also are considered to be true. Behavioral theory is based on the assumption that human beings are like machines or are born blank slates. What people become is a result of environmental and biological influences alone. They contribute nothing from within themselves to their own development.

Based on the assumption that "man is a machine," behavioral models were developed to explain why people do what they do and how they get to be the way they are. One model, operant conditioning, has enough research support (i.e., replicated findings) that a whole host of principles have been developed. One principle is that positive reinforcement of target behaviors will increase the occurrence of target behaviors. An example is when peers laugh (positive reinforcement) at a student who is clowning around (the behavior). The peers' reinforcement increases the probability that the student will clown around more often.

Another principle is that, in the early stages of developing a new behavior, immediate reinforcement of every demonstration of the behavior will increase the frequency of the behavior more rapidly than intermittent reinforcement. If a teacher wanted to increase the frequency of handing in assignments, she would see a more rapid behavior change if positive reinforcement occurred every time a paper was handed in versus positive reinforcement given intermittently. People who believe that the assumptions of behavioral theory are true (i.e., humans are originally blank slates and become a product of their environment and basic biological factors) also believe that the principles are entirely true. Therefore, if it is difficult to increase someone's behavior with a positive reinforcer, the solution is to change reinforcers until the desired effect is obtained.

Keep in mind the earlier statement: Research-based principles do not make assumptions true. Even though positive reinforcement increases target behaviors, it does not necessarily follow that "man is a machine." If the assumptions are not true, one can also argue that the principles are not universal truths. In other words, the principle that positive reinforcement of any target behavior will increase the behavior may not be universally true.

In contrast, cognitive-behavioral theory is an interactive model and is based on different assumptions. The environment is believed to be important in influencing people's behavior (through, for example, positive reinforcement), but people's cognitions also are believed to influence behavior. What occurs within the person as perceptions of experiences also influences behavior. The reinforcer that satisfies and maintains a behavior may come from within. In the interactive model, the principles of behavioral theory are viewed as strong tendencies that can be mediated by cognitions. In other words, students can thoughtfully take the position never to hand in assignments, regardless of any and all positive reinforcements offered to them.

In summary, each of us believes in certain assumptions or presuppositions, meaning the basic ways we look at life, our basic worldview, the grid through which we see the world. Presuppositions are based on what we consider to be the truth of what exists. We live on the basis of our presuppositions more consistently than we realize. What we believe is what we do.

This becomes more interesting when the dominant cultural beliefs differ from an individual's basic beliefs. Individuals with beliefs that are quite different from those currently popular will often make culturally (i.e., politically) correct belief statements but may not display espoused beliefs in their behaviors. This mismatch may go undetected by the individuals themselves. If they obtain insight into the discrepancy, it may surprise and dismay them. Mismatches between what one really believes and what one says and does become clear to some students during classroom management role playing in college classrooms.

A particularly good example of how role-play behaviors can provide insight into a person's basic beliefs occurred during a classroom management role-playing activity. Note that in this situation we chain backward from a role-play behavior to discover the belief. The retrospective view often helps uncover a belief that might otherwise escape detection.

All of the students in the class had identified what they believed to be their personal management styles and all had been trained in the procedure of transitioning students from one place to another in the school (e.g., moving from a large group to small cooperative groups in the classroom, moving from the business classroom to a computer lab). A preservice teacher, who volunteered to play the role of the teacher, previously had identified her management style as humanistic (e.g., believed in respecting students' abilities to make good decisions and problem solve their own behavioral difficulties in supportive environments).

The teacher was modeling for middle school students the procedure of going quickly and quietly to the library from English class. As she led students from the college classroom and down the corridor to the make-believe library, several of the students began loudly laughing and talking. The teacher turned around and looked at them. When this cue went unnoticed and the students continued to talk and laugh, the teacher said, "Let's keep it quiet in the hallway." One student continued to talk and laugh and the teacher, obviously ruffled, grabbed his arm and said, "You need to follow directions."

This was an insightful experience for the preservice teacher who discovered that she became authoritarian—not humanistic—when she felt she was losing control of the situation. That teacher's behavior did not match her stated beliefs. She did try to maintain a pretense of being humanistic by making the necessity for following directions a desired outcome for students: "you" and "need" rather than "must" or "Be silent or else." Still, the nonverbal accompaniment made the communication a demand. What we say with our nonverbal behavior often speaks more loudly than our words.

An Ecological Approach to Management

Having adopted the interactionist theory of management for this text, we also briefly note here the importance of understanding ecological systems theory. We believe that a presentation of ecological systems theory as a framework for management decision making in schools can be helpful in broadening our view of external influences on students. Bronfenbrenner (1979) postulated an ecological model of four major systems that comprehensively describes the multiple influences on child and adolescent behavior in schools. The macrosystem, exosystem, mesosystem, and microsystem levels of influence on students are to be considered by educators as they flexibly select management strategies.

The macrosystem represents the cultural beliefs, patterns, and institutional policies that affect the behavior of individuals. An example of how cultural beliefs affect the behavior of individuals is noted in the Asian culture. Asian families tend to be more authoritarian than other ethnic groups and, thus, authoritarian style in schools appears to be seen as less negative by Asian children (Dornbush, Ritter, Leiderman, Roberts, & Fraleigh, 1987). If Jerad were Asian, there would be less of a tendency for his mother to object to the school's requirement that he phone home. However, it is never a good idea to make global, sweeping decisions on the basis of ethnicity alone. We are merely pointing out tendencies as cited in the literature. Note below how thinking ecologically at the macrosystem level could have prevented some of the home difficulties surrounding Jerad's case.

The exosystem consists of the outside influences and demands in adults' lives that affect students. Parents' work demands, financial stress, or major illnesses influence student behavior. Occurrences in teachers' home lives such as marital conflict also impact student outcomes. The degree to which the interventions of managers are successful is moderated by macrosystem and exosystem influences. These influences may cause some interventions to be more feasible or effective than others. However, educators have less direct control over macro- and exosystem influences than they do over meso- and microsystem influences. As managers develop more community partnerships, the influences of macrosystems and exosystems may be more feasibly addressed.

Educators and parents need to focus their primary management efforts on the microsystems of school (e.g., classrooms, playgrounds, lunchrooms) and home and the mesosystems of relationships between various microsystems (e.g., home–school, teacher–teacher). All of these systems (i.e., school, home, and school–home) represent the student's learning environment (Ysseldyke & Christenson, 1993–1994). Children and adolescents learn in many microsystems; the total learning environment considers the powerful effect of shared responsibility between educators and parents for educating and socializing students. Fantini (1983) labeled the separation of home and school as miseducative. Hess and Holloway (1984) found that collaboration between school and home produced greater gains than either system accomplished separately. In Jerad's case, the teacher would be advised to give guardians an opportunity at the beginning of the year to indicate their acceptance of classroom consequences. If that condition had been met, Jerad's mother could have indicated that she preferred an adult to phone her about problems Jerad was having.

Blame is circumvented with the concept of the total learning environment. Educators are unable to point the finger at the other system, "the home," and parents are unable to point the finger at the other system, "the school," when the student is having learning or behavior problems. Rather, the mesosystem or school–home partnership has joint responsibility for defining a common effort toward a common goal (Seeley, 1985).

Let's summarize the application of ecological systems theory to the case of Jerad. School–home partnerships may have prevented the situation from occurring, or at least prevented it from escalating once it had occurred. At the beginning of the year, Jerad's mother would have indicated the lack of acceptability of the school policy of students' phoning home to discuss behavior infractions. Both school and home would have a jointly agreed-on plan or resolution for the bullying of Jerad during the previous days. The teacher would have a plan acceptable to others (e.g., administrators, fellow teachers, parents, students) for how to handle students who leave the room without permission.

With all of these procedures in place, educators and students are better problem solvers when situations like Jerad's occur. The goal of problem solving is to keep students with academic and behavior problems in regular classrooms. The use of problem solving in the schools has become a prominent trend with more and more educators being prepared to engage in problem solving. Why do educators need to be prepared to problem solve? Aren't all people natural problem solvers?

PROBLEM-SOLVING MODELS

All people are problem solvers. For many, the problem-solving process is implicitly known and followed. However, problem-solving processes and solutions clearly separate novice and expert teachers (Swanson, O'Connor, & Cooney, 1990) and suggest that there are aspects of problem solving that can be taught and learned.

A number of problem-solving models are used at an explicit level in schools. All have the same basic steps: (1) Identify the problem, (2) define the problem, (3) explore alternatives, (4) apply a solution, and (5) evaluate progress. The steps are easy to learn. The thinking skills necessary to be expert problem solvers are more difficult to acquire (e.g., working from elaborate systems of knowledge for understanding problems, integrated sets of principles, metacognition). These skills develop more slowly as educators gain professional expertise.

Professional development in problem solving can be viewed as a continuum of novice to expert skills. Professionals who are experts select several complementary strategies to achieve a more lasting solution to a problem. They select quick-fix solutions when something must be done immediately before things get out of hand. But experts realize that they are temporary and partial solutions.

Novices, when faced with a problem, immediately focus on a quick-fix solution rather than the systematic hypothesis testing of several possible solutions (Swanson et al., 1990). Experts focus on problem definition and apply thinking skills based on principles, pattern recognition, automaticity, and metacognition. An example of the differences between novice and expert problem solvers follows. A novice observes a student not paying attention and immediately decides on a solution:

1. Tell the student to pay attention.

Contrast this with the expert problem solver who thinks through the problem using a prototypical process that emphasizes problem definition and hypothesis testing:

1. Identify that a student is not paying attention to directions.
2. Define not paying attention as gazing out the window and not writing down assignment directions.
3. Hypothesize about the reasons why the student is not paying attention (e.g., has a hearing problem and teacher did not provide visual directions, teacher did not adequately call for the attention of all class members prior to beginning oral directions, student is having difficulty concentrating on

Teachers and principals at Price Laboratory School learn how to implement the IDEAL problem-solving model.

schoolwork because his mother is ill in the hospital, it is spring and the birds are singing outside the window).

4. Select the most likely hypothesis and match the solution to it (e.g., student has a hearing problem and teacher determines that a visual prompt is needed prior to giving directions).

5. Evaluate the effectiveness of the visual prompts for obtaining and maintaining student attention and cycle back through problem solving if the solution was not effective.

Novices do not have well-developed pattern recognition skills. Pattern recognition takes experience and practice. When educators do not practice using the problem-solving model, they will continue to be novice problem solvers, jumping immediately into solutions that have a high probability of not working because they did not match the actual problem. As a wise man once said, "Doing it that way all your life doesn't make it right. If it was wrong when you started, it is still wrong twenty years later." No one becomes an expert problem solver simply by doing the same thing for twenty years. People become expert problem solvers by accumulating great skill, knowledge, and assured competence in the problem domain.

Two depictions of problem-solving models are offered here. For those learners who like information presented in a verbal and linear, sequential manner, see the IDEAL problem-solving model shown in Figure 1–1. For learners who like visual representations of information, see Figure 1–2 where the Michigan State model is presented. This model is described in detail in the following section. Both models include the same basic problem-solving processes. Study them, select one to commit to memory, and apply the steps to problem-solving situations over the course of the semester (e.g., the case of Jerad at the beginning of this chapter).

Teacher Leadership: A Context-Processing Model

As you proceed through this text, you will acquire the necessary knowledge and skills to help you secure students' cooperation by structuring teaching–learning events that maximize their success. You will become a diagnostician and a problem solver. This may sound a bit academic, but it is a very practical way to label a reflective process that effective leaders use every day. Although many problems may occur outside the classroom itself, the teacher can moderate the impact of these problems by creating a learning community with its own standards of success and ways to fulfill them. An optimistic orientation will help you make good decisions and increase your job satisfaction.

The following example highlights a common type of internal, problem-solving dialogue that produces management insights and interventions.

> At the end of the school day, Ms. Harper is preoccupied with thoughts about the way things went that day. She is reminded of an incident that still troubles her. She begins to relive some of the feelings she experienced when Phillip accused her of "always picking on him." This accusation was particularly disturbing because she thinks that she works hard to be fair and considerate. She begins to wonder what is causing Phillip to feel this way.
>
> She cannot easily dismiss this incident because Phillip's behavior—talking during lecture presentations—is unacceptable. She begins to entertain explanations. "Might it be that he feels uninvolved in the class? Is this just one way to get my attention and that of the class? What would happen," she reasons,

Figure 1–1
Prototypic IDEAL
Problem-Solving Model

1. *I*dentify the problem.
2. *D*efine the problem.
3. *E*xplore the alternative.
4. *A*pply the solution.
5. *L*ook back and evaluate progress.

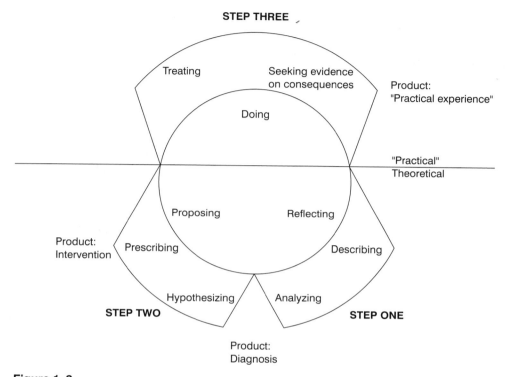

Figure 1–2
Michigan State Educational Diagnosis and Problem-Solving Model

Source: Adapted from *Michigan State Final Report, Behavioral Science Elementary Teacher Education Project, Vol. 1* (1968). U.S. Department of Health, Education, and Welfare, Office of Education, Bureau of Research. Project 8–9025.

"if I were to give him more attention when his behavior matches the class expectations?"

Ms. Harper remembers that Phillip usually arrives early for class. She could engage him in conversation then. As the class begins, she might call on him to highlight a point from the previous day's lesson. Questions scattered throughout the lecture, occasionally directed to Phillip, might provide him with another positive source of recognition. "It's worth a try," she concludes.

After a week of using such tactics, Ms. Harper notes that there are no more accusations of being unfair and that Phillip is being quite cooperative. Now he volunteers observations about the previous day's class and/or assigned homework before class gets under way. He still speaks to others during the class but does so when called on to share topically related remarks.

This process of educational diagnosis—describing an incident, identifying a solution, and trying it out—is the basis for a teacher preparation model developed at Michigan State University (see Figure 1–2). The model delineates the process as follows:

1. Reflecting
2. Proposing
3. Doing

The key elements in the model have since become the foundation for efforts to prepare the reflective educator in preservice programs [see the theme issue of *Educational Leadership,* March 1991, 48(6)]. By taking a classroom challenge, you can begin to see how an educator goes about using the teaching–learning context as the basis for selecting appropriate interventions. You may find the abbreviated and concrete example of this process, presented as a management problem in Table 1–1, a useful way to prepare for more involved discussions of the model in later chapters.

Let us use, as a starting point in understanding the model, the previously discussed case of Jerad.

Step 1: Reflecting

The teacher begins by *reflecting* (lower right section of circle in Figure 1–2) about the characteristics of the situation itself. First, Mr. Fix describes what was going on in the classroom: The students were moving to their cooperative groups and two boys in Jerad's group seemed to be making teasing comments about him. Second, Mr. Fix continues his reflection by analyzing the situation: Jerad intermittently has been the object of teasing by these two boys and he is usually upset by it and tries to get away from them.

This process will be the basis for examining three fundamental management functions: content, conduct, and covenant. Prevention, maintenance, and correction interventions associated with each of these functions offer the teacher-leader a vast variety of management techniques. Grounded in the reflections of this chapter, the teacher-leader is better prepared to see the boundaries that define the problem formation stage in personal theory development.

Thus, personal *reflection* sets the stage for *diagnosis* (between steps 1 and 2 in the figure). Diagnosis helps identify the management function and the form of intervention that would be most appropriate, that is, given the conclusions reached by way of reflection.

Step 2: Proposing

Now the teacher-leader begins to speculate about possible courses of action. Given the *diagnosis,* what would seem to be reasonable ways to deal with the possible impact of this condition in the classroom? This textbook is largely a synthesis of answers to this question. Before explaining the three types of interventions and the

Table 1–1
Schematic Application of the Educational Diagnosis and Problem-Solving Model

---

Theoretical

Reflecting

Describing: Several members of the class request seatwork help immediately after the independent study period begins.

Analyzing: Generally, the requests for assistance are due to confusion about how to proceed rather than inadequate knowledge or skill.

Proposing

Hypothesizing: (IF) students have to rely on the teacher to clarify directions (after a seatwork assignment has been given), (THEN) measures must be taken to make directions explicit and to make students more accountable for them.

Prescribing: Express directions as a series of concrete action steps. Have selected students review the steps while the group completes an example exercise.

Practical

Doing

Treating: Put action steps for a seatwork assignment on the chalkboard (seeking clarity). Assign the steps to those students who frequently seek directions and assistance (seeking accountability).

Collecting Evidence on Consequences: Keep a record of the number of direction-assistance questions students ask after the intervention has been implemented and of those students who ask the questions.

---

corresponding management functions, let us conceptualize the problem as one requiring conduct management and a corrective intervention.

At this point we can cast the problem into an if–then statement, that is, a *hypothesis*. By hypothesizing about the problem, we establish a connection between a situation and a plausible response to the situation. In other words, *if* Jerad has to cope with peer teasing and work cooperatively with all students in the room, *then* measures must be taken to assist Jerad and peers with the required prosocial skills. The *proposing* section of Table 1–1 (see also lower left section of circle in Figure 1–2) reformulates this hypothesis. The hypothesis is a prediction of what we think will happen, given our *analysis* of the problem and our history of dealing with similar problems. We use the *hypothesis* to *prescribe* a specific treatment or intervention.

Numerous paths are available to a teacher-leader for assisting Jerad and his peers in improving their social skills. In this instance, a conduct and corrective management *intervention* will help students work cooperatively and contribute to their learning of the subject. A conduct management intervention relies on solutions that involve teaching replacement behaviors or prosocial skills.

Step 3: Doing

We have now constructed a *theoretical* basis for acting (section below intersecting line of circle in Figure 1–2). It is theoretical because we have yet to try it out in the classroom. Our plan of action is based on our *diagnosis* of a situation, and our intervention is our best "educated guess" about how to deal with the situation most effectively. The diagnosis is based on *describing* and *analyzing* the classroom context of the problem; the intervention is based on a process of *hypothesizing* and *prescribing* based on the context considerations. This suggests a way of *doing* (upper section of Figure 1–2 circle) that we believe will increase the probability that students will choose responsible behaviors conducive to learning. Because we have selected a corrective intervention, we may wish to seek assistance from the special services team, which is prepared to teach prosocial skills and corollary skills such as anger reduction techniques.

Some of you using this text will be enrolled in a collateral field experience. Others may be veteran teachers who can draw on practical experience to judge the wisdom of using various treatments presented in this text. Still others will be practicing teachers who can immediately test various treatments against the daily realities of teaching. In the absence of direct school-related experiences, you may use simulated activities, case studies, or role playing, or you may even apply these techniques in other relationships.

By being engaged in the *doing* phase of this model, you will be able to *treat* and then *collect evidence* (outside of Figure 1–2 circle) to determine the effectiveness of various techniques. As you try various treatments, you will learn that the success of each depends on many factors. Your decisions will be influenced by how you size up a situation, based on the participants; the preventive and supportive techniques that might be used to head off disciplinary problems; the corrective measures that seem plausible, given selected teaching aims frustrated by student misbehavior; the skills required of the student and you to implement a chosen course of action; and the likely outcomes of selecting a given solution. Over time, you will develop techniques that are fashioned from decisions that have produced good results for you.

The evidence-collecting activities that occur each day will produce the data for revising your theory of management. Generally, success will not be total. To be more successful, you will need to look for flaws in your original description and analysis and for faulty logic that may have contributed to an ill-advised hypothesis and prescription. Your next intervention will be based on a better conception of the challenge and more refined management skills.

CONCLUSION

Someone once said that there is nothing as practical as a good theory. The wisdom of this observation will become strikingly apparent as you begin to build your theory of classroom management. You have been challenged to reflect on your personal beliefs about why children and youth do what they do and how they get to be the

Management Challenge 1–1

Reflective Problem Solving

Use the format in Table 1–1 to diagnose, prescribe, and gain practical experience in solving the following management problem:

Ms. Gardiah allows her students to speak with one another during independent seatwork. She encourages them to use process-helping skills so that they do not merely give one another answers. Students appreciate this cooperative and collaborative approach to learning.

This year, however, three of Ms. Gardiah's students who are close friends often use this time to socialize. When Ms. Gardiah reprimands them, they are very polite and apologetic. As a result, social interludes are scattered within task-oriented conversations during the next several days, but soon socializing again dominates their conversations. Ms. Gardiah is distressed because these students are submitting low-quality and incomplete work. The aggravation of giving constant reminders is also making it difficult for her to be pleasant to these three students.

1. Describe the problem as you see it.
2. As you analyze the problem, alternately examine it as a teacher-caused and student-caused problem by accounting for antecedent conditions (what occurs before students socialize), consequent conditions (what occurs after students socialize), and event conditions (what occurs during the cooperative learning activity).
3. Entertain several hypotheses that reflect differences in the causes of the problem.
4. Prescribe solutions that place primary responsibility on the teacher, then prescribe solutions that shift responsibility to the student.
5. Select one of the treatment alternatives aimed at prevention and correction and apply it.
6. Collect evidence that the treatment resulted in desirable outcomes.

way they are. After you accurately describe your own beliefs and compare them to major theories about the nature of people and how they learn, you will begin to build your theory of classroom management. Your theory will be composed of generalizations that help visualize, summarize, explain, and interpret your experience. These generalizations will shape your decisions and guide your responses to the new and the familiar. Your theory base will grow as your experience suggests pertinent variables and the weight to give them when working on the problem diagnosis and prediction. You will begin to see that the process reveals patterns that give shape and substance to classroom events. You will begin to see that management problems are part of a pattern.

Each subsequent chapter will help you understand the patterns or conditions that shape management decisions. This understanding is prerequisite for grasping principles and practices that will enable you to deal with the complex conditions in the nation's schools. In the following chapters, practices are presented as specific techniques and are accompanied by exercises designed to help you acquire the skills to become an effective educator-leader.

SUPPLEMENTARY QUESTIONS

1. Select one or more of the theoretical models discussed in the chapter and identify the underlying assumptions. Do you think these assumptions shape the thinking and practices of most educators, including classroom teachers?
2. Select a problem that you would like to examine objectively and systematically. Using Table 1–1 as an example of how to process the problem, prepare a similar analysis of the problem you have chosen.
3. The authors do not mention specific types of disciplinary problems in this chapter. However, during your reading, specific disciplinary problems may have occurred to you. Brainstorm some common disciplinary problems and determine how different theories might address them.

SUPPLEMENTARY PROJECTS

1. Identify a professional journal read by educators whose professional preparation is similar to your own. Looking at the journal's table of contents for the last year, select an article that deals largely with the classroom management/ discipline issues discussed in this chapter. Determine the theoretical model that best represents the author's belief system. Be prepared to compare and contrast the views of the author of the article and those of the other models in this chapter.
2. Check students' views of discipline by asking several students this question: "What is it like being a student?" Extract the statements that describe aspects of classroom management and discipline. What conclusions and implications can you draw from this compilation of statements? Or, check teachers' views of discipline by asking several teachers to describe the good and bad feelings they experience as they interact with students. Isolate the feelings that appear to be associated with classroom management and discipline. What conclusions and implications can you draw from this activity?
3. Although the steps in the Michigan State problem-solving model are generally followed in the order given, these three processes—reflecting, proposing, and doing—could be reversed to look at the wisdom of using various treatment practices. Identify a common method for dealing with a disciplinary problem. Try to reconstruct the reasoning behind this method; that is, how must the problem be viewed to arrive at this treatment? What do you find in the reasoning that is defensible? That is faulty? Prepare a paper to summarize your analysis of the treatment and your evaluation of the logic that appears to justify the treatment.

REFERENCES

Aitken, J. L., & Mildon, D. (1991). The dynamics of personal knowledge and teacher education. *Curriculum Inquiry, 21*, 141–162.

Batsche, G. M. (1996, October). Implementing a comprehensive program for students with difficulties with anger control and aggression: Building on classroom strategies. Paper presented at the Iowa Behavioral Initiative Conference, Des Moines, IA.

Bridges, E. (1986). *The incompetent teacher*. Philadelphia: Falmer Press.

Bronfenbrenner, U. (1979). *The ecology of human development*. Cambridge, MA: Harvard University Press.

Calderhead, J., & Robson, M. (1991). Images of teaching: Student teachers' early conceptions of classroom practice. *Teaching and Teacher Education, 7,* 1–8.

Canter, L., & Canter, M. (1976). *Assertive discipline: A take charge approach for today's educator.* Santa Monica, CA: Lee Canter and Associates.

Canter, L., & Canter, M. (1992). *Lee Canter's assertive discipline: Positive behavior management for today's classroom.* Santa Monica, CA: Lee Canter & Associates.

Chamberlin, C., & Vallance, J. (1991). Reflections on a collaborative school-based teacher education project. *Alberta Journal of Educational Research, 37,* 141–156.

Charles, C. M. (1992). *Building classroom discipline* (4th ed.). White Plains, NY: Longman.

Charles, C. M. (1996). *Building classroom discipline* (5th ed.). White Plains, NY: Longman.

Dornbusch, S. M., & Ritter, P. L. (1992). Home–school processes in diverse ethnic groups, social classes, and family structures. In S. L. Christenson & J. C. Conoley (Eds.), *Home–school collaboration* (pp. 111–125). Colesville, MD: National Association of School Psychologists.

Dornbusch, S. M., Ritter, P. L., Leiderman, P. H., Roberts, D. F., & Fraleigh, M. J. (1987). The relation of parenting style to adolescent school performance. *Child Development, 58,* 1244–1257.

Dreikurs, R. (1968). *Psychology in the classroom: A manual for teachers.* New York: Harper and Row.

Educational Leadership. (1991, March). Vol. 48, Issue 6.

Emmer, E. T., Evertson, C. M., Clements, B. S., & Worsham, M. E. (1994). *Classroom management for secondary teachers* (3rd ed.). Boston: Allyn and Bacon.

Fantini, M. D. (1983). From school system to educative system: Linking the school with community environments. In R. L. Sinclair (Ed.), *For every school a community* (pp. 39–56). Boston, MA: Institute for Responsive Education.

Florio-Ruane, S., & Lensmire, T. J. (1990). Transforming future teachers' ideas about writing

instruction. *Journal of Curriculum Studies, 22,* 277–289.

Glasser, W. (1969). *Schools without failure.* New York: Harper & Row.

Good, T. L., & Brophy, J. E. (1984). *Looking in classrooms* (3rd ed.). New York: Harper & Row.

Gordon, T. (1974). *TET: Teacher effectiveness training.* New York: David McKay Company.

Gore, J. M., & Zeichner, K. M. (1991). Action research and reflective teaching in preservice teacher education: A case study from the United States. *Teaching and Teacher Education, 7,* 119–136.

Hess, R. D., & Holloway, S. D. (1984). Family and school as educational institutions. In R. D. Parke, R. M. Emde, H. P. McAdoo, & G. P. Sackett (Eds.), *Reviewing child development research: The family* (Vol. 7, pp. 179–222). Chicago: University of Chicago Press.

Hyman, I. A. (1997). *School discipline and school violence: The teacher variance approach.* Boston: Allyn and Bacon.

Iverson, A. M. (1996). Management strategies in inclusive classrooms. In B. Stainback and S. Stainback (Eds.), *A handbook of practical strategies for inclusive schooling,* 296–312. Baltimore, MD: Paul Brooks.

Kagan, D. M. (1992). Professional growth among preservice and beginning teachers. *Review of Educational Research, 62,* 129–169.

Lee, S. W. (1994). *The flex model classroom management planning system.* Lawrence, KS: Child Research Institute.

McCaslin, M., & Good, T. L. (1992). Compliant cognition: The misalliance of management and instructional goals in school reform. *Educational Researcher, 21,* 4–17.

McDaniel, J. E. (1991, April). Close encounters: How do student teachers make sense of the social foundations? Paper presented at the annual meeting of the American Educational Research Association, Chicago.

McLaughlin, H. J. (1991). The reflection on the blackboard: Student teacher self-evaluation. *Alberta Journal of Educational Research, 37,* 141–159.

Pigge, F. L., & Marso, R. N. (March, 1989). A longitudinal assessment of the affective impact of preservice training on prospective teachers. Paper presented at the annual meeting of the American Educational Research Association, San Francisco.

Raths, L. E., Harmin, M., & Simon, S. B. (1966). *Values and teaching.* Columbus, OH: Charles E. Merrill Publishing.

Schaeffer, F. A. (1982). *The complete works of Francis A. Schaeffer: A Christian worldview. Volume 1: A Christian view of philosophy and culture.* Wheaton, IL: Good News.

Seeley, D. S. (1985). *Education through partnership.* Washington, DC: American Enterprise Institute for Public Policy Research.

Shapiro, B. L. (1991). A collaborative approach to help novice science teachers reflect on changes in their construction of the role of science teacher. *Alberta Journal of Educational Research, 27,* 119–132.

Swanson, H. L., O'Connor, J. E., & Cooney, J. B. (1990). An information processing analysis of expert and novice teachers' problem solving. *American Educational Research Journal, 27,* 533–556.

Tucker, L., Plax, T. G., & Kearney, P. (1985). Prospective teachers' use of behavior alternative techniques. Paper presented at the communication theory and research interest group of the Western Speech Communication Association Conference, Fresno, CA.

Unruh, L. (1994). *The effects of teacher planning on classroom management effectiveness.* Unpublished doctoral dissertation, University of Kansas, Lawrence.

Veenman, S. (1984). Perceived problems of beginning teachers. *Review of Educational Research, 54*(2), 143–178.

Wang, M. C., Haertel, G. D., & Walberg, H. J. (1993). Toward a knowledge base for school learning. *Review of Educational Research, 63,* 249–294.

Weinstein, C. S. (1990). Prospective elementary teachers' beliefs about teaching: Implications for teacher education. *Teaching and Teacher Education, 6,* 279–290.

Woolfolk, A. E. (1995). *Educational psychology* (6th ed.). Boston: Allyn and Bacon.

Ysseldyke, J., & Christenson, S. (1993–1994). *The instructional environment system—II: A system to identify a student's instructional needs.* Longmont, CO: Sopris West.

CHAPTER 2

Foundations of Management: Schoolwide Discipline

An understanding of the material in this chapter will help you do the following:

❏ Appreciate the contribution of the schoolwide, ecological system to the management of student behavior.
❏ Plan and implement schoolwide discipline policies.
❏ Administer out-of-class consequences appropriately.
❏ Seek assistance from specialists to help problem solve on behalf of students who are repeatedly given out-of-class consequences.

The final bell rang, signaling the beginning of the first period of the day. Ms. Doe noticed Tony, who was obviously late for his class but walking very slowly down the hall. The teacher shook her head slightly as she thought about Tony's future. "After all," she thought to herself, "How could anyone with such badly groomed hair, unbrushed teeth, and raggedy shoes and pants be successful in school or in life? To add insult to injury, here he is late and not making much of an attempt to get to class. He probably slept in or was hanging out on the corner with that bad crowd of boys who smoke every morning. He has one bad attitude for me to manage."

Ms. Doe walked quickly down the hall to stop Tony and ask him why he was still in the hallway. She used her best tone of voice to communicate scathing sarcasm and suspicion of his motives. He responded with profanity and turned around and left the building. Ms. Doe proceeded to the office and reported Tony's insubordination and truancy. In her verbal report to the principal, she added that Tony's behavior was just as she had predicted, "He will never be successful here."

Hyman (1997) applied an ecological/systems management approach to a case similar to the one just described. Educators who think ecologically would be interested in how the system contributed to the outcome of Ms. Doe's and Tony's interaction. An ecological, systems-level approach to schoolwide and classroom management is based on the belief that student misbehavior is a function of the interaction among people and every aspect of the environment. An ecologist would determine what influences in the school contributed to Ms. Doe's beliefs about students who look like Tony: (1) Did administrators or other staff previously model subtle comments or bold statements about some students? (2) Has school been disrupted by students who dress like Tony? (3) Have parents of students like Tony caused problems for the school?

Systems-level problem solvers search for the solution to discipline problems within the system. They analyze the system, rather than the individual, in order to diagnose the problem. When the target problem is identified, interventions focus on empowering staff to make curriculum adjustments and change teaching styles, correcting and changing organizations, and self-renewal. For example, if administrators were to make demeaning comments about students like Tony, they would be the target of the intervention (e.g., they might be asked to implement positive approaches to managing students like Tony.) Those who adhere to systems thinking believe that schools and classrooms are to be orderly. Educators are to carry out discipline policies.

This chapter prepares educators to think and function at a systems level in matters of discipline. Preplanning of schoolwide discipline policies and procedures is the focus. Some preplanning criteria presented here may seem antithetical to what educators with certain presuppositions (see Chapter 1) might want to address. If so, the educators are faced with a dilemma. Do they integrate the recommendations of this chapter into their management plan? Do they ignore the recommendations and develop what they think might be a better plan? Whatever they do, it should be done in an informed manner, with careful reflection and preplanning of positive systems-level management practices.

PREPLANNING AT THE SYSTEMS LEVEL

Professional educators need to think about management at a systems level (e.g., ecological systems theory). This means fitting classroom management plans into the schoolwide discipline policy, the culture of the school, and the culture of the community. Accordingly, educators need to study the school district or school building discipline plan. If educators disagree with the building discipline plan, they can precipitate change. Teachers will experience difficulty when attempting to carry out classroom management plans that do not fit with building discipline plans. (Consider a teacher who allows food and drink in the classroom at any time even though the building discipline plan states that food and drink can be consumed only at designated holiday observances with administrator consent.) When teachers are knowledgeable about building discipline plans, they can write better, tentative classroom management plans. Teachers should give copies of their tentative plans to building principals and obtain support for the plans.

Recall that schoolwide discipline policies from the early 1900s were based on punitive and exclusionary practices. At that time success in school was not a prerequisite to getting a job. Schools did not have the goal of educating everyone and graduated only 6 percent of the population. Accordingly, schools were oriented toward children and adolescents who were academically inclined and had socially acceptable behaviors. Discipline policies were based on punishment for breaking the rules and included suspension and expulsion. Such policies were a major way to exclude less able, less motivated, or poorly behaved students.

School discipline policies based on suspension and expulsion, however, are no longer appropriate in today's world. Young people today need high school educations for life success. Since the 1960s, nearly 100 percent of all children attend school and 75 percent of them complete school. Schools can no longer function with discipline policies that, in effect, cause them to be exclusive systems. Some educators believe that punitive and exclusionary discipline policies served us well and should continue to be acceptable practices. On the other hand, some assert that traditional approaches will fail today because they are based on assumptions that were more true for the 6 percent of children in school in the early 1900s than for the 100 percent of children in school in the 1990s.

The first faulty assumption of an exclusionary mentality is that children attending school today know the right way to behave and are making a choice to be defiant. Based on the assumption of defiance, educators think that punishment will stop inappropriate and increase appropriate behavior. Unfortunately, some students come from homes where education is not valued, parental guidance is limited, interactions are disrespectful and hostile, and fighting is encouraged as a way to solve problems. Thus, educators are not making a good choice if they implement discipline policies that discriminate against students from homes where guardians do not know how to or do not care to prepare their children with the socially acceptable behaviors needed to follow school rules. The issue becomes this: Do educators punish disrespect and irresponsibility or teach respect and responsibility?

The second faulty assumption is that all students have a strong desire to be in school; therefore, discipline policies of suspension or expulsion will serve as deterrents for all students. This is not a reasonable assumption for many students who are suspended or expelled. They actually may not have a strong desire to be in school at all. The threat of punishment by suspension or expulsion is no threat at all.

This assumption and its ensuing disciplinary practices of suspension and expulsion are tied to legal concerns, also. Provisions of IDEA 97 and Section 504 of the Rehabilitation Act protect students with disabilities or those who are at risk for academic failure. Exclusionary discipline practices may violate the following provisions of these laws: (1) the right to a free and appropriate education, (2) the right to prescribed procedures prior to a change of placement, (3) the right to an education in the least restrictive environment, and (4) the right to stay in the current placement while due process is pending.

Educators who take a revised view of discipline can develop effective, nonexclusionary schoolwide discipline policies for all students experiencing social, emotional, and behavioral problems, including those identified as behaviorally disordered. One step toward a revised view is a change in attitude. For example, ask educators to define discipline. The most common response will be that discipline is punishment of those who do not obey or follow the rules. In other words, discipline is concerned with punishing misconduct. Educators further talk about lists of prohibitive rules and hierarchies of increasingly severe punishments.

Contrast the common response with an additional definition of discipline that most forgot or never knew: preventing misconduct through "training to act in accordance with rules" and "instruction and exercise designed to train to proper conduct or action" (Barnhart & Stein, 1962). The attitude change that will yield a new view of discipline is that the primary focus of discipline is training, instruction, and teaching. In learning basic reading and math skills, students are carefully instructed, given plenty of opportunities to practice, and provided corrective feedback and encouragement. Teachers respond to academic errors with corrective teaching. Students make social errors every day. Should educators automatically respond with punishment or should they use the same instructional concepts that facilitate academic learning: direct instruction, practice, encouragement, and corrective feedback?

The revised view of discipline is instructional with a focus on teaching students to behave responsibly in school. Educators must be able to view misbehavior as a teaching opportunity. This viewpoint helps educators remain objective and not react defensively or punitively. Contemporary schoolwide discipline plans provide joint procedures for negative consequences (punishment) and instruction or teaching replacement behaviors.

Sprick (1985) developed a prototype of a schoolwide discipline plan. His recommended policies and procedures set forth common expectations for student behavior and consistent guidelines for dealing with misbehavior. Implementation of the comprehensive plan helps students learn that staff share basic expectations for student behavior whether they are in the classroom, halls, cafeteria, or rest rooms.

The schoolwide discipline plan's creed is a positive greeting to everyone who enters the school building.

Building a Safe and Happy Community

This phase of planning may be difficult for educators with either a psychodynamic or a humanistic set of assumptions. Educators who hold psychodynamic assumptions may approach schoolwide discipline planning with an exclusionary attitude. Essentially, these educators may expect students to come to school with all the prerequisite social skills and rule-governed behaviors instilled by guardians. Students who do not follow school building discipline policies with total success may be punished, suspended, expelled, or sent to alternative resources for their education and other assistance. The biggest attitude shift for these educators is the willingness to offer school-based, prosocial education to students who are not successfully navigating the discipline or management plan.

Educators with humanistic assumptions may believe that developing a positive school climate characterized by an abundance of adult acceptance and support of all students would be the necessary and sufficient condition to meet in schoolwide policy planning. Given optimally supportive school climates, it is believed that students will make good choices for themselves. Rules, guidelines, and expectations will not need to be explicitly stated by the adults in the environment. It is preferred that students generate these on their own. This approach to schoolwide discipline planning, however, is flawed. First, the probability of efficient systems-level management of hundreds of culturally diverse students without a uniform set of expectations is low indeed. If systems wait on hundreds of students to generate their own common guidelines, a long period of confusion will result. Here are a few examples of expectations that might need clarification: (1) Some students carry weapons in their neighborhood to be safe. Weapons on school grounds are considered unsafe. (2) In the home, some students know that it is acceptable to be loud and noisy, talk back to their guardians, and refuse to follow directions. In schools, learning environments are disrupted when students exhibit these same behaviors.

Second, students are accustomed to following numerous rules that they had no part in developing in the community external to schools. There is an understanding that community rules are developed to keep the environment and people safe. Most people are not irritated by the rules. They follow them. Students read on the restaurant entrance "No shoes, no shirt, no service" and know that they cannot enter without shoes and a shirt. Consider the notice posted in the U.S. Post Office lobby, "No loitering." You will not see students or adults hanging out there. At the swimming pool, people read, "No running. No glass containers. No street clothes. No talking to lifeguards while on duty." Those who break the rules lose their privilege of using the swimming pool.

School environments need be no different from communities in terms of communicating rules clearly. Systems-level management plans that keep environments and people safe should be developed, implemented, and upheld for culturally diverse student bodies. The keys are to teach the rules explicitly and to teach students the prosocial behaviors they need to follow the rules successfully.

School personnel interested in developing or revising building discipline policies may wish to use Sprick's model (1985) as an exemplar. Administrators, teachers, parents, and students need to work together closely to establish policies and procedures that will work for their school. Remember to include broad-based student representation in the democratic process of policy planning. Broad-based representation means that students of various backgrounds and interests participate: the athlete, the musician, the actor, the mechanic, the scholar, the potential dropout. This increases understanding and acceptance of the rules by student leaders who can communicate with their peers accordingly.

The basics of Sprick's schoolwide plan include the following: a school building statement of positive expectations for student behavior that is discussed with students, teachers' classroom rules, lists of consequences and procedures for implementing them, guidelines for office referrals, action guidelines for student lawbreakers, record-keeping procedures, and follow-up procedures for repeated problems. These important components of any schoolwide discipline plan are described below.

Statement of Positive Expectations for Student Behavior

Rosell (1986) found that most schools do not have simple, general statements of expectations. It is critical that school discipline plans clearly articulate the behaviors necessary to ensure a positive learning environment. An example follows of an overall statement of expectations for behavior. Illustrations of how to teach the responsibilities to students are provided later in the chapter.

> Your parents and community provide you with buildings, equipment, and staff to prepare you for success. We will give you the best education we can. We know that you will proudly keep our school "Blue Ribbon" by assuming the following responsibilities:
>
> 1. Attend class regularly and on time.
> 2. Give every assignment your best effort.
> 3. Treat all students, teachers, and property with respect.
> 4. Follow the specific rules in each class.

Educators can be guilty of assumptive teaching, that is, assuming that students know the expectations or appropriate behavior as a function of age: "He's twelve years old; he should know how to behave at school." Regardless of age, troublesome youth may not have learned acceptable social behaviors. Explicitly teach behavioral expectations through direct instruction, modeling, use of rationales, role playing, rehearsal or practice, and reinforcement.

The culture of school buildings is determined by the staff. Positive cultures can be created and maintained by informed, educated staff. Provide staff development to ensure that all school personnel—from bus drivers, custodians, and cooks to associates, teachers, and principals—are giving students positive feedback for following school expectations. Research shows that the rate of three positive feedback statements to one negative feedback statement of adults to students relieves 20 percent of the behavior problems occurring in the building (Batsche, 1996).

Write the School Discipline Plan

Discuss the plan with students and include their input. Include a description of positive expectations like those described earlier. Include misbehaviors that will lead to immediate referral and predetermined consequences. Both of these points are comprehensively described later in this chapter. Distribute and discuss the building plan during homeroom or all first-period classes on the first day of school or prior to implementation. Do not assume that students or personnel will remember all the policies after hearing them once. Periodic reviews are typically necessary every quarter or semester.

Teach and Uphold Classroom Rules

Sprick (1985) reported that students tend to have no difficulty working within a variety of rules as long as each teacher has outlined clear expectations for behavior. Batsche (1996), whose research was conducted in schools with culturally diverse populations and high incidences of behavior problems, recommended that teachers collaborate to write mutual rules common to all classrooms. Batsche's recommendation is sensitive to demands placed on students' memories when different teachers or areas of the school building have different rules and expectations. Examples of common classroom rules and how to teach them explicitly are presented later in this chapter. Teachers can add rules specific to their particular classrooms as necessary.

Determining In-Class or Out-of-Class Consequences

Teachers may rely heavily on the consequence of sending students to the office for administrators to handle. This is frustrating for building principals who have only a slim menu of consequences (e.g., "lecturing," suspension) from which to choose. Their choices of consequences are limited to relatively punitive ones and these are not appropriate for minor misbehaviors. Schoolwide discipline policies must emphasize that the majority of inappropriate behaviors will be handled in the classroom.

Teachers need to document their attempts to resolve minor misbehaviors within the classroom. Attempts to resolve minor misbehaviors include reteaching rules and procedures, class meetings, student-centered problem solving, time owed, parental contacts, isolation within the classroom, and written behavior improvement entries. These consequences are described in this and subsequent chapters. Office referrals are reserved for major misbehaviors, as cited in the next section.

Referrals to the Administration

Referrals should be made to the office only when the misbehavior cannot be handled in the classroom. If severe misbehaviors are identified as part of the school policy, then there will be no question as to whether a behavior should be referred or not. The following examples and nonexamples can be used to guide your own discussion of what misbehaviors should result in office referrals.

❑ *General examples:* behaviors that completely disrupt the learning environment, threaten the safety of others, demonstrate direct and persistent defiance, break the law
❑ *Actual examples:* use of drugs, fighting, throwing furniture, possession of a dangerous weapon, refusal to comply with a direct teacher command that was given when the student was disrupting the learning environment completely
❑ *Nonexamples:* talking back in class, a loud and disruptive student in class who will stop when requested to do so, verbal argument between students in class, swearing in class

Office Referral Forms

Office referrals should be accompanied by a completed referral form and a guardian contact. The following points should be entered on the referral form:

1. Specify what the problem was and describe what happened.
2. Describe your response to the problem and what has been done previously to solve the problem.

Consequences for Office Referrals

Sprick (1985) offers a partial menu of consequences from which to select at the office referral level. These consequences are familiar to most people; however, Sprick innovatively revised some of them. Referring parties need to respect the judgment of building principals in selecting the most appropriate consequences. If referring parties tend to disagree with the pattern of consequences selected by the principal across several referrals, they should resolve conflicts with the administrator using the same respectful, peaceable strategies students are expected to use when they disagree or have conflicts with others.

Discussions.   Procedures should be in place that will eliminate students' waiting in the office to see the person in charge of discipline. For instance, someone should always be "on call" to handle discipline problems or the waiting area should be non-stimulating (i.e., student cannot talk to or watch others).

Use discussions for the first minor offense only. If a discussion can help a student change her behavior, the student will not be back in the office again. A discussion should include the following steps:

1. Identify the problem.

2. Determine whether the misbehavior is partially caused by inability to handle the classroom work (if so, provide appropriate academic follow-through).
3. Explore alternative ways for the student to handle a similar problem in the future.
4. Assist the student in recognizing that she has the ability to choose her responses.

After-School Detention.   Most people are familiar with the consequence of after-school detention (ASD). ASD is often selected as a consequence even though there are problems with implementation. If ASD is used, one recommendation is that schools run an ASD room every day with teachers rotating duty for one week at a time. Resolve transportation problems by having the student report to detention the day after the student has been referred. This allows ample time to make transportation arrangements.

Guardian approval and support is needed for this plan to work. Letters home the first day of school can garner guardian support (see Figure 2–1). Guardians need to provide phone numbers where they can be reached or where messages can be left in order to inform them of ASDs.

When individual teachers supervise their own after-school detention, this classroom consequence is sometimes referred to as *time owed.* Time owed is considered to be a more natural consequence than after-school detention served with some third party. Consequences are considered natural if they are reasonable and likely outcomes of behaviors. When students are not following classroom rules, they are usually wasting class time. Teachers who use time owed require students to spend additional time in their classrooms as a natural payback. This consequence is the most effective form of ASD and should not require the use of the formal referral procedure (Sprick, 1985).

In-School Suspension.   In-school suspension (ISS) is another popular and often-used consequence. Its use should be restricted to severe misbehaviors that merited an office referral. When school records show that students are receiving ISS for mild problems, it is an indication that systems-level problems are present and need to be solved. For example, teachers may need in-service training in classroom management.

ISS has potential for great misuse, but when applied to severe misbehaviors it offers a number of benefits. Sprick (1985) cites the benefits of ISS as follows: (1) It removes students' problems from the classroom, (2) it keeps students within the school, (3) it reduces the likelihood that suspension is a student holiday, (4) it demonstrates to students and guardians that the school will deal with misbehavior, (5) it usually meets with guardian support, (6) students are not turned onto the street, and (7) ineffective guardians are not asked to handle problems that schools cannot handle.

To implement ISS effectively, educators need to preplan the parameters. The weaknesses of typical applications of ISS are enumerated below, as well as innova-

Dear Parents/Guardians,

I am pleased to have your child in my room. We are going to have a challenging and interesting year. You as parents or guardians are important to your child's progress in my class and it is important for us to communicate. The best time to reach me is between 3:00 and 3:45 p.m. at 555-5555 or you can call the central office for an appointment. I will return your call as soon as possible.

To have the best learning environment, the students and I selected four rules that students are expected to follow at school and in my classroom:

1. Act with respect in our actions toward all people and property.

2. Be on time, prepared with all materials, and ready to learn.

3. Promptly follow directions.

4. Follow all school rules.

The students and I have talked about the rules and practiced them in class. It would be very helpful to me if you would also discuss the rules to make sure your child understands them.

Special problems may call for consequences such as keeping your child after school or requiring your child to phone you to discuss a problem. Check the box to indicate your permission to use these rules and consequences with your child. If you have concerns, please write them in the space provided and I will work with you to decide on acceptable consequences.

I am pleased to have your child in my room this year. I look forward to a year of growth.

Sincerely,

_____

____ Agree with rules and consequences   ____ Do not agree

_____(Name)

Concerns: _____

_____

Figure 2–1
Example of a Letter to Parents/Guardians Explaining School and Classroom Rules and Procedures

tive adaptations. Here are Sprick's (1985) recommended parameters for implementing ISS:

1. Select a completely isolated area at least eight feet square with walls from floor to ceiling.
2. Determine how long students will spend in ISS and how the time will be spent.

Weaknesses of the typical three-day ISS are as follows: (1) Out-of-school suspension (OSS) is usually recommended on the third offense (following two ISSs). Students with significant problems could quickly accumulate a third offense and quickly receive an OSS. School discipline plans should avoid the use of OSS as much as possible. (2) Difficulties in only one class cause students to be removed from all classes for three days. (3) Subsequently, all teachers are required to design independent assignments for the student. (4) Under these conditions, the following questions tend to arise: Who determines whether assignments have been completed satisfactorily? What happens if the student fails to complete work during the three-day ISS? What happens if the student lacks the academic ability to do the work independently?

Alternate ISS programs have graduated schedules of consequences. An example follows:

1. *First referral:* fifteen minutes in ISS with student doing nothing
2. *Second referral:* one hour in ISS with student doing nothing
3. *Third referral from same class:* three days in ISS during the class period where problems occurred with class assignments from the teacher who has referred the student
4. *Fourth referral:* Three full days in ISS with assignments from all classes
5. Option of using automatic three-day ISS for certain severe problems such as use of drugs or violence.

The strengths of an alternate ISS program are multiple. First, the mild consequences on the first and second referrals are aversive to students because they are not allowed to do anything. The mild consequences also serve as a buffer zone against the possibility that a particular teacher was having a difficult day and overreacted to a possible misunderstanding.

The ISS program may be an inherently weak deterrent for some students who want to get out of class. ISS becomes a positive consequence for students who find classrooms aversive places. Alternative consequences (e.g., time owed, Saturday school) should be selected for these students.

Second, the graduated schedule of consequences provides extra steps prior to the use of out-of-school suspension. This extra time gives staff additional opportunities to assist the student in learning prosocial behaviors. Third, students do not miss out on large amounts of class time. Compare two referrals on the alternate plan (one hour and fifteen minutes of missing the class in which the behavior occurred) to two referrals on the three-day plan (six full days of missing all classes).

In-school suspension supervisors should reflect on the following criteria when determining guidelines for behavior and how to handle misbehavior in ISS:

1. Clearly state to students and guardians that any abuse of ISS results in out-of-school suspension.
2. Clearly communicate rules to students. Sprick's examples include:
   • Stay quiet.
   • Stay seated.
   • Raise your hand quietly if you need to use the rest room. Rest room breaks can be taken only during times listed on the board.
   • If completing assignments, the supervisor can give you assistance two times each hour.
3. Decide who will supervise ISS. Train them and give them written guidelines to follow. Sprick's examples include:
   • Remain neutral.
   • Do not try to counsel the students.
   • Interact as little as possible with students.
   • Tell the student the rules when the student checks into ISS.
   • Ask for questions and assign a seat.
   • If the student talks or makes noise, the time owed in ISS starts over.
   • Contact administration if student becomes violent or defies a direct instruction.
   • With more than one student, do not allow interactions. Place desks so that students cannot look at each other. Start the time over if students turn to each other or interact in any way.
4. Evaluate the effectiveness of the ISS program on the basis of repeated referrals.

Saturday School.   Some schools dedicate Saturday mornings to in-school suspension or time owed rather than Monday through Friday for the following reasons. Some students do not find missing classes during the week to be enough of an abrasive event that they would change their behavior rather than serve an in-school suspension. The purpose of negative consequences is to decrease the occurrence of inappropriate behaviors. Saturdays are considered precious time by most students who might monitor their behaviors in school better if they knew adverse behavior would result in spending time at school on a Saturday. Additionally, schools may not have a room available for in-school suspension during the school week.

Schools may pay teachers extra salary in order to have staff to cover Saturday school. Sometimes teachers take turns supervising Saturday school without extra pay rather than take their time to supervise students in or after school Monday through Friday.

Saturday school should not be considered an intervention that will dramatically change the behavior of most habitual offenders in in-school suspensions. It is simply one more option of natural, negative consequences that is used to gain students' attention and communicate that their behaviors are not acceptable. To that end, the negative consequence of Saturday school should not be used for minor offenses (e.g., tardiness, not following instructions, talking out of turn in class). Do not make the mistake of following up a few detentions for the same minor offense with in-school suspension or Saturday school. Teachers who are unable to find a successful intervention for repetitive, minor misbehaviors should seek assistance from colleagues, child or building assistance teams, or others who can brainstorm alternative interventions with them. Remember that students are not sent to the office for minor offenses even if they are repeated offenses. Minor offenses are managed in the classroom.

Some may question why such a large portion of preplanning is devoted to managing a small minority of students whose inappropriate behaviors merit referral to the office. The answer is that school personnel who are prepared for management at every level of the system will be prepared to deal most effectively with various misbehaviors. Recall the case of Jerad at the opening of Chapter 1. Effective management practices at the following levels could have prevented the melee and subsequent bad press in the local newspaper: letter home at the beginning of the year, guardian agreement with negative consequences, teacher's explicitly taught classroom rules and consequences, appropriate referrals to the office, and appropriate consequences at the office level.

Instructional Interventions

Batsche (1996) criticized school management for attempting to decrease negative behaviors without getting at the source of the misbehaviors. Often the source of negative behaviors is that students do not know how to display the positive behaviors that are required. He urged managers to overcome this critical flaw by teaching replacement behaviors. Sprick, Sprick, and Garrison (1993) developed a user-friendly set of materials for educators who have little or no background in teaching replacement behaviors. School counselors and school psychologists tend to have more extensive training in interventions for various behavior problems and can assist building principals and teachers with the following: structured reinforcement systems, increasing positive interactions, self-control training, self-monitoring, teaching desired behaviors, assessing and teaching social skills, restructuring self-talk, and mentoring. These are described more fully in later chapters.

Students who have already been referred to the office or are at risk for office referrals need to receive instruction in prosocial behavior. School policies may address the need to provide instruction to such students versus merely meting out negative consequences.

Implementing Consequences for Office Referrals

It is of paramount importance that personnel immediately process behavioral referrals and consistently implement consequences. Be creative with resources in order to accomplish this. Schools get ineffective results from office referrals when students wait in the office because their misbehavior is reinforced: They get to spend time out of class, interact with people passing through the office, and enjoy being on display as troublemakers.

Record-Keeping Procedures

Batsche (1996) reported building plans in which school psychologists were responsible for entering data from office referral records and graphing results. Graphs helped the staff determine whether current policies were working for individual students and teachers. For example, with graphs, personnel could determine answers to the following questions:

1. How many referrals were made by an individual teacher?
2. What grade level had the most referrals?
3. What period of the day had the most referrals?
4. What time period of the year had the most referrals?
5. What percentage of referrals was for problems outside the classroom?
6. What category of misbehavior led to the most referrals?
7. How many students had more than five referrals? Two referrals?
8. Given an individual student who had several referrals:
   a. Who referred the student?
   b. What consequences were implemented?
   c. What procedures were implemented to get the student more motivated or to teach the student prosocial behaviors?
   d. What was done to get parents involved?

Analyzing these kinds of data can lead to more effective systems-level interventions. For example, if the month of October yielded the most office referrals over two or more years, school personnel might want to emphasize citizenship during the month of October. They may wish to focus on teaching school rules and how to follow them, recognize student attempts to follow the rules, or participate in developing school spirit through a variety of activities.

If a Student Breaks a Law

This portion of the schoolwide policy should be completed in conjunction with local officials. Police, juvenile authorities, and a judge can give recommendations on when to involve authorities in offenses of vandalism, use of alcohol or other controlled substances, truancy, possession of weapons, and physical violence. Police can state at what point behaviors in school should be turned over to civil authorities.

Repeated Referrals

Record-keeping assists administrators in identifying students who need an additional support system. Four or more office referrals indicate obvious trouble adjusting to the school rules and expectations. Students who are repeatedly referred require the ongoing intervention support of various professionals (e.g., school guidance counselors, school psychologists, adult mentors). As mentioned earlier, intervention support could take the following forms: structured reinforcement systems, increasing positive interactions, self-control training, self-monitoring, teaching desired behaviors, assessing and teaching social skills, restructuring self-talk, and mentoring. These interventions are described in later chapters.

Teachers who refer large numbers of students from their classrooms may need help with classroom management. If many office referrals come from a particular place such as the cafeteria, staff can design procedures to decrease misbehaviors for that area.

CRISIS MANAGEMENT PLANNING

In addition to a schoolwide discipline plan, buildings need an explicit and comprehensive crisis management plan. Comprehensive crisis management plans include policies and procedures for managing (1) natural disasters (e.g., floods, hurricanes, earthquakes, fires); (2) deaths of students or school personnel, suicide and suicide attempts of students or school personnel; and (3) aggressive behaviors in the classroom and on school property (e.g., physical fights, threats with weapons by students, school personnel, or outsiders entering the building).

Teachers and principals on this school's problem-solving team collaboratively write the building's crisis management plan.

Policy and procedural planning for crisis management at the building level is not presented in this text. However, in the section on conduct management in Chapter 3, teachers will learn to manage aggressive behaviors in their classrooms. Each classroom teacher needs to develop a crisis management plan for aggression that matches the building crisis management plan, obtain the principal's approval for the crisis management plan, and file it in the principal's office.

CONCLUSION

Understanding misbehavior as a symptom of the system suggests that schoolwide discipline practices are critical. We have discussed the importance of preplanning schoolwide and classroom management from a systems-level perspective. The perspective is eclectic; it uses what works best in the ecological context. Educators must be completely familiar with the school building discipline plan and be able to implement it with integrity. Teachers who are sensitive to the impact of the entire system on students will want to file their crisis management plan and tentative classroom management plan in the office after approval by the principal. Positive schoolwide management practices are foundational to effective classroom management, as presented in upcoming chapters.

SUPPLEMENTARY QUESTIONS

1. What questions about schoolwide discipline practices in a school district should a recent undergraduate ask when interviewing for a teaching position?

2. If you were employed as a teacher in a school district that had ineffective schoolwide discipline policies, what could you do to make improvements?

SUPPLEMENTARY PROJECTS

1. Obtain the written schoolwide discipline plan of a school, perhaps where you are completing a field experience, and critique it using Sprick's recommendations in this chapter.

2. Interview some middle school and high school students to find out what they know and their opinions about their school's discipline policies and practices.

REFERENCES

Barnhart, C. L., & Stein, J. (Eds.). (1962). *American college dictionary*. New York: Random House.

Batsche, G. M. (1996, October). Implementing a comprehensive program for students with difficulties with anger control and aggression: Building on classroom strategies. Paper presented at the Iowa Behavioral Initiative Conference, Des Moines, IA.

Hyman, I. A. (1997). *School discipline and school violence: The teacher variance approach*. Needham Heights, MA: Allyn & Bacon.

Rosell, J. (1986). *An analysis of school district policies for disciplinary action with handicapped students*. Unpublished manuscript.

Sprick, R. (1985). *Discipline in the secondary classroom: A problem-by-problem survival guide*. West Nyack, NY: The Center for Applied Research in Education.

Sprick, R., Sprick, M., & Garrison, M. (1993). *Interventions: Collaborative planning for students at risk*. Longmont, CO: Sopris West.

CHAPTER 3

Foundations of Management: Basic Classroom Management Plan

An understanding of the material in this chapter will help you do the following:

❑ Plan for content, conduct, and covenant management of the first two weeks of school.
❑ Teach students classroom procedures.
❑ Teach students the procedures for managing physically dangerous behavior.
❑ Develop and teach classroom rules and consequences.
❑ Build positive classroom relationships.

Research in classroom management pinpoints the quality of management during the first two weeks of school as a critical indicator of successful management during the rest of the school year (Emmer, Evertson, Clements, & Worsham, 1994). Quality management indicators included in this chapter are content, conduct, and covenant management preplanning for the first two weeks. The importance of knowing and applying quality management criteria throughout the year, and especially during the first two weeks, cannot be overemphasized.

Some quality management criteria presented here may seem antithetical to what educators with certain presuppositions (see Chapter 1) may wish to address. If so, the educators are faced with a dilemma. Do they integrate recommendations from this chapter into their management plan? Do they develop what they think might be a better plan? Whatever they do, it should be done in an informed manner, with careful reflection and preplanning.

PREPLANNING AT THE CLASSROOM LEVEL

Reflective preplanning is a necessary condition for quality management, especially for first-year and novice teachers. Do not be misled by the common justification for "winging" it: "I do my best work under pressure." There is no scientific evidence that educators do their best work by "winging" it at the last minute. They may get their work done and it may be adequate to the point that they are not embarrassed about a public display, but it is rarely their best work. It would be far more accurate for people who "wing" it to state: "I do my only work under pressure" (Lucas, 1996) because, in actuality, some people rarely or never do their work until the last minute. People do their best work when they have ample time to develop ideas, lay them aside for a while, return to evaluate them critically, and refine them. In fact, teachers' sense of self-efficacy is related to formal planning (Unruh, 1994).

Preplanning at the building level was presented in Chapter 2. It is now time to introduce the second phase of preplanning: preplanning at the classroom level. This phase of management preplanning includes management of content (setting and instruction), conduct (behavior), and covenant (relationships) in the classroom during the first two weeks. The plan for the first two weeks of school can be refined at any time and used throughout the school year.

Much of a teacher's effectiveness and credibility is established on the first day of school. It is then that the teacher and students begin to know each other, classroom routines are defined and practiced, and patterns of lesson presentation are experienced. Let us begin our consideration of these elements of content and covenant management with an account of how one (fictional) teacher-leader set the stage for a successful school year.

> Looking in on the first day of school, we see Mr. Harmon moving among small groups of students, briefly engaging them in conversation about the previous summer. While doing so, he keeps an eye on the door so he can greet additional students as they enter the classroom. He listens carefully for

common summer adventures and privately notes special events on colorful T-shirts.

When the bell rings, Mr. Harmon begins class by using a few common experiences from the small-group conversations as a launching pad for discussing a few of his own memorable summer activities. He tells the class that last June he was ready for a summer break, but now, refreshed after the summer, he is excited about beginning another school year. He relates some of the highlights from the previous school year and shares his optimism about this year's plans. He also confides in students by telling them about a few topics and activities that fell flat last year; this year, he says, he will drop them in favor of some new, more promising possibilities. Mistakes are a source of growth, he tells the class, and they will frequently look for the growth opportunities in mistakes.

Mr. Harmon again uses some of the information he collected during the informal period before class to ask students about their summertime activities. As students volunteer experiences, he asks if there are others who did similar things and invites students to question classmates about their summer adventures. He inquires about unique and first-time experiences. Some of his remarks and observations are meant to establish rapport with students whose cumulative records suggest previous difficulties adjusting to school. Mr. Harmon balances the exciting stories of some highly spectacular trips with accounts of the simple pleasures derived from family gatherings and less costly leisure-time activities. Everyone in the group participates in the conversation.

This get-acquainted activity is followed by a handout designed to find out about student interests and accomplishments, which may later prove useful as subject-matter entry points. Mr. Harmon encourages students to be spontaneous as they respond to each item, and he informs them that their responses will be used to plan individual and group activities. He wants to make the class interesting, one that students will like regardless of their previous experiences with the subject, he explains. Students are encouraged to use the comment section on the handout to describe aspects of school life that they like and dislike.

Examples of instruments that can serve these purposes are presented later in this chapter.

Content Management

There is much more to setting and instructional management than is encompassed in this brief episode in Mr. Harmon's classroom. However, it should help the reader visualize the way these coordinated and integrated functions contribute to effective content management. This episode emphasized (1) typical management demands and decisions that occur prior to and during the first day of classes, (2) a few aspects of management that are common to both elementary and secondary school teachers, and (3) the importance of planning, that is, operating according to a schedule and appropriately distributing activities according to predetermined objectives and allocations of time.

Additional content management functions take up the remainder of this section and Chapter 5. Content management includes planning (1) use of the physical environment, (2) procedures that occur during the instructional day, and (3) instruction.

Many provisions for learning can be made before students are ever assembled for instruction. Teachers characteristically spend several days before school begins readying the classroom, organizing materials, testing equipment, and planning procedures that will support the instructional program. So, what are these important matters that need managing so that students get started on the right foot?

Effective Room Management

Teachers can make a powerful statement about how they feel about themselves, their students, and their job by the way they prepare the classroom (Grubaugh & Houston, 1990). Obviously, there are some givens, some institutional decisions about what a classroom should look like and how the space should be used, but there are also subtle ways to convey dedication or indifference.

Some teachers will be working in spaces that are already pleasantly painted, well illuminated, and temperature controlled. Teachers might be content with an already favorable setting and do little to add a personal touch. Others will work in buildings in a state of disrepair and in dark, dingy, stuffy classrooms. Teachers might try to transform the dismal setting into an inviting space by using the walls and bulletin boards to display the everyday work of previous students, to generate excitement, and to communicate behavioral expectations. An "at home" atmosphere of warmth and caring is created by displaying plants and personal decorative items that invite inquiries about the teacher's life outside of school.

Make the classroom a place where children feel at home. They can be their best and do their best because it is obvious someone feels they are important and wants them to succeed.

Floor Space and Seating Arrangements

Teaching is a constant quest for student attention. Careful student seating arrangements can maintain attention and facilitate overall monitoring of student behavior. Despite criticisms of neatly ordered rows of seats, this arrangement does provide for a single focal point in the room. With row and column seating, research indicated an increase in work completion. The quality of work remained the same (Bennett & Blundell, 1983). Having rows of seats, however, may not be an effective way to promote whole-class and small-group discussions (Rosenfield, Lambert, & Black, 1985). For this purpose, teachers generally design a classroom configuration that permits greater visual contact with speakers (e.g., circle or semicircle).

When teachers are actually making seating assignments, they should remember that school is a social event for most students. Being seated close to a friend can be helpful to some, detrimental to others. It is important to distribute the models of good behavior throughout the class. The social significance of modeling and the powerful effects of imitative behavior have been well documented by Bandura and Walters (1963).

*Careful seating arrangements
can maintain attention and promote small-group discussions.*

Traffic Areas

Students are not as well coordinated in the classroom as on the playground; they bump into furniture and one another. Clumsiness can provoke laughing and shoving. Heavily traveled lanes should be free of obstacles and wide enough to accommodate the flow.

Teachers can identify the traffic routes by "walking through" the activities likely to occur during the course of a school day. They can plan a typical schedule, list the kinds of behaviors required of students to fulfill its requirements, and then execute these requirements. A little imagination is also helpful to identify the ways students can deviate from planned procedures. Student behavior can be directed in subtle ways (e.g., arranging space so there is only one way to occupy and use it) or in more forceful ways (ensuring that traffic proceeds on signal and according to the rules of the road) (Guerney, 1989).

Supplies and Materials

Storage, Collection, and Distribution.   The organization of supplies and materials should be directly related to their educational functions. Materials for activities that occur frequently and involve the entire class must be most readily accessible and must be governed by the simplest procedures. For example, elementary teachers might prefer to have students keep selected workbooks in their desks. Secondary teachers might want to store basic or supplementary texts on a shelf just inside the classroom door so that students can select the appropriate book as they enter and exit the classroom each day. Use row dismissals to avoid congestion when students put books back on the shelf at the end of class.

There are never enough closets in a home and seldom enough cupboards in a classroom. Seldom-used materials that serve special learning objectives or are used

Management Challenge 3–1
Seating and Socializing

On the first day of school, Ms. Rodriguez prefers to let students select their own seats. She believes that students feel more secure and confident when they are surrounded by people they know and enjoy. This conviction is not without its problems. Some students enjoy one another's company too much. They engage in behaviors that often distract other members of the class. Their socializing also prevents them from getting their own work done.

1. Given Ms. Rodriguez's preference for self-chosen seating arrangements, what might she do to minimize the problems and still maintain the goodwill that often accompanies this practice?
2. When students who are seated by their friend(s) are unable to behave acceptably, what measures might be taken to correct the problem? How might students be involved in solving the problem?
3. Some students have few, if any, friends. They are often viewed as intruders when seated in the vicinity of a friendship group. What can the teacher do to influence the friendship patterns in a class so these individuals feel included?

for short time periods should not occupy prime storage space in the classroom. Supplies that are expensive and might be indiscriminately used by students should be kept out of the room's more public areas.

Many storage problems can be solved by systematic collection and distribution routines. Loading and unloading zones, with no "parking" in either, can reduce student traffic. Teach students the distribution routines so they can assist. A table at the front of the classroom might serve the functions of collecting and distributing. Teachers who are fortunate enough to have a door at the front and one at the back of the room might choose to distribute materials from the front table and collect them at the back table.

Timing can be an important factor in the collection of materials. When teachers can collect material on student time, before and after the bell rings, they should do so. When doing this creates other problems, such as delaying the starting time of class or causing congestion that results in ill will, the teacher should try to handle simple management routines during the "downtime" just beyond the halfway point in a class session or at the end of a class period. At both of these times, students are least likely to be task oriented. Collecting materials just after the halfway point is supported by studies of retention, which show that we are less likely to remember things that occur just beyond the middle of a learning sequence or period. The second suggestion takes advantage of a student habit: Students "pack up" their things and shut down their minds just before the class period is over. Of course, teachers can change this habit by the way they use this segment of time.

Teachers should not use the first few minutes of a class session to collect materials. Students are potentially most alert and receptive to instruction when a new activity is begun. Collecting materials at the beginning of a session can cause the informalities that precede the bell to spill over into class time. When there is no clear demarcation between work and leisure periods, there is a tendency for more leisure to creep into each class session. Of course, teachers can pick a point from the social conversation to draw students into the work of the day.

Assessment of Needs, Acquisition, and Management.   Conduct an inventory of existing equipment and supplies and the policies for their use. Each instructional activity will require previous arrangements for equipment and materials. Teachers can ensure the availability of these items by examining various activities for common material and equipment requirements.

Generally, most materials are supplied by the school district, with the balance supplied by students. Schools may send home a list of specific items that are students' responsibility to provide. Teachers often keep a small supply of these items on hand for students to "borrow." Loaning and borrowing can become a source of irritation and friction among classmates. Some teachers require collateral (e.g., student's watch, shoe) when supplies are loaned from their private store. When the loan is returned, the student gets the collateral back.

Equipment and materials that students do not purchase may be provided for all classrooms. For these items, the teacher need merely conduct an inventory and replenish the supply as needed. Other items, such as scissors and staplers, that are periodically used by students might be allocated on a so-many-units-per-student basis. Once again, teachers secure the equipment on the ratio established by the central office.

Teachers are generally given a modest amount of money to purchase equipment and materials. This money is used to purchase items that the school does not provide or items it supplies in insufficient quantities. Sometimes teachers will use their personal funds to augment the supply of less expensive items; they find that avoiding the hassle associated with sharing some items is worth the expense. Elementary teachers are likely to use their own money to purchase such items as activity packages to augment a unit of work, holiday decorations, and stickers to reward accomplishments. Secondary teachers are likely to use their own funds to buy products to support equipment acquisitions for an extracurricular program and certificates to recognize meritorious achievements.

Teachers may be asked, on short notice, to identify uses for school district funds unencumbered at the end of the school year. Keep a "wish list" ready that includes catalog information and you will be in a good position to secure part of this windfall.

Generally, the amount of material that teachers can draw from a central supply is restricted. Teachers need to organize their program by units of instruction and ascertain material needs to stay within these restrictions. Whether teachers use learning centers, learning packages, or a wide variety of other supplements to teacher presentations, resourceful and careful management of materials is important. Teachers must devise methods for using materials, prepare written instructions, demonstrate and practice these routines, and assign certain students to assist in their implementation.

Effective Instructional Management

Instruction during the first two weeks of school typically consists of review of the previous year's curriculum. Review is important for a number of reasons. First, review at the beginning of the year serves as an intellectual warm-up, much like calisthenics before strenuous athletic exertion or "ah-h-hing" before a vocal solo. Review "warms up" students' prior knowledge and they can then hook new learning onto it, organizing and elaborating (Woolfolk, 1995). Academic review gets students ready for more rigorous academic exercises that require new and great skill.

Second, review serves as informal pretesting and teacher appraisal of skill levels of individual students. Results of this appraisal should be used in future instructional planning. Third, review for students provides an opportunity for immediate success in a new and, therefore, less comfortable or even threatening environment. Success leads to a sense of comfort and confidence and subsequent motivation to engage in learning.

Lastly, review of prior knowledge affords most students the opportunity to function with automaticity in the academic area. This frees them up to process new stimuli (e.g., learning how to relate to the teacher and classmates, how to follow new procedures and rules) (Sternberg, 1985).

An additional aspect of content management is managing all the procedures students engage in throughout the instructional day. During the first two weeks of

---

Management Challenge 3–2

Transitions and Socializing

Mr. Greene sympathizes with students who find it difficult to remain quiet for an entire class period. He recalls his own student days when he was always preoccupied with finding opportunities to share important bits of information with others—humorous observations, plans for after school, and choice morsels of gossip.

Mr. Greene believes that students can be so consumed with exchanging social news that they are unable to concentrate on the task at hand. He sees no harm in letting students get these items of social significance off their minds so they can give their full attention to academic work. Thus, he thinks that such conversation might be allowed when assignments are being collected, when materials are being distributed, or when papers are being exchanged for correction.

1. What is your impression of Mr. Greene's analysis of the situation and his justification for permitting students a brief respite from academic concerns?
2. What do you think of his solution?
3. What provisions must his solution include if it is to succeed?
4. What kinds of problems do you think this solution might create? Do these problems more than offset the benefits of the practice Mr. Greene advocates?

Use this checklist to identify classroom management procedures that should be followed in your classroom. To analyze your personal management:

1. Check the space for each item for which you do have a set procedure to teach.

2. Put an asterisk next to those items for which you do not have a procedure but feel you should.

3. Circle those items you feel should be taught in the beginning days of a class.

Beginning Class
___Roll call, absentees
___Tardy students/policy
___Academic warm-ups or getting ready
    routines
___Distributing materials
___Expected student behavior
___Readmitted students

Room/School Areas
___Shared materials
___Teacher's desk
___Water fountain, bathroom, pencil
    sharpener
___Student storage/lockers
___Materials needed for class
___Lack of materials procedure
___Seating arrangement
___Location of classroom materials

Setting Up Independent Work
___Defining working alone
___Identifying problems
___Identifying resources
___Identifying solutions
___Scheduling
___Interim checkpoints

Instructional Activities
___Teacher/student contacts
___Student movement in the room
___Signals for students' attention
___Signals for teacher's attention
___Student talk during seatwork
___Activities to do when work is completed
___Student participation
___Laboratory procedures
___Student movement in and out of small
    group
___Expected behavior in group
___Movement in room/area

Ending Class
___Putting away supplies, equipment
___Cleaning up
___Organizing materials
___Dismissing class
___Chairs up last period

Interruptions
___Rules
___Talk among students
___Conduct during interruptions or delays
___Passing out books, supplies
___Turning in work
___Handing back assignments
___Getting back assignments
___Out-of-seat policies

Figure 3–1
A Checklist for the Beginning of the School Year

school, it is important to teach these classroom procedures. Figure 3–1 provides a relatively thorough checklist of all the procedures teachers must manage during any given school day. To manage procedures effectively, teachers must plan how to carry out each procedure and how to teach it to students. Effective teaching includes direct instruction, modeling, guided practice, independent practice, and corrective feedback.

Academic Feedback
___Rewards and incentives
___Posting student work
___Communicating with parents
___Students' record of grades
___Written comments on assignments
___Progress reports

Other Procedures
___Fire/tornado drills
___Lunch procedures
___Student helpers
___Safety procedures
___Teacher resource availability

Work Requirements
___Heading on papers
___Use of pen or pencil
___Format for homework
___Neatness, legibility
___Incomplete work
___Late work
___Missed work
___Due dates
___Make-up work
___Supplies
___Lab steps to follow
___Typed or handwritten papers

Communicating Assignments
___Posting assignments
___Orally giving assignments
___Provision for absentees
___Requirements for long-term assignments
___Assignments
___Returning assignments
___Homework assignments

Monitoring Student Work
___Total in-class oral participation
___Completion of in-class assignments
___Completion of homework
___Completion of stages of long-term assignments
___Monitoring all students

Checking Assignments in Class
___Students exchanging papers
___Marking and grading assignments
___Turning in assgnments
___Students correcting errors

Grading Procedures
___Determining report card grades
___Recording grades
___Grading stages of long-term assignments
___Extra credit work
___Keeping records of papers/grades/ assignments
___Grading criteria
___Contracting with students for grades
___Student-kept grade log

For example, to teach procedures for appropriate behavior at the opening of class, the elementary teacher might do the following on the first day of class.

Script

"Students, beginning today we will learn to follow classroom procedures for starting work at the beginning of the class. On the projector screen I'll show a brief assignment to complete while I am taking roll and lunch count. You will have about three minutes to work independently on the activity. Your work typically will serve as the basis for the next activity of the day. You are to be on task, doing your best work, even if you are not sure of what you think I want. If visitors walked in at the beginning of this class, they would see you in your seats writing and thinking on your own. What would it sound like to them?"
(Students should respond that it would be quiet.)

"Let's try it now. When I turn on the projector, read the assignment on the screen and work for about three minutes while I take roll and lunch count. When I am through, I will turn off the screen. I will give you feedback on how I think you did and you can ask questions about the procedure. Before we begin, are there any questions about what you should be doing?"

(Turn on projector.)

Educators who plan to use cooperative learning structures should also teach students the procedures and skills needed for successful group learning. These skills include appropriate social skills for participating in a peer group.

It may take the entire first two weeks of class to teach whole-class procedures and complete reviews. Educators may wish to teach cooperative learning and social skill procedures after the first two weeks. Chapter 5 presents procedures for cooperative learning and social skills training.

To assist in planning procedures for the first two weeks of school, recall that a common sequence of classroom instructional activities is:

1. Opening routine
2. Checking
3. Content development
4. Seatwork or discussion
5. (Repeat steps 2 through 4 for each new content introduced in a single class period.)
6. Closing

Conduct Management

The stage is also set for conduct management during the first two weeks. Conduct management includes establishing explicit rules or guidelines for individual and group behavior while on school property. It also includes establishing positive and negative consequences for following or not following the rules, respectively. Figures 3–2 and 3–3 show typical lists of classroom rules at the elementary and secondary levels, respectively.

Students come from diverse cultural backgrounds and, consequently, have varied expectations for their own behavior. Not every student will have the same

Figure 3–2
Elementary Classroom Rules

- Be polite and helpful.
- Respect other people's property.
- Listen quietly while others are speaking.
- Respect and be polite to all people.
- Obey all school rules.

Figure 3–3
Secondary Classroom Rules

- Be in your seat with all necessary materials and ready to learn when the bell rings.
- Respect all people and their property.
- Follow directions promptly the first time given.
- Obey all school rules.

conduct experiences or expectations as the teacher. When there is a mismatch between the students' conduct behaviors and the teacher's expected conduct behaviors, conduct management problems occur. It is the teacher's responsibility to manage the mismatch by making management decisions that bring about a better match.

On the first or second day of class, the teacher facilitates a student discussion of what they think appropriate conduct in the classroom should be. Indicate that the purpose of the discussion is to brainstorm and then define brainstorming (e.g., all students' ideas are valued and recorded without discussion or judgment). As the discussion occurs, write student comments and input on the board or large sheets of butcher paper taped on the wall. Students will offer similar ideas but use different words to describe them. Record everyone's comments, even if it seems like duplication.

After the discussion is completed, the teacher and students indicate which ideas seem to be targeting the same behavior. This group of ideas will sound like one of the rules in Figure 3–2 or 3–3. The teacher states the rule tentatively and asks students if that rule seems to represent what they would like to follow in their classroom. This procedure continues until all student comments have either resulted in a rule or been set aside as mutually agreed on by students. Sometimes students will generate a new or different rule than those described above. Accept and record their rule. Sometimes students will not generate any ideas that could form a rule like the ones on the lists. The teacher can determine how important the particular rule is to the classroom and subsequently either lead the students in a discussion about the "forgotten" rule or not.

After the list of student-generated rules is finalized, the teacher directs the class in examining how the rules define appropriate and inappropriate behavior in the class. She teaches by example and nonexample. Nonexamples should be close or borderline behaviors that students may have difficulty distinguishing from appropriate behavior. After the teacher models specific examples and nonexamples, she asks for various students to offer additional examples and nonexamples, respectively.

Some readers may argue that the procedures described here are too time consuming. They are, indeed, time consuming. However, dealing with student behavior problems is even more time consuming, not to mention frustrating to the point of burnout for many teachers. Cotton (1990) found that approximately one-half of classroom time was taken up with noninstructional activities. Discipline problems were responsible for a significant portion of this lost instructional time.

Time spent in preventing student behavior problems is time well spent. The value of student collaboration in defining the classroom rules is multifaceted. Students feel a sense of ownership and pride when they have a voice in important management decisions. They are more likely to remember the rules, to value the rules, and to adhere to the rules themselves while encouraging their peers to follow the rules. They are more likely to take a positive role in group problem solving should a peer have difficulty following the rules. Finally, they build skills in the democratic process of negotiating behavioral expectations for a diverse social group of which they are a part.

Although some preservice teachers will be comfortable with the process just described, other preservice teachers will be uncomfortable facilitating the rules discussion their first year of teaching. It seems overwhelming to those who express a need for more teacher control at the beginning of their professional careers. It is desirable to have insight into your own need for control both in this management situation and in all others. A consistent need for high levels of control can be problematic in schools. Educators who are most comfortable under conditions of high control will need to develop leadership skills that give students some sense of control, also. On the other hand, there is nothing wrong with starting the first year of teaching with a set of teacher-developed classroom rules and consequences that are taught to students during the first day or two of class.

Preservice teachers who are comfortable with collaboration can write a script for collaboratively developing rules and practice delivering it. Others who intend to begin their first teaching job with their own rules can write a script for already developed rules and practice it. As these teachers grow more comfortable with managing student conduct they can develop collaborative rules in future years. An example of a script for collaboratively developed classroom rules follows. See Figure 3–4 for a list of one teacher's possible classroom rules and positive and negative consequences for this script. The script and consequences were developed by an undergraduate student who had completed her student teaching and intended to work collaboratively with students to develop rules and consequences during her first year of teaching.

Script for Collaboration on Determining Classroom Rules

"To start off class today, I want to give you one minute of quiet time to think about an important question. There's no right or wrong answer, just your opinion. I'll ask the question, then we'll have one silent minute to think, and we'll discuss our answers. Ready?"

"If eighth graders had to live by just one rule, what should that rule be?"

(Encourage all to share ideas, listing them on the blackboard. Note similarities, ask for specifics, and contrast them until all willing students have contributed. Post the classroom rules.)

"[Name], will you read rule one for us?"

"Act with respect toward all people and property."

"Can anyone think of an example of someone following that rule?"

(Listening while someone is talking, not touching other people's belongings, using school supplies carefully, talking with words and tone that show respect, etc.)

"How about times when a person might be breaking that rule?"

Rules

- Act with respect toward all people and property.
- Be on time, ready to learn, with materials.
- Promptly follow directions to the best of your ability.
- Follow all school rules.

Positive Consequences

- Verbal and written praise from school personnel to student or parents
- Music during individual work time
- Free time
- Time outside room (library, computer center, outside, hallway, etc.)
- Student choice (soda during video, read on floor, teacher read aloud, games, etc.)

Negative Consequences

- Verbal and written reminders or warnings
- Time owed on own time
- Planned discussion on own time
- Exclusion from daily positive consequences
- Other as appropriate (e.g., clean up mess, redo work, apology, school service)
- Parent contact at any time by note or phone call to recognize or alert to student's behavior

Figure 3–4
Classroom Rules and Positive and Negative Consequences

(Put-downs, writing on the desk, teasing, taking someone's belongings, talking while another person is talking, etc.)

"[Name], will you read rule two for us?"

"Be on time, ready to learn, with materials."

"Most of that rule is self-explanatory, bring your book, paper, and a pen, and don't be late. How about the ready to learn part? Can anyone explain that? [Name]?"

(Read the assigned material, do homework, pay attention, quit talking when class starts, etc.)

"Why is this rule important? What happens when some people are not ready with all their materials?"

(Some people hold back the rest of the class by being unprepared.)

"[Name], please read the third rule for us."

"Promptly follow directions to the best of your ability."

"What does promptly mean?"

(Quickly.)

"What are some ways that we work to the best of our ability?"

(Neat writing, staying on task, concentrating, asking questions, using strategies, and following all steps of a task.)

(Do the same teaching activity with the school rules, whatever they may be.)

"Good thinking! I can tell that this class understands the rules. Please ask if you have any questions about the rules or ideas to change or replace the rules we just talked about. When we follow the rules of our class, I know that we can handle more privileges because I can see mature behaviors.

Positive consequences that might happen after the whole class, a small group, or a person follows the rules consistently might be verbal praise or a written note of recognition, listening to music during work time, a few minutes of free time, having class outside our room, or other things you think of, like soda during a video, playing a game, and so on. We will be working on a list of things that you consider positive consequences a little later on."

"We also need to have consequences for someone who chooses not to follow the rules so that they can correct their behavior. If I see students not following a rule, I will remind them of the rule or warn them that they are breaking the rule. The next step could be time owed to me before or after school or a planned discussion about the problem on the students' free time. What other consequences can you think of that would be fair for not following each rule? Let's start with acting with respect. If someone broke that rule, what would be a good consequence?"

(Apologize verbally or in writing, fix or replace property, do service in the school, clean up a mess, etc.)

"Those sound pretty logical to me; let's look at the next rule. How about being on time, ready to learn, and prepared? What should we do about breaking that rule?"

(Owe time, redo work, lose points, lose privileges for the day, etc.)

"The last one is a little harder. What do you think I should use as a consequence for someone not following a direction right away?"

(Warn, owe time, etc.)

"I'm happy with the consequences we have thought of—does anyone want to change or add to these?"

"You will be glad to hear that any problems we have with following rules in this class will be resolved by the involved parties in this class—with one exception. If anyone is disruptive to learning and teaching and will not stop, I will send that person to the office. Consequences in the office are determined with the help of the disciplinary officer in charge that day. Here is a list of the consequences that you can expect."

(Give list of out-of-class consequences.)

"The goal of the school is to help you be successful here. Even when negative consequences are used, all of us are committed to carrying out a plan that will help students solve problems in a positive manner. Now that you know what some possible consequences might be, you won't be surprised when I implement one for not following a rule."

"In the next few days, I will be sending a letter to your parents or guardians that explains the rules and consequences this class has developed. I will ask them to discuss the list with you. I want to make sure that everyone understands and agrees to our plan. If parents or guardians disagree with anything, they can complete an attached form and return it. I will give you a copy of the letter in class so you will know what I said in it." (See Figure 2–1.)

Positive and negative consequences can be brainstormed and determined using the same teacher–student collaborative process outlined in the preceding script. Emphasize the positive aspects of following classroom rules by brainstorming positive consequences first. Figure 3–5 provides a list of commonly brainstormed positive consequences. Note that students see things that adults call responsibilities as positive consequences. Consequences are presented in categories: classroom and schoolwide tasks (social responsibility), things that cost money, verbal feedback,

---

Positive Consequences

Classroom and schoolwide tasks (social responsibility)
- Special jobs—student helper, peer tutor
- Student teaches a portion of the lesson
- Homework pass (excused from a homework assignment)
- Pass to computer lab, gym, etc.
- Choices in lesson activities

Financial costs
- Food—pizza party, snacks
- Field trip
- Grab bags

Verbal and written feedback to students and guardians
- Tell the student what was well done
- Send a special note to the student or present a certificate of merit
- Call the guardian and explain what the student did well
- Send a positive note to the guardian

Freedoms
- Class gets free time
- Computer time
- Free read time
- A few extra minutes of recess
- Hold class outside
- Short class party

- Play music during seatwork
- Movie time
- Learning game day
- Tickets to student lounge, pop room
- Dress up/down day
- Student choice of activity
- Other privileges

Public recognition
- Compliment the student in front of another staff member
- Ask a staff member to acknowledge the student's accomplishments
- Post the student's work in a public place
- Read the student's work to the class
- Shake the student's hand
- Give the student extra adult time

Negative Consequences
- Ignoring
- Gentle verbal reprimands
- Verbal cues and warnings
- Delaying
- Parental contacts
- Time owed
- In-class time-out
- Behavior improvement form
- Natural consequence (e.g., fix it if you broke it)
- Referral to office

Figure 3–5
Menu of Positive and Negative Consequences for Classroom Use

freedoms, and public recognition. Teachers should be prepared in advance to set boundaries on positive consequences and know whether and how they are going to fund positive consequences that cost money.

A discussion of rules for conduct in school buildings or classrooms may be met with dismay by those who hold philosophical beliefs about the nature of humans as good. Cultures go through periods in which it is not acceptable or popular to talk about rules for behavior. Rules may be viewed as oppressive and stripping away the dignity of human beings by indirectly communicating that it is a given that students will do the wrong thing without explicit rules in place. Rules may be viewed as designed to trip up students so that they can be punished. It would be easy, however, to view rules in a helpful, positive reframed manner. For example, rules serve as a common standard to which disparate people can ascribe in order to promote safe, respectful, organized, and efficient environments that are mutually beneficial to all.

An additional reason for rules of conduct is to encourage respectful behavior toward others. Often we do not intend to be disrespectful, we are just busy. In a *Cathy* cartoon, we noticed rules posted in the employee lounge where she worked. The rules consisted of how to use the coffee room. Why? Isn't it taking a negative view of adults? After all, they are responsible people. Wouldn't it be assumed that adults know the common expectations for behavior in an employee lounge? Perhaps lounges become unkempt because employees are busy. Perhaps they think that one lone cup left in the sink of the coffee room will not matter. After twelve busy workers leave cups scattered around, it becomes a problem for someone (e.g., the secretary, the custodian, colleagues). Rules serve as reminders to busy people with many important matters on their minds and, thus, assist in maintaining respect for others.

If the word *rules* is offensive, call rules by a different name. Try *standards of excellence, policies,* or *guidelines.* But have them, teach them, model them, discuss them, and uphold them. State rules in a positive manner. Contrast the rules about pets in public places that you see in Figure 3–6. Does one manner of stating the rule make you more defensive or rebellious than the other? Does one sound more positive? If you are a pet lover, you may not feel too good about either of the rules. But if there is going to be a rule about your pet in public places, which one makes you feel more welcome or accepted?

You probably selected the better rule as being the one that says "Please have pets on leashes at all times." The rule that stated "No pets without leashes" was probably not your favorite. Note that both rules provide the same boundaries, yet the first rule uses a communication style that is more positive than the other.

Albert (1994) suggested that behavior problems develop when schools rely on rules for managing student behavior. She stated that students tend to see *rule* as a four-letter word signifying "how adults control kids." Her solution is to replace rules with a code of conduct that defines how members of a community are expected to interact with each other. Call it rules, call it code of conduct. But do it. In studies from the 1960s through the 1990s, researchers found that the active teaching of rules paired with specific praise and feedback optimally increased appro-

Figure 3–6
Stating Rules Positively

priate behavior of students (Johnson, Stoner, & Green, 1996; Madsen, Becker, & Thomas, 1968; Paine, Radicchi, Rosellini, Deutchman, & Darch, 1983). A description of one of these studies follows.

Johnson et al. (1996) served as school psychology consultants to a group of teachers dealing with the unruly behavior of a class of seventh-grade students in a rural public school. No individual children were referred as more problematic than others. The focus was on the entire class. Unruly behaviors included students talking without raising their hands, tripping or chasing each other, throwing paper, engaging in activities other than the one assigned, and leaving the classroom to gather supplies needed to complete classroom assignments. Teachers stated that these behaviors often disrupted classroom activities and decreased the amount of time spent in instructional activities.

Three of the teachers agreed to work on a team and use an experimental school society orientation that emphasized collaboration and data-based outcomes for decision making rather than advocacy of any particular solution. All team members agreed that the interventions should emphasize educating students to prevent problems rather than react with negative consequences. Baseline observations of student behaviors in the three classes were completed and the team met collaboratively to select interventions: (1) use of a class syllabus along with individual student achievement assessment in language arts, (2) active teaching of classroom rules in math, and (3) student self-monitoring of behavior in reading.

None of the teachers believed that active teaching of the classroom rules as an intervention would be successful, especially for an entire class. All three teachers believed that students were aware of their classroom rules and that the rules had been taught sufficiently already. Interventions occurred for five days and student behavior data were collected across all five days. The team met to discuss the efficacy of the interventions and concurred that active teaching of classroom rules in the math class resulted in the greatest increase in appropriate behavior. For the next five days, the three teachers and the science teacher used the rules intervention. Appropriate behavior reached the 90 to 100 percent level in all classrooms across the last five days.

Proactive approaches (e.g., organizing classroom procedures to promote student engaged behavior and minimize student misbehavior) have replaced reactive approaches or responding after individual student misbehavior (Gettinger, 1988). The proactive intervention of emphasizing classroom rules was shown to be the most effective intervention, particularly in terms of time and effort for teachers compared to other interventions. Actively teaching rules serves two important functions. Rules communicate exactly what is expected and teachers can attend to students when their behavior is consistent with the rules.

The final stage in preparing for conduct management in the first two weeks of school is implementing the crisis management plan for aggressive behaviors in the school environment. A 1995 Midwest newspaper showed a photo of a middle school teacher carried on a stretcher out of a school building, after he was shot by a seventh-grade student during a social studies class. During 1996 in the northwest region of the United States, a fourteen-year-old, ninth-grade student came to algebra class and shot and killed a female teacher and two male students. A female student received a gunshot wound that nearly severed her arm and damaged her liver, diaphragm, and kidneys. Plan ahead by having educators and students trained to respond to threats.

Managing Physically Dangerous Behavior

Sprick, Sprick, and Garrison (1993) provided a model for dealing with student behavior that posed threats to another's physical safety—other students, adults, or the dangerous student. Although educators cannot be sure that implementing any one model will successfully resolve all incidents of physically dangerous behavior, a plan of action that is rehearsed can help establish a calmer atmosphere during a crisis. Calm, thoughtful action is always better than panic. Law enforcement agents in communities are often trained to assist in developing safety procedures to follow during aggressive episodes. Schools can invite them to offer staff development courses in managing aggressive behaviors. The Sprick et al. model (1993) for managing physically dangerous behaviors is described here.

Physically dangerous behaviors include fighting, head banging, hitting windows, self-biting, self-pinching, assault, out-of-control behaviors, and verbal threats. The goal of the crisis plan is to help staff respond swiftly and professionally and with objectivity and consistency.

Several principles should guide the implementation of a crisis plan for physically dangerous behavior:

1. Safety is the first consideration. Staff are not required to put themselves in direct physical jeopardy. There are only two options:
   a. Get everyone out of the way.
   b. Adults physically restrain the student.
2. Intervention must be immediate. There are two priorities:
   a. Ensure that no one is hurt.
   b. Do not reinforce student for behavior.
3. Follow-up intervention must be intensive and it will be time consuming.
4. Early intervention has a higher probability of helping to resolve the problem. Do not hesitate to intervene. Many educators think that the first occurrence will be the only one. They "sweep the problem under the carpet" and hope that it is the last they will hear of it. Educators must take every occurrence of an aggressive act seriously and seek professional assistance in carrying out interventions.

Additional truths to be mindful of include these: (1) Nothing can be done to make the situation pleasant. (2) Intense incidents are stressful and exhausting for everyone. (3) Injury has potential legal repercussions. (4) Successful intervention requires the resources and cooperation of many.

Teachers should not be expected to develop or complete interventions alone. Effective interventions include the following five components implemented concurrently: ensure safety, involve guardians, keep records, determine referrals, and instruct students. An abbreviated version of the Sprick et al. plan (1993) is listed in Figure 3–7.

Beginning in the first week of school, teachers typically assist students in drill and practice of safety routines for such things as fire and tornado threats. The same drill and practice must be completed for safety from other threats such as out-of-control behavior of a peer. Teachers should periodically repeat drill and practice throughout the school year. Once a month is not too often to rehearse safety routines when threats occur frequently and students have difficulty remembering or following the procedures. If one time through the routine does not go smoothly, immediately try it again.

An example follows of a script that teachers can use to introduce safety instruction for managing physically dangerous behavior. The script should be followed by role play or drill and practice of what students are to do in case of a threat. Before the role play begins, the teacher selects a student who agrees to play the aggressive role. The teacher introduces the safety lesson as in the script, states the prompt "Students, room clear," tells students to imagine that someone in the middle of the class is angry and turning over desks, and then has students practice clearing the room.

The script includes instruction in how to obey the prompt "Room clear." Teachers will use this prompt to cue students to complete the prescribed safety rou-

---

Establish policies for responding to physically dangerous behavior:

1. Develop record-keeping procedures for all incidents of such behavior.

2. Involve the student's guardian(s).

Determine whether the student should be referred to special education, and whether other agencies should be involved.

Determine whether there will be consequences for the dangerous student.

Teach the student to manage her or his own behavior.

Safety Procedures

1. Use "room clears."
   - Where will students go and what will they do during a "room clear"?
   - How will the dangerous student be supervised?
2. Use physical intervention with caution.
   - Can students be dispersed so there is no need for physical restraint?
   - Will verbal interventions work (before physical interventions)?
   - Did we call for help before beginning physical interventions?
   - Is restraint necessary? Will it be helpful?

Figure 3–7

Classroom Plan for Managing Physically Dangerous Behavior

Source: Sprick, R., Sprick, M., & Garrison, M. (1993). *Interventions: Collaborative planning for students at risk.* Longmont, CO: Sopris West. Reprinted with permission.

tine. The prompt can be written on a sign and displayed on classroom walls, along with the prompts for tornado and fire drills.

Teachers may determine that they can use variations of this prompt. For example, the prompt "Students, move away" may be used to direct students away from a danger zone when (1) the path to the door and the hall is obstructed or (2) the threat is great enough to necessitate moving students out of the way but not so great that students need to exit the room. For example, if someone is brandishing a weapon in the doorway, students will not be able to escape from the room.

Teachers will often be busy with the out-of-control student or assisting the other students. Therefore, teachers should train two or three responsible and dependable students in how to get help. The teacher may send only one student for assistance, but alternates should be available should a trained student be absent on a given day. Options for getting assistance include directing a student assistant to contact the principal's office via the intercom, telephone, or beep system in place in the school. Before teaching the script about physically dangerous behavior, choose the two or three students that will contact the principal for help and train them in their procedures. Select one of them for the role play when teaching the crisis procedure to students.

Script for Teaching Procedures for Physically Dangerous Behavior

"There may be times when it is not safe in school, not because of a fire or a tornado, but because somebody is upset and doing unsafe things like fighting and hitting. Can you think of some other unsafe things that somebody might do when they are upset?"

(Discuss student responses.)

"When someone is doing things that are not safe, it is very important for the rest of us to act very quickly to keep everybody safe. I am going to tell you the steps to keep safe and then we will practice them. When I notice that somebody, for example, Shawna, is upset and doing dangerous things, I will say 'Room clear.' When you hear me say 'Room clear,' each of you will stay calm and move away from the danger. What does staying calm mean?"

(Discuss student responses.)

"To move away from the danger, you are to leave the room and wait in the hallway for an adult to come. The two steps are (1) the teacher will see the danger and will say 'Room clear' and (2) students will stay calm and quickly move away from the danger, go out of the room, and wait in the hall.

"Let's practice the 'Room clear' drill. Everyone cannot get out of the door at the same time. I will show you how to take your turn leaving the room and where to stand in the hallway to wait for an adult. When we have finished our first practice, I will answer any questions that you have."

(When drill is complete and students are back in their seats, Shawna is in the office continuing the role play. The teachers says the following to the students in their seats.)

"Shawna has had a very difficult time. Shawna will probably feel very uncomfortable about what has happened and it will be important for all of us to help her feel like a regular sixth grader. Everyone of us will need to continue working as a community/group. Everyone in here has a special goal to work on, not just Shawna. For example, I have to work on being patient. Shawna will be working on controlling her angry feelings."

When a "Room clear" prompt has cleared the room, teachers can step into the hall right outside the door and monitor the disruptive student until help arrives. Sometimes teachers may be able to use their communication skills to calm the student and deescalate the situation.

School personnel must take steps to ensure the safety of everyone through a well-articulated and well-understood crisis management system. Do not confuse having school rules and policies about violent behavior with having staff trained and assigned to implement a plan and procedures when a rule is violated.

Educators may hold beliefs that practicing safety procedures frightens students unnecessarily and, therefore, no practices are conducted. This is a grievous error when there is a student in the classroom who engages in physically dangerous behavior. Classmates who do not know the steps to keeping themselves safe are at a disadvantage. They are more frightened by aggressive acts when they have not been prepared to keep themselves safe.

Guidelines for School Building Policies and Procedures.   In addition to the overall plan shown in Figure 3–7, teachers should receive additional help rapidly. They should use a prearranged signal indicating that a crisis is occurring. School buildings should have a plan for who will respond immediately, a chain of command in case the first person is unavailable, and a communication process to ensure that everyone involved will be kept informed. This plan must be carefully designed and rehearsed occasionally.

Staff must be trained to implement the plan. Training should include which behaviors to ignore and which require intervention. Adults who supervise should be trained to stand at the door, to determine what actions to take if the situation escalates, and to implement proper physical restraint techniques.

It is critical to recognize that consequences for out-of-control behavior tend to have little effect on prevention but may be part of a comprehensive plan. Appropriate consequences include owing time and restitution. Suspension for special education students cannot be instituted without due process.

Guidelines for Location of the Class During "Room Clear" Procedures.   Students should go to the hallway and wait for an adult. If dangerous behavior occurs on the playground, students should be taught to move away from the source of disruption. When an adult arrives, the class goes to a predetermined location. Prepared-in-advance, relevant instructional tasks are stored at the location and the class completes them.

Guidelines for Use of Physical Restraint.   There are a number of parameters to keep in mind when contemplating the use of physical restraint. The use of a room clear without physical restraint is preferred because it helps ensure everyone's safety more so than physical restraint without a room clear. Furthermore, physical restraint is more likely to result in injury to someone than a room clear. For some students, physical restraint can result in heightening the emotional intensity. The students are reinforced for out-of-control behavior due to the physical interaction with an adult. Use of physical restraint is less likely to teach the student that she can control her own behavior.

Physical restraint is not an option when the adult is not large or strong enough, the adult is unable to restrain the student easily, there is no other adult to assist, and the adult is not adequately trained/experienced in restraint procedures. Instead, try verbal interventions first. Use a firm and loud command. "Roland, stop beating on the window and move to this side of the room, now!" When more than one student is involved, direct each one to a different location. "Roland, move over to the doorway! Aaron, move over to the lockers!"

Guidelines for Working with Guardians.   After the first incident of physically dangerous behavior, request that parents attend a conference. Parents of a disruptive student often do not know what to do and it will be important for educators to take a positive, problem-solving approach. At the conference, complete four critical activities: (1) Communicate staff's willingness to help the student, (2) mutually determine the severity of the problem, (3) begin joint problem solving, and (4) involve other social agencies as appropriate.

Home–school partnerships that have already been developed will be a good foundation for crisis work. Phone calls home (see later section on Covenant Management) and letters home (see Figure 2–1) during the first week of school represent two positive contacts that teachers have initiated. Based on these school efforts, guardians are more likely to have a sense of a positive relationship with the school.

Guidelines for Record-Keeping and Reporting Procedures.   Record keeping is necessary for these reasons:

❏ Assist staff in developing and evaluating interventions.
❏ Needed if a special education referral is initiated.
❏ Needed if any legal issues arise related to a student's behavior (e.g., assault charges filed by an injured student, school sued for negligence, parents object to confinement, school personnel accused of discriminatory practices if student is an ethnic minority).

Anecdotal logs should detail all past and current incidents and include the following items:

❏ Date and time of day
❏ Location of incident
❏ Adult(s) supervising at the time of the incident
❏ Events that occurred prior to the incident
❏ A detailed description of the student's behavior during the incident, including duration of the incident and specific behavior observed
❏ Action(s) staff took to prevent physical injury
❏ Consequences given to the student (if any)
❏ Action(s) taken to minimize future occurrences of the behavior

Administrators should provide teachers with an opportunity to debrief. Logs need to be filed in the central office, and summary records of number of incidents per week or the number of minutes per week can be used to chart progress.

Guidelines in Teaching Students to Manage Their Own Behavior.   Self-management of behavior typically involves self-control training. Consider implementing one or more of the following interventions: academic assistance, restructuring self-talk, signal interference cueing, mentoring, goal setting and contracting, self-monitoring, structured reinforcement systems, stress management, and increasing positive interactions. Several of these are described in the chapter on conduct management. All of the interventions are thoroughly described and scripted by Sprick et al. (1993).

School psychologists, special education teachers and consultants, school guidance counselors, and other school personnel with advanced training and expertise in managing severe conduct problems can be used as resources to develop or refine existing classroom and schoolwide plans.

Management Challenge 3–3

Procedures and Self-Management Skills

Ms. Koch believes in the importance of teaching students the routines associated with various classroom activities. She has established procedures for entering and leaving the classroom, forming small groups, distributing and collecting materials, and a number of other activities that occur during the school day. Whenever a new activity is introduced, she takes time to (1) identify the procedures associated with the activity, (2) specify and demonstrate responsible ways the students are to behave, and (3) have students practice the appropriate behaviors.

The school principal comes to observe Ms. Koch's class the third day of school. On the occasion of her visit, Ms. Koch is introducing the procedures for using a piece of equipment. When the principal meets with Ms. Koch to evaluate the class session, she is quite critical of the time spent introducing students to the piece of equipment. She believes altogether too much importance was placed on discussing and practicing equipment-handling procedures.

1. Speculate about the arguments the principal used to justify her criticism of Ms. Koch's introduction of the piece of equipment.
2. Build a defense for Ms. Koch, and be sure to include what you understand about the teaching of self-management skills.
3. Use this incident and the material generated by your responses to items 1 and 2 as the basis for a role-playing exercise.

Covenant Management

The final domain of classroom management that requires preplanning for the first two weeks of school is covenant management. Covenant management is about managing relationships: school–home, teacher–student, and student–student. Effective covenant management relies on communication skills and the synergistic effects of quality content and conduct management.

Positive and proactive school–home relationships are developed during the first two weeks of school by using at least two strategies: telephone calls and open houses. These help lay the foundation for a positive school–home relationship. Telephone calls to the guardian(s) of each student should be rehearsed for brevity and positive content. The contact is one or two minutes long, spoken clearly, and not hurriedly. Teachers ask no questions and expect no responses. The guardian may say little or nothing. When the message is concluded, say "Good-bye" and hang up. An example of a script follows. Note the components of the call. The caller greets, identifies himself by name and role, identifies student by name and one positive behavior, invites future contacts, alerts hearer to letter, welcomes family to open house, thanks hearer for time, and closes.

Telephone Script for Teachers' Initial Call Home: Covenant Management

"Hi, I'm [name], your son's/daughter's [subject] teacher. I have only had [student's name] in my class for a few days, but I really appreciate how [helpful to others, hard working, etc.] he/she is. Feel free to contact me here at school anytime regarding [student's name] progress. You will be receiving a letter if you have not already concerning the rules of the classroom. I wanted to remind you of our Open House on [date, time] and I hope to see you and [significant other] there. Thank you for your time. Good-bye."

Let us now look at some of the subtle yet significant differences between conditions at home and school. It should become apparent that behavioral problems common to both settings may occur with greater frequency and intensity at school because of setting circumstances. Accenting these distinctions may help teachers more fully appreciate the enormity of their task and make them less apologetic when seeking home support for their endeavors.

Teachers might casually introduce these ideas into conversations and conferences with parents, not to evoke parents' sympathy but rather to help them obtain a better understanding and appreciation of a teacher's situation. Parents are less inclined to be critical of teachers with disciplinary problems and are more receptive when called on to help if they also grasp the enormity of the teacher's task.

Silberman and Wheelan (1980, pp. 172–173) offer five observations about classroom and family differences, which are described in Figure 3–8. Although unlikely topics for a single parent conference, they can make quite an impact whenever they are presented. Let us look at these observations in greater detail.

Classrooms Are Crowded Places. Parents would be hard pressed to identify another workplace where so many people are squeezed into such a small space. Adults would rebel, overtly or covertly, if they had to work in such close conditions. Yet children are expected to work harmoniously and productively, five days a week, in proximity to one another. Obviously, an adult must be present to manage the movement and interactions of students. Without rather strict, conscientiously enforced rules, student misbehavior would spill out into the aisles of the classroom and into the corridors of the building.

Figure 3–8

Open House Presentation Outline to Inform Parents of Differences Between Home and School

Source: From Silberman, M., & Wheelan, S. (1980). *How to discipline without feeling guilty: Assertive relationships with children.* Champaign, IL: Research Press. Reprinted with permission.

> I. Classrooms are crowded places.
>
> II. Classrooms allow very little privacy.
>
> III. Classroom relationships are not as intimate or close.
>
> IV. The menu of rewards and punishments is not as rich.
>
> V. Teacher authority is more easily undermined.

This classroom is an example of a crowded workplace. Skillful management is required if children are to work harmoniously.

Contrast this crowded setting with the size of most family homes. Sometimes each child has his or her own room. Even when everyone is at home, each person can occupy a different space. In the summer, when kids are outdoors much of the time, the amount of space per person greatly exceeds that of the typical classroom. Yet parents find children underfoot. Homes, yards, and neighborhoods are spacious when compared to classrooms, and adults have fewer children to cope with than teachers.

Classrooms Present Little Opportunity for Privacy.   This point has important implications for dealing with disciplinary problems. The most obvious is that lack of privacy can turn minor incidents into problems. An adult supervising a group of three children, for example, can permit much greater latitude in the behavior of each group member because fewer people are affected when the individual chooses to assert his or her wishes. Each member is also better able to discern the others' wishes and intentions and can better choose compatible behaviors. As the group gets larger and more diverse, it becomes more difficult to express oneself without infringing on the desires or preferences of another person. The work is complicated and difficult for the individual who must monitor the differences.

When a disciplinary problem does occur, it is difficult to ignore it as the group size increases. When a person refuses to abide by the rules in a small group, the group chooses either to ignore it or do something about it. If and when an adult is called on to settle the problem, the adult's actions are more likely to be sanctioned by the other participants in the incident. If the adult refuses to intervene and tells the participants to settle the dispute among themselves, this action is generally not regarded as a failure in leadership. However, when a teacher ignores too many rule violations, students often lose respect and challenge the teacher's leadership. Students are constantly observing the teacher's ability to lead, and from these observations they draw conclusions that govern their subsequent behavioral choices.

The best way to deal with some disciplinary problems is to remove the student from the classroom. Unacceptable behavior is often instigated and fueled by social stimuli. But where does the student go? Sitting in the hallway, the student may become a problem to someone else. Often the problem is not one the principal needs or wants to handle. The dilemma is finding a place where neither the teacher nor the student feels compelled to save face or play to the crowd. Unlike parents, teachers cannot send the other children away or deal with the offending child in a private place. And because classrooms are crowded places, returning the student to the group can reintroduce the conditions that provoked the original problem. Thus, teachers often create many problems while trying to solve one. One-on-one solutions often occur after school, long after the impact of the situation has diminished.

Classroom Relationships Are Less Intimate.   Parents share so many high and low points of their child's life that these experiences create a common bond transcending momentary disagreements and occasional conflicts. When there is a conflict of wills and the parents decide that they will prevail, there is usually a backlog of goodwill to assuage hurt feelings and reestablish damaged relationships.

Teachers work at building good relationships with students, but they are seldom able to form close attachments like those that bind parents and children. In a classroom composed of twenty-five to thirty students with whom the teacher is associated for only one year, the teacher can hardly be expected to secure from all pupils the full cooperation and enduring goodwill that parents build over a child's lifetime.

Fewer Means of Rewards and Punishments Are Available.   As noted earlier, teachers have very few positive reinforcers at their disposal, and the use of punishment to exact appropriate behavior can have unfortunate side effects. Many high school teachers rely heavily on grades to induce good behavior. Yet a large number of students are indifferent to this form of incentive. Others may be content to "get by" with a C so that they are not subject to most of the demands for responsible behavior. Thus, a teacher's grades are not a very effective form of control.

Teachers often use social reinforcers as an inducement to good behavior. Students thrive on the recognition and approval of their teachers. But exclusive or extensive use of verbal and nonverbal expressions of approval diminishes their power. Students soon take them for granted or are content to get fewer such rewards. When this happens, they may engage in unacceptable behavior. The teacher must then find other reinforcers to manage student behavior. The options are often expensive, less acceptable, and difficult to deliver in a consistent and systematic way.

Parents control many more and stronger reinforcers. They also control more powerful aversive consequences and are less subject to public scrutiny when they punish their child. In fact, most parents fully expect other parents to use punishment to manage behavior. Thus, it is not uncommon for parents of teenagers to ground them for a weekend, revoke telephone privileges, or deny them use of the family car. With younger children, parents may remove TV privileges and the use of prized toys. Parents provide more things for their children, and they are in a position to determine the use of these things. Parents also have greater control over the way their children use time. Outside-of-school time is not scheduled, or when it is, the schedule often includes privileges that have been given and can thus be taken away.

Teacher Authority Is Easily Undermined.   A teacher's authority is conferred and can be taken away by members of the community. When parents make or repeat disparaging remarks about particular teachers or take their child's side in a dispute with a teacher, they diminish the teacher's authority to make and enforce standards. Certainly there are occasions when schools and teachers make mistakes. Education consists largely of making and exercising value judgments, and teachers are not immune from errors in both areas. But there are ways to deal with these breaches in confidence that will preserve the teacher's stature and confidence. All too often the ways to adjudicate differences between home and school pit the teacher against the parent. Children can only conclude that the teacher is mistaken, because parents are generally presumed to be omnipotent, and all too often it is the teacher who has to back down.

Parents are less likely to undermine another parent's authority. They may disagree with the way other parents fulfill the parenting role, but they acknowledge their right to be wrong. When their children try to use another family's practices as an argument for why they should be allowed to do something, not infrequently they are told something like "I don't care how Mr. and Mrs. Smith handle their children—that's their business. However, as long as you live in this household, you will be at home, and in bed, by 10 o'clock on a school night, and that's final!"

Although parents can dismiss what other parents do, teachers often find it difficult to disregard what their colleagues do, even when they find their practices less satisfactory. The opinions of coworkers may be magnified because of a teacher's need for acceptance from other adults in the workplace. Thus, teachers may be inclined to bend to pressures from others and learn to live with personally objectionable compromises.

Parents' expectations of teachers should be shaped by the unique, demanding realities of the classroom. They can be helped to understand and appreciate these realities when teachers point out the similarities and differences between home and school management conditions. With their firsthand experience as disciplinarians, parents can readily empathize with the teacher and will more likely lend their support when called on to do so.

Positive Teacher–Student Relationships

In the development of positive teacher–student relationships, beginning with the first day of school, teachers can concentrate on the following strategies: greet students at the door, demonstrate interest in each student by making one personal comment to them each day, note to students their good efforts in all aspects of classroom life and not just academics, and monitor favoritism.

Monitoring favoritism is paramount. Brantlinger (1995) interviewed low- and high-income adolescent students and asked them about social isolation and relationships with teachers. Although low-income students are believed to not care about school and teachers, the findings revealed that low-income students had strong feelings and cared very much. It was hypothesized that the pretense of not caring was a defensive reaction to possible rejection. In fact, low-income students were particularly sensitive to teachers' attitudes toward students. Many low-income students stated that teachers liked preppies (high-income) and disliked grits (low-income). They believed that teachers were the high-income group and viewed a number of teacher behaviors as snobbish, rejecting, uncaring, and humiliating. On the other hand, they expressed appreciation for the few teachers who had been kind.

Teachers can demonstrate interest in all students by asking them to complete interest inventories during the first two weeks of school. Interests of students with academic weaknesses or low motivation can subsequently be used to develop lesson plans. Figures 3–9 and 3–10 illustrate examples of interest blanks that can be used at the elementary and secondary levels, respectively.

Classrooms are social settings in which many young people and usually one adult, all with diverse backgrounds, are expected to spend harmonious time together in a very small space. The teacher is the leader in developing the group covenant. Students form impressions of their status in the group during the first few weeks of school. For many, first impressions are lasting impressions. This makes it imperative that teachers preplan and implement strategies in covenant management from the first day of class.

CONCLUSION

Management during the first two weeks of school emphasizes the preventive features of classroom control. Preactive teaching—or the planning that teachers do prior to the resumption of another school year, before and after school, and during free periods and weekends—can have a profound effect on the ecological aspects of instruction, behavior, and relationships. The fact that a circumscribed set of management routines can be planned before the school year begins and then introduced during the first few days and weeks of school highlights their significance. Few management matters can be dealt with so expeditiously and can have such widespread effects.

If you can successfully respond to any item from the following list, you are well on your way to successfully managing a real classroom during the first two weeks of school:

1. Am I completely familiar with the school building discipline plan, to the point that I can implement it with integrity?

What Do You Like?

Name _____ Date _____ Grade _____

Please answer every item completely.

1. When you are not in school, what three things do you really enjoy doing?

   _____

   _____

2. When you cannot watch television at home, what do you most like to do?

   _____

3. If you could do anything that you wanted to do this weekend, what would you

   choose? _____

4. If you could learn about anything that you wanted to learn about, what would it be?

   _____

5. What is your favorite television show? _____

6. Do you like to do your best work in groups or alone? _____

7. Which school subjects do you like best?

   _____

8. What three things do you like to do most in school?

   _____

9. If you had 30 minutes of free time at school each day to do what you really

   like, what would you do? _____

10. What three jobs would you enjoy doing in class?

   _____

Figure 3–9
Elementary Interest Inventory

What I Like

Name_____ Grade_____ Date_____

Complete these sentences to express your own feelings and thoughts.

1. I am very proud that I _____.

2. A reward I like to get is _____.

3. My two favorite TV programs are _____.

4. One thing I do very well is _____.

5. My favorite school subject is _____.

6. When I read for fun I like to read stories about _____.

7. One of my better accomplishments is _____.

8. If I had $10 I would spend it on_____.

9. When I have free time I like to _____.

10. I know I can _____.

11. I enjoy _____.

12. Something I want to do more often is _____.

13. One of the things I like best about myself is _____.

14. A good thing my teacher could do for me is _____.

15. In schoolwork my best talent is_____.

16. Something I really want is _____.

17. I feel satisfied when I _____.

18. An important goal for me is to _____.

19. If I did better in school, I wish my teacher would _____.

20. If I could get the chance, I would like to try _____.

Figure 3–10
Secondary Interest Inventory

2. Are my crisis management plan and tentative classroom management plan approved by the principal and on file in the office?
3. Have I organized the physical environment of my classroom to prevent content management problems from occurring?
4. Have I planned lessons for the first two weeks of class that review prior knowledge in ways that increase the likelihood of academic and social success for every student?
5. Am I ready to teach classroom procedures to students?
6. Are my tentative rules and consequences ready to be disseminated, discussed, taught to students on the first or second day of class, and reviewed throughout the first two weeks?
7. Have I developed the props that I will use for consequences?
8. Have I developed a tentative letter to send home explaining the classroom rules and consequences?
9. Do I have every student's name with guardian name(s), address, and telephone number?
10. Do I have a phone home script prepared to use?
11. Are my rapport-building activities developed?

SUPPLEMENTARY QUESTIONS

1. Lawrence, Steed, and Young (1984) used their research in British secondary schools as the basis for discovering the conditions associated with disruptive behavior. They noted, for example, that reported incidents of disruptive behavior peak toward the middle of the week and occur more frequently during afternoon sessions. Given your understanding of setting management, what do you think accounts for these findings? What remedies could you suggest?
2. Persons who observe classrooms with a mind toward the efficient use of time are sometimes appalled by teachers' lack of attentiveness to time management strategies. What aspects of classroom life do you suppose they view as time wasters? What measures would they propose to use classroom time more effectively?
3. When teachers speak of providing good "structure" so that students feel safe, secure, and purposeful, what do they have in mind? How can structure become so confining or oppressive as to actually constitute an impediment to learning?
4. A student's feelings of security rest in large measure on being able to "read" the environment for cues that certain events are about to happen. Confusion about where things are or when things happen encumbers a student's attempt to make sense of the surroundings. What do you make of this statement? What are the implications for content, conduct, and covenant management?

SUPPLEMENTARY PROJECTS

1. "Settling kids down" is a practical aspect of management. Observe in several classrooms, at different grade levels and across different types of classroom activities, and make a record of the ways teachers typically handle this management challenge.
2. Delays and breakdowns in the flow of events in a classroom are often the precursors to discipli-

nary problems. These "breaks in the action" are often time-outs from good behavior. Divide a sheet of paper into two columns. Head one column "Delays/Breakdowns" and the other column "Incidents of Unacceptable Behavior." Observe several class sessions and keep a record of instances when interruptions in the flow of events are an invitation to behavior problems.

3. The tenor of the class period or the school day can be influenced by a teacher's verbal and nonverbal behavior. Make a videotape of the first five minutes in several classrooms. List the messages, and speculate about their affective impact on students. Compare your notes with one or more persons who have made a similar critique of the tapes.

4. Design an elementary or secondary school classroom that you think would be both functional and attractive. Keep a record of the thoughts, particularly assumptions about teaching, learning, and students, that guided your selection and arrangement of furniture, equipment, and materials. Prepare a paper explaining the rationale for your plan and presenting its merits.

REFERENCES

Albert, L. (1994). Discipline tips from the experts: Rule is a 4-letter word. *Teaching Kids Responsibility, 1.*

Bandura, A., & Walters, R. (1963). *Social learning and personality development.* New York: Holt, Rinehart & Winston.

Bennett, N., & Blundell, D. (1983). Quantity and quality of work in rows and classroom groups. *Educational Psychology, 3,* 93–105.

Brantlinger, E. (1995). *Social class in school: Students' perspectives.* Research Bulletin 14. Bloomington, IN: Center for Evaluation, Development, and Research.

Cotton, K. (1990). *Schoolwide and classroom discipline.* School Improvement Research Series. Portland, OR: Northwest Regional Educational Laboratory.

Emmer, E. T., Evertson, C. M., Clements, B. S., & Worsham, M. E. (1994). *Classroom management for secondary teachers.* Needham Heights, MA: Allyn & Bacon.

Gettinger, M. (1988). Methods of proactive classroom management. *School Psychology Review, 17,* 227–242.

Grubaugh, S., & Houston, R. (1990). Establishing a classroom environment that promotes interaction and improves student behavior. *The Clearing House, 63*(8), 375–378.

Guerney, M. A. (1989). Classroom organization: A key to successful management. *Academic Therapy, 25*(1), 55–58.

Johnson, T. C., Stoner, G., & Green, S. K. (1996). Demonstrating the experimenting society model with classwide behavior management interventions. *School Psychology Review, 25,* 199–214.

Lucas, R. (1996, September). *Scholarly and grant writing.* Presentation at the University of Northern Iowa, Cedar Falls, IA.

Madsen, C. H., Jr., Becker, W. C., & Thomas, D. R. (1968). Rules, praise, and ignoring: Elements of elementary classroom control. *Journal of Applied Behavior Analysis, 1,* 139–150.

Paine, S. C., Radicchi, J. S., Rosellini, L. C., Deutchman, L., & Darch, C. B. (1983). *Structuring your classroom for academic success.* Champaign, IL: Research Press.

Rosenfield, P., Lambert, N. M., & Black, A. (1985). Desk arrangement effects on pupil classroom behavior. *Journal of Elementary Psychology, 77,* 101–108.

Silberman, M., & Wheelan, S. (1980). *How to discipline without feeling guilty: Assertive relationships with children.* Champaign, IL: Research Press.

Sprick, R., Sprick, M., & Garrison, M. (1993). *Interventions: Collaborative planning for students at risk.* Longmont, CO: Sopris West.

Sternberg, R. (1985). *Beyond IQ: A triarchic theory of human intelligence*. New York: Cambridge University Press.

Unruh, L. (1994). *The effects of teacher planning on classroom management effectiveness.*

Unpublished doctoral dissertation, University of Kansas, Lawrence.

Woolfolk, A. (1995). *Educational psychology* (6th ed.). Boston, MA: Houghton Mifflin.

ADDITIONAL RESOURCES

Interventions: Collaborative planning for students at risk, Sopris West, 1140 Boston Avenue, Longmont, CO 80501; phone: (303)651-2829.

Training in physical restraint, David Mandt & Associates, Richardson, TX; phone: (972)495-0755.

CHAPTER 4

Foundations of Management: Communication Skills

An understanding of the material in this chapter will help you do the following:

❑ Recognize the strengths and weaknesses in your own communication skills.
❑ Develop body language, listening, and sending skills of communication.
❑ Implement restructuring self-talk in positive ways.
❑ Adhere to ethical and legal guidelines for communication.
❑ De-escalate conflict using communication skills.

Words Are Arrows

Words are arrows
and can pierce you hard.
Anger drips
from the
wounds
of
words
used like
arrows.
And pain
is remembered
in the
scars.

—*White Deer of Autumn*[1]

A word aptly spoken is like apples of gold in settings of silver.

—*Proverbs 25:11*

What people say and how they say it powerfully affects themselves and those to whom they speak. The old adage "Sticks and stones may break my bones but words will never hurt me" is only true if the hearer has learned to ignore hurtful words. Most young people typically have not learned how to cope effectively with the hurtful words that are heard in school buildings. When adult messages to students have been hurtful over the years, by middle school or junior high age those same students will appear to be no longer listening. They are turned off and tuned out. Undoing the harm will take repeated, consistent, and persistent use of effective communication skills.

This chapter presents numerous communication skills that can be implemented by educators to help themselves and their students. The skills are not only helpful but also necessary at the prevention, intervention, and remediation levels. Although the nonverbal and verbal interventions described here are necessary in all situations, they are not sufficient to resolve all problems. The skills introduced in one chapter cannot satisfy all needs or fulfill all expectations. Additional chapters will build on the foundation introduced in this one. Educators should seek additional professional assistance for themselves or students when their communication behaviors significantly and chronically impede success in the work and school environments.

---

[1] White Deer of Autumn. (1992). *The Native American Book of Change* (Vol. 3, Native People, Native Ways Series). Hillsboro, OR: Beyond Words Publishing. Reprinted with permission.

OVERVIEW OF COMMUNICATION

Definition of Communication

Communication is defined as the transmission of information through listening and speaking. Communication has various forms: body language and spoken and written messages. In this chapter, skills in positive self-talk (e.g., positive attributions), listening, and talking to others through verbal or written form are emphasized.

Communication skills are foundational for management at the three levels of prevention, brief intervention, and remediation. Effective communication in schools prevents problems from occurring. An example of communication at the prevention level is giving students school handbooks that contain the schoolwide discipline policies and procedures and teaching them periodically throughout the school year. This prepares students to meet expectations. Intervention that requires communication skills might be the use of peer mediation programming. Rehabilitation efforts that rely on the foundation of communication skills include knowing how to use communication to de-escalate a crisis situation with an angry, acting-out adolescent and forge a partnership to learn new ways of managing anger.

Importance of Communication

Ginott was one of the first to draw attention to the importance of educators' communication skills (Charles, 1996). In fact, Ginott (1971) wrote the following often-quoted words, which appear widely in teachers' portfolios and on bulletin boards, often without attribution:

> I am the decisive element in the classroom. It is my personal approach that creates the climate. It is my daily mood that makes the weather. As a teacher I possess tremendous power to make a child's life miserable or joyous. I can be a tool of torture or an instrument of inspiration. I can humiliate or humor, hurt or heal. In all situations it is my response that decides whether a crisis will be escalated or de-escalated, and a child humanized or dehumanized. (p. 13)

Ginott offered a model of communication with a simple underlying principle: When speaking to students, adults must always address situations, not the students' character or personality. Ginott asserted that communication interventions had to be used repeatedly over time for their power to take effect. This is an important concept that bears repeating. Many individual communication efforts are necessary over a long period of time to reap success. And it is worth it. Do not give up. Keep rehearsing and role-playing effective communication skills.

In class discussions and role plays of management scenarios, one of the problems that both undergraduate and graduate students face is using effective communication skills. They have a tendency to display Ginott's communication no-no's, which drive wedges between speakers and listeners (Charles, 1996):

❑ Label students negatively (e.g., "Some students are being pretty lazy this morning." "Are you hard of hearing?").

❑ Ask students "why" questions (e.g., "Why did you trip her?" "Why is your assignment always late?").

❑ Lecture (e.g., "What's the problem back there? This is math class, not the bus ride to the game tonight. If you expect to play in the game, I would suggest that you do your own work and stop bothering others who are trying to learn something. I want quiet. If you have a question, ask me.").

❑ Make sarcastic remarks (e.g., "Good move, Juan." "Oh, so you remembered something for once.").

❑ Demand cooperation (e.g., "Class, this morning I will not put up with any nonsense. All eyes on the guest lecturer now.").

❑ Lose self-control (e.g., "I have had it with you! I have asked you repeatedly to get to work. Go to the office now!").

❑ Manipulate students with nonspecific praise (e.g., "You are super!").

Readers who have used any of these negative communication behaviors will find the skills in this chapter critical to master. Good communication skills are the foundation of effective management in schools. They are a necessary condition for successful management but they are not entirely sufficient.

Educators who seek to improve their communication skills must cultivate an overall attitude of respect for themselves and children and adolescents. Educators adhere to the following guidelines described by Grossman (1995) and Jones and Jones (1995):

❑ First, educators never prejudge or hold grudges, both of which color communication and cause it to sound negative. Respectful educators hold positive attributions for students and believe that students want to be and are responsible most of the time.

❑ Second, educators at their best are communicating dignity versus preaching. Educators at their worst are belittling students.

❑ Third, educators describe situations and what needs to be done versus bossing. Educators do not perceive the goal of an adult–student confrontation to be adult wins and student loses. Rather, they allow students to share responsibility for resolving problems.

❑ Fourth, in recognition of cultural differences, educators adjust communication patterns to students' needs and clearly explain and teach the various communication skills that will be used in the classroom.

Novice educators often lack confidence and feel insecure and timid about communicating with students. Novices have special needs for praise and recognition. They are often preoccupied with themselves. "How am I doing? How am I being regarded?" dominates much of their thinking. Like everyone else, they want their own needs for recognition and approval met. Because of these needs at this particular time in their professional careers, novices find it more difficult to communicate successfully. Developing effective communication skills takes lots and lots of practice for most but does wonders for building confidence. Paradoxically, when novices use communication skills that meet the needs of others, their own needs for self-validation are better served also.

After completing a communication skills unit during a classroom management course, preservice teachers wrote brief descriptions of their own communication profiles, including strengths and weaknesses (Iverson, 1996). Most of the preservice teachers in the sample demonstrated accurate awareness of their own communication strengths and weaknesses. They also selected appropriate strategies that could be used to improve their weaknesses. Lastly, most indicated that, prior to the instructional unit on communication skills, they could not remember receiving procedural training in how to communicate effectively during uncomfortable interpersonal situations in schools. Six examples are included here to demonstrate how varied people's communication styles are. The examples also indicate that most educators have a need to equip themselves with new and better communication skills.

Example 1

I can talk to parents calmly. I talk a lot but I might get passive if someone is upset. I would be quiet and let them be in total control. I would lose control of the situation if someone is very irrational. I would like to improve professional talk like saying "yes" for "yup." I need to avoid arguments with children and not say so much. I most need to work on principles to follow if someone gets upset or irrational or argumentative.

Example 2

I become too empathetic or sympathetic and dwell on how horrible something is for a parent or child. I need to engage in emotional separation and still be pleasing and respectful. I most need to develop the skill of reframing.

Example 3

Trying to be calm and confident is difficult. I overcompensate by being authoritarian. However, being authoritarian is very uncomfortable for me. I need to be better prepared for the different scenarios that could come up and not get defensive. I need to practice the skill of positive self-talk in order to maintain objectivity versus subjectivity. I need to practice reinforcing what others say versus getting defensive.

Example 4

I tend to be passive. It takes awhile for me to determine an appropriate response, be professional, and know where to go next in my response. I think that there is probably a list of generic responses that can be adjusted to fit about any situation.

Knowing how to begin to respond seems very important, after that the follow-through comes more naturally. I think I am good at telling things straight but still padding it.

I need to remember that it is okay to take my time to construct a response. I could generate a list of generic responses and practice using them as ways to begin responding.

Example 5

My natural reaction is to arch my back and my neck hair stands up when others are belligerent. I should think ahead about how to handle difficult situations and the need to create a calm atmosphere for me and the other person.

Role playing and having steps written down would help. The more you practice the more natural it will feel.

Example 6

I sometimes have difficulty getting the right ideas across. I like to be blunt and shoot straight. Good communication processes are unnatural for me and don't sound real. I need to work on listening to the other person and practice skills of clarifying and summarizing. They need the most work.

Rogerian theory, with roots in humanism, has shaped some of the basic communication skills presented in this chapter. Rogerian theory is based on assumptions that people are able to solve their own problems by talking about them with an accepting, supportive, and nondirective other. According to the theory, nondirective listeners exhibit unconditional positive regard and reflect the speaker's thoughts back. This process assists the speaker in reaching her own problem resolution. Communication skills from this theoretical position include body language basics and listening.

Behavioral theory has yielded a number of communication skills also. Recall that behavioral theory yields strategies that are environmentally based and directive. The listener directs the strategies and problem solving rather than emanating from the speaker. Ethical behavior demands that the speaker agree with the strategies and that they not be applied to the speaker without informed consent. These strategies include body language and sending verbal message skills.

Interactionists also rely on some basic communication skills. In addition to the skills already mentioned, interactionists would include the strategy of positive self-talk. Three important categories of communication skills are differentiated from sending verbal messages, the category that we tend to think of first when thinking about what communication is. The three skill areas of self-talk, body language, and listening will receive a great deal of attention in this chapter. Educators need to cultivate skills in these three areas as the foundation for sending effective verbal messages.

COMMUNICATION SKILLS

Positive Self-Talk

All of us use self-talk every day. Self-talk influences how we think and feel about ourselves and it influences our behavior. Consider the following example. Several ninth-grade students are ignoring teacher directions and laughing and talking among themselves. The teacher may engage in positive or negative self-talk about the students' actions. The affective direction in which the teacher's self-talk takes him will affect his thoughts, feelings, and outward behavior. When the affective direction is positive, teachers' self-talk could take on many forms but might sound like this:

> They are sure enjoying themselves but I need to use a strategy to obtain every-one's attention. I will call on one of them (Berry) to repeat the directions for the class. Berry may not have heard me but it will gain everyone's attention. If she cannot repeat the directions, I will remain neutral and simply ask for a vol-unteer from the class to repeat them. That will probably be a successful strat-egy for now. If the same students continue to have the same kinds of behaviors in the future, I may need to try a different strategy.

It may seem a little ridiculous to take the time to go through that much self-talk. Some may say that it makes no sense and is not practical for teachers who need to make split-second decisions to rehearse all of the above prior to halting the off-task behavior of talking and laughing. However, this is precisely the kind of talk that occurs following an incident or during the quiet and reflective times before and after school. Without self-talk, people tend to jump into solutions immediately, solutions that are high control and punitive. Novices actually do need to take the time to run through that much self-talk. Experts in positive self-talk will actually say an abbrevi-ated version that resembles the following: " . . . having fun . . . need attention . . . Berry repeat . . . volunteer . . . pattern, different strategy. . . . "

Contrast the above with the following negative self-talk of a teacher:

> I know those kids are laughing and fooling around because they think that I am stupid and the assignment is stupid. I'll show them who's stupid. I'll call on each one of them by name and ask them to repeat the directions. The entire class will sit here until they can come up with them.

People do process this many statements or more when engaging in negative self-talk. Take a moment and think about your own personal experiences and recall instances of negative self-talk. Did the negative self-talk ultimately affect your thoughts, feelings, and outward behavior? When self-talk is chronically negative, restructuring self-talk or attribution retraining may be effective interventions.

Restructuring Self-Talk

Changing the way people talk to themselves is helpful when people experience excessive criticism, negative attitudes, putting themselves down, and self-control problems. Negative self-talk is associated with feelings of frustration, powerlessness, and anger. When negative self-talk occurs across situations and time, it creates bar-riers to success.

Educators who recognize these behaviors in themselves or in students may want to use a restructuring self-talk intervention in order to resolve problems successfully. It is usually a good idea to seek assistance from school counselors and school psychologists when implementing self-talk interventions with students. They often will take the lead in developing the intervention but, obviously, need the assistance of the teacher for prompting students and monitoring improvements in the regular classroom.

Support services staff can help teachers by conducting assessments to detect the patterns of students' faulty assumptions underlying negative self-statements. Nine types of cognitive errors or faulty assumptions that students make follow:

1. *Overgeneralizing:*   "If I am not good at geometry, I am not a good student at all."
2. *Selective abstraction/self-criticism:*   "I am only a good student if I don't make any mistakes."
3. *Excessive responsibility:*   "I am responsible for all failure or bad things that occur."
4. *Assuming temporal causality:*   "If I did it poorly in the past, I will always do it poorly."
5. *Self-references:*   "I am the cause of all bad things that happen to me" or "Everybody should like me."
6. *Awfulizing:*   "All bad things happen to me and nothing will ever change."
7. *Dichotomous thinking:*   "Everything is perfect." The next day, "Everything is ruined."
8. *Demanding:*   "People should always listen to me."
9. *Low frustration tolerance:*   "Things should always come easily to me."

Restructuring self-talk may need to be paired with other interventions that address problems in a comprehensive manner. Support services staff can assist with determining the nature of paired interventions, also.

Sprick, Sprick, and Garrison (1993) offer step-by-step procedures, scripts, and props for conducting self-talk interventions. The intervention procedures of Sprick and his colleagues typically follow the same format. That format is briefly summarized to illustrate all aspects of the intervention: (1) a preplanning phase for the educator(s) to define the problem before discussing it with the student, (2) working with the student to define the problem and determine a plan, and (3) implementing the plan. An example follows of a teacher and a school psychologist working together to develop a self-talk intervention for a student. Any educator who has the skills can carry out this intervention. It does not necessarily require a support person to conduct the three phases. Note the importance of the preplanning phase of the restructuring self-talk intervention.

Preplan

The teacher describes for the school psychologist all the conditions surrounding the problem.

The teacher lists typical negative statements. (Negative comments have an all-or-none quality and tend to make unrealistic demands. They have key words like "can't ever," "should," "always," "never," "nobody," "everybody.")

The school psychologist analyzes the list of negative statements, identifies the cognitive errors of the statements, and looks for a pattern. (See earlier list of nine types of cognitive errors.) The teacher has the opportunity to confirm the identified pattern.

The school psychologist and/or the teacher write positive statements to replace each negative. (For example, the student says, "I'm never going to be good at math." A positive replacement statement could be "I might do better if I would ask questions when I don't understand.")

The school psychologist and/or teacher identify prompts to signal the student when she is engaging in negative self-talk. (Examples include touching the student's desk, teacher touching her ear, student carrying a stop sign as a physical reminder.)

The school psychologist and teacher collaboratively develop a self-monitoring procedure. They identify who will be the adult case manager and develop procedures to monitor progress.

Collaborate with Student

Meet with the student to collaborate on the final plan. Either the school psychologist or the teacher introduces the tentative plan. The educator's script follows:

> We are meeting today because I am concerned that sometimes you say things to yourself that affect how well you do on an assignment. For example, I think you tell yourself that you are never going to be good at math. Can you think of some other things that you say to yourself that are put-downs? (Pause.) These thoughts fill up your brain with yuk. That makes it hard for you to do well. How do you think I would feel and act if I told myself that I have to get everything right all of the time?

The student then has the opportunity to write positive self-talk alternatives. The teacher and student role-play the self-talk alternatives. Together they select a signal and role-play sending the signal. The student learns how to use the self-monitoring procedure and sets a consistent schedule for practicing positive self-talk.

Implementing the Plan

The student begins using the plan immediately. It is not necessary to wait to start on a Monday. The adults should evaluate progress at the end of five to ten school days and revise the plan if there are any glitches. The plan needs to be faded gradually after the student demonstrates consistent success over time. Most school counselors and school psychologists know how to fade plans and other educators can ask them for assistance with this. Follow up intermittently to check on the student's continued success.

The intervention just described requires the time and effort of a support person, the teacher, and the student. It can be an invaluable exercise for students who are inhibiting their own success due to negative self-talk.

Attribution Retraining

Attribution retraining is a special subtype of restructuring self-talk. Attribution retraining focuses on changing how students talk to themselves about the causes of academic success and failure. A typical goal of attribution retraining is to encourage students to explain failure in terms of lack of effort rather than lack of ability. In real life, students tend to say that a task is too hard and that they are not smart enough. Both statements mean the same thing—that students believe they lack the ability.

Heider's (1958) naive psychology is recognized as the birthplace of attribution theory and subsequent strategies of attribution retraining. Heider stated that a person's behavior is meaningless until we attribute a cause to it. We are constantly trying to navigate the world by understanding cause-and-effect relationships. We like a world that is predictable; we can make better choices when the world is dependable.

For example, when Mr. Wilson wins the Teacher of the Year award, it is a relatively momentary event. What does it even mean to be Teacher of the Year? The

This teacher encourages students to try their best on a task and to say, "I did a good job because I used the right strategy."

award makes sense when it is referred (i.e., attributed) to a relatively permanent property such as his portfolio containing twenty years of evidence of excellent teaching. Most people then feel assured that such an award predicts a successful teaching career. On the other hand, if Mr. Wilson's award is referred (i.e., attributed) to easy judges or easy criteria or no other applicants, most people would not feel assured that the award does indeed predict successful teaching.

The importance of this discussion is that people will behave differently toward the awardee based on their understanding of the Teacher of the Year award. This in turn could influence Mr. Wilson's future teaching performance. In fact, the way Mr. Wilson himself understands his award could influence his future teaching performance.

Attributions then can be defined as a person's beliefs about why she or someone else succeeded or failed at a task. Attributions or beliefs can influence people's self-talk and resulting behaviors. Attribution concepts are introduced here to make educators aware of attributional influences on their own behavior and the behavior of students.

Students can attribute success on assignments either to ability, effort, knowledge, and other internal attributes or to luck, help from others, task difficulty, and other external attributes. Students with learned helplessness attribute failure to lack of ability. Ability is viewed as an internal, stable, and global cause. They are inclined to say to themselves, "I would have passed the test if I were smart" or "I'm just not smart enough to ever get this." Dweck (1975) showed that when students who generally attribute failure to a lack of ability were instructed instead to attribute failure to a lack of effort, they showed more resilience to academic setbacks and disappointments. Multon, Brown, and Lent (1991) reviewed thirty-nine studies of the relationship between self-efficacy beliefs and academic outcomes and concluded that the relationship was positive and causal. Their meta-analytic investigation provided compelling support for the potential value of intervening in low achieving students' attributions. Restructuring self-talk, what a person says about success or a lack of it, has a profound influence on future performance.

Attribution theories have been reformulated since the mid-1940s and have yielded attribution retraining strategies. In spite of a lengthy history, Reeder (1996) found that educators had little knowledge and experience in understanding the importance of people's attributions and how to conduct attribution interventions. When presented with the procedures for attribution retraining, regular educators, special educators, and school psychologists expressed a high degree of interest in learning how to implement attribution interventions.

Educators who teach and encourage effort attributions must be sure that targeted students have *not* been making the necessary efforts. Attribution retraining should be coupled with learning strategy instruction when students lack learning strategies to be successful on a task. In other words, simply teaching students to tell themselves "I tried hard and that's why I succeeded" will not make them more successful academically. They must also use the learning strategies that lead to successful task completion.

Long-term benefits are more likely when teachers incorporate attribution retraining into everyday instructional repertoires. Some intervention procedures follow for paired learning strategy instruction and attribution retraining.

Step 1:   Model the use of the learning strategy to the student (e.g., developing a story web prior to completing the language arts assignment of writing a creative story).

Step 2:   Model correct and incorrect examples of learning strategy use by working through actual examples. Teach learning strategy use until the student can execute the strategy.

Step 3:   Teach the use of positive attributions ("I finished the story because I used our study time to work really hard.")

Step 4:   Teach student to pair positive attribution statements with learning strategy use (e.g., "I used my story web and I worked really hard. That's why I was successful in writing the story.").

Step 5:   Allow student to practice making a positive attribution statement after successfully using a learning strategy and give feedback.

Step 6:   On a daily basis, remind the student to continue monitoring his use of positive attributions paired with learning strategies (e.g., reinforce for making appropriate attributions and challenge when students offer explanations likely to induce helplessness).

Attribution retraining paired with learning strategy instruction is a long-term intervention that will need to be implemented for at least several weeks, if not a year or longer. For the most effective implementation of these interventions, it is important to involve many people who have direct contact with the student (e.g., teacher, parent, principal, school counselor). This will expose the student to as much modeling and practice of the intervention as possible. The ultimate outcome is student attributions that emphasize effort rather than ability as the primary cause for success and achievement.

Influence of Race, Socioeconomic Status, and Gender on Teachers' Attributions

Little research has been done on the effects of race, class, and gender on teachers' attributions for students. Some evidence shows that teachers hold Caucasian, middle-class children more responsible for academic outcomes than minority students. Teachers may also expect African-American and lower-class Caucasian students to fail more than middle-class Caucasian students (Baron, Tom, & Cooper, 1985; Cooper, Baron, & Lowe, 1975; Wiley & Eskilson, 1978). Asian Americans may benefit from beliefs held by teachers. Elementary teachers attributed the academic success of Caucasian, middle-class, and Asian students to internal factors and academic failure to external factors (Tom & Cooper, 1986). The same teachers did not hold the same attributions for lower-class Caucasian students. Asian-American students also have been rated as more academically competent (Wong, 1980) and academic performance has been evaluated more favorably (Tom, Cooper, & McGraw, 1984) compared to Caucasian students.

No research evidence suggests that teachers attribute different causes to male and female students' academic behaviors (Heller & Parsons, 1981; Wiley & Eskilson, 1978). What is known is that teachers label some subjects as more sex-appropriate for males than females (e.g., math is sex-appropriate for males and sex-inappropriate for females) and vice versa (e.g., English is sex-appropriate for females and sex-inappropriate for males). Bernard (1979) found that teachers evaluated male students more highly in English than females when males performed well in the sex-inappropriate domain.

To synthesize, the importance of teachers' attributions is that teachers must put the emphasis on students' effort and acquired skills in explaining academic success. In turn, students will learn to attribute their failures to lack of effort or to needing assistance to acquire the skills.

Body Language

Body language is a visual form of communication and includes body posture, body tension, and facial expressions. When an educator leans forward with hands on hips and has a serious demeanor on her face, no verbal message is needed to communicate to most students that this person means business. That is the power of body language.

People use body language intentionally but it can also be used unintentionally. For example, many people naturally, and without conscious, purposeful intent, cross their arms and move their body away from a speaker when the speaker's message is not accepted or the speaker is disliked, distrusted, or perceived in some other negative fashion. Educators need to become aware of their own body language and monitor its effects.

There are cultural differences in body language or nonverbal communication. The differences, as described by Grossman (1995), are enumerated here in general with specific examples included for each of the body language goals. Emotion is expressed differently across cultures. Some Asian-Pacific people laugh or giggle when they are embarrassed. The Hispanic-American culture displays more physical affection (e.g., touching, kissing, males hugging and patting each other on the back) than the European-American culture. Cultures vary in how they typically express anger and defiance: African Americans roll their eyes, Asian Pacific Americans force smiles, and European Americans give silent stares.

Cultural backgrounds also influence how people show submission. African Americans and Asians avoid direct eye contact. Asians also nod their heads repeatedly and do not make critical comments. Cooperman (1975) suggested that African-American students may be more sensitive to nonverbals. Gay and Abrahams (1973) indicated that African-American children are taught to be suspicious of Caucasians. African-American students may be suspicious of Caucasian teachers' positive behavior initially. This may lessen over time as positive behavior remains consistent.

Body language goals for educators include the following:

1. Relax muscles and posture when sitting or standing (e.g., arms and hands held loosely at the sides, hands resting lightly over each other in front of the body, standing erect without leaning forward or backward).
2. Relax facial muscles (e.g., relaxed versus clenched jaw muscles).
3. Make eye contact (e.g., focus on speaker's mouth rather than steady eye gaze). African-American students may show respect by avoiding eye contact with those in authority (Gilliam & Van Den Berg, 1980). Hispanic Americans may be brought up to look away when they are being reprimanded (Grossman, 1995).
4. Stay outside another's personal space (e.g., when another individual is moving away, they may be indicating that their space has been invaded). Aiello and Jones (1971) reported that African-American students may maintain less physical distance between themselves and others. Hispanic-American and Latino students may also stand closer while Oriental students need more space than European Americans (Grossman, 1984).
5. Nod head and smile to communicate acceptance.
6. When shaking hands use a firm grip, no matter how you are feeling.
7. Breathe at a moderate rate (e.g., slowly and deeply versus rapidly and shallowly).

There are enough cultural differences in the use of body language that educators need to observe, listen, and ask questions about the use of body language in their school culture and subcultures. Do not take anything for granted or make sweeping generalities about issues of body language.

Body language goals are more difficult to demonstrate when the social situation is uncomfortable but these are the times when it is most important to use them. Uncomfortable social situations occur when there are angry, sad, embarrassed, and guilty feelings involved.

For example, a father attends a school meeting to help develop a plan to improve the academic achievement of his tenth-grade son. The father and son, four teachers, the special services director, and the school psychologist are at the meeting. Early in the meeting, the father loudly declares to the science teacher that, if she knew how to teach, his son would not be skipping her class and shirking the assignments.

The science teacher can react in a number of ways. At one extreme, she could cross her arms tightly across her chest, lean forward, tighten her facial muscles and clench her jaw, and just as loudly say something like, "How would either of you know whether I can teach? Your son has rarely been in my class and you, sir, have never been in it." At the other extreme, she could shrink back and try to look small, look down at the floor with a red face, with quivering lip shed a tear or two, and mumble something incoherent or leave the room.

It is time to apply body language basics in the most professional manner. This teacher will be most successful if she practices all of the following behaviors: (1) breathe slowly and deeply, (2) maintain a relaxed posture with arms resting at her sides or on the table, (3) sit in a relaxed but erect position and neither lean forward nor backward, (4) maintain relaxed facial muscles, and (5) establish eye contact with the father (depending on cultural norms). People who are verbally attacked are often caught off guard. Unless highly skilled in effective communication, their quick responses are typically unproductive ones. Momentary silence is a good strategy and other professionals around the table should all be comfortable with it. The teacher is now ready to respond in any number of acceptable ways that will promote problem solving and conflict resolution. For example, she could say, "I did not realize that my teaching style was Darrell's reason for not attending my class or completing assignments. When he was in class, he did the work and the quality of his work indicated that he understood the lesson. If my class is the only one of your classes where you feel this way, Darrell, we should discuss this after the meeting is over or at another time. That way we won't take up everyone else's time. What do you think?"

With practice, educators can learn to use effective body language and effective communication (e.g., listening and speaking) skills. They will experience greater success in any number of interpersonal interactions.

Signal Interference Cueing

Signal interference cueing is a form of body language used to assist students who seem to be unaware that they are engaging in inappropriate behavior. Often, the behaviors that students engage in without being aware appear disrespectful to adults. These behaviors include swearing, blurting out, complaining, sarcasm, criticism, bragging, noncompliance, shouting out comments or rude remarks, being noisy, arguing, talking back, rudeness, and having the "last word." The cueing intervention we are about to discuss is also helpful with misdirected attention and lack of attention to task.

Signal interference cueing is used to help students become aware of and control their own impulsive, excessive, habitual, or off-task behavior. The intervention works on the premise that students become aware of their behavior and learn self-management. Adults provide students with predetermined cues whenever they begin to exhibit behavior that has previously been identified as inappropriate. Cueing is especially effective with students who have the ability to behave appropriately, but tend to act inappropriately without thinking first.

Simply teaching students to respond to a cue will be enough to change the inappropriate behavior for some students but not all. Educators should remember that they can always seek an interventionist's help in implementing signal interference cueing (e.g., educational consultant, guidance counselor, and school psychologist). Reasons to seek help are for assistance in measuring progress and implementing concurrent interventions.

Signal interference cueing should be viewed as a temporary measure until students can learn to monitor their own behavior. When students require intensive training to learn new behaviors, a teacher can couple signal interference cueing with interventions like teaching desired behaviors, restructuring self-talk, mentoring, structured reinforcement systems, and increasing positive interactions (see Chapter

5). Teachers can run one or two individual, signal interference cueing plans at a time. More than that will probably be too demanding on a teacher's time.

Before implementing signal interference cueing, complete a planned discussion with the student (see discussion later in this chapter). It is always important to contact students' parents to discuss problems and keep them informed of all aspects of the intervention plan.

Sprick et al. (1993) provided a set of detailed procedures for implementing signal interference cueing. Procedures follow their typical format of preplanning, final planning in collaboration with the student, and implementation of the plan. The following steps show you how to develop a detailed plan for using signal interference cueing.

The student we are dealing with, Rory, has low rates of eye contact with the teacher and does not pay attention. This results in Rory not being able to follow directions the first time given. The teacher has checked Rory's health records and knows that there is not a hearing problem. The teacher has also checked Rory's skill levels and she knows that her instruction matches what Rory is capable of doing. She believes that Rory's difficulties are chronic inattention or off-task behavior and that he is unaware of how his behavior is causing difficulties in following directions the first time given.

Preplan

First, during the preplanning phase, identify when Rory is likely to have problems. For example, it is determined that direction following decreases in the afternoon, no activity is any more likely to result in inattention, and being grouped with a best friend decreases attention and ability to follow directions.

Second, identify possible signals that might be used to cue Rory to pay attention to directions the first time given. Here are some ideas for signals and you will be able to think of others:

❑ Say the student's name quietly.
❑ Hold up a hand like a stop sign.
❑ Hold up a finger to the lips.
❑ Touch your ear lobe.
❑ Give a quick verbal cue such as "Think."
❑ Stand by the student's desk or touch the student's desk.

Third, Rory will help choose the cue, which needs to be verbal and not visual because Rory does not look at the teacher very often. A visual cue can be used if Rory responds to cue cards placed on his desk. The teacher decides that when Rory responds to the signal and follows directions, she could give him a mark on a tally card that she carries with her. The marks could be graphed to provide feedback to Rory about his improvement. She knows that Rory may have some additional ideas of consequences when they meet together.

Fourth, the teacher tentatively decides on two ways to determine whether the intervention is helping Rory reach his goal of following directions the first time given. The teacher generates the following list of ideas for monitoring progress:

❑ Check with each person in the plan to get their impressions of whether the plan is helping

❑ A student self-monitoring system
❑ A tally of appropriate and inappropriate behavior kept by the teacher
❑ An anecdotal log
❑ Periodic observations
❑ A daily rating system

Fifth, the teacher schedules quick debriefings with parents every two weeks and a quick check with Rory to discuss progress a few times each week. The teacher also determines who will meet with the student to discuss and finalize the plan.

Script

"Rory, I am very glad to have you in class with me this year. For some of my students I periodically set up special goals. A special goal that I'd like to help you with is learning to pay attention and follow directions the first time given. I think that you will get along better at school. I have arranged to meet with you and your mom during math tomorrow. Another teacher will take the class. It's hard to find time to talk with students individually so this is a special opportunity. I'm pleased that we'll have a chance to work on this. Is this okay with you?

"We'll talk more tomorrow. In the meantime, do a little thinking about ways that you might follow directions the first time given. Tomorrow, we will figure out how we can all help you with that goal."

Collaborate with Student

Meet with the student to collaboratively develop the plan. The teacher begins the meeting by involving Rory in reviewing the problem and setting goals.

Script

"Rory, I'd like to help you reach your goal of following directions the first time given. I'll give you a signal when you need to think about what you are doing. For example, if I see you looking away from me, I could say to you quietly "Rory, look and listen" or "Rory, first" or "Think." We can choose one of those or something else. When you hear me say that you will know that you need to listen for directions and follow them the first time given."

(The teacher then helps the student select a signal to use and practice following the signal.)

After role playing, the teacher describes what will happen when the student responds appropriately or fails to respond to the signal. Together they review everyone's roles and responsibilities. Finally, they set up regular meeting times to debrief. The teacher always concludes meetings with words of encouragement.

Script

"Rory, you learn very fast and I'm looking forward to working with you on this. It will be fun for you to see your own improvements."

Implementing the Plan

The key is to get started. Once a plan is developed, do not put it off. The teacher watches for opportunities to reinforce the student for responding to the signal and for not needing the signal.

Script

"Rory, there were several times today that I didn't provide you with the signal. On your own, you were very thoughtful about following directions. You have been respectful toward others and me. Everyone gets through the activity so much faster when I do not have to repeat the directions. I enjoy watching you make good choices."

The teacher continues to monitor progress and makes periodic revisions to the plan as necessary. When the student shows consistency in following directions the first time given, the frequency of providing the signal can be decreased and finally stopped. The teacher continues to make sure that Rory consistently follows directions without a signal and provides continued support and encouragement.

ETHICAL AND LEGAL CONSIDERATIONS OF COMMUNICATION

To this point in the chapter, self-talk and body language procedures have been presented. As skills in listening and sending verbal messages are discussed, it is important to enumerate ethical and legal considerations in communicating. Different professional bodies each have their own code of ethics. Administrators, guidance counselors, school psychologists, and teachers all have ethical codes. Many similarities are seen across professional groups. Teachers' ethical standards are presented here as an example.

The *Code of Ethics of the Education Profession,* adopted by the 1975 National Education Association (NEA) Representative Assembly, provides standards by which educators should monitor and judge their conduct. The first ethical principle focuses on commitment to the student. Three of the criteria under the first principle shed considerable light on the ethics of communication. Specifically, educators are to make reasonable efforts to protect students from conditions harmful to learning, to not intentionally expose students to embarrassment or disparagement, and to not disclose information about students obtained in the course of professional service without a compelling professional or legal purpose. For example, it is unethical for teachers to take their red ink pens and mark a large "F" across the front page of a test. When a student in the class questions, "Why didn't you mark this one wrong? I had it wrong," it is unethical for the teacher to respond in front of the entire class, "You had so many wrong that I got tired of marking them."

It is unethical for educators to embarrass students by telling them that if they are going to act like first graders they can spend the day in first grade. It is also unethical for educators to talk about students' problems in the lounge where few or none of the listeners have a compelling professional reason to be involved.

It is an ethical responsibility for educators to maintain the privacy and confidentiality of all information that students reveal about themselves with two exceptions. First, students may give educators permission to share information. Second, the law requires that educators provide authorities with information when students reveal that they or someone else is in danger (e.g., suspected child abuse, suicidal or homicidal ideation).

NEA's second ethical principle focuses on educators' commitment to the profession. This principle directs educators to not disclose information about colleagues without a compelling professional purpose and to not make false or malicious statements about colleagues. Not only are certain behaviors unethical but they are also subject to legal sanction.

Defamation and Rights to Privacy

Defamation is a derogatory communication to a third person. Derogatory words and insults directed at an individual do not constitute defamation of character. Basically, defamation involves libel or slander. If the untrue statement is written, it is called *libel;* if spread by word of mouth, it is called *slander.* Legislation and recent shifts in the court's approach to defamation suits make teachers vulnerable to both types of suits.

Teachers can be sued for defamatory statements published in students' permanent records. A teacher can avoid culpability in this area by confining record entries to pertinent, factual, and objective observations and by excluding subjective observations and conclusions that may be difficult to prove. The truthfulness of the information should be unquestionable. Objective statements can be easily verified. (The reader may want to review the section of Chapter 9 devoted to anecdotal records as a reminder of the distinctions between factual statements and their interpretations.)

Teachers frequently express their discontent with misbehaving students, often mentioning the particularly disagreeable characteristics during informal conversations with colleagues. The conversations often conclude with both parties feeling a little less favorably inclined toward the offensive students. The teachers' remarks could be construed as slanderous to the extent that they subject the student to the scorn and hatred or to the sorrow and pity of a third party.

At one time, a true statement was considered to be the ultimate and absolute defense against slander, regardless of how damaging the statement might be. However, recent court decisions indicate that if the intent of the statement is to cause harm, irrespective of the truth of the communication, an individual can be held accountable for defamation (Connors, 1981, p. 130). Teachers can be found guilty of slander if they knowingly spread gossip that harms a student's reputation. On the other hand, the courts have given teacher communications a conditionally privileged status if they are made as part of a disciplinary process or administrative responsibilities.

COMMUNICATION: LISTENING AND SPEAKING

Educators need listening and speaking skills in dealing with community members, parents, students, and fellow educators. Most people do not naturally develop effective communication skills but must prepare and rehearse how to listen and how to deliver messages across different situations. In fact, we usually have developed some bad habits because we have not been attentive to what is known about effective communication. Educators are better managers when they are prepared to deliver difficult messages, to mediate and de-escalate misunderstandings of messages, and to know when to obtain the assistance of consultants with expertise in effective communication.

Listening Before Speaking

Students learn more and behave better when they like their teachers. Importantly, students like teachers who listen to them and communicate understanding (Anderson, Evertson, & Emmer, 1979; Kounin, 1970).

Listening is a critical communication skill. Many times conflicts or problems can be prevented or defused simply by using good listening skills. Although it is difficult for many readers to imagine that the use of simple listening skills can have a significant management impact, those who cultivate and use listening skills become believers.

Listening means hearing precisely and helping the speaker feel understood. Gordon (1974) refers to this kind of listening as *active listening.* Specific verbal skills are used to help the speaker feel that she was understood: acknowledging, reflecting, paraphrasing, summarizing, and clarifying (Conoley & Conoley, 1992).

Grossman (1995) reports that students from some ethnic backgrounds (i.e., Asian Pacific Americans, Hispanic Americans, Native Americans) may not be comfortable discussing their thoughts, feelings, and problems with their teachers. That does not mean that educators should not use active listening skills but they should not try too hard to encourage some ethnic minorities to engage in the process. Wei (1980) found that Vietnamese students may be shy and withdrawn around the openness of American teachers. Nguyen (1987) reported that Cambodian, Laotian, and Vietnamese students may find teachers' direct ways rude, even attacking. Therefore, culturally sensitive use of the following listening skills is recommended.

Acknowledging

Acknowledging is a listening/communication skill that many people use everyday. As a communication skill, acknowledging helps build initial relationships. When people make the following types of statements, they are using the skill of acknowledging: "yes," "really," "wow," "right," "good."

Acknowledging is used to (1) encourage others to speak and (2) communicate some awareness of the emotional content of the other person's message. The use of acknowledging statements is especially helpful with those who are hesitant to talk. Educators may wish to use various acknowledging statements with others who feel insecure about their ability to be successful in a given situation. Students experiencing learned helplessness or parents who speak infrequently are two examples. Acknowledging statements are good to use when it is important to let the speaker know she is heard, yet the listener needs to hear more before responding further. Acknowledging statements can serve to "buy" time.

Reflecting

Reflecting means repeating back the words that someone spoke. A person's words may contain two types of message content: cognitive and affective. The listener can selectively reflect part of the message to underscore the importance of some information or to move the conversation in a particular direction (e.g., begin the process of analyzing the problem, direct the conversation toward the speaker's emotional responses to the situation). Teachers and administrators typically need to focus on the cognitive portion of the message. Guidance counselors, school psychologists, and school social workers are prepared by education and training to reflect both parts of the message, based on what seems most appropriate at the time.

Later in the chapter, we give examples of teachers using reflection to communicate with students. The following illustration of reflection is used when a teacher is communicating with a parent. A parent might say to a teacher, "I am really frustrated that Sally is not turning in her assignments. I have tried everything." The teacher as the listener has to decide whether to respond to the parent's cognition (e.g., I have tried everything to assist Sally in turning in her assignments) or the parent's affect or emotion (e.g., I am really frustrated that Sally is not turning in her assignments after all of my efforts).

1. If the teacher reflects by stating "I hear you saying that you are really frustrated that Sally is not turning in her assignments," the focus is on the affective or emotional portion of the message. This reflection emphasizes the importance of the feeling of frustration and could lead potentially to two opposite emotional reactions: the parent crying and feeling hopeless about solving the problem or becoming angry and punitive toward Sally. When this happens, it may reduce the ability of both parent and teacher to problem solve constructively.

2. If the teacher reflects the following, she is focusing on the cognitive portion of the message with the intent of analyzing the problem. "Yes, you have tried many things to help Sally turn in her assignments over the past two weeks. Let's investigate whether there was anything that happened about two weeks ago that caused Sally to quit turning in assignments."

3. The teacher could also focus on doing or intervening by reflecting the other portion of the parent's cognitive message. "You tried a number of things to help Sally turn in her assignments. Tell me what you tried in order and how each attempt worked."

Either choice 2 or 3 is probably a better choice for the teacher than choice 1. The focus is on the cognitive message and leads to constructive problem solving. However, educators should not ignore really emotionally distraught parents or students and reflect exclusively cognitive messages. This would be inappropriate. The other party cannot problem solve without a calm atmosphere, and it is not calm enough to proceed. Educators can reflect the speakers' emotions: "I can see that this is upsetting to you" or "I know that things like this can be frustrating" or "It's okay to cry. Take your time." After reflection, the educator needs to be quiet and comfortable with silence. When parents or students cry or are struggling to control an emotion, educators can offer tissues and then wait patiently. Do not stare at the person. Quietly look away or down or through materials. This gives the person time to regain her composure. You will know when to proceed because you are going to wait for the other person to speak. You do not need to dwell on what just occurred. Take your cues from the parent or student. Often the person is ready to proceed with the purpose of the meeting.

Ethical codes require that the proceedings of such a meeting be kept confidential. In other words, it is not okay for you to report in the faculty lounge the next day that Sally's mom cried during the parent-teacher conference.

Paraphrasing

A third skill that communicates listening is *paraphrasing*. Paraphrasing is more complex than reflective listening, is used to cue the speaker to slight variations in her message, is offered tentatively, and may be used to indirectly challenge but without disagreeing. It involves substituting synonyms that heighten or reduce the power of what is said or slightly change the meaning or make no change. This listening skill resembles therapeutic techniques of counselors and psychologists and is not recommended for use by the untrained. It is explained here to help build awareness of how various listening techniques can impact the direction that interpersonal communication takes.

An example of paraphrasing follows. Here a school guidance counselor is talking to Sally's parent about incomplete assignments. Many teachers bypass this kind of listening and request special assistance from support personnel who are trained in advanced listening techniques.

> *Parent:* "I have tried and tried to help Sally get her assignments done, in her book bag, and back to school to turn in. I remind her every morning as she leaves the house to turn them into you. She just does not pay attention to what I do or say."
>
> *Counselor:* "You seem to be angry with Sally because you think she is not paying attention to you."
>
> *Parent:* "I'm not angry with her. I don't get angry with my children. That's not my job."
>
> *Counselor:* "I may have misunderstood. I know some behaviors do make me angry when I've tried to correct them. I find that my anger is a good barometer of how frustrating a situation is for me."
>
> *Parent:* "Well, that's certainly true. I've been frustrated by Sally."

Counselor: "And I find that the more angry I become, the less creative I am at finding solutions. That's when it's good to get somebody else's ideas."

Parent: "That's probably where I am right this minute with Sally."

Summarizing

Summarizing is a listening/communication skill that pleases and surprises the speaker. The speaker is likely saying to herself, "Someone listened carefully enough to be able to list back most of the important points that I made." It seems to help in making decisions, preserving information, and in ending meetings.

Teacher: "So far, you've told me about Sally's problems with assignments, her behavior problems at home, and some family problems. You think that all these things are probably contributing to her assignment incompletion."

Parent: "You have a great memory. I have told you a lot."

Teacher: "Do you think this might be a good time to choose a high-priority problem to work on? If you do, we could set up a meeting with the student assistance team where team members can help us brainstorm and develop a plan."

Clarifying

Clarifying is asking questions that invite elaboration on previously made points. This is done in order to get such a clear depiction of an event that the listener can see and hear it as if she was right there when something happened. Clarifying questions seek descriptions rather than explanations. Thus, they begin with "what" and not "why." People have difficulty answering "why" questions and often feel defensive when asked why they did something. Clarifying questions ask the person to define terms and ask about what happened before (antecedent conditions) and what happened after (consequences). They are used to gain information. Clarifying questions do not occur rapid-fire but are sensitive to the speaker's leads. They are used to give speakers the opportunity to put their information together in helpful, problem-solving ways.

Consider the fruitlessness of the teacher asking "why" questions in the following scenario. The problem is not clarified at all and, in fact, the student is less able to problem solve as he becomes more agitated while answering "why" questions.

Student: "I was having a good day and then math class came along and spoiled it all. Now I am not interested in anything except getting out of here."

Teacher: "Why is that?"

Student: "Because of that pencil-headed teacher! He really makes me mad. He was so unfair!"

Let's look at an instant replay, but with a "what" question instead of a "why" question. Note that more information is obtained when using a "what" clarifier.

Student: "I was having a good day and then math class came along and spoiled it all. Now I am not interested in anything except getting out of here."

Teacher: "What happened in math class?"

Student: "Mr. Numero wouldn't let me turn in my assignment. And I had it all done. It's not fair."

Teacher: "What happened that you could not turn in your assignment?" (versus "Why did he do that?")

Student: "I left it in the wrong notebook in my locker and when I asked to go get it, he said I couldn't."

Through these examples you should see more clearly just how important clarifying questions can be to the communication process, especially if they begin with "what." As previously stated, "why" questions press the speaker to explain rather than describe. When most of us are immediately asked to explain, we are going to blame the other guy and vehemently. That is just what the student did, in a less-than-respectful manner. On the other hand, when "what" questions were used, the student was invited to describe what happened. The series of well-stated "what" questions led to the student admitting her contribution to the conflict.

Elaborating

Elaborating is a skill that results in building on what has already been introduced. Elaboration allows for more complex and comprehensive plans to be formulated. It makes people feel invested in the process because their ideas have been heard, valued, and used. There are times when elaboration can be used to link listener suggestions to speaker verbalizations. Then the final plan is more clearly a collaborative, joint effort.

Parent: "I think the only way to handle this problem is to get Sally to grow up and take responsibility for getting her own assignments in. I don't have time for this anymore and it's not right that I should keep babying her."

Teacher: "The idea of Sally's independence appeals to you. We could work together to teach her how to self-monitor. Your schedule would have time for helping her be more independent, wouldn't it?"

Compare the following communication skills of teachers speaking to students. The communication skill the teacher used is in parentheses following the response, unless no skill was used from the list given earlier. Note how the first teacher used responses that quickly draw the conversation to a close without gaining insight into the student's real problem. The second teacher uses effective communication skills to increase her insight into the student's problem and her ability to assist in problem solving.

In our first example, the teacher does not use basic listening/communication skills:

Student: I don't have the assignment done.

Teacher: You don't?

Student: No, I don't! It took way too much time and was a stupid assignment.

Teacher: What was so stupid? (clarifying, but focused on the inappropriate affect of the message)
Student: Reading and then writing.
Teacher: Really?
Student: Yeah.
Teacher: Are you serious? (clarifying, but focused on the inappropriate affect of the message)
Student: Yep.

This student has now dug herself into a hole by insisting that the assignment was stupid. This reflects negative attributions for success and the teacher's response patterns helped entrench this student in her way of thinking. The teacher did not remain objective but became defensive and controlling.

In the next example, the teacher reserves judgment, listens, and responds neutrally; in other words, he does use basic listening/communication skills. This creates an atmosphere of safety and the student provides more information that will assist the teacher and student in collaborative problem solving.

Student: I don't have the assignment done.
Teacher: Really. (acknowledging)
Student: No, I don't! It took way too much time and was a stupid assignment. (negative attribution statement, external cause beyond student's control)
Teacher: It seemed time consuming to you. (reflecting cognition, not affect "stupid assignment")
Student: It took all my study time to finish the reading and then there wasn't any time left to write.
Teacher: Show me what you read and tell me how much time you spent on it. (clarifying)
Student: I read this story just like you told us to. I started about 9:00 last night and read until 9:30. By then it was too late to start answering the questions that you assigned and I went to bed.

The teacher is now prepared to ask more clarifying questions to determine why the student left the English assignment until 9:00 P.M. The teacher would not say: "Why did you wait until 9:00 P.M. to start your homework?" This question communicates a feeling of disrespect or judgment. Educators need to avoid "why" questions. Instead, an effective clarifying question might follow a summarization as in the following example: "You told me that you started the assignment at 9:00. A half hour later you had finished the reading but you had to go to bed. What happened before 9:00?"

After complete information is gathered, both the teacher and student can discuss study skills that may prevent problems like this one from occurring in the future. The student needs to articulate positive attributions for failure. For example, it may have been more accurate for the student to state, "I understood what to do but I miscalculated how long it would take me and I ran out of time." This statement reflects an effort attribution and has been linked to higher student achievement. Educators are to assist students in making these kinds of positive attributions; the student links success to effort.

Reframing

Reframing is the process of (1) casting a problem in a new light, (2) emphasizing the positive aspects of the problem over its negative consequences, and (3) highlighting what adaptive purposes the problem serves. In the next example, a student's constant talking or clinging behavior to the teacher can be seen as evidence of the student's positive attachment to the teacher, rather than merely as an annoying habit.

Example

A student's constant talking to the teacher or clinging behavior is seen by the teacher and others as an annoying habit. It can be reframed by casting the problem in a new light. In other words, the student's behaviors are viewed as evidence of the student's positive attachment to the teacher. By emphasizing the positive aspects of the problem (e.g., the teacher can have a positive influence on the student's learning because the student is attached to her) over the negative consequences (i.e., annoys and irritates teacher because the student is constantly demanding attention), the teacher can see how influential she can be in the student's life. Teachers also can highlight the values to students of positive attachments: feelings of security, trust, and so on necessary to students' normal development.

Communication skills to this point have emphasized aspects of sending messages via methods short of verbalizing to others. In summary, those skills included self-talk, body language, and listening. The final form of communication described here is sending verbal messages to others.

Sending Verbal Messages

Effective skills in sending verbal messages facilitate (1) relationships with students, (2) appropriate confrontation of students' disruptive behavior, and (3) specific feedback to students about their academic achievement (Jones & Jones, 1995). Quality student relationships and appropriate confrontation skills are described in this chapter. Communication skills for giving specific feedback about academic performance are presented in Chapter 5.

Schools can facilitate quality relationships by emphasizing positive verbal messages at the schoolhouse door.

Educators need to have positive interactions with students across time and situations in order to promote quality relationships with students. Interactions are those times that adults pay attention to students. Positive interactions include everything from saying hello to students to asking students how they are doing to complimenting students who are responsible and make good choices. See Figure 4–1 for examples of positive interactions.

Positive interactions have nothing to do with the tone or substance of actions; they occur when adults pay attention to students who display appropriate behavior. Increasing positive interactions is best implemented at the systems level. It is desirable that schools include it as a goal in their buildings' strategic plans. All staff in the building should be trained in how to conduct positive interactions. Many educators engage in numerous positive interactions and this helps to define the culture of the building. Staff and students have quality relationships and a sense of community. Behavior problems are less frequent when students believe they have the goodwill of adults. There are times when students do not have the goodwill of adults and the specialized intervention of increasing positive interactions is required.

Positive interactions with students are lacking in school contexts for a number of reasons. First, staff get busy, focus on tasks, and decrease the frequency of interpersonal interactions with students. Second, staff do not recognize the importance of having frequent positive interactions with students. Third, students exhibit behaviors that staff react to negatively. It is the third circumstance that can necessitate development of a specific intervention.

Negative, avoidant reactions lead to reduced positive interactions. For example, staff who view students as sassy and disrespectful often begin to avoid or inter-

Figure 4–1
Examples of Positive Interactions

Greet student as soon as she enters classroom.

Give student a job to do in the class.

Seat the student near the source of instruction.

Make friendly eye contact.

Ask student a question when you know she can be successful.

Go by student's seat and check to see how things are going.

Give student a class responsibility when she finishes her work.

Walk with the student in the hall on the way to another destination.

Ask student how she is, about her weekend, etc.

Wish the student a great weekend, a happy vacation, and so on.

Tell the student that you look forward to seeing her tomorrow.

Visit with student about her interests.

Write a positive note to student.

Write a positive note to student's guardian(s).

Ask additional staff in building to do above activities.

act negatively with them. Some staff respond negatively and decrease their positive interactions with students who have poor self-concepts and seem to cling to adults or act helpless. Staff find it particularly difficult to sustain positive interactions with students who exhibit chronic attention-getting behaviors of arguing, negotiating, teasing, tattling, making excuses, being off task, and disrupting.

When staff members find themselves using the following self-talk or sending the following verbal messages to others about a particular student, it is probably necessary to focus on intense applications of positive interactions. "I can see nothing positive about this student." "This student is always off task." Teachers typically do not have the time to commit to the first phase of this intervention and need assistance. Educators should choose partners to work with them. Partners can be fellow teachers, educational consultants, school counselors, school psychologists, and principals.

Prior to implementing the intervention, partners gather baseline data by observing the educators who want to increase the frequency of positive interactions. Partners also observe intermittently after implementation to see if the frequency of positive interactions is increasing. Ideal ratios of positive to negative interactions have been cited in the range of three positives to one negative all the way to ten positives to one negative. The best recommendation is to achieve the ratio that best assists students in overcoming inappropriate behaviors.

An adaptation of Sprick et al.'s procedures (1993) for increasing positive interactions follows. Note that the procedures follow their typical outline: develop a plan, meet with the student to collaborate on and finalize the plan, and implement the plan.

Preplan

The partner observes and counts the current level of positive to negative interactions of the educator. The educator and partner define the problem and set goal(s). The two list all of the student's negative behaviors, determine best consequences to use for each type of negative behavior, and rehearse how to use the consequences.

Next, they make a list of noncontingent positive interactions. *Noncontingent* means that the interactions will occur regardless of student's negative or positive behaviors.

It is also necessary to make a list of contingent positive feedback. This feedback will be given to recognize the student's positive behaviors. It is important to ask other adults to increase their positive interactions, also. One reason is that students who are targeted for positive interactions often are hungry for positive regard and attention. If the teacher is the only person engaging in positive interactions with the target student, the student may begin to hover around the teacher in a way that the teacher finds stressful. The student has several adults to relate to when positive interactions are coming from a variety of sources.

Last, the partners develop an evaluation plan by which they will judge goal attainment.

Collaborate with Student

The educator and the student collaboratively review the student's problem and set goal(s). The educator then assists the student in practicing actions to take in attaining the goal(s). The educator and student discuss possible consequences for misbe-haviors. They then review the positive interactions menu and the student knows that the two of them will be having positive interactions also. The two of them schedule regular discussions to check progress toward the goals. They review the plan and the educator concludes with words of encouragement.

Implementing the Plan

The educator follows the plan to increase the ratio of positive to negative interac-tions. The partner evaluates how the teacher is doing by making regular checks and the educator makes adjustments as necessary.

The partner helps the educator fade the intervention following consistent student progress. The partner follows up and encourages the educator intermittently. Although this intervention can be faded, it is always important to promote positive interactions!

Educators' Friendliness Toward Students

Preservice teachers often comment that they want students to know they are their friends. Subsequently, preservice teachers ask questions about how best to do that. Educators are advised to be friendly rather than be friends. To be friendly requires (1) being open and approachable, (2) being willing to listen to things not directly related to students' classes, and (3) sharing their own feelings and opinions. Educa-tors who are friendly need also to be the person in charge and provide the leadership that students need. This represents the demarcation between being friendly and being friends. For example, a teacher can demonstrate friendliness in her willingness to listen to a group of juniors planning an event at the local pizza place on Friday night. The teacher might express her own feelings by sharing how much she liked to do those things when she was in high school. However, if the group asks her to join them, the line of demarcation pops up and social distance needs to be established. The teacher needs to say something like the following, "Thank you for thinking of me but I had my time with my friends in high school. It is your turn to have a good time with each other."

Grossman (1995) noted that not all students prefer teachers to be friendly. Certain Asian Pacific American students are used to formal relationships with teach-ers and some students with emotional problems feel threatened by any close relation-ship. Educators need to be sensitive and not push friendliness in these situations.

Problem-Centered Discussions Between Educators and Students

Probably every building administrator, teacher, teacher associate, guidance coun-selor, and other types of educator have had talks with students who were experienc-ing problems in school (e.g., tattling, disorganization, poor listening, disruptive behavior, fighting, cheating). Many of those talks occurred after the problem was chronic or severe and went something like the following:

> "Sherida, we have talked about this many times before. What do you have to say for yourself? (Pause.) What are we going to do? You are constantly com-

ing to class without your materials. I have tried everything and nothing is working. I am tired of talking to you about knowing where your assignments are and getting them in on time. You are starting tenth grade next year and I think it is time for you to take some responsibility. From now on, starting today, you are responsible for bringing your materials to class—no more passes to go get them. I won't remind you anymore about your assignments. If they are late or never get in, you will have to suffer the consequences of low grades. Do you understand?"

Educators often feel that the litany of complaints and threats, like the one in the preceding illustration, constitutes an adequate presentation of the problem. However, active participation by the student is woefully lacking. Interactions that are lecture-like usually do not result in significant behavior change.

Sprick et al. (1993) developed semi-structured procedures that facilitate a collaborative and positive discussion between an educator and student to resolve a particular problem. They called the procedures *planned discussions*. The purpose of planned discussions is to let students know that there is a problem, to get students actively involved in problem solving, and to let them know that the educator is there to help them learn and grow.

Sprick et al. (1993) suggested that planned discussions should be the first step in any intervention plan. They are often sufficient interventions during the early stages of a problem. Problems that can lead to planned discussions include annoying behaviors like tattling and sloppy work. Moderate problems like off-task behavior, disruptive behavior, tardiness, and poor listening should start with the intervention planned discussions. Many teachers do have "chats" with students about these kinds of problem behaviors. Planned discussions ensure that the time teachers spend talking to students about their problem behaviors is collaborative and problem solving in nature. More intensive interventions may never be needed when educators use a series of planned discussions in early intervention work. Planned discussions are used for chronic and severe problems also, but only as part of a broader intervention plan.

Teachers' immediate thoughts will be "When will I ever have time to complete a series of planned discussions?" It is important to realize that approximately one-half of classroom time is taken up with noninstructional activities. Discipline problems are responsible for a significant portion of this lost instructional time (Cotton, 1990). Well-planned discussions could potentially alleviate future discipline problems, thereby freeing up time. Figure 4–2 provides a list of alternative times that teachers should consider using for conducting planned discussions.

For minor problems, and to prevent future problems, teachers may want to schedule several planned discussions per week during independent seat time. This allows teachers to have contact with all students in the class. Teachers could use the time to provide positive feedback and encouragement if a particular student did not have any problems or if a student has improved. By scheduling individual discussions with all students, no particular student feels alienated or singled out. Another benefit of this approach would be early resolution or prevention of a problem, thus

Figure 4–2

Alternative Times That Could
Be Used to Conduct Planned
Discussions

Before school

After school

During recess

During music, physical education, and other special classes
(with prior teacher approval)

During independent seatwork (if the problem is minor)

During study hall

During library time

During free reading time

During a class meeting (if the problem involves several students)

Arrange for someone else to cover the teacher's class (two
teachers may form a collaborative partnership to assist each
other at times like this)

saving time, energy, and frustration. Busy teachers also can ask a support person to partner with them in carrying out planned discussions. School counselors and school psychologists would be pleased to team with teachers and take responsibility for assisting with planned discussions. Teachers should realize, however, that student discussions with them may be more beneficial than discussions with someone outside of the classroom. Teams can determine together who would be the better choice to carry out the planned discussion.

Cultural contexts must be considered prior to implementing planned discussions. Southeast Asians may find this intervention to be too open and direct. Hispanic students may further label the discussion as hostile and disrespectful when teachers seek to ascertain both sides of the situation and facilitate dialogue.

As is typical, the procedures or phases of Sprick et al.'s (1993) planned discussion include (1) a preplanning phase for the educator to define the problem before discussing it with the student, (2) working with the student to define the problem and determine a final plan, and (3) implementing the plan. Two required elements of a successful planned discussion are (1) follow the procedures and (2) use effective communication skills. Here is an example of the planned discussion intervention that could be used, for example, at the earliest signs that a student has weak organizational skills (e.g., arriving in class without materials and assignments).

Preplan

The following form can be used in preparation for discussions:

Describe the problem before discussing with student:

_____

_____

Who is involved? _____

Severity of problem on a scale of 0 (no problem) to 10 (severe): _____

Where does the problem occur?

_____

How often does the problem occur?

_____

Situational factors:

Is the problem academic, social/behavioral, or both? (Circle one.)

Establish a focus. (When the student has interrelated difficulties, introducing too may concerns can overwhelm the student and increase a student's sense of inadequacy.) The specific area that is of most concern is:

_____

Who will participate in the planned discussion? _____

Is this problem minor or severe? (Circle one.)

Does the educator feel a need for assistance? Yes or No (Circle one.)

Check all of those who will participate:

___ Principal (alone when student sent to office from class for discipline)
___ Teacher (alone when problem is minor)
___ Parents or guardians (when problem is more severe or teacher thinks they should be included in developing and implementing plan)
___ Support service personnel (educator feels need for specialized assistance)

Schedule the planned discussion with the student and the parties chosen to participate at a neutral time. A script that can be used with parents and student when making the initial scheduling contact follows.

Educator's Script

"[Name], I need your help with a problem. What I am concerned about is [describe problem]. Let's get together to talk about this on [date]. Before we meet, think about ways that we can work on this problem. I will think about solutions, too. [Name of participant] is invited to come to the meeting. I am sure she will have some good ideas about how to help. I am looking forward to working with you. I am sure that we can come up with some creative ideas."

Collaborate with Student

Conduct a collaborative meeting with the student and complete a discussion record. First, the educator and student collaboratively define the problem.

Educator's Script

"Thank you for meeting with me today to help solve [describe problem]. I am here to help all students with [name type of problem]. Solutions usually turn out better if we work on this together. [Name], what do you think is causing the [name type of problem]."

If the student responds with "I don't know," give the student something concrete to do to help cue him or ask him, "What makes [name the problem] difficult?" If the student still has difficulty answering and a third party is involved in the discussion, request assistance from the third party in helping define the problem.

Next, everyone generates action ideas to solve the problem.

Educator's Script

"We're at the best part now—deciding our plan. Let's list all the things that you and I and [name other participants] can do to help you with [name type of problem]. Let's share as many ideas as we can. Every idea is a good one. After we write them down, we'll pick what we want to try."

(Select an idea or ideas that will be relatively easy to implement.)

"[Name], thank you for your great ideas of things you could do that would help you [type of problem]. Out of all the ideas, let's decide on a few that seem best and we'll talk about how each of the best ideas could be carried out."

Assign responsibilities and set times to carry them out. Schedule a follow-up meeting and send the student off with encouragement.

Implement the Plan

Privately, and on a daily basis, encourage student efforts. Continue periodic discussions of progress with the student and adjust the plan as necessary. Keep that momentum going. Conduct a planned discussion any time it is important to see if more structured interventions are required.

Interventions involving academic assistance, restructuring self-talk, signal interference cueing, goal setting and contracting, self-monitoring, and structured reinforcement systems may be included for intervention plans that need greater depth. (See Chapter 5 for interventions not discussed in this chapter.) The educator needs to provide continued follow-up and encouragement.

Sprick et al. (1993) provide discussion records for educators to use in note taking and comprehensive procedures for the intervention. This intervention takes only a brief time for most educators to master the steps. Although students do participate, they typically do not talk at length. Thus, a planned discussion can take as little as four or five minutes. Educators who role-play procedures of the planned discussion react quite favorably to the intervention and soon report the benefits of the approach.

Direct Confrontation

Additional verbal skills that may be needed include those used in direct confrontation situations. Confrontation is an intermediate to advanced skill that must be used with professional objectivity to be effective. This is a skill that counselors, psychologists, and social workers may feel more comfortable using than teachers or principals. With this communication skill, the listener may be identifying the speaker as the target of the feedback. Using the earlier case of Sally, who did not turn in assignments, the educator might say to the parent: "I see that you did not try the techniques we discussed to increase Sally's turning in assignments. I'm wondering if you are feeling unable to help her and are hoping that someone else will."

Indirect confrontation is conceptualizing the problem as the issue it represents and placing the problem on the issue. "I didn't notice you trying the techniques we discussed to help Sally turn her assignments in. This suggests to me the ideas we developed don't seem to fit as well as I'd hoped. What have you experienced?"

Educators who want to communicate effectively with students who exhibit inappropriate or disruptive behavior must adhere to the practices of (1) confronting only present behavior, (2) talking to the student rather than around the student to someone else, and (3) using "I" messages. Look at these students as if they have a clean slate. This does not mean that educators forget the past nor that they do not use the pattern of behavior problems to help them problem solve. It does mean that educators "bag" past incidents and concentrate on the present ones in order to avoid prejudging or holding grudges against students. Contrast the following two approaches to talking to a student about a late assignment.

Example 1

"Jerad, we have been through this before. Is it going to start again—not getting assignments in on time? I am getting pretty tired of policing you. You are in ninth grade now and need to act like it. Teachers aren't going to babysit you. Figure out how you are going to turn this around and let me know."

Example 2

"Jerad, thank you for meeting with me. The reason that we are meeting is to work together to solve a problem of getting assignments in on time. One of my jobs is to help students learn to be steady workers. For two weeks you have been a steady worker and now you have a late assignment. I am not sure how I can help you, so I thought we could work on this together. Jerad, can you help us figure out why you had trouble getting this assignment in on time?"

"I" messages consist of two types. The first type focuses on educators expressing demands by beginning the message with "I." Examples are "I need you to put the pencil down" and "I expect you to follow rule one in our class: Be respectful to all people at all times." The second type of "I" message requires educators to begin the verbal message with "I," continue by stating their feelings, and end with the effect the students' behaviors are having on the educators. Examples are "I am frustrated because I cannot teach the lesson if you are interrupting" and "I feel angry and uncomfortable with your debates about the value of the assignments I give."

"I" messages require educators to take full responsibility and ownership of their feelings and the effect of student behaviors on them as educators. This intervention moves squarely away from attacking the student and requires educators to be more vulnerable by focusing only on their own feelings. What is responsible for the success of "I" messages? We think it is the lack of attack on the student paired with the concomitant vulnerability of educators who share their own feelings. Ultimately, it is important for educators to recognize that some unpleasant interactions are a part of working with people and to know that they cannot attend to every one of them. Some educators find this difficult to do because of their own angry responses.

Educators' Management of Their Own Anger

Most educators know, without any discussion, that freely expressing their own anger on the job is not an acceptable practice. There are two opposite and extreme methods for managing anger and many people engage in one or the other. First, people let it all hang out and say and act exactly how they are feeling. An example would be the principal who becomes red in the face, shouts at the noncompliant student, and whops the metal trash can by his desk with a yardstick for emphasis.

At the opposite extreme for managing personal anger is to smile and withdraw and act like no one is angry, especially you. An example would be the teacher who is repeatedly engaged by a student in a debate about the value of the lesson and assignments. The student skillfully debates and the teacher is unable to proffer an accepted justification. The teacher smiles after several minutes and walks away but feels angry inside, even raging inside after a few weeks of not only this daily sparring but also no completed student work. Neither of these two methods for managing anger is effective; they are simply not good choices.

Educators' angry, hurt, frustrated, or guilty feelings are natural. Everybody experiences such reactions when interacting with others. The previous discussions of communication skills provided the means for educators to begin to change their attitudes about communication and conflict, thereby reducing the frequency of having angry feelings. Well-developed positive self-talk and attributional thinking skills can be instrumental in reducing anger responses to others' actions. Body language basics of open postures, relaxed muscles, and deep breathing are the exact opposite of the physiological responses of anger. Therefore, when they are practiced they reduce the likelihood of heightened anger responses.

Effective listening skills focus educators' attention on hearing and understanding the intent of a speaker's message, whether the intent is affective or cognitive. Using effective listening skills puts educators in the role of helping speakers solve their own problems rather than educators being responsible for the problems that speakers are sharing. This change in attitude can reduce educators' angry responses to speakers' messages. The skill domain of sending verbal messages is the appropriate domain for educators to express, in effective ways, their personal anger.

Paramount importance is placed on telling the other party how you feel without attacking her. Consider the situation in which the building principal, Ms. Neat, sent a written memo to the curriculum committee members. In it, Ms. Neat named the members who had completed their assignments by the deadline and the one member who had not. That one member is you, Ms. Act. You are angry that Ms. Neat made this information public without first contacting you to obtain your work, especially since the deadline had never been communicated. You feel like your reputation was impacted by Ms. Neat's thoughtless and insensitive memo. How will you respond? (1) You can let her have it. (2) You can smile sweetly and withdraw but feel angry and vengeful inside. (3) Or you can respond somewhere in between by letting her know how you feel without attacking her personally. Listen to the following response that Ms. Act delivers in a quiet tone to Ms Neat.

"Ms. Neat, I did not know what the deadline was. It was never communicated to any of us. You publicly broadcast to the committee that I was the only one who did not make the deadline. That is so like you."

There is something wrong with this message. What? Rather than communicate explicitly how Ms. Act felt, she merely inferred how she felt and personally attacked Ms. Neat by saying, "That is so like you." An attack generally provokes a defensive posture and creates obstacles to communication. Even though this verbal message was delivered quietly, it was not the most effective way to resolve the problem.

Consider a new version of the message that better fits the criteria of stating how you feel without attacking Ms. Neat personally. Remember to focus on Ms. Neat's behavior rather than on her as a person.

"Ms. Neat, I am angry that you announced in a memo to the committee that I was the only one who did not make the deadline. I did not know what the deadline was; I have no record that it was ever communicated to me. I think this type of public announcement hurts my reputation. I would like to discuss with you how to resolve this problem and prevent it from happening in the future. When could we schedule a time to do that?"

Consider another example of angry feelings but this time the interaction is between a teacher and a student. Rudy likes to debate the value of lessons and assignments and will serve as an excellent example because many adults have angry reactions to "Rudy-like" behavior. Some adults will not react with anger to this situation. That is terrific. They will not need to communicate to Rudy that they are angry. However, many adults experience angry feelings and manage it with one of the extreme opposite reactions discussed earlier. The adults either vent their anger on the student (who then feels like she has successfully accomplished her goal of getting an adult to sputter out of control) or smile sweetly and withdraw, feeling angry and vengeful inside. Reflect for a minute on what you would communicate to Rudy if you were angry and compose your response. Then read ahead; it should sound something like this:

"Rudy, I get angry when you persist in asking questions about the value of lessons and assignments. It is good that you think critically about what you study. However, repeated questions disrupt the class for me and other students. This has become a serious problem. We need to schedule a time to meet and collaborate together on a resolution. I see from your schedule that we could both meet during sixth hour. What day would be good for you this week?"

The strengths of this response are several. The teacher communicated his true feelings without attacking the student. In fact, the teacher used the skill of reframing to cast Rudy's annoying debate behaviors in a positive light of thinking critically. The teacher also communicated that problem solving would be collaborative rather than authoritarian. Finally, the teacher structured the time of the meeting but gave the student choices of what day of the week they would meet.

In the preceding situation, imagine that Rudy is an Hispanic American male and the teacher is female. How would communication change? Some male Hispanic American students will listen better to an adult male (Grossman, 1995). When students have difficulty accepting female teachers' authority, teachers may want to try stating requests versus issuing orders. A male administrator may be needed in more severe situations.

Students' Management of Their Own Anger with Educator Assistance

Students' angry, hurt, frustrated, or guilty feelings are also natural. Everybody has them as natural reactions to conflicted interpersonal interactions. However, students' expressions of strong feelings like anger in school contexts are no more appropriate than educators' expressions of anger. Educators are to assist students in learning how to express their anger appropriately. As stated previously, active listening skills can be very effective in helping others regain their self-control. A special focus in active listening requires educators to acknowledge and validate students' feelings. An example might be, "David, I know that it makes you angry when the guys accuse you of cheating. Swearing at them and threatening them are not okay to do at school. Take a few minutes to think about what you could do instead. After that we will talk about your ideas."

Educators can provide appropriate ways for students to "let off steam" also. Physical activities are especially helpful: (1) cleaning areas in classrooms, (2) running errands for teachers, and (3) running laps, doing jumping jacks, or pushups. Nonphysical activities that serve as relaxants are helpful to some students: (1) eating or drinking, (2) listening to music, and (3) talking calmly. Educators must ensure, however, that, when using these activities to help students calm down, students do not respond as if they had been rewarded for getting angry. One way to overcome any possible negative effects of relaxation techniques is to be sure to require students to make up work time that they missed during relaxation activities.

Educators may wish to provide a way for students to escape from the environment in which they are experiencing strong feelings. There may be a place in the building where students can go to calm themselves. Many teachers use signal interference cueing (e.g., teacher says, "distancing" to student and student takes responsibility to go to a special room for calming purposes) with students who may need to escape. The idea is to let students be alone where it is easier to become calm. We all need to have a calm atmosphere before we can problem solve effectively. How do you think this intervention would have worked with Jerad, the boy in Chapter 1 who tried to leave the room and was grabbed around the neck by the teacher?

Natural consequences for expressing strong feelings may include making apologies. Grossman (1995) reported that students from some ethnic backgrounds (e.g., Hispanic Americans) may be more likely to apologize in subtle ways as opposed to overt, direct apologies.

Finally, more specific interventions for students with severe anger control deficits are described in Chapter 5, where we discuss conduct management. Figure 4–3 provides a list of some common school situations that educators can use as the context for practicing body language and communication skills.

Assessment of Professional Communication Skills

Figures 4–4 and 4–5 are examples of rating scales that educators can use to routinely assess their communication skills after a difficult interpersonal encounter at school. Figure 4–4 focuses on listening and Figure 4–5 focuses on how well the educator did at receiving critical feedback from the speaker.

CONCLUSION

Effective communication skills in the domains of self-talk, body language basics, listening, and sending verbal messages are not developed overnight or during the course of a college semester of study and practice. However, readers should have basic knowledge and procedural skills in each of the domains mentioned in order to continue to build on their initial foundation.

Consider the following situations and practice the necessary communication skills to best manage them. When you can select the appropriate communication procedures and role play the situations adequately, you can be assured that you have the foundational communication skills that will help you develop into an expert communicator/manager. Your competence will grow and your appreciation of what you have accomplished will be reassuring.

1. You find yourself making the following comments about a highly distractible student who is often off task: "Rudy never pays attention. I am so tired of him always disrupting the class. I am on him every minute of the day."
2. A student is unable to work cooperatively with peers in small group math lessons but can work better in cooperative groups focused on reading or science. He has a pattern of making negative statements about math assignments: "This is stupid" and "This is too difficult; I can't do it."
3. You are angry with a student who is disrespectful to you.
4. You are angry with a student who is disrespectful to others.
5. You are angry with a student that you have been unable to control.

Administrators

1. Employee is frustrated with administrator for the way a student's behavior problem was disciplined.

2. Female student is suspended for being tardy to class and her parents are in the administrator's office and are emotionally upset but are not showing anger.

3. Female student is suspended for being tardy to class and her parents are in the administrator's office and are angry and loudly threatening to sue.

4. Administrator calls parent(s) to communicate bad news about their child (e.g., student was in a fight or brought a weapon to school or was in possession of drugs).

5. Student was consistently disruptive to classroom learning environment and sent out of class to principal's office. Student is angry, swears at principal, and paces around the office.

6. Student was consistently disruptive to classroom learning environment and was sent out of class to principal's office. Student is argumentative but not angry with principal.

Teachers

1. Student made a low grade for the quarter. It is parent conference time and the parent is feeling discouraged and becomes teary-eyed during the conference.

2. Parent unexpectedly comes by at the end of the school day to talk to the teacher. The parent is angry about an assignment that requires students to write about a historic figure that the parent believes was racist. Parent accuses teacher of being racist.

3. Teacher makes a telephone call to the home and requests a meeting with the parent(s) to discuss student's lack of progress.

4. Student is quietly noncompliant with teacher requests.

5. Student is loud and noncompliant with teacher requests.

6. Student argues with teacher decisions.

7. Student constantly exhibits behaviors that are borderline unacceptable.

8. Student responds to new or difficult tasks with frustration and says something like one of the following: (a) This task is stupid. (b) I can't do this. (c) This is too hard.

Figure 4–3
Practice Scenarios of Common School Situations

(Name) _____

(Grade) _____   (Date) _____

1 = Poor
2 = Fair
3 = Average
4 = Superior
5 = Excellent

Assessment of Listening Skills

1 2 3 4 5   1. I heard precisely.

1 2 3 4 5   2. I helped the speaker feel understood.

1 2 3 4 5   3. I effectively used acknowledging (yes, really, wow, right).
_____used to encourage person to speak
_____used to communicate awareness of emotional content

1 2 3 4 5   4. I effectively used reflecting (repeating back).
_____selected to underline emotional responses
_____selected to begin behavior analysis

1 2 3 4 5   5. I effectively used paraphrasing (offered tentatively).
_____used to cue speaker to slight variations in message

1 2 3 4 5   6. I effectively used summarizing.
_____seemed to help make decisions
_____preserved information
_____used to end a meeting

1 2 3 4 5   7. I effectively used clarifying (asked questions for elaboration).
_____used to get a complete picture, snapshot, or movie
_____used to help speaker put information together
_____used "what," not "why," questions

1 2 3 4 5   8. I effectively used elaboration (building on information introduced).
_____used to link speaker's talk to my suggestions

Yes   No   9. I appropriately gave the speaker credit for having all the best ideas.

Figure 4–4
Assessment of Listening Skills

6. You are discouraged or frustrated with a student that you have been unable to motivate.
7. You do not believe what a student is telling you.
8. A student does not appear to like you even though you have made many attempts to build a relationship.
9. A parent or student communicates in an angry or accusatory way with you.
10. A parent is emotionally upset at a parent–teacher conference when you tell her that her daughter has been skipping class and is receiving a "D" letter grade for the quarter.

Yes	No	1. I used a relaxation response when I became aware that feedback was imminent.
Yes	No	2. I listened closely to everything the speaker was saying and did not begin to formulate a response until I heard the entire message.
Yes	No	3. I tried to catch the essence of the speaker's feelings.
Yes	No	4. Before I spoke, I studied my own feelings and was able to label them.
Yes	No	5. I repeated back what I heard. I asked for clarification. If I was in a group, I checked to see if others saw me the same way.
Yes	No	6. I reminded myself that I have no way to control the way others see me and that I am completely responsible only for my own behavior.
Yes	No	7. I decided to change the behavior, realizing that the person's feelings may not change about me.
Yes	No	8. There is a content misunderstanding between me and speaker. I gave reasons why I behaved the way I did.
Yes	No	9. The misunderstanding is not one of content. I did not get defensive and give reasons why I behaved the way I did.

Figure 4–5
Assessment of Feedback Skills (Received by Educator)

SUPPLEMENTARY QUESTIONS

1. High school students sometimes complain that teachers treat them disrespectfully. Which of the communication tips in this chapter do you remember teachers violating?
2. Some teachers say that they are too busy to communicate through listening and that it is not realistic to expect them to take the time. What do you think? How will you decide when you must take the time and when it is not as necessary?
3. Think about a teacher in your past who was a positive influence on you and your peers. What were her/his communication skills? Was communication the most important skill or were there other reasons that prompted you to select this teacher?

SUPPLEMENTARY PROJECTS

1. Record or videotape your interactions with others to see which of Ginott's communication no-no's you use. Write scripts to replace your current messages and provide evidence of rehearsal. Critique new tapes that show improvement.
2. Use the same tape to listen to your communication skills and gauge your use of body language, listening, and sending verbal messages. Do your predominant communication skills match the philosophical and theoretical beliefs that you identified in Chapter 1? Justify your response.

REFERENCES

Aiello, J. R., & Jones, S. E. (1971). Field study of the proxemic behavior of young school children in three subcultural groups. *Journal of Personality and Social Psychology, 19*, 351–356.

Anderson, L. M., Evertson, C. M., & Emmer, E. T. (1979). *Dimensions in classroom management derived from recent research.* Austin, TX: Texas University, Research and Development Center for Teacher Education. (ERIC Document Reproduction No. ED 175-860)

Barker, K. (Ed.). (1985). *The new international version Bible* (p. 1248). Grand Rapids, MI: The Zondervan Corporation.

Baron, R. M., Tom, D., & Cooper, H. (1985). Social class, race and teacher expectations. In J. Dusek, V. Hall, & W. Meyer (Eds.), *Teacher expectancies* (pp. 251–269). Hillsdale, NJ: Lawrence Erlbaum Associates.

Bernard, M. E. (1979). Does sex role behavior influence the way teachers evaluate students? *Journal of Educational Psychology, 71*, 553–562.

Charles, C. M. (1996). *Building classroom discipline.* White Plains, NY: Longman.

NEA Committee on Professional Ethics. (1975). *Code of ethics of the education profession.* Washington, DC: National Education Association.

Connors, E. T. (1981). *Educational tort liability and malpractice.* Bloomington, IN: Phi Delta Kappa.

Conoley, J. C., & Conoley, C. W. (1992). *School consultation: Practice and training.* Boston: Allyn and Bacon.

Cooper, H., Baron, R., & Lowe, C. (1975). The importance of race and social class in the formation of expectancies about academic performance. *Journal of Educational Psychology, 67*, 312–319.

Cooperman, M. L. (1975). Field-dependence and children's problem-solving under varying contingencies of predetermined feedback. *Dissertation Abstracts International, 35*, 2040–2041.

Cotton, K. (1990). *Schoolwide and classroom discipline. School improvement research series.* Portland, OR: Northwest Regional Educational Laboratory.

Dweck, C. S. (1975). The role of expectation and attributions in the alleviation of learned helplessness. *Journal of Personality and Social Psychology, 25*, 109–116.

Gay, G., & Abrahams, R. D. (1973). Does the pot melt, boil, or brew? Black children and white assessment procedures. *Journal of School Psychology, 11*(4), 330–340.

Gilliam, H., & Van Den Berg, S. (1980). Different levels of eye contact: Effects on black and white college students. *Urban Education, 15*, 83–92.

Ginott, H. (1971). *Teacher and child.* New York: Macmillan.

Gordon, T. (1974). *Teacher effectiveness training.* New York: Wyden.

Grossman, H. (1984). *Educating Hispanic students: Cultural implications for instruction, classroom management, counseling, and assessment.* Springfield, IL: Thomas.

Grossman, H. (1995). *Classroom behavior management in a diverse society* (2nd ed.). Mountain View, CA: Mayfield.

Heider, F. (1958). *The psychology of interpersonal relations.* New York: Wiley.

Heller, K. A., & Parsons, J. E. (1981). Sex differences in teachers' evaluative feedback and students' expectancies for success in mathematics. *Child Development, 52*, 1015–1019.

Iverson, A. M. (1996). *Preservice educators' self-reports of communication skills.* Unpublished manuscript, University of Northern Iowa.

Jones, V. F., & Jones, L. S. (1995). *Comprehensive classroom management: Creating positive learning environments for all students.* Boston: Allyn and Bacon.

Kounin, J. S. (1970). *Discipline and group management in classrooms.* New York: Holt, Rinehart & Winston.

Multon, K. D., Brown, S. D., & Lent, R. W. (1991). Relation of self-efficacy beliefs to academic outcomes: A meta-analytic investigation. *Journal of Counseling Psychology, 38*, 30–38.

Nguyen, T. P. (1987). Positive self-concept in the Vietnamese bilingual child. In M. Dao (Ed.), *From Vietnamese to Vietnamese American: Selected articles*. San Jose, CA: Division of Special Education and Rehabilitative Services, San Jose State University.

Reeder, M. A. (1996). *Acceptability across disciplines of attribution retraining alone and combined with learning strategy instruction*. Unpublished thesis, University of Northern Iowa.

Sprick, R., Sprick, M., & Garrison, M. (1993). *Interventions: Collaborative planning for students at risk*. Longmont, CO: Sopris West.

Tom, D., & Cooper, H. (1986). The effect of student background on teacher performance attributions: Evidence for counterdefensive patterns and low expectancy cycles. *Basic and Applied Social Psychology, 7*, 53–62.

Tom, D., Cooper, H., & McGraw, M. (1984). The influences of student background and teacher authoritarianism on teacher expectations. *Journal of Educational Psychology, 76*, 259–265.

Wei, T.D. (1980). *Vietnamese refugee students: A handbook for school personnel* (2nd ed.). Urbana, IL: Illinois University, Midwest Organization for Material Development. (ERIC Document Reproduction No. ED 208 109)

White Deer of Autumn (1992). *The Native American Book of Change* (Vol. 3, Native People Native Ways Series). Hillsboro, OR: Beyond Words Publishing.

Wiley, M. G., & Eskilson, A. (1978). Why did you learn in school today? Teachers' perceptions of causality. *Sociology of Education, 51*, 261–269.

Wong, M. C. (1980). Model students? Teachers' perceptions and expectations of their Asian and white students. *Sociology of Education, 53*, 226–246.

PART II

Management Tools: Theoretical Models, Principles, and Practices

CHAPTER 5

Content Management: Setting and Instruction

An understanding of the material in this chapter will help you do the following:

❑ Identify teacher errors in the organization and delivery of instruction that can contribute to discipline problems, and cite ways to avoid these errors.

❑ Discuss the importance of teacher expectations on content management, and offer suggestions for equalizing opportunities for all students.

❑ Distinguish between expository and facilitative teaching methods and the content management responsibilities associated with each.

❑ Examine the characteristics of varied instructional activities, and identify the collateral content management requirements.

❑ Manage cooperative learning lessons successfully.

❑ Role-play ways to deal with instructionally related discipline problems.

Minnick (1983) conducted a study of excessive discipline problems at an inner-city junior high school in a large southwestern city. Classes of twenty-one target students who regularly misbehaved were monitored, as were classes of nondisruptive students.

Teachers with a high incidence of disciplinary problems failed to plan and design appropriate instructional tasks, rarely attempted to enhance a lesson with an overview or explanation of the topic's significance, neglected variety in lesson plans, seldom encouraged students to discuss or evaluate the material they were learning, did little to check student comprehension by carefully monitoring seatwork or through assignments and regularly graded papers, and never seemed able to establish enough order to begin to cover material effectively.

In contrast, those teachers maintaining strong and consistent instructional management and organizational skills had markedly fewer classroom disruptions. Minnick concluded that it may be more meaningful to speak of disruptive schools or disruptive classrooms rather than disruptive students. Other researchers whose work will be examined in this chapter support these findings. We label this aspect of classroom management *content* or *instructional management*. How can other teachers duplicate the success of effective content managers?

In this chapter, we focus in particular on models of content or instructional management. Reflecting our position that student behavior in learning contexts is too complex to be addressed by any one theory or model, we offer principles from several models of classroom management. First, strategies from Kounin's research (1977) in movement management during instruction are described. Second, principles from Glasser's quality teaching model (1990, 1992, 1993) provide guidelines for instructional planning to minimize discipline problems. Last, interventions are described to be used with students whose behaviors present additional instructional challenges. These interventions tend to rely on shaping desired behavior (Sprick, 1985; Sprick, Sprick, & Garrison, 1993) and are developed in the context of discipline through dignity and hope (Curwin & Mendler, 1988). In this chapter, you will learn the procedures of effective content management.

CONTENT MANAGEMENT: INSTRUCTION

Teachers are managing content when they manage space, materials, equipment, the movement of people, and lessons that make up a curriculum or program of studies. We have seen that the management of the setting in which this program takes place can affect the availability of time and the attention of students. When efficient setting management procedures reduce the occurrence of problems, students and teachers can concentrate their energies on learning and instruction.

Content or instructional management does not refer to skills peculiar to teaching a particular subject but rather to those skills that cut across subjects and activities. Such skills might be called generic because they are not subject or activity dependent.

Instructional management essentially involves gaining and maintaining the *cooperation* of students in learning *activities* (Doyle, 1980). Note the emphasis on cooperation and activities. Cooperation entails a willingness to adhere to the activity's requirements. Students who are willing participants are not likely to create disturbances that detract from learning (Glasser, 1990; Jones, 1989).

Meaningful student engagement can be increased if the teacher uses a variety of activities. The activities should be tied to student interests and have defensible educational aims (Glasser, 1992). Teachers also need to prepare students to make the most of the activity (Marshall, 1987). While activities serve as a way of achieving relevant instructional goals, they also make demands independent of the material to be learned on the student and impose unique management demands on the teacher (Doyle, 1986; Paine, Radicchi, Rosellini, Deutchman, & Darch, 1983).

Lectures, classwide recitation, small-group instruction/discussion, seatwork, drill-and-practice sessions, role playing, audiovisual presentations, simulation games, and independent and group projects are the common activities that fill the classroom day. Each activity is but a means for teaching a body of material and helping students acquire skills. The subject-matter competence of both teacher and student helps determine an activity's success. Equally important are the teacher's adeptness in organizing and presenting the activity and the students' receptiveness to the activity.

Kounin (1970) has identified three clusters of instructional management skills:

1. *Movement management* refers to the teacher's effectiveness in pacing, maintaining momentum, and making transitions from one topic to another.
2. *Group focus* involves the ability to maintain group concentration.
3. *Avoidance of satiation* enables the teacher to minimize boredom and the feeling that "I have had enough already."

These skill clusters are independent of the subjects and contents customarily associated with instruction. Thus, they are considered management skills that influence the extent to which students participate in activity-related behaviors, maintain a high level of involvement, and preclude the occurrence of disciplinary problems.

Movement Management: Arranging and Directing Activity Flow

Kounin's research highlights the mistakes that teachers make with respect to movement within and between lessons. By using videotapes of thousands of hours of classroom instruction, Kounin discovered two movement management mistakes: jerkiness and slowdowns. Each of these errors is an impediment to student concentration. When students have their concentration broken, they are more likely to engage in unacceptable behaviors.

Jerkiness

Thrusts. *Thrusts* occur when the teacher suddenly bursts into an ongoing activity without warning and gives directions for another activity. For example, imagine a group of students working at learning centers. The teacher, who has been circulating around the room, suddenly says, "Put the materials you are working with back in the boxes and folders and get ready for social studies."

The teacher did not inquire about progress, suggest the need to finish in the next five minutes, or in any way prepare students for a change in activity. Seemingly without regard for the students' involvement in one activity, the teacher instead tried to plunge them into another. The potential for disciplinary problems emerges as students scurry to fulfill the new set of directions, not quite sure what they are, and to culminate another activity at the same time. Experienced teachers report that this is frustrating for students and usually results in chaos.

Dangles.   Jerky transitions can also be caused by what Kounin calls *dangles*. The teacher leaves one activity dangling in midair to go to another, only to return to the first. For example, the bell has just rung; students are seated and quiet. The teacher directs them to get out their math books and turn to the assignment on page 72. She is reminded of an announcement about a special assembly and says, "Before I forget, I have an announcement to read." After reading the announcement, she returns to the math assignment, but student attention has been momentarily diverted. Or perhaps the teacher decides to tell a short story. Students are left wondering what the connection of the story is and find it difficult to refocus on the original task.

How can students be expected to set aside the intrusion and get right back to the former task? Some will visit with their neighbor to discuss the assembly, and a few others will do so vicariously. The disruption has drawn student attention away from the first task and has made it more difficult to return. Is it any wonder teachers dislike those "May I have your attention for a moment please" announcements that are periodically broadcast from the school office each day?

Flip-Flop.   The *flip-flop* is a variation of the dangle. The teacher seemingly terminates one activity, begins a second, and then surprises everyone with a flashback to the first. Students conclude a science activity with a short quiz, which is graded by exchanging papers. Scores are recorded by way of oral reporting. After the class begins a homework assignment, the teacher asks, "By the way, how many of you got all of the science quiz items right?"

Truncations.   Then there are the times when the teacher leaves one activity, goes to another, and never returns to the first. Kounin calls these movement errors *truncations*. In this instance, the teacher, after beginning an activity, is reminded of another activity that may have been neglected earlier and sets aside the present activity to resume work on the earlier one. For example, say students are doing seatwork; the teacher is grading papers and suddenly remembers parent conferences will be held a week from Friday. Since he wants students to write invitations to their parent(s), he instructs them to put their social studies assignment aside so that they can get the letters written today. The letter writing is followed by recess, math, and science. So what does the student do about the social studies? The clamor that the teacher likes to avoid at the end of the school day is likely to include some unsettling solutions to the original social studies assignment.

Slowdowns

The pacing of a lesson is also a crucial factor in maintaining student attention. *Slowdowns,* the second major category of movement management problems, occur when instructional momentum is unnecessarily delayed by what Kounin calls over-dwelling and fragmentation.

Overdwelling. When students characterize teachers as being "a drag," they may well be referring to this movement management problem. Rather than being too abrupt and jerky, the teacher is too ponderous. Kounin has identified several forms of overdwelling: task, behavior, actone, and prop.

Task and *behavior overdwelling* involve spending too much time on directions and explanations. Sometimes the teacher wants to be sure the students follow instructions and gives more instructions than are necessary. At other times the teacher wants the student to stop misbehaving and offers a prolonged discourse expressing displeasure.

In his book *Motivating Classroom Discipline,* Gnagey (1981) features Mr. Harold in this illustration of task overdwelling:

> Mr. Harold had a little verbal routine that he went through every time he gave a spelling test. He repeated it so exactly that his students couldn't tell it from a Memorex tape. "Now clear your desks of everything except your pencil and spelling tablet. Remember that we slant our books a bit to the left, not to the right, unless of course you are left-handed. Your name should be printed, not written, in the upper left-hand corner on the top line. Please number your papers from 1 to 10 in two columns, 1 to 5 in the first column and 6 to 10 in the second. I will pronounce each spelling word twice, and you should write it as neatly as possible. If you want a word defined, please raise your hand after I have pronounced it for the second time. Ready? Here we go!"
>
> After the third week of reruns, students began to show their impatience in many ways. One girl had become expert at lip-synching the act and amused everyone who saw her "speaking" in Harold's scholarly baritone. (p. 66)

Ms. Eckrich is the central character in his example of what is meant by behavior overdwelling:

> "You should know better than that, Ronald," glared Ms. Eckrich. "We always put our books away before we take a test. I have told you over and over again that your desk must be clear during a test. You should have learned that in the fourth grade and yet here you are at the end of fifth and you still haven't caught on." Ms. E's voice had now risen half an octave and the last sentence was delivered at a volume just below a shriek. "If you insist on breaking the rules again and again, I don't see much hope for you. You will probably end up in reform school with all the other dummies who wouldn't listen to their teachers!" By this time some of the other students were rolling their eyes and not taking the teacher seriously: "Here she goes again." Many shifted uncomfortably in their seats. Few if any were ready for the test that was supposed to be the central activity for the day. (p. 65)

Actone overdwelling occurs when the teacher gets so enthralled with details that everyone loses sight of the main idea. Recall the history teacher who talks so incessantly about names, dates, and places that he loses sight of the significant event, or the math teacher so captivated by an elegant solution to a problem that he neglects the principle that can be used to solve a class of similar problems. A teacher's enthusiasm and expertise can be an invitation to student participation, or they can be a deadly weapon, killing interest and annihilating anticipation.

Finally, *prop overdwelling* happens when a teacher becomes so enamored with the physical prop that the lesson goes awry. Mr. Byte was introducing students to a new computer. He wanted to give them a chance to work some math problems and have the benefit of immediate feedback. But Mr. Byte got so carried away talking about the various features of the computer that the students were only able to spend a few minutes working problems.

Fragmentation.   The final form of slowdown, fragmentation, is in a class by itself. *Fragmentation* consists of breaking down, into what seems like an infinite number of parts, an activity that does not require such discrete units. It begs student indulgence. Some teachers think that every activity must be done a row at a time, in five-minute blocks or according to directions given one step at a time. Students are left waiting. They must find diversions of some kind, a task at which they are ingenious, or they will go stark raving mad.

Aggravation and annoyance are the by-products of slowdowns due to overdwelling and fragmentation. Students get fed up and either tune out or cut up. In either case, the student's contribution often provokes a response from the teacher similar to the one that originally prompted the student's misbehavior. Now the entire group is out of sorts, hardly an optimal condition for learning.

Group Focus: Maintaining Group Concentration

The second cluster of instructional management skills involves group focus, the ability to maintain group alertness and effort. Kounin (1970) contended that teachers can be catalysts for a productive group by managing the (1) group format, (2) degree of accountability, and (3) attention.

Group Format

Managing a group format requires organizational skills and techniques that promote a sense of cohesiveness and cooperation. The job to be done becomes a joint enterprise, with everyone sharing their knowledge and skills. Several researchers have offered some interesting insights into how to effectively manage the group format.

Kerman and Martin (1980) completed a three-year study of the relationship between fifteen specific forms of motivational and supportive interactions and the academic performance of low achievers. They found that all of the teachers from more than thirty school districts in Los Angeles County practiced the fifteen interactions more frequently with high achievers. Their work culminated in the model presented in Table 5–1.

Promoting the interactions in Strand A and Strand B of Table 5–1 would appear to be effective ways to facilitate group focus. Examine the first five interac-

Table 5–1
Equal Opportunities in the Classroom Interaction Model

Strand A: Response opportunities	
1. Equitable distribution	"I am going to be called on to perform in this class."
2. Individual help	"My teacher is concerned about me and wants me to succeed."
3. Latency	"I have time to think."
4. Delving	"My teacher is making a special effort in helping me to answer."
5. Higher level questioning	"My teacher really expects me to think."
Strand B: Feedback	
1. Affirmation or correction	"I am going to be told promptly that my classwork is acceptable or not."
2. Praise	"My teacher is especially pleased with my classwork."
3. Reasons for praise	"My teacher is going to tell me why he or she likes what I accomplish in this class."
4. Listening	"My teacher is really interested in what I have to say."
5. Accepting feelings	"My teacher understands how I feel, and that's okay."
Strand C: Personal regard	
1. Proximity	"My teacher is close by, and it doesn't bother me."
2. Courtesy	"My teacher respects me."
3. Personal interest/ compliments	"I am more than just a student to my teacher; my teacher compliments me."
4. Touching	"My teacher likes me."
5. Desisting	"The teacher is upset with what I'm doing, but not with me as a person."

Source: From *Teacher Expectations and Student Achievement: Teacher Handbook* (formerly *Equal Opportunity in the Classroom*) by Sam Kerman and Mary Martin, 1980, Bloomington, IN: Phi Delta Kappa. Copyright 1980 by Los Angeles County Office of Education. Reprinted by permission.

tions in the table and ask yourself why these techniques would not be practiced as frequently with low achievers as with high achievers. Do you begin to see the role of teacher expectations? Can you think of reasons for a teacher to call on "highs" more frequently than "lows"? To prompt or cue a high who does not respond, but call on another student when a low appears not to know? Allow a high time to think when unable to respond immediately, but quickly get the low "off the hook"? Help a high formulate an answer, but ignore an incomplete or inaccurate response from a low? Ask a high questions that call for understanding and judgment, but ask a low to recall simple facts?

Communication of expectations for student performance is related to achievement (Kagan, 1992). Brophy and Good (1970) presented the earliest findings of differences in the expectations teachers held for high versus low achieving students. The frequency of teacher contact was the same but look at the differences in the content of interactions:

- ❑ Criticized high achievers much less and praised them more.
- ❑ Cued and questioned high achievers when they struggled with accuracy.
- ❑ Increased opportunities for high achievers to respond (three to four times as often).

This initial investigation of teacher expectations was based on observation data (e.g., when the student is doing this, the teacher is doing that). Observation data are correlational and do not establish a cause-and-effect relationship. All that could be said on the basis of Brophy and Good's observation data was that teachers praised and called on students who were doing well academically. One could not say that teacher praise and calling on students caused them to perform well academically.

Kerman (1982) conducted a large experimental or cause-and-effect study that is referred to as TESA (Teacher Expectations and Student Achievement). Teachers from thirty California school districts volunteered to participate in the study. Experi-

A teacher masters group format includes all students, regardless of race, class, gender, or disability.

mental group teachers received in-service training on the fifteen strategies from Table 5–1 for interacting with all students equitably. All students in the experimental classrooms made significant academic gains compared to all students in control classrooms. Specifically, the 2000 low achievers whose teachers learned interaction strategies significantly outperformed the low achievers in the control classes whose teachers did not learn interaction strategies. In addition, they had significantly reduced absences and discipline referrals.

Other researchers found that lows were given fewer chances to respond and less time to answer, were provided more negative feedback and less classroom freedom/opportunities, were seated away from the teacher, and received less eye contact (Good & Brophy, 1984; Weinstein, Marshall, Brattesani, & Middlestadt, 1982; Weinstein & Middlestadt, 1979).

Since the question and recitation/discussion are primary instructional tools, it is incumbent on teachers to use them on behalf of all learners. A group format that excludes or only marginally involves a large portion of the pupil population results in apathy and, worse, a loss of self-esteem. Some students may choose to withdraw completely. They drop out but stay in; they have for all practical purposes chosen not to be a part of the group. Others will engage in various forms of attention getting. They want desperately to be a part of the group. If they cannot do so constructively, they will do so destructively. Unfortunately, their behavior does not always seem destructive to other students; the class clown often has a winning way with peers.

Degree of Accountability

Accountability is the second form of group focus. The instructional leader has to create a feeling that everyone is responsible for what happens in the group and for learning the material that is the subject of the group's focus. Note the five interactions under Strand B in Table 5–1. Feedback provides the teacher an opportunity to reward correct answers, help students untangle confusing ideas, and set them straight when they do not understand. Recall that teachers are less likely to give feedback to low achievers; if the number of response opportunities is negligible in the first place, there will be few opportunities to give feedback. When the teacher increases response interactions and the amount of feedback for all students, they experience a sense of fulfillment and accountability. These complementary functions also bolster positive personal regard (see Table 5–1).

Students are more likely to be attentive if they believe that they will derive some benefits, and personal regard is certainly a payoff that matters. When students feel that they matter, they are also more receptive to the ideas and activities the teacher believes to be important. When their welfare and well-being are bound up in the aims and aspirations of others, they are more likely to give their allegiance to the group. Securing and sustaining student attention is not just a matter of being a subject-matter expert; it is a matter of knowing how to use management techniques to optimize pupil involvement (Slade & Callaghan, 1988). When all students are involved and all efforts are pointed in the same direction, teachers find it easier to achieve their goals. Students can cause obstructions or they can cooperate; leadership determines their choice and the way they exercise it.

Averting Boredom: Avoidance of Satiation

Kounin's final category of instructional management skills concerns the teacher's ability to forestall boredom. Progress, variety, and challenge are the hedges against satiation. Let us look briefly at each of these ways to counteract conditions that are potential causes for discipline problems.

Progress

Progress is the feeling one gets when steadily moving toward some significant objective. Certainly the skills associated with movement management and group focus contribute to this sense of accomplishment. However, even with the effective use of these group management techniques, obstacles and setbacks can still arise. How might the teacher act to minimize impediments to progress? Several techniques proposed by Redl and Wattenberg (1959) can be very helpful.

Restructuring the program might be necessary when progress is halted, either by student resistance to the subject matter or by extenuating circumstances that siphon students' energy. Admittedly, some educational goals do not elicit enthusiasm or determination. Under these circumstances teachers might ask whether they control the program or whether the program controls them. When encountering resistance to selected educational aims, the teacher might ask whether these aims are worth fighting for. Can a compelling case be made for what the teacher believes are significant educational aims? Teachers need not capitulate to win student approval and cooperation. Nor should they be staunch advocates for programs and practices because students should be taught to "tough it out." There are times when restructuring the program is the most reasonable way to promote progress.

The extracurricular program, seasonal changes, and holiday periods are extenuating circumstances that might suggest a restructuring of the classroom program. Sometimes it just does not pay to compete with a basketball tournament game on Friday night, the first snowfall of the year, or the winter holiday. This is not to say teachers should relinquish responsibility for teaching during these periods. Rather, they should try to capitalize on the interest in these circumstances and make the program the beneficiary.

Sometimes progress is stymied by intellectual roadblocks. Students are unable to move ahead because they lack the information or skill to fulfill the requirements of a particular task. For this situation, Redl and Wattenberg (1959) propose hurdle help. There is no point in letting frustration grow until students seek a nonacademic outlet. Discipline problems can be averted by knowing how much frustration students can tolerate. Some teachers let students decide; they have a prearranged signal system that enables students to request help when they have exhausted personal resources. Other teachers prefer to use knowledge of and previous experience with a student, along with nonverbal cues, as a basis for making personal assistance decisions. Whatever the detection system, it is wise to help students make steady progress by removing hurdles they cannot jump over and too often try to run around.

Variety

In addition to being the spice of life, variety is also an effective way to avoid satiation. Interest boosting and support from routine are classroom management techniques that Redl and Wattenberg (1959) advocate to help revive a program that might be undermined by insufficient variety.

Restlessness is probably the most reliable sign that interest is waning. Helping a child or class mobilize interest to sustain constructive activity becomes the most immediate problem. Teachers commonly tap an area of interest that has previously produced positive results. A good grasp of age and stage characteristics of students and recalling their individual tastes can be used to pull back anyone teetering on the brink of disinterest.

Routine is the archenemy of variety. Whenever routine has the upper edge, there is a greater likelihood satiation will set in. Students tire easily of repetition, yet practice is essential to some forms of learning. When confronted by daily routines, students go aimlessly through the motions. Yet routines are necessary to preserve order and organization. Teachers must learn to sense when enough is enough. Enterprising activities that invite inquisitiveness and excitement help minimize the diversions from routines that students create for themselves.

Providing structure, without imposing a litany of particulars, can also be liberating rather than constraining. Students need guideposts so that they can monitor their own progress and experience the joy of increasing competence. While teachers do prescribe and moderate the circumstances of life in a classroom, they can also relieve the monotony and tediousness of the routines they create. Achieving accord between the repetitions that serve and those that do not calls for a deft balancing act. Respites from routines may be the only solution in some instances; in others, teachers should periodically examine the purposes served and look for less dreadful alternatives.

Challenge

When the challenge is sufficient to court the best efforts of students, satiation is seldom a problem. Students look on learning as a test of their intellectual powers. They want to succeed because success is evidence of their ability to take on a challenge and come out a winner. Some students will create challenges for themselves. Others may prefer the alternatives teachers propose. In either case, students do not tire of success if the success is a genuine test of their abilities and culminates in personally relevant accomplishments.

Discipline problems are often the by-products of a challenge unaccepted or unrealized. Fear of failure may discourage some students from accepting the challenge. Others may be distressed when they accept the challenge and do not succeed. It is better to moderate these conditions through management techniques that foster competence.

PLANNING AN INSTRUCTIONAL PROGRAM

Deciding on the Appropriate Teaching Structure

Lessons and the activities designed to achieve lesson objectives can be organized around two teaching structures: one that favors expository teaching and receptive learning (Gersten, Carnine, & Woodward, 1987; Rosenshine, 1983, 1986) and one that favors facilitative, inductive teaching and discovery learning (Charles, 1983). Teachers find that some lesson objectives are better attained by using direct and deductive-based teaching methods, whereas other objectives may be better suited to indirect and inductive-based methods. The management requirements depend on the teacher's decision to use one of these primary instructional delivery systems.

Direct or expository teaching is generally characterized as highly structured, efficient, and formal. Advocates of the method generally view the teacher as a scholar and a purveyor of information. The teacher's management responsibilities are aimed at controlling all aspects of the lesson: objectives, activities, materials, assignments, and evaluation.

Charles (1983) identified eleven widely used methods of teaching. These methods can be arranged on a continuum from most to least structured to illustrate the difference between direct and indirect methods. The first five methods are typically used as the basis for direct teaching activities:

1. Diagnostic prescriptive teaching
2. Expository teaching
3. Modeling
4. Read/review/recite
5. Competency-based education

The other six methods, however, are commonly associated with more indirect methods of teaching:

6. Simulations
7. Projects
8. Group process
9. Inquiry/discovery
10. Facilitation
11. Open experience

All of the direct methods of instruction emphasize teacher control. Teachers have few management-of-materials problems. The focus is on the teacher and the textbook as the primary instruments of instruction. Direct instructional methods used with groups of students are subject to weak instructional matches, however. For example, some students do not have the prior knowledge to benefit from the lecture. Behavior problems tend to increase under these conditions. Students become frustrated, disinterested, bored, and inattentive. Management success needs to be based on altering instruction to achieve a better match with learner characteristics.

Indirect or inductive-based teaching methods emphasize process over product. These methods are aimed at eliciting student participation and contribute to divergent rather than convergent production. That is, a lesson does not always have to be aimed at achieving specific objectives but can entertain a myriad of possibilities. Proponents of this position trust the learner to be a responsible participant in the selection of objectives, methods, materials, and evaluation procedures (Pinnell & Galloway, 1987). This approach is in direct contrast to that of direct instruction. Rogers (1977) asserts that teaching that ignores the learners' desire to achieve personal meanings will produce only inconsequential learnings. According to this view, the teacher should become a facilitator rather than a director of learning. Facilitators do not attempt to impart or impose their knowledge. According to Rogers, facilitating the learning process involves the following:

1. Asking questions that tap student interests, concerns, fears, and aspirations
2. Helping students identify what really counts in their lives and then assisting them in their search for human and material resources that discern these matters
3. Establishing a climate that fosters curiosity, allows mistakes, and encourages students to experience all aspects of their environment
4. Using activities that stimulate students to raise questions, search for information, and make decisions
5. Helping students organize and share the results of inquiry with others

This process opens students up to the experiences of themselves and others. Advocates claim this process produces both enduring ideas and ideals.

The facilitative process is distinguished by its emphasis on learner-oriented and -directed methods. It makes use of simulation games, creative problem solving, group and individual projects, and open-ended enrichment exercises to put learners in control of their own learning. Such activities are believed to be sufficiently engaging to sustain the interest and involvement of the learner. The act of discovery (Bruner, 1961) inherent in all of these activities leads to the construction of knowledge that is viable for other types of learning. The student participates in a process of knowledge getting (Bruner, 1966).

Critics of discovery/inquiry and individual/group project methods claim that these approaches are inefficient and unpredictable. The subject-matter expertise of the teacher, they say, is largely discounted or compromised to permit more learner latitude. Thus, the teacher's management role is largely confined to the following:

1. Helping students identify acceptable topics for inquiry
2. Scheduling convenient times for students to meet
3. Assisting students during the planning stages of their investigations
4. Providing students access to resources needed for their work
5. Responding to students' requests for space and help
6. Scheduling time periodically for students to report their findings
7. Designing accountability measures that fulfill schoolwide reporting requirements while allowing students personal appraisals of their accomplishments

The eclectic teacher leader will use expository/direct and discovery/indirect methods of instruction. Curriculum and lesson objectives will determine methods of instruction. Regardless of the methods selected, the teacher must possess a wide variety of management skills.

Analyzing Instructional Activities for Management Requirements

Doyle (1980) offers a useful way to examine the organizational characteristics of an activity and, in so doing, provides a helpful way to analyze activities for the associated management requirements. He proposes that five managerial dimensions serve as planning devices: duration of activity, space required, type and number of students, props/resources needed, expected behavior of students and teacher (p. 7).

Each of these structural components of an activity has management and control implications. The questions listed in Table 5–2 can help you diagnose the demands of an activity, anticipate behavior problems, and institute measures to avoid the occurrence of these problems. Doyle (1986) acknowledged that cooperative learning activities, in particular, are some of the most complex in terms of classroom arrangement and demands on attention. Cooperative learning activities require well-developed classroom management skills. Let's pause and take an in-depth look at the management and control implications of cooperative learning activities.

Analyzing the Management Requirements of Cooperative Learning Activities

Many educators know what cooperative learning is and how it is different from competitive and individualistic learning. They also may know that research suggests that cooperative learning results in (1) a greater effort to achieve, (2) more positive interpersonal relationships, and (3) greater psychological health (Johnson, Johnson, & Holubec, 1990). Educators often can cite that the essence of cooperative learning is positive interdependence or the student mentality that "we are in this together." Educators also know that there are additional components of cooperative learning that are essential: (1) individual accountability, (2) face-to-face interaction, (3) social skills, and (4) processing group effectiveness.

Management of the procedures, steps, and how-to's of the cooperative learning process is often less well known. Expert teachers, with little or no experience in group learning processes, pale at the thought of managing a cooperative learning activity. It is no wonder then that many preservice and first-year teachers prefer to stand behind the podium with a direct instruction plan based on large group lecture and the use of the overhead projector. That is not to say that novices are unable to manage the procedures of cooperative learning methods. Many beginning teachers are able to manage them quite well because they analyzed the activity in terms of its management requirements and planned their management strategies, accordingly. Successful management of cooperative learning simply requires thinking of and planning for all the components of the cooperative learning lesson and the concomi-

Table 5–2
Activity Dimensions and Management Requirements

Duration

1. What are some of the inherently fascinating and controlling features of the activity?
2. How do these features serve to sustain student attention and involvement?
3. What can be done to capitalize upon the activity's inherently attractive characteristics?
4. What age and developmental characteristics of students might influence their participation?
5. How can protection from intrusions, pacing, time of day, season of year, mix of students, supervision, and feedback be regulated to sustain student interest and involvement?

Space required

1. What kind of space elevates the effectiveness of this activity?
2. What can be done with existing space to approximate the ideal?
3. What are the drawbacks of the existing space? What can be done to offset them?
4. Are there administrative or custodial regulations that mitigate against the desired use of space?
5. How can other teachers be involved so that space arrangements can be optimized or so monitoring functions are manageable?

Type and number of students

1. What personal qualities contribute to student receptiveness?
2. What types of skills contribute to student involvement?
3. What type of student mix helps optimize both individual and group attainments?
4. What types of assignments can be given to individual members of the group to maximize their contributions?
5. What are the monitoring and feedback requirements, given the composition and size of the group?

Props/resources needed

1. What types of equipment and materials are essential? What organizational and managerial complexities do they introduce?
2. Must separate prop/resource instructions be given prior to their use?
3. Can these props and resources be shared, or must each student have individual access to them?
4. How will individual and group productivity be increased/diminished by the availability or lack of props/resources?
5. Can the activity be simplified without diminishing the appeal or the hoped-for effects?

Expected behavior of students and teachers

1. How similar or different are the behavior requirements to those generally expected?
2. What are the unique behavior requirements? To what extent do the teacher and students possess the needed attributes and skills?
3. How can the unique attitudinal and behavior demands be conveyed to and practiced by students? Must the practice occur prior to or can it occur during the course of the activity?
4. How will the teacher deal with departures from the stated expectations? What will be the outcomes of having to employ these measures?
5. How will the teacher provide feedback during the course of the activity?

---

tant procedures that students need to know how to follow in order to have a successful cooperative learning experience.

For example, a preservice teacher at a field experience in a language arts classroom wanted to teach a lesson using cooperative learning methods. She received input from her peers and professors regarding how to plan thoroughly and teach her students each procedure of the cooperative learning lesson. Although she did some planning, she decided that she could also rely on informally addressing concerns that came up in the process. She regretted that decision later; there were too many procedural aspects for which she was unprepared. Although she maintained control of the class during the cooperative learning lesson, students did not benefit from the lesson as much as she had anticipated because of management shortcomings. Her lesson will be described here, following a discussion of procedural planning.

In planning a cooperative learning lesson, first list all the procedures that students will need to learn in order to complete an activity. Do some brainstorming of the procedural steps that a cooperative learning lesson would entail. Then look at Figure 5–1, which provides examples that can be used as a master list. What did you consider and what did you forget? Take the list in Figure 5–1 and order the procedures to reflect the approximate place they would occur in a lesson.

Based on these exercises, you should begin to see the need for preplanning the management of cooperative learning lessons. Once you learn the basic management process, there will be few occasions to vary it. After some opportunities to manage cooperative learning lessons, you will carry out procedures automatically. That will free your thinking for planning the cognitive aspects of learning and instruction.

Students who have not participated in structured cooperative learning or social skills activities may not be able to learn all the procedures the first time you want to use cooperative learning structures. You may need to divide the procedures of the cooperative learning process into units and teach the units over a period of days.

Now we present the following case study of a preservice teacher's management of cooperative learning. The presentation is explicit; novices should be able to use it as a model for facilitating their own successful management. This preservice teacher's cooperative learning lesson was presented in a game-like format but it is important to point out that all cooperative lessons are not game-like. It is not our intent to comprehensively educate readers about the methods of cooperative learning but rather to familiarize them with the management considerations. There are seventeen relatively separate features of cooperative learning lessons to attend to in preplanning. The features (Johnson et al., 1990) are represented in the following bulleted list as a brief review for those who have little background in cooperative learning:

❑ Instructional objectives and the academic task
❑ Task assistance
❑ Size of the groups
❑ Assignment to groups
❑ Lesson closure

Figure 5–1

Brainstormed List of Procedures to Teach in a Cooperative Learning Lesson

goal of lesson

end product, expectations

which students assigned to which groups

roles of group members

how and when to assign roles

directions for moving from large group to cooperative groups

directions for material use in group

directions to complete lesson (model task, guided practice, follow-up questions)

when to move to small groups

when to give directions

time limits

accountability

social skill

how to evaluate social skill

how to evaluate group process

what to do when group is finished

how to return to large group

dispersal of materials

how to seek assistance

rules for group work

managing the student who is not an effective group member

❑ Evaluation of learning
❑ Room arrangement
❑ Instructional materials that promote interdependence
❑ Roles that promote interdependence
❑ Positive goal interdependence
❑ Individual accountability
❑ Intergroup cooperation
❑ Criteria for success
❑ Desired behaviors
❑ Monitoring behaviors
❑ Collaborative skills interventions
❑ Evaluation of group functioning

You now have the opportunity to study the preservice teacher's management procedures during her cooperative learning lesson. Management and instructional processes are intertwined in many lessons, and particularly in cooperative lessons.

Therefore, many instructional aspects of the lesson will be presented and critiqued for their contributions to management outcomes.

The teacher we will be studying, Ms. Hammer, was a preservice, language arts teacher completing a course in schoolwide discipline and classroom management. A requirement of the management course was to participate in a classroom-based field experience. After spending four weeks in a seventh-grade classroom observing aspects of the expert teacher's classroom management, Ms. Hammer was ready to teach her first lesson to the class while also practicing her newly acquired management skills. She decided to go for the gusto and attempted to teach and manage a cooperative learning lesson.

The students were completing a unit on six folk tales and were to take a test on them the following week. Ms. Hammer decided to conduct a review of the main characters by grouping students cooperatively and having them play a game she created: Folk Tale Taboo. Ms. Hammer planned the lesson and management procedures in advance. She now stands in front of the twenty-two students to begin the lesson with some confidence based on her preplanning and advanced preparation. Following is a description of her instructional management. After you study it carefully, note what she planned and managed well. Make a list of problems that you foresee her having because of inadequate management planning. Reflect on how you would manage the cooperative learning lesson if you were in front of the class of seventh graders.

Lesson: Folk Tale Taboo

Ms. Hammer is in front of the class; students are in rows and columns. Ms. Hammer has her materials for the lesson on a nearby table, and materials for the cooperative learning activity are already on the tables where the groups will gather. There are two sheets of butcher paper taped to the blackboard with directions on them. Directions are placed on each of the cooperative learning tables, also. Ms. Hammer begins:

"Good morning. Have you ever wanted to describe something to someone else so they would know exactly what you meant, but you just couldn't find the words? For example, let's say that I want to tell you about a character in a folk tale and I cannot remember the character's name! I could start describing the character to you and then you might figure out who I was talking about. Let's try that. I am thinking of a folk tale character but I cannot say the name. I want you to help me out. Listen to my description and anyone call out at any time who I am talking about.

"It's this little boy. He can fly all over. There's a bad guy with a hook on his arm that the flying boy is afraid of. . . . "

(Students call out Peter Pan.)

"That's right. That's who I was thinking of. Good job. Today you will have an opportunity to develop communication skills as you describe folk tale characters to each other. This is also an opportunity for you to review characters from your six folk tales. Toward the end of the class, you will be writing descriptively about how well you worked with others to communicate about the characters.

"Now I want you to think of the name of a character in one of the six folk tales we have been studying. After you have the name in mind, think of four good descriptive words or phrases for that character. I am going to pass out cards and you will write down the name of your character and the four descriptive words or phrases under the name. Place the character's name at the top of the card. Below the name, number down the side of the card with one, two, three, and four. Then write a descriptor next to each number. J. D., would you retell the directions for everyone. (Pause.) Before I pass out the cards, are there any questions? (Pause.) While I pass out the notecards, you can be thinking of a character and four descriptive words or phrases."

Note that the teacher obtains student attention and interest in her opening. In stating directions before she passes out writing materials, she maintains their attention to the directions. She makes sure that everyone understands the directions prior to passing out cards. While students write on cards, she circulates and helps those who are having difficulty.

"Everyone has completed their cards. Pass them to the person in front of you and I'll pick them up from the first person in each row."

Ms. Hammer picks up cards quickly and moves to the front of the room to conduct a large group discussion.

Ms. Hammer asks, "Who has played the game Taboo before?" A student responds and is asked to explain the rules of the game. Ms. Hammer asks another student to restate the rules to check for comprehension. She moves to the blackboard by the butcher paper with the directions for the cooperative learning lesson. Students have heard the rules presented verbally. They will now see the rules presented visually. Repeated presentations of the directions for a lesson decrease behavior problems during the completion of tasks.

"For fifteen minutes you will be playing Folk Tale Taboo, a wonderfully fun game that you and I created just for you. I made some game cards before class and I am adding the ones that you just now completed."

(Ms. Hammer reads through the rules written on the butcher paper.)

"Rules: (1) You will be assigned to your regular base group and each group serves as a team. (2) Two teams compete with each other to see who can earn the most points. (3) Each time a card is played, you will set a timer for one minute. Describe as many cards as the other team can name in a one-minute period. When one minute is up, the timer is reset and a member of the opposite team draws a card to describe. It is important that the describer work quickly so the other team has a chance to guess the name. Remember, you only get one minute. (4) The name at the top of the card and the four words or phrases listed below the name are Taboo words and cannot be used when giving a description. If the describer says a Taboo word, the timer is reset and the describer draws another card and begins again. (5) Teams record each others' points.

"Just for practice, let's run through how to play a card. Here's the first card. Jess, Shamu, and Eric are on a team together and will be guessing the name of a character that I am describing."

Ms. Hammer turns to the group to model how to play the first round with a card. She holds up a large version of a card that all students except the three can read from their seats. A student holds up his hand and Ms. Hammer calls on him. He indicates that he would like to try describing the character instead of Ms. Hammer providing the description. She agrees. The students play the card. Ms. Hammer asks if there are any questions about this aspect of the game.

Ms. Hammer steps to the second piece of butcher paper taped to the blackboard and goes over the learning goals and the social skill of the lesson. The learning goals are to practice (1) thinking skills, (2) speaking skills, and (3) character recall. The social skill is to practice teamwork, which she describes as working together to solve problems and showing respect for the person trying to describe.

Ms. Hammer tells each student what group they are in and assigns one person per group as reporter. The reporter is told to draw the first card and begin describing. She then tells them what area of the room to go to and what materials they will find there: timer, cards, paper, pencil. There are four people per group, which places eight people around each table.

Ms. Hammer tells the students to go to their area. While they are seating themselves, Ms. Hammer interrupts to tell them that the first group to obtain fifteen points will be the winner. The teams begin the competition. There is some jostling and debating about who will run the timer, who will record the points, and who the players will be each time a new card is drawn. Some team members are engrossed in the game, some stare off, and some talk with each other. Ms. Hammer interrupts several of the groups during the competition to teach them how to use the timers.

(Pause here and brainstorm what poorly managed procedures caused problems during the Taboo game. Use the seventeen features of cooperative learning lessons listed earlier to help you decide what could be problematic. Indicate the strengths of the teacher's management procedures. A critique will be provided at the end of the narrative about the cooperative activity.)

When fourteen minutes have passed, Ms. Hammer reminds the groups that they have one more round before time is up. She waits for the final round to be completed and asks the students to go back to their seats. As they are returning to their regularly assigned seats, she speaks over the noise and commotion and asks them to get out paper and pencil for the writing assignment. When all are seated and ready with materials, she asks them to pick one of the three learning goals or the social skill for a writing topic. Students are directed to write for five minutes about how the experience helped them practice attaining a goal or the social skill. Papers are turned in after five minutes and class is dismissed.

Add to the list you started earlier the strengths of Ms. Hammer's instructional management. Brainstorm and record any components of her cooperative learning lesson that led to management problems. When you have your lists, continue reading the critique of management strengths and areas for improvement.

Critique of the Management of the Cooperative Lesson

The teacher's first planning requirement is to determine the academic and collaborative or social skills objectives. It is a common error to indicate academic objectives and ignore collaborative skills objectives. Omissions lead to management problems because students need to be taught how to work cooperatively with each other. Cooperative interactions do not happen naturally.

The instructional objectives and the academic tasks were clear. Both were orally and visually presented by the teacher. She asked students to repeat directions for the task and gave them opportunities to ask questions. She also placed directions for the task on the competition tables. The teacher modeled the task once and provided guided practice once. The use of all of these instructional strategies decreased the likelihood of management problems later during group work.

On the other hand, students did not know how to use timers and this caused groups to be off task and disruptive as they argued with each other. Ms. Hammer interrupted some groups in the middle of the game to demonstrate how to use the timer accurately. She should have assigned the task of timekeeper to someone in each group and taught them the use of the equipment. The role of recorder of points also needed to be assigned. Because it was not, students were off task, arguing with each other about who should perform this task. Ms. Hammer had a collaborative skill of the day that she briefly described. More time modeling and discussing the skill with thorough checks for understanding would prevent problems in the group later.

Clear objectives help teachers decide the best size for learning groups, which tend to range from two to six students per group. Johnson et al. (1990) advise beginning teachers to start with pairs. The larger the group, the more social skills students need to be successful and the more behavior management problems surface. Regardless of teachers' skills in facilitating cooperative learning groups, they should not have students working in groups of more than three until students have the skills to do it competently. Finally, the less time there is for group work, the smaller the group should be. Everyone needs the opportunity to contribute. Given the advice of Johnson and his colleagues, Ms. Hammer would have been a more successful manager if she had made her groups smaller. Two people per group would be advisable for this activity. That would place four people around the competition table. When one person is describing, there is only the one partner who could be sitting there uninvolved. Out of every describing team of two, only one has potential to be uninvolved. Thus, there would be more opportunities for each student to be actively involved in the lesson the majority of the time. Ms. Hammer's teams of four meant that when one was describing, as many as three teammates might be sitting idly by. Three idle students potentially increase the occurrence of management problems. Smaller teams also mean that fewer people in a group have to practice the social skill at any one time.

Teacher-made groups typically are more task oriented than student-selected groups because teachers place nontask-oriented students with task-oriented students. Students prefer to be in groups with peers that they like. Some teachers allow students to complete a peer nomination form (see Figure 5–2) on which each student indicates three peers with whom they most like to work. Then, teachers sometimes can place students in groups with one of their choices and one or two others that the teacher selected. Groups should stay intact until they can successfully work together. Then it is appropriate to interchange group membership.

Ms. Hammer had a management problem with lesson closure that could be labeled a *truncation* (Kounin, 1970). She terminated the cooperative learning activity and never asked groups to share the number of points they earned. She told them previously that the team with the most points would win. The criteria for success was presented but was not addressed at the end of the lesson. The groups were not required to evaluate their group functioning either.

There was no large group sharing time in which to talk about cards that were difficult to describe, to process how difficult it is to describe things, or to share tips with each other on how to describe. The evaluation of learning and individual accountability factors were addressed by requiring students to descriptively write about their attainment of a goal area or the social skill. The final writing activity provided some lesson closure but it was not sufficient.

If Ms. Hammer had interrupted their writing and said, "Oh, by the way, which team obtained the highest number of points for Folk Tale Taboo?," she would have executed another management *faux pas,* Kounin's undesirable flip-flop. However, following the writing activity, she could have acknowledged teams' efforts. This management strategy would help students cooperate in future lessons.

Ms. Hammer's setting management was adequate: She planned ahead, had the room arranged for cooperative learning, and had materials ready. Circles are usually the best management of the physical environment. The key is to place students so they can see all their materials, see each other, talk without raising their voices, and make exchanges comfortably. In other words, the closer, the better. Ms.

Figure 5–2
Sociometric Exercise for Forming Cooperative Learning Groups

Circle the names of three students with whom you would most like to do group work in the classroom.		
Adrianna	Del	Omar
Andy	Grant	Patisha
Azim	Jerome	Schwanda
Bathsheba	Lil	Weldon
Carlos	Miguel	Zach

Hammer used circles and students were close to each other. She gave no instructions about using quiet voices. Fortunately, she had no difficulties with noise level.

She potentially could have had management difficulties in moving students from large to small groups because she did not provide students with instructions in how to proceed to their tables. Perhaps she was relying on their knowing that they only had fifteen minutes for the tournament. The time limit could potentially influence them to go quickly to their tables and begin the game but she forgot to tell them about the time limit. It was not until they were moving to their work areas that she committed a dangle (Kounin, 1970) by reminding them of something she forgot to tell them earlier.

Instructional materials, planned to promote interdependence, also prevent management problems. New groups with few collaborative skills can be given one copy of the materials. This increases the likelihood that students will work together. In Ms. Hammer's classroom, the nature of the task promoted interdependence for the team that was trying to guess the name on the card. They could share ideas and work together to obtain the correct answer.

If the describers had been given one minute to work as a team to come up with descriptors, then interdependence would have been present for them also. Interdependence can also be achieved by structuring intergroup competition. In intergroup competition, groups usually prepare their members to compete in a tournament with other groups. Students of the same ability level across teams compete against each other. Ultimately, the group wins whose members' combined score is best. Positive goal interdependence was present because Ms. Hammer used outside enemy interdependence (Johnson et al., 1990). In order to promote interdependence without using outside enemies, Ms. Hammer might have required that every member of the listening team record the name of the character being described. Disagreements would be discussed and resolved by the team members. Another option would be to have each listener record the name and for every correct answer, a point would be added to the group score.

Interdependence also is ensured by assigning interconnected roles to each member of the group. Roles include the following:

❑ Summarizer who restates the group's major conclusions or answers
❑ Checker who makes sure that all members can explicitly describe how to arrive at an answer
❑ Accuracy coach who corrects mistakes in another's explanations
❑ Elaboration seeker who asks others to relate current information to prior studies
❑ Researcher who gets materials for the group and communicates with the teacher and other groups
❑ Recorder who writes down group decisions and edits group reports
❑ Observer who notes how well the group is collaborating

Roles were not clearly assigned or described; therefore, roles did not promote interdependence. Subsequently, some students not directly involved in the game were noisy and off task. A lack of role assignment in cooperative learning tasks generally results in management problems for the teacher to solve.

In summary, Ms. Hammer's management of the cooperative learning activity was generally successful. Her management strengths included clear lesson presentation, obtaining group interest, checking for understanding, and organization of materials. Although she did not prepare students thoroughly for every procedure they needed, students remained on task and cooperative for the most part.

Ms. Hammer needs to improve her management of cooperative learning in the following ways. First, she needs to become more skillful at managing group work that promotes interdependence and individual accountability at the same time. Specifically, she needs to assign roles and ensure that students are taught how to fulfill their roles.

Second, she needs to consider the developmental level of her students in her management of time limits. Her criterion was that the team who obtained fifteen points first would win. She provided a fifteen-minute time period. That meant that a team would need to get one card right every minute. Many seventh-grade students struggled to provide even one descriptor in the sixty-second period. That did not give the listening team an opportunity to make a single guess. Perhaps the following instruction would be more appropriate: Give the describing team sixty seconds to pool their ideas about descriptive words and another sixty seconds for the describer to communicate the descriptions. Finally, she needed to manage closure activities to ensure that students would continue to participate and take the learning activities seriously.

This cooperative learning lesson demonstrates how novice teachers can successfully manage complex instruction. Careful management planning ensures that students will stay on task, cooperate with each other, learn a great deal, and have fun.

Sequencing and Integrating Additional Instructional Activities

Teachers who can entice students to become active participants in the educational process will have fewer discipline problems. This educational process is largely a matter of selecting and sequencing appealing activities and helping students make the most of their participation in them. Removing restlessness, passivity, and boredom from the classroom also removes potential discipline problems (Glasser, 1992).

Envisioning activities that will spark interest and sustain student involvement is an important instructional function and an equally significant management function (Parker & Gehrke, 1986). Students who are meaningfully involved are less likely to seek other outlets for their energy and imagination. Sequencing and coalescing several activities builds momentum and a commitment to learning. Units of instruction and daily lesson plans serve this integrating function. They contribute to the critical mass that students bring to each new learning event. Teachers who ask themselves the questions listed in Table 5–2 for developing and implementing activities will also find an activities-based lesson plan a useful device for making the most of each activity.

Good and Grouws (1979) conducted a number of teacher effectiveness studies and used their findings to formulate a sequence for teaching basic mathematics skills. Outlined in Table 5–3, the sequence provides a series of activities in lesson-plan format that can be easily adapted to other subject areas. The categories and specifications within the table can be used to visualize the preventive disciplinary characteristics associated with this format for content management.

Table 5–3
Activity Sequence Outline

Daily Review: (First 8 minutes except Mondays)

Review the concepts and skills associated with the homework.

Collect and deal with homework assignments.

Ask students to do several mental computation exercises.

Development: (About 20 minutes)

Briefly focus on prerequisite skills and concepts.

Focus on meaning and promoting student understanding by using lively explanations, demonstrations, process explanations, illustrations, and so on.

Assess student comprehension by using process/product questions (active interaction) and controlled practice.

Repeat and elaborate on the meaning portion as necessary.

Seatwork: (About 15 minutes)

Provide uninterrupted successful practice.

Build momentum—keep the ball rolling—get everyone involved, then sustain involvement.

Alert students; let them know their work will be checked at the end of the period.

Promote accountability—check students' work.

Homework Assignment:

Assign on a regular basis at the end of each math class except Fridays about 15 minutes of work to be done at home, including one or two review problems.

Special Reviews:

Conduct weekly review/maintenance during the first 20 minutes each Monday.

Focus on skills and concepts covered during the previous week.

Conduct monthly review/maintenance every fourth Monday.

Focus on skills and concepts covered since the last monthly review.

Managing Daily Review Sessions

Students need opportunities to practice and apply what they learn. Homework affords students that opportunity, as do review sessions at the beginning of the class. Generally, each lesson begins with a review of seatwork and/or homework, and the review sets the stage for new learning. It may be tempting to forgo the time devoted to review in favor of the new lesson, especially when students performed well during the guided practice session the previous day, but the review session should not be omitted. Regular homework assignments, even if in modest amounts, followed by a daily review session are not only a good accountability measure, but they also provide a predictable academic environment.

Plan for management of the review so that it is not boring, repetitive, or a cursory treatment of the topic. If a game-like format is used, ensure that all students are accountable and participatory throughout the lesson. An example of a game-like, unit review follows that took an entire class period. This review was poorly constructed; note what not to do in a review.

> The social studies teacher prepared eighth-grade students for a unit exam by conducting a social studies bee. The students began the class period by standing beside their desks. The twenty-four students waited their turn to answer questions posed by the teacher. When a student responded incorrectly, the student sat down for the rest of the period. The last person standing was the winner. Can you imagine what seated students were doing during the remainder of the bee? Of course you can! They visited, laughed, passed notes, scuffled over pencils, grew frustrated with each other, and even began name calling.

The form of the daily review session is often dictated by the type of material to be learned. Skills might be demonstrated by sending several students to the chalkboard and using their work to review the steps in a process. Recitation of factual information can be made more lively by creating game-like conditions—an element of competition adds excitement. Checking for understanding might involve dividing the class into groups to share their ideas and the basis for arriving at their conclusions. Brief reports from each group can be used to summarize key points.

Managing Lectures/Presentation Sessions

Because teaching is often equated with talking, it is not surprising that the lecture is often chosen to deliver material. Lectures can be an efficient way to dispense information if well conceived and delivered in an interesting fashion. Students also need to be equipped with skills in note taking. The following suggestions should enhance the effective use of this technique:

1. All teaching techniques require collateral learning skills. Teachers who lecture must help students learn how to listen and take notes. The first step in developing both skills may be to supply students with the key points in outline form. Students can later compare the points they have recorded under each section with those given by the instructor.

2.   Ausubel (1963) coined the term *advanced organizers* to refer to concepts and methods that a teacher uses to connect a new lesson to previous learnings. When the advanced organizer is a part of a written outline or is displayed on a transparency, students can readily see the connection between a previous and new lesson. Beginning a new lesson always involves a risk, but the teacher can reduce initial anxiety by showing students how this lesson is built on things they have previously learned.

3.   The lecturer must be attentive to nonverbal cues from students and must likewise give nonverbal cues to help students stay on track. Pace, voice gesticulation, gestures, and eye contact can maintain attention. Well-placed questions and brief discussions can provide an occasional respite from teacher talk.

4.   The use of audiovisual media and a variety of written supplements can also embellish the delivery of a lecture. Illustrations and applications of the lecture can be presented through audio- and videotape, films and slides, or records. Portions of the lecture might be delivered by other speakers.

5.   Some teachers vary the distance between themselves and students by moving about the room. If students must shift focus as the teacher changes positions, they are more likely to be attentive. A voice emanating from nearby is also likely to command greater attention.

6.   Nothing commands our attention more than hearing our name interjected into a conversation. Teachers can capitalize on this tendency by interspersing names of students within the lecture. This can be done in a speculative way: "Suppose Mary was convinced . . . ," or in a retrospective way: "Recall the other day when Jim. . . . "

7.   Periodic checks on student understanding and comprehension can help maintain attentiveness. If students are confused because the teacher refers to something they were supposed to have learned earlier, are perplexed by the terminology, or are frustrated because they cannot keep up with the pace of delivery, they are likely to throw in the towel. Teachers can lace the lecture with open-ended queries and pointed questions to check for presentation clarity and coherence.

Managing Seatwork

Students spend considerable instructional time engaged in independent seatwork assignments. Teachers may work with a subset of students during these times. Learning to manage seatwork is an important feature of the teacher's day. There are essentially four instructional and managerial tasks associated with seatwork (Anderson, Brubaker, Alleman-Brooks, & Duffy, 1983), each of which is accomplished through the use of routines: selecting, presenting, monitoring, and evaluating.

Selecting Assignments.   Typically, teachers give whole-class seatwork assignments and use small groups for remedial work. The selection of seatwork assignments can create problems for low achievers. Students who encounter difficulties in completing the seatwork become discouraged and look for outlets for their frustration. Teachers can overcome this problem by conducting remedial instruction with a small group. The rest of the class can be completing independent seatwork.

Students engage in independent seatwork when they use computers. Teachers manage the selection of computer lessons.

Presenting Assignments.   Some of the problems that students encounter doing seatwork originate in the way that assignments are presented. Anderson et al. (1983) analyzed teacher explanations for seatwork assignments to ascertain the types of information given to students. They found that the majority of explanations (79 percent) included procedural directions and/or isolated hints to help students focus their efforts. Teachers gave fewer explicit explanations about the purposes of the work (5 percent), specifically what benefits would accrue to the student, and even fewer explicit descriptions of the cognitive strategy to be used to do the assignments (1.5 percent). Iverson and Stack's review (1996) of the literature also showed that teachers rarely provided instruction in the cognitive strategies needed to complete learning tasks. Although information about purposes and strategies might not be essential for all assignments, these are precisely the motivational and task cues needed by students who exhibit discipline problems.

Monitoring Performance.   Seatwork is often performed while the teacher is working with another group. Monitoring the performance of students completing individual seatwork must also occur. What can teachers do to maintain the benefits of working with one group while the remainder of the class is engaged in seatwork? Anderson et al. (1983) recommend the following:

1.   Do not begin work with a small group focused on content, skill, or a project immediately after the seatwork assignment is given. Allow five minutes to circulate among students, making a special point to pass by students who revealed some signs of difficulty while the assignment material was being presented and/or who typically have problems with this type of instruction. Only after everyone has gotten started should a small group be convened.

2.   Circulate among students after dismissal of one small group and before engaging in an activity with another. Again, concentrate on students who may have

problems. If it appears that several students are having a similar problem, a short lesson may be called for. Take a few minutes between the groups. Sometimes the assignment may have to be changed or the student may need to be given other work until the teacher can provide more extended assistance.

3. Troubleshooting rounds can be more productive if the teacher provides help in the form of questions. Students learn to be more reflective and less dependent on the teacher for answers. They also learn that the process of problem resolution can be just as important as the end result, the answer.

4. The teacher need not be the only source of help. Peers can be taught how to provide assistance without giving answers. Or a student can use a "help card" (Paine et al., 1983) to indicate that assistance is required the next time the teacher is free. The reverse side of the help card that faces the student might be labeled "keep working." Another method is a folder of "surefire" work, often drill-and-practice sheets for elementary students, or "waiting work," incomplete assignments or supplementary reading assignments for high school students. Finally, the teacher may devise a set of signals for letting students know when it is acceptable to interrupt small group instruction.

5. As the year progresses, students should begin to value themselves as independent learners and seek help only after exhausting self-help strategies that they have been taught throughout the year. Thus, early in the school year the teacher should systematically integrate self-help activities into regular lessons. The strategies that students lack can often be discovered by paying close attention to the questions they ask and those needed to lead them toward greater understanding of a task. Devoting time to building self-help attitudes and skills early in the school year can save time and reduce competition for a teacher's attention throughout the year.

Evaluating Assignments. Routines for evaluating seatwork should emphasize getting information about student thinking processes and comprehension. Some teachers may be more interested in the completeness and accuracy of work. Thus, their feedback to students is often confined to reporting the number right or wrong and some brief indication of their satisfaction with the work. Little may be done to help students understand why an answer is incorrect and what needs to be done so that the error is not repeated. Without such encouragement and help, students tend to think that the most important thing is to have an answer, any answer. Since seatwork occupies so much classroom time and is an instrument that teachers rely on to deepen understanding and develop or refine skills, teachers should design defensible ways to select, explain, monitor, and evaluate this type of work.

Managing Homework

Homework is a distinctive learning activity because it takes place largely outside the teacher's purview and provides students an opportunity for solitary study. Although the beginning stages of a homework assignment might be done in class, this step is generally to ensure that directions are understood and that initial efforts are error free.

Standards for assigned homework should be discussed and reasons given for them. Students should record the standards in their notebooks, and the standards should be periodically reviewed during the early weeks of school. A projector can be used to show examples of well-done homework from previous classes, or exemplary work can be displayed on a bulletin board. Standards might address the type of writing instrument to be used, the kind of paper, the type of notebook, the required heading, and allowances for erasing. Such standards help students develop good work habits and become more proficient in the subject covered by the homework. They learn how to learn and how to manage themselves in the classroom.

The amount of homework will vary with grade level and lesson objectives. Homework composed of drill-and-practice exercises, in which boredom and fatigue can undermine performance, should be limited to twenty to thirty minutes. Assignments that challenge the critical and creative abilities of students will require longer time periods. The amount of work given should be tempered by the frequency of assignments. Regular assignments, requiring modest amounts of time, are preferable to huge assignments followed by long periods without homework. When planning lessons, teachers look for ways to capture and sustain student attention. This is also an important consideration for homework assignments. The following positive steps are commonly used by teachers to minimize the use of punitive controls (e.g., marking the student down or giving a zero or a demerit as procedures for handling incomplete work) (Cangelosi, 1988; Chernow & Chernow, 1981):

1. After you are confident students understand what has been taught, demonstrate the connection between the day's lesson and the homework assignment.
2. Find imaginative ways to introduce homework assignments, to make worksheets attractive, and to make the homework itself challenging but doable.
3. Teach students procedures for budgeting time and routines for completing work.
4. Design charts and graphs to provide a graphic record of achievement and progress.
5. Motivate by example; share your homework experience with students.
6. Appeal to the current interests and activities of students when designing assignments.
7. Motivate by the way you respond to completed homework. Develop an extravagant vocabulary for expressing your satisfaction. Written comments on papers and occasional notes home elevate student persistence and performance.
8. Check most work. Students will be less lax and are less likely to gamble that work will not be collected or read if work is regularly checked for completeness and accuracy. Diligence should be rewarded.
9. Since students are test-conscious, homework that consistently contributes to test success will be taken more seriously.
10. Develop intermediate steps for long-range assignments and set short-term deadlines and dates to check progress. Completed homework promotes class control and self-control.

Students who learn to handle work without direct supervision are more likely to exercise self-control in the classroom as well. The time required to check homework may discourage the use of this practice, particularly when the teacher must correct every piece of assigned work. Thus, the following techniques may prove to be helpful:

1.   At the beginning of the class period/day, students may be sent to checking centers to mark their own paper or that of a classmate. Meanwhile, the teacher can do some spot checking at the centers. Special marking pens will help the teacher quickly go over all the papers to check the success rate of students.

2.   With some subjects and some assignments, correct responses can be placed on the chalkboard or on an overhead transparency. Students can check their work at their seats during the review session preceding the daily lesson. After the day's lesson, the teacher can look at these prechecked papers while circulating and assisting students with their homework for the next day.

3.   Correction may be limited to selected items each day. While students are working on a seatwork assignment, the teacher can check all or some student homework assignments, perhaps concentrating on those who generally have problems or who are negligent about completing work. Conscientious students may be given reinforcement during the discussion. Some of the work that the teacher sees while circulating can be collected and displayed to reinforce responsible homework behavior.

4.   A perfect paper can be rewarded with helper status. A student is told that a perfect paper tomorrow will be rewarded by being able to assist someone who has not completed their work. This procedure can be an incentive to those who frequently submit incomplete work. A surprise selection each day might keep everyone on their toes.

5.   The teacher can provide each student with a folder or notebook for homework and assign everyone a number between one and five. On a given day, all number-three students would submit their folders or notebook for correction. The teacher could read this subsample during seatwork.

Some homework assignments serve as a synthesis experience in which the ideas and skills taught during an earlier unit of instruction must be applied. Generally this kind of assignment is best accomplished in parts, with each part corresponding to a section of the unit. Thus, periodic progress checks can be made by collecting student work and checking specified parts of the assignments. Each section might be graded separately, or the student might have to demonstrate a predetermined level of sufficiency or mastery before proceeding. In either instance, the teacher would only have to give cursory attention to the previously evaluated work when checking the final product. Homework can play an important role in the amount and quality of student learning, but it can also be a hassle for both students and teachers. Some of the procedures suggested should help both parties deal more effectively with this instructional tool.

Managing Discussion Sessions

Students need opportunities to process ideas from teacher presentations, reading assignments, and other activities. Discussion sessions help students attach personal meaning to ideas, validate understanding, and find out how others perceive a point. These sessions also help make ideas more memorable by connecting them to the personal experience of the participants. Many human relations and communication skills are practiced as students exchange ideas. Discussion sessions can be more productive if planning takes into consideration the following suggestions:

1.   Maintaining the attention and involvement of all students during whole-class discussions can be facilitated by seating arrangements that permit everyone to see everyone else. The small amount of time required to move furniture can be more than offset by favorable speaking and listening conditions. Early in the year the teacher might have students practice moving furniture into several types of grouping arrangements.

2.   The teacher should not assume at the beginning of the year that students know how to participate in discussions. Procedures for this activity need to be devised and taught. As the school year progresses, directions may need to be reviewed periodically. Since certain skills increase and distribute participation, early discussion sessions might emphasize one of these skills. Prior to the discussion, a small amount of time might be devoted to presenting and demonstrating the skill so that students become aware of it and practice using it.

3.   The focus of the discussion can be sharpened if the teacher lets students know its purpose. It is easy to stray from the topic when there is ambiguity about the end product. When several questions are to be answered, the group might begin with those that are to elicit factual responses. This procedure permits early success, promotes a sense of progress, and creates a positive expectation for subsequent questions. As the group entertains more open-ended questions, the facts collected may be the springboard for answering subsequent items.

4.   Teachers orchestrate whole-class sessions by determining who speaks, the length of time allotted to an individual, the order of turns, the type and amount of assistance provided reticent or struggling participants, and the termination points within the topic. The study by Kerman and Martin (1980), discussed earlier in this chapter, addressed several aspects of this situation. Note the variety of ways teachers influence the participation of students and the effects of their decisions on pupil expectations (see Table 5–1). The amount and quality of student participation can be adversely affected by how teachers perceive the potential contributions of students and how they act out these expectations. Even nonverbal cues can encourage or discourage a student.

5.   Discussions are an effective way to promote retention and transfer, the twin problems of teaching. Some discussion sessions should involve the integration of material presented earlier. It is imperative that students be given directions that structure the discussion and provide progress checks along the way.

6. Listening is just as crucial during discussions as during teacher presentations, but students may not think so. This is generally due to a belief that when it comes down to tests and grades, what counts is teacher talk. Teachers can enhance respect for student contributions by being respectful listeners and using student contributions as the preface to some of their own. Or students may be asked to summarize a peer's remarks before offering their own. And, of course, teachers can do more to ensure that evaluation instruments are designed to elicit information and skills acquired during group discussions.

Managing Projects and Problem-Solving Sessions

Teachers generally use what have come to be called higher order questions to promote problem solving. The "cognitive taxonomy" of Bloom, Engelhart, Frost, Hill, and Krathwohl (1956) might be used to frame questions that require application, analysis, synthesis, and evaluation processes. These processes are more intellectually demanding and require conditions unlike those appropriate for recitation sessions. Guidelines for helping students stretch their intellect and imagination follow:

1. Students must be given periods of silence to think. To reduce their initial feelings of uneasiness during these periods, the teacher might provide for very short periods of silence and less involved questions at the beginning of the year. Over the school year, the length of silent periods and intellectual demands can gradually be increased.

2. Students might be encouraged to record, in abbreviated fashion, their thoughts during these periods of silence. Rather than writing paragraphs, students might jot down key words and phrases, use arrows to show a progression of ideas, or develop a diagram of key parts. This practice increases the likelihood that students will participate in the public forum and will be able to make a more straightforward presentation. A teacher who circulates while students are at work can check the responses of students for what should be included in the discussion, look for particularly meritorious points, and begin to chart the direction of the discussion. If students are going to be placed in small groups, the written responses can be used to make grouping decisions.

3. When silence and written responses are a prelude to a whole-group discussion, the teacher might want to make some preliminary remarks about the steps in the problem-solving process. Students may be directed to submit their ideas without any expectation of group reactions. Only after the teacher has recorded the products of everyone's thinking on the chalkboard does the group engage in a critical examination of the output. When the group works with a summary, the focus is on achieving greater clarity, looking for relationships, and forming generalizations. There is a concerted effort to evaluate the data rather than the person who offered it. Students begin to value the diverse ways of looking at problems, and the prospect of more than one successful solution.

4. As students discuss the material on the chalkboard, the teacher underscores the significance of some points by offering speculative remarks and raising

questions. The teacher's "I wonder if . . . ," "Did you consider . . . ?," "Does this mean . . . ?," and "How about . . . ?" queries are aimed at getting students to mine their initial thoughts for new possibilities. The teacher's attitude should be one of helping students make the best use of their ideas rather than supplementing the material with ideas of his or her own.

5.   Teachers need to be aware that students like some form of closure at the end of a problem-solving session. Sometimes the teacher may have to reassure students by promising to reopen the discussion at a specific time or during the study of a related topic. However, closure can generally be accomplished by scaling down the problem. For example, students can work on selected aspects of much larger problems. Or problems may be selected to illustrate a curriculum theme that connects a collection of units of instruction. "Managing Our Environment" might be the theme with units and problem-solving activities devoted to various aspects of our environment. In this way, closure achieved by solving one problem serves as groundwork for dealing with the next problem. Students are much more motivated to engage in problem-solving activities when they can experience the satisfaction of growing competence.

Managing Special Review Sessions

Teachers commonly use units of instruction and/or a collection of chapters in a textbook to organize a program of studies. Units are typically topic oriented, and textbook chapters are typically theme oriented. But methods of organization provide direction for creating daily lessons and the structure for drawing these lessons together. Such special review sessions serve as a culminating experience, bringing together pieces of the puzzle to form a picture.

Special review sessions require considerable teacher planning and direction. The direction might be confined to framing discussion questions aimed at retrieving information that can be used to formulate generalizations and conclusions. Direction might also be supplied through well-structured problem-solving activities or simulated games, with problem resolution depending on appropriate application of prior learning.

If divergent production is the aim of the review, students might be challenged to use creatively what they have learned. This might involve making a product or a plan that can be traced to salient features of the topic or theme, or it might require critiquing the topic or theme and comparing and contrasting competing views.

Special review sessions ought not to be passive affairs. Teacher lectures highlighting key points may be efficient, but they do not challenge learners to analyze, synthesize, and evaluate what they have learned. These cognitive processes promote longer lasting learning and prepare learners to make connections between school and life. In addition, students are less likely to engage in these processes in daily lessons.

In closing, the Instructional Environment System–II (Ysseldyke & Christenson, 1993–1994) provides a list of specific teacher behaviors to cultivate as you develop instructional management skills. They are adapted here for your use:

❏ Determine each student's current level of performance and expect ambitious growth. Communicate this by helping students set high but realistic goals. Develop ways to graph progress and require students to do the graphing. Keep portfolios of work products that include the baseline level of performance and subsequent products. Intermittently, request the student to look back and evaluate their progress.

❏ Clearly communicate objectives of each lesson and make sure that every student knows what is to be learned. Objectives can be written on the blackboard, overhead projector, or butcher paper on the wall. Students can write them in their notebooks and objectives can be referred to at various times throughout the lesson.

❏ Teachers consistently model using class time well by starting on time, being prepared with all materials, and managing smooth and short transitions. Teachers explicitly communicate to students that they are to be on time with all necessary materials and be ready to learn. Some teachers record on the blackboard the materials needed for the lesson beside the objectives of the lesson. Then they set a timer and ask students to be ready when the timer rings. Teachers explicitly teach students how to transition smoothly and efficiently. Teachers also explicitly communicate their expectations for the use of in-class study time.

❏ Clearly communicate your standards for performance. Provide models of expected performance and teach students how to use them to guide their own performance. Clearly communicate the consequences of not achieving the expected standards of performance. For example, students can be told that products that meet the expected standard will be considered final pieces of work. Those not meeting the standard will be considered drafts and students will redo work until it meets the standard.

❏ Call on students equally and expect them to answer. Use a class roster to check who has been called on. Another method is to put each student's name on a stick. All sticks are placed in a cup and sticks are drawn randomly; no student knows who will be called on until a stick is drawn. It is very important to ask low achievers questions that are most likely to provide success experiences. Therefore, when names are drawn, teachers may need to modify the question that they were going to ask next. After low achievers have experienced some initial success, ask them moderately difficult questions and be prepared to prompt and cue them just as much as you would prompt and cue a high achieving student answering a moderately to very difficult question.

❏ Explicitly communicate that you expect all students to be actively involved in learning. Purposefully structure learning activities to provide low achievers opportunities to respond actively. For example, the boy with a learning disability has difficulty reading the text and recording group members' responses during cooperative learning in language arts. However, he is one of the best artists in the school. Structure the cooperative learning activity in a way that can lead to either verbal or visual responses. Another example is telling a struggling reader ahead of time what passage he will be reading before the class. With time to prepare, he is able to succeed.

Implementing these guidelines for communicating teacher expectations is important to effective instructional management. As found in the Kerman (1982) experimental study, you can expect a reduced number of disciplinary referrals.

Dealing with Instruction-Related Discipline Problems

When students exhibit behavior problems during the learning and instruction process, teachers need to problem solve on behalf of those individuals. The teacher's first step in problem solving is to check her own classroom management plan. She should ask herself: "How is my plan working? Have I sufficiently taught the rules and how to follow them? Do I need to reteach any of the rules? Does every student know the rules and how to follow them? Have I been consistent in following through with the appropriate use of both positive and negative consequences?" If teachers can answer these questions satisfactorily and a particular student is still having problems in the instructional setting, teachers need to analyze the contributions of the instructional environment to the problem. The environment includes setting, movement management, group focus, instructional presentations, and activities.

Sometimes teachers can analyze the instructional environment to isolate the cause(s) and then select effective solutions on their own. Sometimes they will be more successful in developing appropriate intervention strategies if they participate in group problem solving with the designated team in the building. These teams are referred to by such names as Child Assistance Teams, Student Assistance Teams, or Building Assistance Teams (BAT). Building principals, school counselors, and veteran teachers can tell you how to gain access to problem-solving teams.

To assist educators in problem solving, we next discuss guidelines from Sprick (1985) for the following problem areas:

- ❑ Off-task behavior
- ❑ Talking without permission (during lectures, during class, failing to raise hand)
- ❑ Poor listening and not following directions
- ❑ Not bringing materials to class
- ❑ Late or incomplete assignments
- ❑ Tardiness or absenteeism
- ❑ Failure to be motivated/doing nothing
- ❑ Cheating
- ❑ Test anxiety

These problems are listed in a somewhat hierarchical order. It is hierarchical in the sense that the problems first in the list tend to occur more frequently and are usually, but not always, easier for the teacher to solve without team assistance.

Off-Task Behavior

This discussion of off-task behavior is based on the work of Sprick (1985). The greatest proportion of off-task behavior occurs during independent seatwork. For example, the science teacher, Mrs. Suce, provides twenty minutes of class time for studying assignments and writing lab reports. Most students are off task, talking, doing nothing, resting their heads on desks, reading for pleasure and so forth. Mrs. Suce reminds the students periodically to get to work and most do for a few minutes following the reminder. Mrs. Suce wants to problem solve and she asks herself why students behave this way in her science class. She knows that the same students use their study time well in Mrs. Vander's math class. Several times she stood outside the math classroom and observed all students on task during their study time. Mrs. Vander rarely says a word to the students.

There are several reasons students are off task during study time: (1) It is normal to relax versus work, (2) students have difficulty with time management, and (3) students may be unable to do the work independently. The first two points will be discussed as a pair. The third point will be addressed separately.

It is natural and normal for students to want to socialize or relax rather than work. It is also typical of students not to be adept at managing their time and not to understand that effort in the classroom leads to success. Pair these two and it should become apparent that teachers must learn how to set up structures that help students take responsibility for using time productively.

Mrs. Suce's structure to get students on task was to remind, remind, remind. In other words, Mrs. Suce actually took the responsibility for getting students to use time productively. In her class, students learned to relax, have a good time, and wait for the next signal from Mrs. Suce to get to work. Additionally, some students like any kind of attention, whether positive or negative. Mrs. Suce's criticism or nagging to get back to work may serve as a reward for off-task behavior. What should she do in setting up a new management structure? The emphasis is on devising strategies that are not punitive and can be integrated into learning activities. When the management structure is determined, present the problem of off-task behavior and the plan to the entire class before implementing it.

The plan might look something like the following. First, give one reminder to the whole class. Most will get to work. Look directly at any students remaining off task until all are back at work. Intermittently provide acknowledgments to all students who are on task, "Elana, at the rate you're going, you should not have homework tonight." Be quiet. Be brief. Be matter of fact. Be adult like. Be sure to verbally acknowledge students who have a history of poor work habits. With these students, strive hard to meet the recommended ratio of three positive comments to every negative comment.

Second, do not become engrossed with other activities. Establish the practice of visually scanning the room, especially when you first implement a plan to increase on-task behavior. Scan using an unpredictable order.

Third, teach students how to continue working while waiting for teacher assistance. Students need instruction about how to proceed with other parts of the assignment. They also need a way to cue the teacher without holding their hands up for prolonged periods. An example of a cue is standing a partially opened book on their desk in a vertical position. Elementary teachers have successfully used the help card described earlier in this chapter. Whatever signal is used, inform students that they are to use the signal and work quietly in order to obtain help. Make sure to do room scans frequently or students will give up on the system. They will begin calling out for help or being off task. Students may also serve as assistants. Train them in how to assist, let them know when you want them to assist, and rotate assistants so they can get their work done also.

Fourth, use a class roster to mark off-task behaviors with an "O" beside student names when you do class scans. A logical consequence for not using class time wisely would be time owed. Time owed means that the student would stay after class or spend time with you at another time during the day to complete the assigned work. For example, a student who earned three O's during class would owe you three minutes at another time during the day. Such a short amount of owed time may seem a bit ridiculous to you but it can be very effective in helping students take responsibility for managing their class time well. It is not convenient to have to return to a teacher's class for three minutes when a student wants to be with her friends.

Students who actually seek one-on-one time with adults may enjoy time owed. Their on-task behavior in class will not increase and their off-task behavior will stay the same or increase. If this happens, you should hold a planned discussion (see Chapter 4) with the student that emphasizes obtaining the goal of using class time well. Time with an adult can be earned by increasing time on task and off-task behavior will be ignored. Be creative in providing time with an adult. The student may have favorite adults in the building and those people may have tasks to do during the day that would benefit from student assistance.

Based on the tips just outlined, develop your management plan for dealing with off-task behavior. Be sure to present it to the students before implementing it. Let them know that you will be aware of their efforts to be on task and will acknowledge them. Remember to acknowledge students' efforts to take responsibility for using time well. For example, when you first implement the plan, let the whole class know that you are pleased with their efforts. After a ten-minute period of whole-class on-task behavior, say, "Each of you has worked hard for ten minutes. Everyone is showing how good your concentration is." Give five minutes of free time after several days of all on-task behavior.

The second major reason that students are off task during study time is that they may be unable to complete assignments independently because of insufficient instruction. Insufficient instruction takes various forms. It may be that students did not listen to or did not remember instructions. It may be that the instructional presentation did not match student skill levels. Thus, they did not profit from instruction.

Let's return to Mrs. Suce's science class during the lab sessions that occur twice a week. Half a dozen students have questions at one time as they work on lab exercises. Mrs. Suce is busily trying to help each student but some have to wait several minutes for her to have time for them. Students grow weary of waiting and holding their hands up. They begin to visit and wander around. Lab feels chaotic to the teacher and to observers. Mrs. Suce describes the students as immature and unable to work independently. In actuality, Mrs. Suce's conclusion should be: "Many students are asking for assistance. That must mean that we need to work on clarity of instructions or that there was not a match between my instruction and their skill level. Uh-oh. It's time to check out where the problem is. Then I can provide more and different instruction prior to expecting them to work independently."

Note the difference in the attributional statements the teacher made for the same group of students. The negative attribution was that the students were immature. The positive attribution, though unspoken, was that students were capable of working independently when the teacher provided an instructional match.

Let's return to the teacher's self-talk statement: "Many students are asking for assistance. . . . " In order for Mrs. Suce to check out where the problem was, she should take inventory of the kinds of questions students asked as she circulated the room. Questions generally will fall in one of several categories. The categories guide the teacher to adapt instruction in certain ways in order to achieve a match. Consider the following categories and how the teacher uses the category information to change instruction.

In the first category, basic questions about the assignment are asked such as which pages to read and which questions to answer. Explicitly inform students that you will give the assignment once and will ignore questions regarding information that you already addressed. You would be right to ask if this is fair to students who have language processing problems. One good solution is to write assignments on the board, read them to students, and require students to copy them across the top of their papers. Tell students that assignments must be written across the top before you will accept papers. Anticipate the typical student questions that accompany assignments and include the information in the assignment as you give it. For example, students may ask if they can answer the question with one or a few words rather than a complete sentence.

When students can complete this copying strategy accurately over a period of a week, try giving assignments orally and requiring students to write them across the top of papers. Be careful to monitor student success with oral presentations of assignments minus the visual presentation. Many classrooms have at least one student who profits most from visual presentations of assignments.

In the second category, basic questions are asked about procedures or use of equipment. This may be a good time to not only teach equipment use but also note-taking skills. Be explicit as you teach equipment use or procedures. This means that you will have to analyze the task and break it down into as many steps as possible. Proceed slowly through the steps. Provide comprehensive and explicit instruction at each step, paraphrase the instruction, and write the paraphrase on the board. Require students to copy the paraphrase for each step. After you have modeled paraphrasing several procedures across several days, begin to call on students to paraphrase and write their versions of the procedures on the board. Remember to call on lower performing students; ask them to paraphrase the easiest steps and write their paraphrases on the board. As students become comfortable and successful with paraphrasing, discontinue writing on the board and require that they write paraphrases on their papers after listening but not seeing. Periodically, check their work to see who is having difficulty. Consider assigning points for note taking. Before students begin their independent work, ask hypothetical questions. Allow students to answer from their notes and cite the step that would answer the question.

Basic questions are asked about meaning (e.g., important concepts or vocabulary) in the third category. Make sure that you go over assignments during instructional planning and try to anticipate where problems will arise. Specifically plan to emphasize these areas through methods like drill and practice prior to independent work. A few students may still not be ready and teachers need to work with them further in a small group while others are working independently.

Talking Without Permission

Iverson (1990) found that teachers reported talking as one of the top three problems demonstrated by students in classrooms. Achenbach (1991) also reported that teachers rated talking as one of the most frequent behavior problems in their classrooms. Accordingly, educators need a way to think about this prevalent behavior and a way to intervene when talking is disruptive.

It is helpful to observe and think about talking behaviors in learning contexts of humans across the life span. It is particularly enlightening to begin with adults. We have presented, and attended, numerous workshops and in-services for adult learners who engaged in high rates of talking to each other during the lectures and transitions. At one national conference on religion with more than 300 attendees, guidelines and instructions for conference participation were mailed to registrants two to three weeks in advance. Attendees were specifically asked to refrain from talking during presentations. It did not stop most adult learners from talking to each other whenever they wanted. That was one noisy conference. We have also taught young adult learners in college classrooms where talking occurs frequently during transitions.

Do these descriptions of adult talking behaviors sound like the ones teachers provide of child and adolescent learners in our schools? We think there are a few differences. Talking appears to be a high-frequency behavior in learning environments for all age groups. It is critical that people learn the social skill of listening when another person is speaking and to take turns speaking. In Chapter 3 you read that some classrooms make this a rule. Positive and negative consequences were provided for following the rule and breaking the rule, respectively.

Remember that transitions appear to pull people into talking behavior. Chapter 2 included information on how to teach students to behave during transitions. If educators do not want students talking to each other during the change from one activity to another, they need to provide explicit instructions about not talking during transitions. If these transition rules are learned by students, off-task behavior and talking will occur infrequently and instructional time will be increased.

Well-taught rules and procedures for transitions are usually sufficient for decreasing the frequency of talking. However, some students continue to have difficulty managing their talking successfully. The question becomes how to better manage instructional settings in order for students to take responsibility for talking at appropriate times only. Management of talking will be examined in terms of talking during lectures, one or two students talking during class, more than just a few students talking during class, and failure to raise hands.

Talking During Lectures. Let's look at Mrs. Suce's science class again. The students continually talk during her lectures. It is not just a few students but all students talk at one time or another. Mrs. Suce teaches the same class three times a day and the other two sections do not talk during lectures. Therefore, she does not think that the explanation is that she is presenting boring lectures. The other two sections responded to the basic classroom management plan that included the rule of no talking when others are speaking. She has tried the usual negative consequences: issuing a whole-class directive, eye contact, proximity control, gentle verbal reprimands, time owed, and telling students to listen. All of these strategies helped, but only for a few minutes each time. The talking is now a pattern for most students, having occurred over a period of several weeks.

Mrs. Suce needs to emphasize accountability for talking with applications of both positive and negative consequences as appropriate. The teacher may want to devise a plan during a class meeting (see Chapter 7) in which students help make decisions. It will be important for the class to clearly and explicitly state the guidelines for student behavior during lectures. One way to do this is by eliminating confusion about who can talk. The rule can become no talking without raising your hand and being granted permission. All other talking is unacceptable and results in negative consequences.

The class can determine the negative consequences together. It is recommended that the mild consequence of verbal reprimands be used the first day the plan begins. After that, consequences should be moderate in nature but never severe. Excessive talking, although frustrating, is a relatively minor misbehavior. Severe consequences would be inappropriately matched to the misbehavior and they are usually more difficult to implement consistently. Teachers need consequences that are reasonable and moderately aversive. More than likely, classes like Mrs. Suce's are made up of students who like to socialize. They like to talk to each other. Natural positive consequences would be giving them permission to socialize at appropriate times after they have demonstrated an increase in following the rule. Natural negative consequences would be removing them from the social environment for short periods of time for breaking the rule.

How would negative consequences work? There are two basic choices: in-class time-out and time owed. Remember that students may have ideas of their own that will serve even better. One group of students decided that talkers would lose the privilege of sitting in their chairs for seven minutes after the first warning. In other words, the student who talked had to stand up beside her desk for seven minutes. Any student who reacted (e.g., laughed, pointed) also had to stand up for seven minutes. In less than a week, students were assuming responsibility for listening while others were speaking. It is important to note that the students agreed among themselves to try this consequence. The teacher had them role-play it a few times to help them decide how they would feel about standing up for seven minutes. All students participated in role plays and determined that they wanted the teacher to use the consequence. Without student participation in such decisions, students may interpret consequences as unfair, humiliating, or punitive. The end result is large-scale rebellion against the teacher.

The choices of in-class time-outs and time owed can be described for students during a class meeting and discussed as options. An in-class time-out is isolation of a student in the classroom setting for a period of time. Time-out usually consists of one minute per years of age and not more than five minutes total. In other words, a three-year-old would have a time-out of three minutes and a five-year-old would have a time-out of five minutes. A six-year-old and a sixteen-year-old would also have a time-out of five minutes. The exception to the five-minute maximum rule is giving longer time-outs to students who are not able to calm themselves by the end of five minutes. When students return to the group after five minutes and are upset and likely to misbehave immediately, the length of time-out should be extended. This is not done to punish students more severely but to provide them with ample time to calm themselves and be successful in class upon their return.

An example of how a time-out works follows. A teacher taught in a classroom that had a refrigerator in it. The students agreed that an in-class time-out was a negative consequence that would be appropriate to use for talking without permission. They helped the teacher move the refrigerator away from the wall and placed a chair behind it and away from the class. (Of course, the teacher checked the wiring and so forth for safety.) The students made a big sign for the front of the refrigerator that said "Siberia" on it. When an in-class time-out was the consequence, the teacher would say, "Five minutes in Siberia." Whole-class planning and participation in developing the consequence created camaraderie and students were good natured about going to Siberia. Classmates were supportive of each other's efforts to decrease talking.

Again, this may seem a strange occurrence to some but it illustrates how creative students can be in deciding how best to help themselves assume responsibility. Negative consequences like those just described have been constructed by students and therefore seem to be less threatening and more palatable than those constructed by a teacher. They are mutually agreed-on cues that say, "Pay attention to your behavior. Monitor your behavior."

An in-class time-out for talking may be difficult to manage since talking often involves two students and there may be only one time-out setting. In that case, teachers may need to rely on time owed. A logical consequence for wasting time by talking is to pay back time out of minutes that students value. One episode of talking during a lecture could result in one minute of time owed. Such a brief time owed could be done immediately after class. This may seem such a minor consequence that it would have no impact. However, brief time owed after class may be very effective with students who like to socialize. They just gave up the few precious minutes between class when they can always socialize without negative consequences. All other students are allowed to leave while the student remains seated for an extra minute. The student is to sit quietly without talking or studying. Time starts when the student is quiet. Time owed in larger blocks (e.g., five minutes) can be conducted before school, after school, during a break, and so forth.

Talking Incessantly During Class: One or Two Students. Sylvia has always been a talker at school and has been reprimanded repeatedly in the past. This year she has been talking more than ever. She has so many things that she wants to say to her girlfriends about boys and going to the movies and so forth. During independent seatwork, she constantly talks even if no one is listening.

Every teacher is having the same problem with Sylvia: getting her quiet and on task. They have tried many things, including sending her to the office. She is not fazed and laughs cheerfully about the negative consequences. This may be an example of a chronic talker, one who talks out of habit. Talking is reinforcing in and of itself, regardless of the reactions of people around her. Sylvia may know that she is in control, too, because her behavior has adults so upset.

It will not be easy to change Sylvia's behavior. It will take concerted effort and patience. The following plan to help Sylvia decrease her talking may seem severe but it can be successful with chronic talkers. Before all of her teachers implement the plan, one or two teachers need to hold a planned discussion with Sylvia to collaborate on the development of the plan and gain her cooperation in carrying out the plan. Sylvia needs to know that her excessive talking is a habit and that her peers and others will listen better to her if they know that when she speaks, she is saying something important. Tell her of the sequence of consequences you will be using.

She is told that she will spend time in an isolated area of the classroom where she is not to talk even during class discussions. Decide together what you will call it. For instance, it could be called "quiet time."

Assign her a desk among her classmates but close to the teacher's desk for monitoring purposes. None of the peers around her should be her close friends with whom she most likes to talk. Consistently give her positive feedback when she is quiet but do not comment on her lack of talking. Instead, focus on her effort and participation in learning. Arrange an isolation area in the classroom that is as far away from peers as possible. The students who are nearest the isolation area must be able to ignore anyone in isolation. Determine the sequence of consequences for talking.

Here is one example of a sequence that could be used: (1) Give one verbal reprimand and warning per period. "Sylvia, you are breaking the rule of talking without permission. Next time you talk without permission, you will go to quiet time for this period and our next class period." (2) At the second occurrence of talking without permission, say, "Sylvia, you need to go to quiet time for the rest of the period and all of our next class. You may return to your desk after one entire period of no talking." Be calm, do not argue or negotiate, and ignore student comments. (3) For each incident of talking during quiet time, the student owes an additional fifteen minutes but this time is owed before or after school or during lunch. "Sylvia, for talking you owe another fifteen minutes during your lunch time today." (4) After successfully remaining quiet during an entire class period, say, "Sylvia, you may return to your regular seat tomorrow. I am pleased that you were able to follow the rules for quiet time." (5) Reward the student's efforts: Write a note to the parents, have leaders that Sylvia looks up to congratulate her on her growth, or give her a responsibility in your class.

Talking Incessantly During Class: Several Students.   The major difference between this situation and the previous one is that these students are all enjoying talking and listening to each other so much that the usual negative consequences have not deterred any of them. They do not have a history of being chronic talkers to the point of talking when no one is listening. It is important to meet with the several students together and explain the plan. Again, be neutral, calm, and ignore student complaints. Students in the company of each other during a discussion may be more prone to complain about being treated like babies when you explain the consequences. Tell the complaining student that you will impose consequences only if he does not act maturely.

During the discussion, make a list of appropriate talking during class time and another one of inappropriate talking. Examples and nonexamples should come from their past behaviors. Consequences for inappropriate talking could be moving their seat assignments to separate the students for a week. Talking in the new seat could result in time owed. As always, catch the students being good and give positive feedback. If there is no improvement with this plan after two weeks of implementation, develop a reinforcement system (see Chapter 6). Ask the parents to participate in this plan.

Failure to Raise Hands.   Many teachers attempt to conduct class informally and allow students to participate freely and with spontaneity. This can become a problem when a few assertive students dominate class discussions or call out for help during seatwork while less assertive students remain silent and unassisted. Under these circumstances, teachers will need to designate periods in which students are expected to raise their hands and periods in which it is not necessary to raise hands. Even with designation tactics, developmentally younger children will tend to have a difficult time remembering that during such and such a time period, they are to raise their hands. When reminded, they will initially follow the procedure but will forget as the time period progresses. Be careful in your applications of differential times to raise hands. You do not want to give negative consequences to students who are excited about participating and cannot remember that this is the time to raise hands versus calling out.

Even with older students, when calling out is a habit, students may have difficulty remembering to raise their hands. Structured teaching procedures will need to be implemented to correct this. Begin by clearly communicating teacher expectations at the beginning of a class period. Here is an example of what you might say:

> "During certain activities in our class, it is important that everyone has an equal opportunity to talk or ask questions. Therefore, we will be using a new procedure in our class but one that you are familiar with from previous classes—raising hands for the opportunity to participate. I will let you know when the activity of the day requires raising hands and when you can participate without raising your hands. Generally, in small group work I will not require you to raise your hand. With fewer students, there is time for everyone to participate and we need to be able to freely share. However, in most large

group discussions, I will require that you raise your hand and wait to be called on so that everyone has an equal chance to contribute."

Teachers who are used to responding to students who call out will have some difficulty ignoring call-outs at first. Teachers may also momentarily forget that this is a time period in which hands are to be raised and call-outs ignored. But ignore they must as they strive to be consistent. They are not to use a student's call-out, even if it is polite and at a convenient time, as a teachable moment in which they remind the student of the rule and then allow them to share. Students will not learn to follow the rule 100 percent of the time if teachers do not consistently ignore call-outs. Instead, teachers need to quickly call on students whose hands are raised. Students who have more difficulty remembering to raise their hands should be called on quickly also. Teachers' responses to them should be prefaced with statements like the following: "Mark, your hand is raised. What would you do if you were Horton the elephant hatching the egg?" The first two weeks will be the most difficult but teachers who are consistent for that length of time will have most students raising hands appropriately.

Poor Listening and Not Following Verbal Directions

It is important to have a classroom rule about listening such as "Listen when other people are speaking." When you are ready to make an important announcement such as verbal directions and you do not want to have to repeat them, it is critical to begin with a verbal prompt such as "Everyone please listen." Then give the verbal directions. Students who were not listening will ask teachers questions about what they said later in the period. Now comes the consequence and it must be used consistently with every student. Ignore the questions and tell students that you cannot answer because you already gave that information. As students improve in listening, let them know you appreciate their efforts.

Not Bringing Materials to Class

Materials for class include paper, writing utensils, textbooks, homework, and any other supplies. The reasons why students do not bring needed materials to class range from forgetting to bring them to attempting to avoid consequences for not being prepared. Interventions for not bringing materials vary considerably. Some interventionists advise a structured plan in which students lose points toward their final grade and owe time for forgetting textbooks. Others use a barter system. Students who need to borrow supplies (e.g., paper, pencil, textbook) from the teacher do so before class begins and give the teacher a valued personal possession (e.g., watch, ring, wallet, shoe, jacket) as barter. At the end of class, students can get their possessions back if they return the supplies they borrowed. We prefer the latter intervention because it does not penalize students who have legitimate and significant difficulties with organization and memory for details. Students who consistently use the barter system can be targeted for individualized interventions to improve organizational skills. Interventions for students who come to class without their homework are addressed in the next section.

Late or Incomplete Assignments

Problems with receiving completed homework from students vary from turning work in late to turning in incomplete work to not turning in work at all. The number of students in a classroom that have the problem can range from one or two individuals to many. Just as the nature of the problems vary, so do the reasons for late or incomplete assignments vary. Sprick's (1985) interventions are described here.

Contributing factors to late or incomplete assignments fall into three general categories: (1) Students grow lax in timely productivity because teachers are inconsistent in collecting, recording, and returning work; (2) consequences for late work are negligible; and (3) students lack skills to do the work. The first two categories will be addressed together. The third category, skill deficiency, will be presented at the end of the discussion.

Before the school year begins, teachers need to plan how to deal with homework. In addition to tips on managing homework presented earlier in this chapter, we offer the following suggestions teachers can consider as they develop their homework plans. Students need a well-designed grading system in order to know exactly what they need to do to pass the class. Parents need information about the homework routine in order to support their children. Accordingly, teachers need to develop consistent routines for assigning, collecting, recording, and returning homework.

From week to week, students and parents should be able to count on about the same amount of homework that is due on a regular schedule. Students who have not learned to pace themselves on long assignments need explicit instruction in how to complete portions of an assignment across a number of days.

Always collect homework at the beginning of the period. This will prevent students from putting off homework and trying to finish it during class time. Collecting homework in person as students enter the door also encourages timely homework completion. Give students feedback and send notes to parents when students hand their work to you on time. Have a policy for late work and explicitly communicate it to your students. Define late. For example, "Late work means the work was turned in after the teacher began the class." Obviously, teachers will need to start classes on time if they are using that definition. Define the consequence. For example, "The consequence for late work is a loss of ten percent of the points for each day the assignment is late."

Students need some in-class time to begin new or difficult assignments. This provides time to ask questions and seek teacher assistance. Students with academic skill deficiencies also may not know how to manage homework: may not write assignments down, may not keep track of what they have completed, may not know due dates, may not pace themselves on long assignments, may not understand grading practices, and may not have time management skills. Determine whether the student has the academic and management skills to complete assignments. If not, ask all the other teachers to work with you. Make arrangements for the student to get help with any areas of deficiency. Develop a homework routine and obtain parental support.

Tardiness or Absenteeism

According to Sprick (1985), several factors may contribute to chronic tardiness. First, there may be insufficient consequences for tardiness. Second, many teachers do not begin instruction immediately, often tarrying even ten or twelve minutes to begin the lesson. Students do not believe that they are missing out on anything important and they either slip in a bit later or tarry in the hallways to socialize. Some schools develop schoolwide discipline policies that include a hierarchy of consequences designed to deal with chronic tardiness. In addition to school policies, teachers should have their own classroom policies in place (which, of course, should not contradict school policy). Teachers may be successful in decreasing tardiness at the classroom level by incorporating the following strategies.

One thing that teachers can do is construct grading systems that award points for participation and effort. Opening activities that begin as soon as the class begins earn participation points for students who are present. These activities and their points cannot be made up by tardy students. A second thing that teachers can do is stand at the door and greet students as they come in, even taking attendance. Students will learn that such teachers are prepared and ready to go when the bell rings.

Failure to Be Motivated/Doing Nothing

Nylan is a student who fails to turn any work in to his teachers. Since first grade, he has had a history of doing little or nothing but it seems worse this year. Teachers say that he sits in class doing and saying nothing. In language arts, the teacher tried extra hard recently to develop a unit that would motivate Nylan. It involved World Wide Web searches on the computer and, indeed, Nylan showed an interest in the project and immediately went to work in the library. However, when the teacher came by his computer station to monitor his progress, he was cruising the web in an area that had nothing to do with the project. He was unable to demonstrate any progress on the actual project.

Passive resistance and poor motivation in the area of academic achievement are some of the most difficult problems to solve. Sprick (1985) stated that students with this profile definitely need intensive help and offered the guidelines described here. Typically, it will be necessary to involve support services: school counselors, school psychologists, and social workers. There are potentially many causes for the problems and it is difficult to even speculate on the causes of Nylan's behavior without more information. It is most likely true that Nylan, and students like him, are discouraged and have given up. Sometimes a factor in the problem is that students either do not have, or think that they do not have, the skills to complete assignments. Problem solving will be based on identifying the student's skills and helping the student develop and obtain realistic goals.

Although Nylan has exhibited passive behavior since first grade, some students' withdrawn behaviors represent a recent change. It is important for teachers to approach students with recent behavior changes differently. Recent changes suggest that students are going through something difficult. Such changes may be indicators

of suicidal ideation. When teachers suspect that students are experiencing significant feelings of hopelessness or suicidal thoughts, it is time to seek the assistance of
the building assistance team or counselors or psychologists.

After establishing the history of withdrawal, teachers must obtain accurate information about students' skill levels. The best way to do this is to work with Nylan individually. If he can complete the majority of the work without assistance, you can proceed with a plan to increase motivation. If he cannot complete the work accurately, he
will need remediation of basic skills. In this case, Nylan has the basic skills that he needs
to accomplish the tasks. In fact, his skills are better than those of many of his peers.
Incidentally, Nylan's parents wondered if their son was gifted and, therefore, bored with
the curriculum. Psychological assessment did not support their hypothesis of giftedness.

Teachers can record Nylan's specific behaviors over the last few weeks that
have been of concern. Teachers need to be as detailed and specific as possible. First,
record all concerns. In Nylan's case, concerns might include these: Does not participate in discussions, does not speak to anyone, does not bring materials to class,
does not turn to the page in the book, does not take notes or work on problems on
the overhead projector, does not use time in class to work on new assignments,
rarely uses class time to start homework, does not turn in assignments, sits pas-
sively, stares ahead or at hands, acts bored or apathetic.

Second, select a target behavior from the listing. The target behavior should be
the one that is most critical to success. For example, the teacher might select "does
not complete assignments" as the target behavior. Now the teacher must clarify
exactly what she expects Nylan to do, write a goal, and assign responsibilities to
obtain the goal. Educators will be most successful when they hold planned discussions with students and write goals collaboratively (see Chapter 4). Figure 5–3
shows a sample form that could be used for goal setting and attainment.

The teacher is now ready to hold a planned discussion with Nylan. Nylan
probably will make few contributions to the discussion; do not be discouraged. It is
a beginning to engage him in the process of solving his own problems. Now the
hard work begins. Busy teachers must clear time in their schedules to make frequent
contact with Nylan. If he shows any improvement, it must be noted by giving him
positive feedback. If he makes no effort to meet goals, hold another brief planned
discussion at the end of the first week. Be calm, be supportive, and restate your
expectations that he will make the effort to reach the goal. If Nylan has not made
any efforts after two or three weeks, teachers probably need to develop a highly
structured reinforcement system. In the meantime, support services personnel
assigned to the building should be conducting problem-solving assessment that will
direct additional intervention development.

Cheating

Cheating is a common problem with several underlying causes (Sprick, 1985). The
most basic explanation for why students cheat is that students want to succeed.
Adults come back with the comment, "Then work hard and you will succeed." It is
necessary to look beyond that simple belief to student beliefs about why they cannot

Student_____ Teacher_____ Date_____

Goal 1 _____

Student Objective a_____

Student Objective b_____

Student Objective c_____

Teacher Support a _____

Teacher Support b _____

Teacher Support c _____

Evaluation Process _____

Date of Goal Evaluation _____

_____

Student Signature

_____

Teacher Signature

Figure 5–3
Goals and Objectives

succeed without cheating. First, many truly do not have the academic skills to succeed. Second, some are under tremendous pressure to excel and, thus, succumb to cheating. The third group better fits the adult adage of "Work hard and you will succeed." The students in this group either did not take enough time to prepare or have learned that cheating is a quicker, easier route to success than studying. Regardless of the reason, there are supportive strategies for teachers to use that reduce incidents of cheating.

First of all, teachers should monitor the environment to prevent cheating. Test security, seating arrangements, cleared desks and floors around desks, teachers' visual scanning and moving about the room, and removal of baseball caps are good starting points for reducing cheating. Baseball caps? Yes, the underside of the bill offers a nice place to anchor critical points of information. Try one on and you will see how handy a cap can be during an exam.

Just as important as cheat-proofing the environment is the academic preparation of students that will help them be successful. Determine why the student thought she needed to cheat. Based on your determination, provide one or more of the following: basic skills training (e.g., note taking, highlighting, distributed practice, test taking skills), peer tutoring, and time management training.

The first time a student is caught cheating, discuss it privately and not publicly with her. Give her an opportunity to earn alternative credit, determine the reason, and match your intervention to the reason. Tell the student that, although you do not expect her to have another episode of cheating, a further incident automatically results in a failing mark.

Test Anxiety

Various factors can contribute to the debilitating feeling of panic called test anxiety that students experience when taking exams (Sprick, 1985). Pressure from parents and self may be a factor leading to test anxiety. Students who experienced early difficulty in their test taking histories may think they cannot take tests and test anxiety develops. Tests may actually be difficult to take because students have never learned test taking strategies and approaches.

To problem solve how to best help students reduce their test anxiety, consider the following guidelines. Teachers should unobtrusively observe the strategies test-anxious students use and record them. Teachers need to meet with parents and seek their support in the problem-solving process. Parents can support their children by reducing any pressure to excel. They can give permission for their children to receive support help (e.g., relaxation training). Teachers then begin an instructional program that prepares all students to use strategies of completing easy items first while marking difficult items to return to later, using answers from easier items to help answer harder items, using the process of elimination strategy, taking a brief break to relax, and guessing on blank items at the end of the session. Teachers may take it for granted that students already know how to use the described strategies to take tests but many do not know them. They need explicit instruction in test taking strategies. Giving frequent, short tests also reduces the stress of completing infrequent, comprehensive exams.

CONCLUSION

Instructional management takes you a step closer to the teacher's primary function, the actual teaching of the curriculum. Instructional management refers to a set of generic skills that cuts across subjects and activities. The observation checklist in Appendix A summarizes the critical instructional management behaviors presented in this chapter. Turn to the appendix now and use the list as a summary and review of the chapter. Use the list to assist you in observing various aspects of content management in classrooms. The list can also be used as a self-rating form as you prepare to teach a lesson or to critique your lesson presentation after you have completed it.

SUPPLEMENTARY QUESTIONS

1. Some teachers hesitate to use debates, role playing, panel discussions, group projects, field trips, and a host of other procedures that add variety to the question-and-answer recitation pattern. Their reluctance may be due to fears about a loss of control. Speculate about the loss-of-control factors that might be inherent in these activities and the ways to counter the anxieties associated with using each of these activities.

2. Workbooks and worksheets may be used as control measures because they keep students occupied. However, because students often regard these assignments as busywork, they often race through them, giving cursory attention to the material, or seek relief from the boredom by engaging in unacceptable off-task behavior. How can a teacher capitalize on the educational and management benefits of workbooks and worksheets without incurring the adverse effects of negative student attitudes?

3. Anticipating what could go wrong can be an effective way to evaluate a prospective lesson activity. Select a lesson delivery activity, and identify potential management considerations for its use. What can be done to minimize the likelihood that there will be management difficulties?

4. Consider this technique: After placing all students' names in a tin can, the teacher asks a question and pulls a name out of the tin can. If the student answers correctly, the student's name is left out of the can. If the student answers incorrectly, the name is put back in the can. What are the advantages and disadvantages of this technique? What are some ways it can be used (e.g., every fifth name drawn is eligible for an individual or group reward)?

5. "Goofing off" is a common way teachers characterize pupil misbehavior. These behaviors often occur during seatwork. What explanations can be given for these behaviors? What preventive and supportive measures might be used to minimize the incidence of these behaviors?

SUPPLEMENTARY PROJECTS

1. Elementary teachers often deliver lessons using a teacher's manual. Secondary teachers often lecture while using the textbook as a content outline. Interview students to secure their reactions to these two lesson development practices. You might camouflage your intentions by including these practices within a discussion of several other practices.

2. Make a list of common methods of instruction, for example, teacher presentations, class discussions, debates, and so on. Prepare an instrument to discover student perceptions about why each method succeeds or fails. Students could respond to a series of open-ended statements, such as the following: "Teacher presentations are an effective teaching tool because. . . . " or "Teacher presentations often fail because. . . . "

3. Teachers sometimes believe they have taught something well, only to find out later that many

students did not learn. Interview several teachers about their explanations for the occasional discrepancy between their perceptions of student attainment and actual results. Which explanations are grounded in the management aspects of the lesson?

4. Teachers may be the cause of disciplinary problems: Flaws in the planning, organization, and delivery of instruction can be the impetus for disciplinary incidents. Ask a teacher to identify two or three students who present chronic behavior problems. Observe their behavior over a period of several days, paying particular attention to the instructional antecedents of on- and off-task behavios. Do your observations suggest some connections between student behavior problems and the teacher's management of instructional functions?

5. In many cases, students can help one another with particular educational tasks. One student

may teach a subject to another for designated periods of time. A teacher gains a more individualized program of instruction without adversely affecting the learning of the tutor or the tutored. Work with a classroom teacher to organize a short-term peer-tutoring program, possibly with a subset of students in a particular classroom. Keep a record of student achievement during the period of the program. Compare student performance with that obtained prior to instituting the peer-tutoring program.

REFERENCES

Achenbach, T. M. (1991). *Manual for the teacher's report form and 1991 profile.* Burlington, VT: University of Vermont Department of Psychiatry.

Anderson, L., Brubaker, N., Alleman-Brooks, J., & Duffy, G. (1983). *Student responses to classroom instruction: Final report* (NIE-G-80-0073). East Lansing, MI: Institute for Research on Teaching, Michigan State University.

Ausubel, D. (1963). *The psychology of meaningful verbal learning.* New York: Grune & Stratton.

Bloom, B. S., Engelhart, M. D., Frost, E. J., Hill, W. H., & Krathwohl, D. R. (1956). *Taxonomy of educational objectives. Handbook I: Cognitive domain.* New York: McKay.

Brophy, J. E., & Good, T. L. (1970). Teachers' communication of differential expectations for children's classroom performance. *Journal of Educational Psychology, 61,* 365–374.

Bruner, J. (1961). The act of discovery. *Harvard Educational Review, 31,* 21–32.

Bruner, J. (1966). *Toward a theory of instruction.* Cambridge, MA: Belknap Press of Harvard University Press.

Cangelosi, J. S. (1988). *Classroom management strategies: Gaining and maintaining students' cooperation.* New York: Longman.

Charles, C. (1983). *Elementary classroom management: A handbook of excellence in teaching.* New York: Longman.

Chernow, F. B., & Chernow, C. (1981). *Classroom discipline and control: 101 practical techniques.* West Nyack, NY: Parker.

Curwin, R., & Mendler, A. (1988). *Discipline with dignity.* Alexandria, VA: Association for Supervision and Curriculum Development.

Doyle, W. (1980). *Classroom management.* West Lafayette, IN: Kappa Delta Pi.

Doyle, W. (1986). Classroom organization and management. In M. C. Wittrock, (Ed.), *Handbook of research on teaching* (pp. 392–431). New York: Macmillan.

Gersten, R., Carnine, D., & Woodward, J. (1987). Direct instruction research: The third decade. *Remedial and Special Education, 8*(6), 48–56.

Glasser, W. (1990). *The quality school: Managing students without coercion.* New York: Harper & Row.

Glasser, W. (1992). The quality school curriculum. *Phi Delta Kappan, 73,* 690–694.

Glasser, W. (1993). *The quality school teacher.* New York: Harper Perennial.

Gnagey, W. J. (1981). *Motivating classroom discipline.* New York: Macmillan.

Good, T., & Brophy, J. (1984). *Looking in classrooms* (3rd ed.). New York: Harper and Row.

Good, T. L., & Grouws, D. A. (1979). Teaching and mathematics learning. *Educational Leadership, 37,* 39–45.

Iverson, A. M., & Stack, D. (1996). *Preservice teachers' use of learning strategy instruction.* Unpublished manuscript, University of Northern Iowa.

Iverson, S. J. (1990). *Cognitive behavioral interventions for students in the regular classroom setting: Grades four through eight.* Unpublished manuscript, Heartland Area Education Agency, Johnston, IA.

Johnson, D. W., Johnson, R. T., & Holubec, E. J. (1990). *Circles of learning: Cooperation in the classroom* (3rd ed.). Edina, MN: Interaction Book.

Jones, V. F. (1989). Classroom management: Clarifying theory and improving practice. *Education, 109*(3), 330–339.

Kagan, D. M. (1992). Implications of research on teacher beliefs. *Educational Psychologist, 27,* 65–90.

Kerman, S. (1982). *Teacher expectations and student achievement* (Workshop handout). TESA Training.

Kerman, S., & Martin, M. (1980). *Teacher expectations and student achievement: Teacher handbook.* Bloomington, IN: Phi Delta Kappa.

Kounin, J.S. (1970). *Discipline and group management in classrooms.* New York: Holt, Rinehart & Winston.

Kounin, J. S. (1977). *Discipline and group management in classrooms* (rev. ed.). New York: Holt, Rinehart & Winston.

Marshall, H. H. (1987). Building a learning orientation. *Theory into Practice 26,* 8–14.

Minnick, B. (Ed.). (1983). Student disruption: Classroom chaos linked to teacher practices. *R&DCTE Review, The Newsletter of the Research and Development Center for Teacher Education, 1,* 2–3.

Paine, S. C., Radicchi, J. A., Rosellini, L. C., Deutchman, L., & Darch, C. B. (1983). *Structuring your classroom for academic success.* Champaign, IL: Research Press.

Parker, W. C., & Gehrke, N. J. (1986). Learning activities and teacher decision making: Some grounded hypotheses. *American Educational Research Journal, 23,* 227–242.

Pinnell, G. S., & Galloway, C.M. (1987). Human development, language, and communication: Then and now. *Theory into Practice, 26*(special issue), 353–357.

Redl, F., & Wattenberg, W. (1959). *Mental hygiene in teaching.* New York: Harcourt, Brace, & World.

Rogers, C. (1977). Forget you are a teacher. *Instructor, 81,* 65–66.

Rosenshine, B. (1983). Direct instruction. In T. Husen & T. N. Postlethwaite (Eds.), *International Encyclopedia of Education* (Vol. 3, pp. 1395–1400) Oxford: Pergamon.

Rosenshine, B. (1986). Synthesis of research on explicit teaching. *Educational Leadership, 43*(7), 60–69.

Slade, D., & Callaghan, T. (1988). Preventing management problems. *Academic Therapy, 23*(3), 229–235.

Sprick, R. S. (1985). *Discipline in the secondary classroom: A problem-by-problem survival guide.* West Nyack, NY: Center for Applied Research in Education.

Sprick, R., Sprick, M., & Garrison, M. (1993). *Interventions: Collaborative planning for students at risk.* Longmont, CO: Sopris West.

Weinstein, R. S., Marshall, H. H., Brattesani, K. A., & Middlestadt, S. E. (1982). Student perceptions of differential treatment in open and traditional classrooms. *Journal of Educational Psychology, 74,* 678–692.

Weinstein, R. S., & Middlestadt, S. E. (1979). Student perceptions of teacher interactions with male high and low achievers. *Journal of Educational Psychology, 71,* 421–431.

Ysseldyke, J., & Christenson, S. (1993–1994). *The instructional environment system–II: A system to identify a student's instructional needs.* Longmont, CO: Sopris West.

CHAPTER 6

Conduct Management: Student Behavior Choices

An understanding of the material in this chapter will help you do the following:

❏ Use the assertive/authoritative communication style.
❏ Describe the characteristic ways of expressing the nonassertive and hostile response styles.
❏ Describe the reasons teachers adopt a dysfunctional leadership style.
❏ Distinguish between minor and moderate/severe behavior problems and select appropriate interventions.
❏ Access building assistance teams to resolve behavior problems.
❏ Select behavioral interventions that match target problems.
❏ Monitor progress in order to evaluate the success of a conduct management plan.

What you believe about the nature of people will affect your conduct management. Before beginning this chapter, you should stop and reexamine your personal beliefs about the nature of human beings and your philosophy of management. Have you developed more insight into your beliefs and philosophy? Are you talking or writing about them differently in any way? Continue to critique your basic beliefs throughout this chapter. We recommend that you reflect and elaborate on your knowledge of the four theoretical models discussed in Chapter 1 by (1) rereading; (2) presenting the models to an "audience" and taping the presentation, listening to the recording, and redeveloping weak points; and (3) writing a one-page paper that compares your personal beliefs about discipline to the models that best match your beliefs. Once again, our position in this chapter is interactive. We offer a menu of techniques extrapolated from all the models; many of them are quick, efficient, and directive.

This chapter emphasizes helping you develop the procedural skills you need to resolve discipline problems. In this chapter, we examine schoolwide and classroom conduct, mistakes that educators make when trying to preserve order, ways to secure adherence to school and classroom rules, common ways in which students behave contrary to the rules, interventions that require assistance teams, and criteria that can be used to judge the effectiveness of a conduct management plan. Communication skills are revisited, specifically in terms of assertive, nonassertive, and hostile styles of communication. In the previous chapter, you learned that good content management prevents classroom discipline problems. How do you then explain comments from many frustrated preservice and novice teachers that the high-quality lessons they prepared could not be presented because students were "out of control" from the moment they entered the classroom?

RATIONALE FOR DIRECTIVE CONDUCT MANAGEMENT

Research supports the preceding comments of preservice and novice teachers. For example, Mcneely and Mertz (1990) found that secondary student teachers had a high sense of efficacy and spent a great deal of time planning lessons that had more than one activity at the beginning of their student teaching experiences. By the end of student teaching, they spent their time on classroom control and planned lessons with single activities in order to reduce disruption. In another study, Hoy and Woolfolk (1990) concluded that student teachers grew more controlling in social problem solving during the student teaching experience.

Kagan (1992) suggested that preservice teachers need to come to student teaching already equipped with the basic procedural skills and strategies like the ones that you learned in Chapters 2 through 5. Then you will be able to teach high-quality lessons while using external, teacher-directed, high-control techniques appropriately. In other words, desirable student teaching outcomes would result if preservice teachers could continue to plan high-quality lessons and use directive management techniques effectively rather than spending large amounts of time on disciplinary problems.

Swanson, O'Connor, and Cooney (1990) analyzed differences between expert and novice teachers' problem-solving approaches to classroom discipline. Expert teachers were master teachers identified by building principals. Expert teachers were more likely to solve discipline problems using direct or external controls (e.g., establish and enforce rules, end action immediately, separate students, proximity control, modify instruction, model behavior, time-out, confront student, contingencies). Novice teachers' solutions were more likely to rely on internal decisions of students (e.g., provide maximum freedom, counsel students, encourage, reason, empathize, discuss, involve students more). The expert teachers were significantly more likely to place a priority on defining and representing the problem prior to intervening. Novices tended to represent problems in terms of possible solutions.

An inference that could be made from the studies mentioned is that it is possible to teach high-quality lessons with the appropriate use of external, directive behavior techniques. Doyle (1986) concurred with this position in his review of classroom management. A common theme was that the teacher's management task is more one of maintaining work systems than remediating misbehavior. Order is not achieved once and for all. The teacher continually protects the work systems by using quick, efficient, nonintrusive directive techniques.

Study the following vignettes and use them as pretests to evaluate your skills in problem-solving behavior problems. In the conclusion section of the chapter, you will return to them and problem solve again to see if you would manage them any differently.

You walk into your first-hour class several minutes before the bell rings and see a group of students who have arrived early. Several of them are teasing a lone student who is crying. This student has never been a problem for you. How would you solve this problem?

You have a student who spends a great deal of class time either joking around or debating the inherent value of your lessons and assignments. Classmates laugh at his jokes and seem to like him. Today is no exception. During the first few minutes of the lesson, he first cracks a joke about it and then remarks that it is a waste of time and has no relevance to life outside of school. How would you solve this problem?

You are leading the students in a review of some difficult course material. Two students seated toward the back of the room are quietly talking to each other. You have asked them once already to stop talking. Now they are talking again. How would you solve this problem?

You are explaining the distribution of grades on the exam you have just passed back to students. You describe how the grade on this exam fits into your grading system. One bright student begins to criticize your grading policies, saying that they are unfair. How would you solve this problem?

Class is over and students are exiting the room. Two students begin to argue and one pushes the other with enough force that the student falls into nearby desks. How would you solve this problem?

Record what you would do now. As you study the content of this chapter, revise your solutions if you think of better ones. Compare your responses at the end of the unit to your current responses as a check of what you already knew and what you learned.

THE ASSERTIVE MANAGEMENT STYLE

The most fundamental condition of effective teaching, to be preserved at all costs according to Canter and Canter (1976, p. 2), is the right of teachers to get their personal and professional needs met in the classroom. This position hardly needed to be stated and certainly was not an issue in the not too distant past. Teachers had legitimate power, conferred basically as authority, and students were to behave in accordance with teacher expectations. Teachers could act, with a reasoned regard for student needs, without looking over their shoulders to see if the courts and the community were scrutinizing their decisions. They could act confidently because there was a reasoned consensus about what constituted acceptable behavior, and they were given considerable latitude in the use of measures to ensure compliance with these behavioral standards.

Today, educators' management measures may be challenged or disregarded by students. Parents also seem to be more inclined to support their children and ask educators to account for their actions. Thus, when educators are called on to defend their decisions, they may become more cautious and, possibly, more compromising. They may be more willing to overlook disruptive behavior and to disregard the student who causes problems. They may reconcile themselves to teaching in a situation that is less than what they want, or believe desirable, to avoid the conflict of wills that often accompanies disciplinary actions. Cautious teachers are less likely to get their needs met in the classroom because they defer to the threat of accountability or compromise for the sake of convenience.

Teachers who do not get their needs met in the classroom are more likely to become discontented and disenchanted with their jobs. They will view themselves and their students less kindly and will experience a sense of powerlessness that stems from lack of confidence and skills. As a consequence, they are likely to be reticent about taking charge of their classrooms. With their confidence undermined and their capabilities undernourished, they do not know how to express their needs, much less how to fulfill them.

Canter and Canter (1976) proposed a philosophy to help teachers express and meet their needs through the use of assertiveness training skills. According to Canter (1978; 1979, p. 34), assertive teachers, those who know how to express their needs, assume a position characterized by the following stances:

1. I will not allow any student to stop me from teaching for any reason.
2. I will not allow any student to stop another student from learning for any reason.
3. I will not permit students to engage in behavior that is not in their best interests and the best interests of others.

4. Whenever students choose to behave appropriately, they will be recognized and supported for that behavior.

This assertive discipline position espoused by Canter and Canter, and similarly advocated in *How to Discipline without Feeling Guilty: Assertive Relationships with Children* (Silberman & Wheelan, 1980), and *Toughlove* (York, York, & Wachtel, 1982), provides one striking way for teachers to express their commitment to young people. Teachers acknowledge at the outset that learning is hard and demanding work. Enjoyment and satisfaction sometimes accompany the process and are frequently associated with the outcomes, but the hardships and hassles are many. Teachers who faithfully discharge their responsibility believe that it increases the chances students will fulfill their needs. Thus, the first two stances complement one another. Together, they provide for the reciprocal arrangements that justify the teacher's use of legitimate power.

A commitment to each individual, the third assertive proposition, also addresses the satisfaction of student needs. Students should be helped to be an asset to themselves. Although learning is ultimately an individual attainment, each learner needs all the help that a teacher can give. A teacher can use expert power to devise instructional arrangements that increase student productivity and satisfaction and can use legitimate power to regulate student conduct and increase the incidence of behaviors that support learning. Some students are disposed to choose behaviors that do not advance educational aims. They would rather talk with another student about last night's TV program, a new student, or plans for the weekend.

The fourth stance dictates that assertive teachers support good behavior and make this behavior the springboard to more and more success. Some students enjoy considerable success in mathematics but do not enjoy similar triumphs in history. The adversity in one area can be offset by good fortune in the other. Other students will not be very successful in any part of the standard curriculum. Expert power helps the teacher individualize to improve performance.

How can teachers remain in control while being reasonable human beings (Canter, 1979)? First, teachers can recognize that noncompliance can be created by the way that adults communicate expectations. Teachers who do not really know what to say or how to say it and mean it are bound to be frustrated and sometimes furious with student responses to the message. Students who receive ambiguous messages are bound to think that the teacher is not really serious and continue to operate on this perception.

Canter and Canter (1976, pp. 162–166) have suggested four assertive communication techniques that can be easily learned:

1. Broken record
2. Active sending
3. Active receiving
4. Yes-or-no

The *broken-record technique* is one of the most effective ways for a teacher to keep a demand at the front end of a verbal exchange. In this instance, each student response is met by a phrase such as "I understand, but. . . . " or "That's not the point" followed by a statement of what the teacher wants or expects. The exchange might occur as follows:

> *Teacher:* "Jim, I want you to return to your seat."
> *Jim:* "But I have finished all my work and need something to do."
> *Teacher:* "I *understand, but* you do not leave your seat without my permission when I am presenting the lesson to the group. Return to your seat."
> *Jim:* "How can I get permission when you are busy?"
> *Teacher:* "*That's not the point;* you do not leave your seat without permission. Return to your seat."

Note that the teacher is not deterred from her original request. The student's remarks do not distract her; she will continue to uphold the rule. If a third such exchange does not get the job done, another action is called for. The teacher should have a follow-up position in mind when the broken-record technique does not produce results. Jim either returns to his seat or he suffers another consequence that underscores the teacher's intentions to have directions followed.

You have no doubt heard some frustrated person say, "What do I have to say to get through to you?" The second technique, *active sending,* is a variation on this theme. With this technique, the teacher secures a semblance of compliance by asking the student to repeat the request, framed as a "What did you hear me say?" question. By repeating the message, the student must substitute the teacher's words for his, acknowledge that he heard what was said, and at least subliminally accept the message.

> *Teacher:* "Sue, return to your seat. There are already two people at the pencil sharpener."
> *Sue:* "I can't do my work. I broke my pencil and don't have anything else to write with."
> *Teacher:* "Sue, what did you hear me say?"
> *Sue:* "Go back to my seat because there are already two people at the pencil sharpener."
> *Teacher:* "Yes, return to your seat."

Once again, the teacher remains true to the original request. The teacher wants the student at her desk being productive rather than standing in line at the pencil sharpener. The teacher taught students how to use work time effectively while waiting for assistance of any form and Sue is not following procedures for being an effective worker. The student appeals to the teacher's desire to get work done, but the teacher is not distracted from the procedure that needs to be followed.

Active receiving is a technique that the teacher uses to let students know that she has heard them but chooses to disregard their position. This technique is based on the disposition "I don't care what you say, it's what you do that counts." The teacher refuses to be dissuaded from her request, regardless of the justification the student might offer. Let us return to Sue's justification and use active receiving to deal with her response.

Sue: "I can't do my work. I broke my pencil and don't have anything else to write with."

Teacher: "I realize you broke your pencil and have nothing to write with" (active receiving). Now the teacher decides to state her request. "That's not the point, there are already two people at the pencil sharpener" (broken record). "Return to your seat" (original request).

There would be no resolution without the addition of the broken-record technique. Of course, the teacher could permit an exception to the rule. The teacher could also restate Sue's position, followed by silence, to encourage her to rethink her stance. This takes more time and may not be appropriate during fast-paced instructional periods. The teacher needs to be prepared for the exception-making rhetoric that students may use to sidestep the rules.

"I want to know, will you or won't you do what I asked?" is a familiar way for an exasperated teacher to bring a confrontation to a close. The fourth assertive communication technique is a variation of this common query. Rather than "Will you or won't you?" the teacher substitutes a more emphatic *yes or no*. The teacher is not interested in having the student ponder the options; the teacher merely wants to know what the student intends to do.

Teacher: "Jack, put the water pistol in your desk."
Jack: "I wasn't doing anything with it."
Teacher: "Are you going to put the water pistol in your desk? Yes or no?"
Jack: "Yes."

If Jack said "No," the teacher must be prepared to say, "Then hand it to me." This technique saves words. The teacher restricts the options so that there is no room for conversation or debate: Do it or do not do it. You have chosen to defy my request if you do not do it. The consequence for a no response may vary, but noncompliance is always met with a consequence, not a conversation.

Each of the four assertive communication techniques is to be used in a matter-of-fact manner. The teacher insists that students abide by the rules and procedures that were established and taught at the beginning of the year. Teachers who consistently stretch the rules through pointless verbal exchanges are eventually driven out of the classroom.

DYSFUNCTIONAL ALTERNATIVES TO ASSERTIVE LEADERSHIP

The Nonassertive Leadership Style

The nonassertive teacher permits some students to meet their needs at the expense of the teacher and other students. According to Canter and Canter (1976, pp. 20–26), the nonassertive teacher generally engages in one of five forms of behavior:

1. Hedging
2. Requesting an explanation

  3. Making threats
  4. Describing
  5. Ignoring

The most common form is *hedging on enforcement* by asking the student to accomplish an intermediate behavior:

❏ "I want you to *try* to stop pestering your neighbors."
❏ "You had better start *thinking* about losing recess before you sharpen your pencil without getting permission."
❏ "You had better start *being* more *concerned* about completing your work assignments."

In these examples, the teacher approaches the incident with an attitude of "Let's reach an informal agreement on this matter. I will not impose a penalty for the rule violation if you promise to be good." The promise is aimed at getting the student to *try* to be better or to *think* before engaging in unacceptable behavior.

A *request for an explanation* for the bad behavior is the second form of nonassertive behavior: "I want to know *why* you persist in roaming around the room when you are supposed to be doing seatwork." The teacher presumably believes that bad behavior is excusable if, first, the explanation warrants it or, second, there is reason to believe that in the absence of an excuse a student will desist from such behavior in the future. Both alternates work best when the student makes all the right noises and then is careful to escape detection in the future.

In the third form of nonassertive behavior, the teacher *makes threats* without informing students of the consequences that will follow repeated instances of the objectionable behavior: "You had better not let me catch you taking Barbara's pencil again." Students accustomed to idle threats ignore them. They wait for the teacher to settle down and then resume the same behaviors.

An observer does not have to spend much time in classrooms to witness examples of these nonassertive ways of dealing with disciplinary problems. In each instance, the student is not asked to stop or change behavior but to alter some internal condition that supposedly accounts for the behavior. The teacher permits the student to engage in good intentions rather than insisting on good behavior.

Some teachers believe that they are in command when they employ the verbal trappings of an assertive approach and simply *describe* the misbehavior, the fourth form of nonassertive behavior. Frequently they also add a request to stop: "Brett, you pulled Ellen's pigtail. Please do not do it again." On another occasion they demand compliance without indicating what will happen if the child refuses: "Brett, stop pulling Ellen's pigtail."

Sometimes they threaten consequences but do not follow through: "Brett, if you continue to pull Ellen's pigtails, I'm going to have to keep you after school." Brett cannot resist the challenge and gives Ellen's pigtail another jerk. His teacher says, "I've had it up to here with you," signaling to a point just below her chin. "Now stop it!"

In the fifth form of nonassertive behavior, teachers avoid a confrontation by *ignoring* unacceptable behavior: Ellen reports Brett's pigtail-pulling behavior. The teacher acknowledges that she saw it but tells Ellen that things will just get worse if she disciplines Brett. She tells Ellen to stay out of his reach and ignore him when she cannot. "He will soon tire of the whole thing" is the only reassurance Ellen gets.

Note that in each instance the student does not learn to choose and practice good behavior. The teacher, by requesting a change in motives rather than an improvement in conduct, avoids a confrontation or a contest of wills at the expense of another student. There is no reason to believe that Brett will change his ways. Other students will be his victims because the teacher has been victimized.

Why does a teacher choose to assume a nonassertive response style? The nonassertive style may have its origins in teachers' need for acceptance, which makes them particularly vulnerable to rejection. The fear of being rejected persuades them to avoid conflict and confrontations. When coupled with a high need to nurture, this disposition may contribute to a tendency to indulge students and promote dependency.

Rinne (1984) has used Berne's *Games People Play* (1964) to provide a provocative analysis of student game-playing behaviors, complete with illustrations and useful "functional routines" to counteract these "dysfunctional games." The fifteen games that Rinne identified, shown in Table 6–1, provide a particularly effective way to visualize situations that might evoke a nonassertive response style. Note that the student words that initiate each game are likely to evoke a defensive posture from the teacher. Can you imagine a teacher's response to each game with one of the five forms of nonassertive behavior?

Because students generally perceive teachers as having the upper hand, they must find rather subtle and indirect ways to turn a situation to their advantage. The nonassertive teacher is likely to capitulate, thereby selecting a dysfunctional response to the dysfunctional games of the student. Although the conflict may be resolved to the immediate satisfaction of both parties, the nonassertive solution permits each to evade responsibility, a practice that will gradually reduce their commitment to one another and to time spent on learning.

The Hostile Leadership Style

The hostile leadership style may actually evolve from the nonassertive one. In this approach, ideals grounded in the inherent goodness of young people become suspect. The teacher's anger is fueled by feelings of incompetence, and being liked becomes less important than being respected. Teachers conclude that respect is fostered by rigorous standards, but students resent and resist the "unreasonable" standards. As a result, teachers express indignation through verbal harassment and physical abuse.

Canter and Canter (1976, pp. 26–28) identify five ways in which hostile teachers attack students. These are similar to the communication no-no's of Ginott in Chapter 3. First, the "you" statement expresses the teacher's exasperation. The teacher's outrage is conveyed with a negative "put-down" message devoid of information that would help students change their ways:

- ❑ "You act like a first grader."
- ❑ "You do absolutely nothing unless I am on your case."
- ❑ "You persist in doing just the opposite of what I ask for."

Table 6–1
Games Students Play

Dysfunctional Game	Key Words
Who me?	"Who me? [What did I do?]"
I have an excuse.	"I left it in my locker."
Irrelevant comment.	"Hey, did you hear about ...?"
Let me help you.	"Let me do that [for you]."
You're neat.	"I learn a lot in this class."
Shocking behavior.	"This class stinks!"
I gotta go.	"Can I get a drink of water?"
Time for the bell.	"Is it time to go yet?"
Helpless.	"I can't!"
Why do we have to?	"What good is this to me?"
Why don't we ever have any fun?	"Why does the other class get to ... and we don't?"
It's your fault.	"You didn't tell us!"
Teach me if you can.	"I don't wanna."
You can't make me.	"Who do you think you are?"
Teacher's gone.	"Is she gone yet?"

Source: From *Attention: The Fundamentals of Classroom Control* (pp. 293–314) by C. H. Rinne, 1984, Columbus, OH: Merrill/Macmillan. Copyright © 1984 by Merrill/Macmillan. Reprinted by permission.

Note the negative value judgment that focuses on what the student does or does not do. There are no clues as to the desired behavior.

Second, the teacher retaliates for a personal affront by cutting a student down to size.

Third, the teacher makes uncomplimentary remarks denigrating the student's character:

❑ "You act like an idiot."
❑ "You are so childish."
❑ "You couldn't act intelligent if your life depended on it."
❑ "You are the worst person I have ever had in class."

Fourth, hostile teachers threaten dire consequences, without consistent follow-through. Teachers out of control often promise to impose harsh penalties (e.g., clean every window in this classroom, stay after school the remainder of the semester, scrub the locker room for a week), but they are neither able nor inclined to carry them out. Their outbursts are not taken seriously by students who know the costs to the teacher would be too great.

The threat of legal penalties sometimes forestalls physical abuse, the fifth form of abuse, but teachers who feel pinned against the wall may come out swinging.

Sometimes the physical abuse is difficult for others to detect (pinching, squeezing); at other times it is so provocative (banging a student against a locker) as to make others cringe at the sight.

Regardless of the reasons for this style, it tends to provoke resentment, hostility, and frequently revenge. The conflict escalates, and battle lines are drawn. There is seldom a graceful way for either party to retreat. Sides are chosen, and the derision and divisiveness further undermine the climate for learning. As the climate deteriorates, so does the morale of all participants. Further aggression is minimized by a truce that lowers the expectations each party has for the other. Peace prevails, with occasional skirmishes and upheavals, as long as rewards are easily come by and punishments are not overly severe.

SPECULATIONS ABOUT THE PROGRESSION OF MANAGEMENT STYLES

Beginning teachers rarely use the hostile management style as a dominant leadership approach. They are more likely to be nonassertive because of their desire to promote and preserve harmonious relationships at all costs. They visualize a classroom where congeniality and cooperation abound and students intuitively understand and appreciate the teacher's role in sustaining this pleasant state of affairs.

The teacher who is intent on harmony chooses immediate measures without regard to long-term consequences. He may temporarily win a student's goodwill by telling her to be concerned about a bad behavior rather than insisting that she behave in a previously specified way. However, the student still does not know how she is supposed to behave and what will happen when she does not. Thus, the student misbehaves again and again to find out. Soon the teacher, exasperated and disappointed because the student has taken advantage of his patience and goodwill, lashes out at her for being a perpetual problem. This hostile outbreak, often provoked by a minor incident, seems totally unreasonable and unfair to the student and her classmates, who have forgotten the preceding infractions.

A teacher can only pack so many frustrations into a barrel of restraint before blowing the lid. Thus, the nonassertive response style, which seemingly produces temporary solutions, magnifies the problem while mollifying the student. Is it any wonder the hostile response style is more characteristic of experienced teachers who continue to take their job seriously? We believe that the hostile response style is often the eventual penalty that teachers and students pay for nonassertive leadership.

STUDENT REACTIONS TO DYSFUNCTIONAL LEADERSHIP

Sidetracking Tactics

The use of a dysfunctional leadership style is more likely to evoke student behavior that is also dysfunctional, at least from the teacher's point of view. Regardless of the nature of the offense or the severity of the consequences, some students will try to downgrade the disruption and avoid the penalty. Some are also ingenious at escaping detection. Canter and Canter have suggested that students caught red-handed will often plead their case by using one of four sidetracking tactics (1976, pp. 82–87):

1. Saying, "You don't like me."
2. Crying
3. Pleading, "I'm sorry, give me another chance."
4. Being belligerent

These tactics tend to move the teacher into a nonassertive response style, and each tactic has proven effective because teachers prefer to forgive and forget.

"You don't like me" is the favorite ploy of children who sense that the teacher places a premium on being liked and liking. These teachers are generally overprotective and fair to a fault. They underestimate the resilience of children and are overly concerned about the harmful psychological effects of rejection. They believe that children cannot distinguish between rejecting the deed and rejecting the doer. Children find it convenient to capitalize on this disposition and drive the teacher into a defensive posture. Rather than insisting on compliance with the rule, the teacher enumerates the student's good qualities and laudable behaviors and becomes trapped by a preponderance of evidence that favors a light sentence, usually a verbal rebuke. The student has succeeded in escaping appropriate negative consequences by using the adult's vulnerability.

Crying, another tactic that provokes a nonassertive response style, is effective because it makes the teacher feel either helpless or guilty. Teachers feel helpless because the other person has suddenly taken charge of the situation; they feel guilty because they assume responsibility for the student's plight. Moments ago the teacher was in control of the situation and was about to discipline a student who had behaved inappropriately. Now the teacher has been placed in a position that calls for giving comfort or receiving absolution. The student has been able to escape negative consequences by using the adult's vulnerability to hurt feelings.

"I'm sorry, give me another chance" is a third sidetracking tactic that appeals to fair-minded teachers. They are ready to back down when students acknowledge wrongdoing and promise to mend their ways. They equate acquiescence and assurances with a genuine intent to improve. However, pledges made under duress are not to be trusted. It is far better to build trust through trustworthy behavior.

Belligerence, a fourth sidetracking tactic, provokes an educator's hostile response style. There can be no truce because both parties have decided that they must win to save face. The standoff position favors the individual least able to fight back. Generally, the teacher can win the battle, but the teacher's win often contributes to a student's declaring war. The more frequent and prolonged the battles are, the more likely the teacher will lose.

Reasons Why Manipulative Tactics Work

Many teachers are unfamiliar with assertive communication strategies or have not developed the skills to use them. Therefore, it is not surprising that students win many verbal squabbles and often escape from disciplinary incidents unscathed. Despite teachers' being in the communication business, little is done to develop their communication skills. Teacher-educators talk about the importance of using class discussions to advance selected educational aims but then do little to help teachers acquire the communication skills associated with this activity. Similarly, they teach that good management requires an explicit statement of the rules. Then they neglect to demonstrate, develop, and refine communication skills that ensure that the rules will be enforced. Teachers' lack of preparation in communication is therefore one reason why the manipulative tactics of students are effective.

Another reason is the very nature of the adult–child relationship, which is often predictable and seldom egalitarian. Teachers are just too busy to follow-through on their demands (Greenberg, 1969; Wayson, 1980). Students know that they can ignore a teacher reprimand and resume the offensive behavior because the teacher's attention is soon devoted to other matters. Or they can conveniently forget to observe a consequence because teachers often prefer to do the same. Teachers cannot afford to dwell long on a single incident. Negative consequences can be as bothersome to the teacher as they are to the offender. The sheer magnitude of the teacher's task favors students. The latter soon learn that there are some situations in which rule violations are not easily detected and others in which only cursory attention is given to them.

The hectic pace and myriad responsibilities of teachers also favor students who are adept at creating confusing and conflicting accounts of a disciplinary incident. Students may accentuate the details that shift the blame to the other party, which forces the teacher to adjudicate the matter through a lengthy line of questions for which he or she has neither the time nor the patience. Unwilling or unable to sift through details and distribute responsibility, the teacher drops the matter with a mild rebuke to the offending parties.

Much of what happens in school is arbitrarily decided by adults. Many adults are not comfortable with this arrangement and feel uneasy about imposing their will on students. Being so disposed, they are less inclined to insist on compliance with their standards of judgment and codes of conduct. Students who sense this ambivalence will use it to their advantage. All of the sidetracking tactics cited earlier are partially effective because adults are uncomfortable with and unsure about their use of authority.

Many students avoid negative consequences by portraying themselves as defenseless and helpless victims of this arbitrary system. They find that pleading for understanding and mercy is not nearly as effective as expressing their contempt for the system and their regrets for those who have to administer it. When teachers are confronted with contempt for the system, they wonder about the reasonableness of both the rule and the punishment. Their confidence in their leadership role and in the system is undermined.

As we have seen, educator–student interactions are complex. Most of the transactions between educators and students are problem free and serve the needs of both parties. However, students do sometimes choose behaviors that are not in their own or others' best interests. These occasions call for an assertive leadership style. Teachers can use assertive communication to minimize the occurrence of these problems and to solve them with a minimum of disruption.

DIRECTIVE CONDUCT COMPETENCIES: THE BASIC CLASSROOM MANAGEMENT PLAN

Dreikurs and Cassell (1972) rely on the use of logical consequences, which are impersonal and not based on personal authority, and on encouragement to assist students in positive behaviors. Their approach assists educators in using democratic principles in democratic schools, while remaining assertive and directive according to the demands of each situation. This section will prepare you to assertively, yet democratically, and competently manage classroom discipline plans.

In addition to developing an assertive communication style, teachers need competencies in administering their basic classroom management plan. Sprick, Sprick, and Garrison (1993) describe the competencies as follows. The essence of the first competency is this: Know at all times what you want your students to do. In Chapters 2 and 3 you learned to set the limits—and involve students in doing so—by stating schoolwide and classroom rules in explicit terms. The more precisely stated and taught rules are, the less room there is for error. The more latitude there is with respect to what is acceptable, the more students will seek clarity by testing the full range of possibilities. Teachers should restrict the possibilities when there are certain behaviors that they want without exception. However, a teacher's rules cannot violate those set by the principal, superintendent, school board, and state department of education (Gathercoal, 1990).

Rules are in effect throughout the day and there are additional procedures for specific activities. You are acquainted with procedures that are used to minimize disruptions and maximize time on task when, for example, students are asked to form a reading group or to exchange papers for grading purposes (see Chapters 3 and 5). As discussed earlier, such procedures increase student performance.

Note that some of the rules leave room for interpretation. For example, how can the teacher be certain students know precisely what is meant by "Be respectful of all people and property"? Planning and review sessions that teach examples and nonexamples can help clarify behavioral standards. This increases the probability that teachers will act assertively with respect to these standards. Students are not sure when teachers are not sure. Students who are not sure test the rules to ascertain teacher intentions; teachers who are not sure tend to be too lenient. Thus, the teacher may have to teach a rule by correcting instances of unacceptable behavior. But it is even better to teach what a rule means by way of a preventive or prosocial approach (Schloss, 1983) rather than with a corrective strategy.

The essence of Sprick et al.'s second competency (1993) is this: Teachers' control and administration of consequences (Rich, 1988) are an important feature in a conduct management plan. Educators and students typically manage behavior by managing consequences and implementing educational interventions. Both positive and negative consequences and education are used to increase the probability

Responsible behaviors are posted in a middle school classroom.

that students will exhibit rule-governed behavior. When students need additional support beyond the use of positive and negative consequences, interventions that emphasize teaching-desired replacement behaviors are used to support students. Teachers may work with assistance teams to implement such interventions.

Acknowledging Responsible Behaviors

Consequences for misbehavior are needed but rarely turn behavior around without also acknowledging responsible behavior. This is the most powerful element of the basic classroom management plan. It must include both positive interactions (see Chapter 4) and other structured procedures for acknowledging responsible behavior.

To be able to acknowledge appropriate behavior, you must monitor whether students are meeting expectations. Visually scan the room on a frequent basis. Move about the room during independent and cooperative group work times. Some teachers like to take notes on a record form. Notes can be used to identify students who deserve recognition for special or sustained efforts. You can acknowledge appropriate behavior by observing, smiling, and nodding. Notes can also be used to identify problem areas. For example, when some students have similar problems on activities, teachers may need to clarify their instructions (see Chapter 5). Notes can be used to identify students who have problems that require minor interventions. Finally, notes can be used to provide documentation of problems that may require referral.

Verbal praise for successful behavior can be used and should be relatively brief, age-appropriate, and frequent. The following examples are for a first grader and an eighth grader, respectively.

❑ "Kevin, you are being responsible for your behavior. I can see that you are listening and watching."

❑ "Jerod, your contributions to our discussion really added to our understanding of the issues."

Acknowledge responsible behavior with written feedback to a student by sending a "Special Note from Your Teacher's Desk." You can use a phone call or written feedback to parents or guardians for responsible behavior, a job well done, or general appreciation. Certificates of merit can be used intermittently throughout the year or be given to a few individuals each week in a regularly scheduled five-minute ceremony. These need to be used equitably by acknowledging all students for their merits, not just high achieving or popular students.

Educators seldom give responsibility to students who have difficulties, but meeting a responsibility yields a greater sense of responsibility. Look for ways to give students additional responsibility. Figure 3–5 includes a number of activities and social responsibilities that can be used as positive consequences. The following comment shows how a social responsibility was used to acknowledge responsible behavior.

❑ "Nasha, you have turned in your homework for three days in a row. How would you like to be my homework checker this week? During attendance and lunch count, you would collect the papers and check them off."

Finally, it is important to remember that infrequent, major rewards given to a few students tend to be less effective than frequent recognition of daily efforts.

Correcting Irresponsible and Inappropriate Behavior

Misbehavior is generally a mistake and constitutes a learning opportunity. When you treat misbehavior accordingly, students will begin to view mistakes as learning opportunities, also.

A first step in managing inappropriate classroom behavior is to brainstorm a list of all potential misbehavior that could occur in a day's time. Make sure each item on the list is an observable behavior (e.g., disrespectful to each other is observable in terms of putting each other down or making sarcastic comments).

The second step is to determine whether brainstormed misbehaviors should be handled with ignoring, consequences, or corrective education. The third step is to brainstorm all possible negative consequences and determine which ones you feel comfortable using. Mentally or verbally rehearse how to handle different situations using various negative consequences. That way you can base your decisions on some experience before you prematurely determine that you will always or never use certain negative consequences.

To be effective, consequences must be implemented consistently, fairly, and calmly. Students must also be informed in advance that certain behaviors will lead to predetermined consequences. Some in-class consequences that teachers can choose from include ignoring, proximity control, gentle verbal reprimands, cues and prompts, positive practice, time owed, time-out, behavioral contracting, and goal setting. These strategies are described on the basis of Sprick et al.'s work (1993).

From the following menu of consequences, select the ones you think you would be most comfortable using to teach students to behave responsibly. They should also be the least intrusive in the classroom. Select mild classroom consequences for mild misbehavior that cannot be ignored. Try to have some logical association with the inappropriate behavior. Stay calm and consistent when you use them.

Ignoring

Sometimes students engage in misbehavior because they need attention. Any correction at all from the teacher serves as a form of attention and actually increases the misbehavior. This is because some students find negative teacher attention just as reinforcing as positive attention. Sprick et al. (1993) suggest the following guidelines when using ignoring as a conduct management technique. First, if misbehavior increases with verbal reprimands, ignoring should be considered. Another rule of thumb is to ignore student misbehavior that does not get in the way of teaching or in the way of students' learning.

Ignoring is the only response to misbehavior that does not require teacher time. If you plan to use ignoring with a student, hold a planned discussion and collaborate with the student. The teacher must also seek opportunities to interact positively with the student. Therefore, tell the student that you will pay a lot of attention to her when she is following the class rules but that you won't be able to see or hear her when she engages in irresponsible behavior. Be sure to give examples of responsible and irresponsible behavior. Consistently ignore misbehavior in both body language and talk. Do not interrupt instruction. Keep teaching. Student behavior will get worse before it gets better. Plan to give ignoring two weeks before you judge its effectiveness.

Proximity Control

Proximity control occurs when the teacher moves into the space of a student who is not following the rules. This may be sufficient to assist the student in monitoring his own behavior.

Gentle Verbal Reprimands

According to Sprick et al. (1993), gentle verbal reprimands are used when students do not know that a behavior is inappropriate. These reprimands are also used when students are unaware that they are engaging in inappropriate behavior. Teachers can give gentle verbal reprimands alone or follow them with instructions that provide positive practice of an alternative behavior. A suggested script follows that can be used at the beginning of the school year when teaching students how you will be using the consequence of gentle verbal reprimands. The second example of a script is used later in the year after students are familiar with the use of gentle verbal reprimands.

Script for Use at Beginning of Year

"Class, sometimes a student will do something that is not acceptable or not okay in our room. For instance, one student may make a sarcastic remark to another person or about another person. First, I will quietly tell the student that the comment may have been meant to tease but it felt hurtful to the peer. Second, I will remind the student of the class rule 'Treat everyone with dignity and respect.' Then I will suggest a different comment to make in the future. For example: Cora, that comment was hurtful. It would be better to tell Ben 'thank you' for the assistance he was giving you or not to say anything."

Script for Use Later in the Year

"Andrea, you need to watch the film. Remember our rule, 'Be ready to learn.'"

Go over to the student; do not give reprimands from across the room. Use neutral or supportive tones. Avoid increasing the emotional intensity if feedback is repeated.

Verbal Cues and Warnings

All too often a teacher deals with a minor incident like this:

- ❏ "Harry, what are you doing?"
- ❏ "What are you supposed to be doing?"
- ❏ "Well, why aren't you doing it?"
- ❏ "What if everyone were to behave that way when they wanted to be first?"
- ❏ "Harry, you know better than that."
- ❏ "How many times do I have to tell you?"

The teacher wants Harry to change his behavior. She has already tried using eye contact and proximity control. A brief assertive statement will suffice if she does not think that Harry knows what he is doing or what he is supposed to do: "Harry, I need you to follow our rule of being respectful to all people." A statement like this will probably be unnecessary after a few planning and review sessions. Harry will know what he is doing and what he is supposed to be doing.

Verbal cues and warnings are appropriate consequences prior to giving a more severe consequence such as in-class time-out. For example, the teacher might say, "Sonya, your tone of voice is starting to sound impatient. You need to take a deep breath. Then lower your voice."

Note that the cue makes allowances for misbehavior but does not excuse it. The teacher does not sanction the unacceptable behavior, but there is no retribution. A warning helps to reestablish order without making a demand on either party. It is a signal to students to regain control and take charge of their behavior. It also helps the nonassertive teacher who may be more willing to press claims for decent behavior if the student has had the benefit of one departure from the norms.

Delaying

Delaying is used when a student engages in excessive misbehavior to get attention. The teacher might say, "Sonya, that was a complaint. We can talk about it later during your discussion time." Another example is, "Monny, you are starting to tattle. Remember you are to write it down, place it in the box, and wait until Response Time."

Preferential Seating

Assign the student to sit in a different section of the room. Seat students close to the source of instruction when they have hearing or visual problems and when they have difficulty paying attention or need more teacher assistance to be successful. Seat students away from peers with whom they get in trouble and with peers that have good classroom social skills.

Time Owed

Time owed communicates to the student that misbehavior wastes class time and needs to be repaid during a time that is valued by the student. It is recommended that you set up small amounts of time owed for each infraction. For example, do not have students owe an entire recess for each infraction. Instead, keep a student in from recess, one minute per infraction. Teachers need to decide what the student should be doing during time owed. There are two basic options: Discuss the problem or sit doing nothing. The more boring, the better. Here is an example of what a teacher would say when giving a student time owed as a consequence: "That was an example of not listening. You owe one minute of after-class time." Secondary teachers and librarians, physical education teachers, or music specialists who have the student for only one period may need to consider in-class time-out.

The loss of minutes from recess, eating lunch alone, or having to remain after class/school are social deprivation consequences. Time owed is a natural consequence for not using time in class well. At the beginning of the year, teachers need to talk to students about the times of the day that they can return to her classroom to pay back the time owed.

Let's consider how time owed would work with Vanessa, a student who talks when she shouldn't. The teacher first uses eye contact. She then moves to proximity control. If neither of these negative consequences is effective and Vanessa continues to talk, the teacher gives a gentle verbal reprimand: "Vanessa, I need you to follow our rule of listening when someone else is speaking." This does not stop Vanessa either. Soon she is whispering to the boy next to her. The teacher now says, "Vanessa, you owe two minutes." The amount of time owed generally depends on how much time the teacher thinks Vanessa has been off task. Sprick et al. (1993) recommend starting quite small. For example, two minutes of time owed could be completed between classes at the middle school and high school levels. This is enough time to be an inconvenience for students and gets their attention that you are serious about following classroom rules.

For some students, staying in the classroom and missing several minutes of recess or staying after school may not be a negative consequence. They like teacher attention and do not have to compete with others for it during these times. If this appears to be the case, select a different negative consequence. During very hot or cold days elementary students may also prefer to lose recess time and remain indoors. Teachers can manage these situations by arranging for students with time owed to sit quietly in their seats doing nothing or to stand outside by the school building wall during recess.

Some would argue that a student who has to do assignments during time owed will be less favorably inclined toward the area of study because of the emotional distress associated with the situation. However, the time owed penalty should be evaluated by looking at the circumstances that provoked it. Insisting that the student use the time to work on missed assignment time would be a logical consequence (Dreikurs & Cassell, 1972) if the rule infractions had prevented the student from completing the assignment in class. The logic: If students choose to spend class time unproductively, then the lost time will be recouped on the topic that suffered because of the irresponsible behavior. Allowing a student to sit idly after school teaches another lesson—one that may be more harmful than doing an assignment under protest.

Staying after school, even for a few minutes, takes away a precious commodity from most students; after-school time includes a great variety of options, which have to be temporarily set aside. Worse yet, the student is left behind. After the allotted time, friends may have already left the customary gathering place; even if everyone is there, the latecomer has already missed all of the preliminary excitement associated with after-school activities. Penalties imposed by coaches and extracurricular activity sponsors also can increase the inducement to abide by the rules.

Time-Out

In-Class Time-Out.   Time-out is to be used with care. It is typically reserved for students who engage in misbehavior frequently (Sprick et al., 1993). Time-out serves essentially the same purpose as a warning. Students are removed from the social stimuli most want. Time-out may consist of any of the following: Student sits with head down on desk, is unable to participate in a group activity, is seated toward the back of the room and turned away from the group, or is seated in an area of the room that is screened or partitioned so that the student can hear but not see the events taking place in the classroom.

Duration of time-out is one minute for each year of age with no more than five minutes total. Some teachers have students set a timer when they enter time-out. Other teachers prefer to have the student return to class when they are ready to follow the rules. The open-ended time frame puts the student in control; the door is always open to those who are prepared to return and act responsibly.

Determine the length of time in advance. Five minutes total for sixth grade and above is recommended. Five minutes or less is recommended for younger students, according to age and sophistication. Kindergarten and first graders should have one minute. Use a timer so that you do not forget the student in the time-out location. Some students do not go to time-out immediately but dawdle, argue, and even refuse to go. Escort younger students to time-out. Tell them that the timer begins when they are in time-out and quiet. Inform older students that the amount of time they take to get to time-out will be recorded and they will owe that time after class. If students misbehave after returning from time-out, calmly send them back. Students with serious behavior difficulties may need to return to time-out repeatedly in the same morning or afternoon. This is not something that many educators experience but if you do, stay calm and consistent. Consider these scripts:

- ❏ "That was an example of not following directions. Go to time-out and think about other ways you might have handled that situation. You may return to your seat when the timer rings."
- ❏ "That was an example of not following directions. Go to time-out and think about other ways you might have handled that situation. You may return to your seat when you have filled out a Behavior Improvement Form."

The teacher can facilitate students' using time-out for reflection on their behavior by preparing a form for students to fill out before returning to class. The form can simply ask the student to state the unacceptable behavior (What were you doing?), the desired behaviors (What should you have been doing?), and the consequences of future misbehavior (What will happen if you continue to misbehave?). The student can return with the form when the time elapses. Nothing is said when the student returns. Later, it is advisable to hold a planned discussion. Some students who need a time-out also need ongoing problem solving to help them learn replacement behaviors.

Time-Out in Another Location.   Time-out in a place outside the classroom is reserved for behavior that is highly disruptive (Sprick et al., 1993). Examples of this include overt defiance toward adults, noncompliance, loud sustained disruptions, highly aggressive behavior, and sustained screaming. As you write your plan for the use of time-out outside of the classroom determine what behaviors will result in removal from your classroom. Decide where the student will go, how long the student will be there, what the student will do there, who will provide supervision of time-out, and what the student needs to do to reenter your classroom.

Some teachers seat students in the hall or send them to the principal's office for time-out. Neither of these settings is as desirable as an isolated place in the classroom. There are just too many interesting things happening in the halls and the principal's office. There is no incentive to behave acceptably when a student is singled out for attention and becomes a party to events that may be a sharp and interesting contrast to the classroom. Keeping a student just out of reach of an enticing classroom activity, without being able to participate, is much more effective.

Notification of Parents/Guardians

The purpose of a parental or guardian contact is to keep them informed and to have them encourage the student to behave more responsibly. Educators need to suggest that guardians talk to their children. Make it clear that the school will take care of the consequences and do not lead the parents to believe that they should do the punishing. Guardian contact should never be considered an effective consequence for chronic misbehavior. However, it is effective when the student rarely engages in misbehavior and is from a home with firm but supportive parents.

Very few students want their guardians notified of their problems in school. Guardians generally tell their children to mind the teacher and generally feel let down when they do not. A guardian may not always agree with the teacher's rules or their application, but most guardians want their children to be respected and respectful.

When a parent or guardian contact is used as a consequence, the student should immediately go to the principal's office. Arrangements for this contingency should be built into the management plan so that the consequence can be carried out without delay. A delay gives students time to think of ways to report the incident in a less objectionable light.

When the teacher and student arrive at the office, the student should be asked to name the behaviors that have made this call to the parents necessary. The response is corrected for accuracy, if needed. Having reviewed these matters, the student is prepared to answer the two questions almost any parent will ask: "What did you do?" and "What will you do to follow the rules next time?" Parents want to understand the magnitude of the problem and to know how subsequent plans might involve them.

Unless the guardians have indicated they disagree, the student should be the one to place the call, for a number of reasons. First, the teacher does not absorb the parent's initial displeasure. Second, many children come from single-parent homes or from homes where both parents work, and a student is more likely to get through to a parent at work. The person who receives the call, when hearing a student's voice, is much more likely to interpret the situation as an emergency and bring the parent to the phone. Third, the student begins the conversation with a description of the problem and what she contributed to it. The parent is less likely to come to the student's defense under these circumstances. When the student talks about what she will do the next time, it serves as a verbal rehearsal and commitment to the parent.

The parent is now a part of helping the student be accountable. Parents are likely to influence their children and say, "You get back in that class and behave yourself. I don't want to have to come to school to pick you up." An inconvenience to parents is one way to get immediate cooperation.

Requiring students to call guardians should not mean that educators expect guardians to solve problems alone. Problem solving is expected to be a collaborative effort between guardians and educators. Educators with knowledge and skills in schoolwide and classroom management have many interventions to try. They realize, however, that ecological theory suggests that forging home–school partnerships increases the success of school-based interventions.

Written Behavioral Contract

The least severe consequences contain an element of choice and are generally behavior improvement plans requiring teacher–student, and occasionally teacher–student–parent, cooperation. The *written behavioral contract* best illustrates this cooperative solution to a disciplinary problem. The contract is often used when the regular classroom conduct code and allied positive and negative consequences do not work.

The behavioral contract generally includes at least three items: behavioral expectations, negative consequences, and a specific time period. First, behavioral expectations should be explicitly stated. The behaviors that are direct opposites of the behavior that the teacher will not tolerate should be specified first.

Second, negative consequences that will be applied for failure to exhibit the aforementioned behaviors are stated. Some teachers like to include a corresponding list of positive consequences for conduct becoming a responsible student. Students may be invited to participate in making both lists of consequences. Sometimes a well-intentioned student will choose overly severe negative consequences for bad behavior and too little compensation for good behavior. Teachers have to be a moderating influence during this consequence selection process.

Finally, a time period for the contract should be specified. Remember that students who require more severe measures are generally unable to handle long-term commitments. Abiding by the terms of a contract for a single class period may be a big achievement for some students. Success should be the occasion for another contract. The same contract may be reinstated, or a new contract changing the positive and negative consequences might be written.

Teachers who use contracts have to teach contract-writing skills to students. Students soon become proficient at stating goals as specific behaviors because they are increasingly sensitized to the behaviors that help and hinder. Lists of positive and negative consequences can be used to assist students in preparing their plans. Students can be helped to choose and administer their consequences. They should get more satisfaction from the by-products of their good behavior as they become more responsible. Completed seatwork assignments enable them to participate in class discussions, answer more test items correctly, and get better grades. These achievements produce a sense of self-satisfaction that endures long after the short-lived pleasure that accompanies receiving five more minutes of free time, being excused from a quiz or an assignment, or serving as a hall monitor for a day. Students are ready to write contracts that cover longer periods of time after having successfully fulfilled the requirements of several assignments. Keep in mind that students can tire of negotiating contracts, too. There are various types of behavioral contracting, some less structured than others that prove useful.

Example of Using Negative Classroom Consequences

To illustrate how educators can use in-class consequences to manage behavior problems, let's look at Sprick's plan (1985) to reduce swearing. Students need to learn that swearing is unacceptable in some settings and will be offensive to many people. Sometimes swearing is against the rules. Some people are not offended by swearing but others are. In the teaching process, teachers should not make a big issue of swearing, but they do need to help students see that swearing is not acceptable.

Students swear for a number of reasons: They hear swearing a lot in their environment; it is a habit and is hard to break; swearing makes students feel more sophisticated or tough; students swear to antagonize adults; and students are hooked on emotional conflict.

It is recommended that the teacher first discuss the problem of swearing with his class. The discussion might go something like the following:

Script

"I am concerned about the amount of swearing that I have been hearing throughout the building. My own feelings about swearing are irrelevant; they don't count. What does count is that many people believe that swearing in a public setting is not okay. Public settings are schools, places of employment, and so forth. Swearing is offensive to many people and these people will judge you solely on the basis of your language. If you choose to swear, other people will conclude that you are a 'bad' person, that you have no regard for others, or that you are illiterate. You may not be welcome in their homes. They may not want you to date their daughter. You might not be selected to represent the school or a club. Many opportunities will be given to others and not you because people are afraid that you will embarrass them. You could lose a job opportunity because of your swearing, especially if it becomes a habit.

"I need for you to not use bad language in school. I am telling you about this so that you can work on improving your language. If everybody works on it on their own, great. If not, I will need to set up a consequence for swearing."

When the situation begins to improve, tell students, "I am pleased that you were able to handle the problem of swearing. It's great that I do not have to impose a consequence." If the situation does not improve within a week, use a mild consequence. You do not want to make a big deal out of swearing. An example of a mild consequence would be owing five minutes from their lunch period, break, after school, or from any enjoyable class activity. The amount of time does not need to be excessive. Another example would be filling out a behavior improvement form. Walking the length of the hallway could be used for out-of-class swearing behaviors.

The teacher would discuss the problem and future consequence with students. Let students know that they seem to need help in breaking their habit of swearing in class. Explain the consequence. If you use owing time, specify the amount of time that will be owed for each incidence of swearing and when the time will be paid. Provide students with examples of exclamations that are acceptable by generating them with the students. Tell students that any questionable comments will be considered swearing. Make sure that students understand the consequences and ask if there are any questions.

It is critical that you stay calm, unemotional, and consistent when giving consequences. Do not argue or debate with the student. Tell the student to talk with you after class. Praise the class for their self-control if swearing has been a large group problem. Praise individuals if only a few students have been a problem. When a large number of students are unmotivated to meet expectations, or if only one or two students are unmotivated, it may be time to investigate the wisdom of structured reinforcement systems (see discussion later in this chapter).

Setting Limits Outside the Classroom

As Sprick et al. (1993) point out, large numbers of students move from one place in the school building to another many times a day. Halls are crowded and chaotic with running, shouting students and slammed locker doors. It is easy for students to carry their boisterousness into the classroom. It is hard to calm down and be ready to learn with all materials when the bell rings.

It is important that teachers remind themselves that this behavior is natural for students. They are very interested in spending time with friends and they must talk loudly to be heard above the hallway commotion. On the other hand, the fewer the consequences for hallway behavior, the faster and louder students become. Sprick (1985) offers the metaphor of adults speeding on highways that are not frequently patrolled. Does the metaphor get your attention? Sprick offers some helpful tips on setting limits outside the classroom. We will look at improving hallway and cafeteria behavior, specifically. Those two examples should help you be creative in planning your management of other areas outside the classroom.

Supervising hallway behavior can accomplish the goal of getting the student body to take pride in adult-like functioning. Here's how it works. Seeing faculty in hallways prompts students to have appropriate behavior just like seeing a police car prompts adults to drive at the speed limit. Students who break the rules are more likely to pay the consequence and this results in quieter hallways. Last, but not least, supervision time prompts staff and student interaction. Supervisors should be relaxed and friendly and talk, greet, and joke with students.

First, staff must meet as a group and come to consensus on expectations and procedures. They will need to list unacceptable behaviors (e.g., running, shouting, slamming lockers, swearing, racial slurs) and agree on ways students can acceptably engage in frequently occurring borderline behaviors (e.g., affection in public, name-calling, disagreements).

Second, staff must list consequences for each misbehavior keeping in mind that minor misbehaviors (e.g., running, slamming locker doors, shouting, swearing, and inappropriate intimacy) should have mild and easily implemented consequences with no paperwork. An example of a mild consequence for running would be to go to the end of the hallway and walk back. More serious misbehaviors, like talking back and noncompliance, should be referred to the office. (See Chapter 2 on Schoolwide Discipline.)

Third, staff need to determine how they are going to provide ongoing hallway supervision. For about the first week of hallway supervision, it is recommended that every teacher be in the halls during passing times (Sprick et al., 1993). Massive supervision changes behavior rapidly. If the first week goes well, change to each teacher assigned to the halls during two or more passing periods per day. Structure this so that teachers have been assigned times in a way that every passing period is covered.

Write a positively stated rule that is part of the schoolwide rules. Use this rule to teach students the expectations for hallway behavior. Remember to teach the rule using examples and nonexamples. Also teach the negative consequences.

Provide students with positive feedback when improvement is noted (e.g., announcement over intercom or at a pep assembly, article in school or community paper, announcements in parent newsletter).

Student conduct in the rest rooms, cafeteria, playground, and buses can be subject to the same procedures. For example, cafeteria behavior is not learned by osmosis—these behaviors must be taught too. Teaching them in a chaotic twenty-minute lunch period is seldom effective or efficient, but a planning session five to ten minutes before lunch time and a review session immediately following is recommended. Once again, the teacher must describe and simulate the conditions, create episodes, ask students to role-play model behaviors, and use the review session to augment them.

Similarly, other self-management skills can be taught through planning and review sessions. Investments early in the year will increase dividends at the end. Capital gains will be counted in teachers' own emotional well-being and that of their students. Achievement gains will also accompany this investment in good behavior.

All of the consequences discussed in the preceding sections are merely illustrative. The teacher may have to alter consequences for some classes or some individuals. Some students might get a negative consequence for the first infraction. Although students start each day with a clean slate, some students may merit more consequences sooner. This decision can be communicated during planning and review sessions, when creating individual behavioral contracts, or during individual conferences with students.

For example, neither a gentle verbal reprimand nor taking away play objects reduced the incidence of Allisa's unacceptable behavior. The teacher knew that Allisa had all the necessary skills to complete assignments. Allisa was therefore informed that beginning tomorrow, she would owe time during recess (or after school) if she played with objects at her desk rather than completing her assignment. Allisa did not like to stay after school and was eager to go home and play. The same menu of consequences was used, but getting to the potent ones faster was viewed as the best solution in Allisa's case.

Some teachers decide to change the specific consequences after some experience with their plans. A warning may result in a student missing the next session on the computer, for example. Time owed could mean a student eats lunch in a designated "no talking" area or a student must remain in the classroom five minutes after other students leave for recess or home. Choosing effective consequences can be almost as important as consistently applying them when inappropriate behavior warrants their use.

Criteria for Choosing and Using Consequences

The unpleasant consequences ought to be ones that a teacher feels comfortable using. Teachers may have been told "good" teachers do not punish an entire class for the misdeeds of a few recalcitrant students. Yet a teacher may want to use the practice if the unacceptable behavior is a group occurrence. Some teachers might be reluctant to impose the consequence because they fear reprisals from the innocent parties. Yet group consequences may be the most effective way to teach the principle "We are all partially responsible for one another's behavior."

Some teachers might put "call parents" on their list of consequences, even though they are not comfortable taking this step. They may think that calling parents is an admission of incompetence. Or the teacher might feel insecure when dealing with parents and is dubious about their support. This consequence may be anxiously avoided and the teacher may use the nonassertive response style because the plan includes a consequence that he or she is reluctant to use. Students will sense that the teacher is apprehensive about applying this consequence.

Finding consequences that students do not like but that are not physically or psychologically harmful is another test of appropriate negative consequences. Naturally, the teacher's power to manage should be exercised in humane ways. Choosing negative consequences that are meaningful to students and, at the same time, humane is a rigorous test of a teacher's leadership role. Generally, the loss of something that really matters will be a sufficient cause for better behavior. Not all students respond to the same corrective measures.

Negative consequences should always be presented to students as a choice. Teachers cannot insist that students behave, but they can insist that students pay the price if they choose to misbehave. Teachers should work earnestly to help students "be on their best behavior." When students see that negative behavior is clearly a choice that they made and will be connected to an unpleasant consequence, a disciplinary incident will ideally lead to positive behavior change.

Prolonged use of negative consequences, in the absence of positive behavior changes, can result in poor teacher–student relationships. It is recommended that educators typically pair negative consequences with positive consequences, positive interactions, and interventions that teach desired behaviors.

Students find it easier to accept negative consequences and make adjustments in their behavior when violations of the rules are treated in a matter-of-fact manner. When painful consequences are used as a form of revenge, the student feels obliged to respond in kind. Hostility seems to provoke hostility. It is best not to add to the burden by telling students who they resemble or where they will end up. A succinct statement of the behavior a teacher will not tolerate, followed by the penalty for noncompliance, is generally all that is required.

Severe-Clause Measures

Most rule infractions involve minor offenses: Students talk during seatwork or shout answers without being recognized, they shove and push in the lunch line, they make wisecracks or swear or chew gum, or Al begins wandering around the room ten seconds after a seatwork assignment has been given. We have considered negative consequences that seem to fit these ordinary misbehaviors and have discussed the criteria for selecting and using these consequences. Now let us look at what is done when students are persistent troublemakers or engage in unacceptable behaviors that are more than ordinary offenses.

When a student willfully inflicts harm on another or destroys property, overtly refuses to comply with a command, or stops an entire class, these are severe-clause behaviors that call for more drastic action. The criteria for selecting consequences are still good guidelines for dealing with these behaviors, but out-of-class consequences, reflecting a teacher's resolve to change a situation without delay, are needed. These behaviors result in office referrals, described in Chapter 2.

In addition, some behaviors are chronic and not in the students' best interests. They are resistant to intervention strategies presented in the text thus far. In these cases, teachers may need to seek help from colleagues at the building assistance team level. This team supports the teacher's problem solving, intervention planning, and implementation.

Teaching Desired Behaviors

Most behavior problems in classrooms will be prevented by consistent implementation of effective instructional management, the basic classroom management plan, and related positive and negative consequences. The rest of this chapter is devoted to the how-to's of managing behaviors that do not respond to these general management strategies. We want to assert that this is not the time for relying on punishment alone to turn student behaviors around. This is a time for discussing and collaborating with students in a problem-solving format. It is a time to teach some students appropriate replacement behaviors.

Teachers may need to develop lessons to help students manage situations that cause difficulties. Lessons should include positive practice and feedback. Examples include (1) working with the class on conflict resolution strategies and (2) conducting lessons on social skills. Teachers should never hesitate to seek assistance from the problem-solving team in the building. Team members can help develop lessons and support the teaching. When students do not know how to meet schoolwide and classroom expectations, educators need to teach desired behaviors. Common problems include the following: (1) student does not know how to handle poor peer relationships, (2) student does not know how to be respectful to or accept corrective feedback from adults, (3) student has bad habits like making noise or masturbating, (4) student is chronically off task because of daydreaming or a short attention span, or (5) student is aggressive.

Reinforcement Systems

Classroom or individual reinforcement systems are considered to be highly intrusive interventions and, therefore, must be used wisely. Structured reinforcement systems are based on the premise that external rewards can motivate students to improve their behavior. Those who hold to humanistic philosophy and theory, in particular, object to the use of external motivators (Kohn, 1997).

Those who ascribe to behavioral and interactionist or ecological/systems theories support the appropriate use of structured reinforcement interventions. They define appropriate use as those short-term, structured reinforcement interventions that are applied to deeply ingrained, inappropriate behaviors resistant to other or simpler solutions (Sprick et al., 1993). Appropriate use targets students who are not motivated intrinsically to do their best in meeting expectations.

The rationale for the appropriate use of structured reinforcement is multifaceted. Targeted students should meet one or more of the following rationales: (1) Students need additional motivators because changing behaviors requires a lot of effort, (2) students are not motivated by success in school or do not value it, and (3) students' needs appear to be better met by inappropriate behavior than doing what is expected or appropriate.

It is important to consider the concerns about reinforcement systems when developing a plan so that your interventions do not fall prey to certain weaknesses. First, a highly structured reinforcement system assists in getting the student's attention fixed right away on changing a behavior. Once the student has improved, the system must be faded gradually while carrying out a carefully designed component of teaching students to value success. Do not terminate reinforcement systems all at once or students will probably stop working on the target behavior. They will rapidly revert to previous behaviors.

Second, you do not have to worry that students will always ask what they will get for doing something if you fade reinforcement systems and teach students to value their own success.

Third, do not consider reinforcement to be bribery. This is a common understanding that is misleading and inaccurate. Bribes occur when someone offers something, usually money, to someone else to influence them to do something wrong. For example, giving money to a presidential campaign in order to obtain protection of your business interests constitutes a bribe. On the other hand, reinforcement is used to encourage someone to engage in behavior that is equated with success. An example of a reinforcer is awarding continuing education units (CEUs) toward maintaining professional licensure to teachers who attend a one-day workshop. Likewise, awarding coupons toward a free lounge pass to students who set and attain work completion goals is an example of a reinforcer.

Fourth, other students will not object to some getting reinforcers if you follow at least one of three guidelines. These guidelines include keeping the reinforcement plan private, getting the nontargeted students to support the plan, and occasionally reinforcing the entire class for their support of a student's success.

Fifth, do not tell yourself that all students should be motivated and should behave without rewards. Remember that some students need to learn to value target behaviors (e.g., timely work completion) and without a structured reinforcement system they will continue to exhibit inappropriate behavior.

Sixth, remind yourself that reinforcing is no different from encouraging and facilitating. All students need different strokes. Teachers' encouraging words through positive interactions are more valued by some students than others. Teachers' reinforcements will work better for other students because that is what they currently value. Your job is to be sensitive to what students currently value and to use that to help them be immediately successful. Changing values takes time.

Educators who have little to no formal educational preparation in the implementation of structured reinforcement systems are urged to request help from their building assistance team. School counselors and school psychologists are the two professionals in the building who are most likely to have the skills to help teachers implement a plan tailored to their needs. With these caveats in mind, an overview of the implementation of structured reinforcement systems follows.

Implementing a Reinforcement System

As you get ready to implement a reinforcement plan, clearly define behaviors you want to change and establish boundaries between acceptable and unacceptable behaviors. Name your reinforcer(s). You can have a class brainstorming session to identify things they might enjoy working for as a group. Give them ten minutes to suggest as many things as possible. Tell students that no idea is stupid. Write all suggestions on the board and allow no discussion. At the end of ten minutes, go through the list with students and eliminate unrealistic suggestions. Have students vote on the remainder, tally the votes, and arrange the list in order of preference. The first item on the list will be the first goal and so forth.

Specify what students must do to earn the reinforcers and set up a reinforcement schedule. For example, a class problem of tardiness is resolved by giving one point every day when no one is late. When the class earns four points, they get five minutes of free time. Set up a record-keeping system (e.g., keep information on a chart or a corner of the board where everyone can see).

Discuss and finalize the plan with students. Implement the plan. Share their progress at the end of the first week. You might say, "You have just earned your first point. That gives you one point out of four. You are working very hard and will reach your goal by the end of the week at this rate."

If there is an individual who keeps the whole group from earning points, take steps to change that person's behavior. Try any of the following plans. If the student is hooked on negative feedback, carefully explain this to the whole class and that they need to work on ignoring. The student may need a consequence of isolation. Reinforce him for cooperating in the group plan. You can also exclude the student from the class plan so that his behavior no longer affects classroom efforts. Set up an individual reinforcement system that will allow him to earn the right to become part of the group again.

Example of a Reinforcement System

The following case study will acquaint you with the process of team problem solving that may be in place in your school building. Notice that the classroom teacher first tries to help the student by using in-class consequences and teaching desired behaviors. The teacher keeps records of the target behavior and the success of interventions. The teacher knows when her consequences and interventions are not producing the desired results and how to access more support.

In the following case study you will also see the importance of ecological systems theory, especially at the mesosystem level where home and school need to work together to help the student. You will see how structured reinforcement systems were implemented and paired with teaching desired behaviors. There also is an example of how to monitor the progress of a student using simple graphing procedures. Educators are expected to keep records of student behavior change so that it can be graphed and monitored to gauge intervention success.

Ms. Gloria Jackson is the kindergarten teacher of Aaron, who is aggressive at school. He hits, stomps, chokes, kicks, and pushes other children down. Gloria met with Aaron's mother and developed a plan. Gloria has tried the following in-class consequences for aggressive behavior: (1) verbally sent to time-out and more often (2) physically carried to time-out. Time-out is five minutes long. He is then asked if he is ready to return to class. Five minutes has been long enough for him to quiet down and he returns to class successfully. Gloria reports that the other students ignore him and continue with their work when he is being disruptive. She has paired the time-out intervention with lessons on how to solve problems with peers. The guidance counselor has come into the class to help with the lessons and has scheduled Aaron in her supervised peer playgroups for additional instruction in conflict resolution.

Aaron's aggressive behaviors continue and Gloria decides to refer the problem to the building assistance team for support in ongoing problem solving. Gloria can describe the problem clearly and, in addition, has kept records of Aaron's aggressive behavior. The team can quickly graph the frequency of aggression (see Figure 6–1). You can see the baseline of Aaron's target behavior, aggression, averages two aggressive acts per day. Success of forthcoming interventions can be judged by continuing to count the frequency of aggressive behaviors and comparing it to the baseline.

On a scale from zero to ten, where a zero indicates no problem and a ten indicates a severe problem, Gloria rated Aaron's physical aggression as a ten. He attends morning kindergarten only and typically has two angry outbursts each session. Aggressive behavior ranges from three to five minutes in duration. She believes that Aaron's behavior is a result of not getting his way. The behavior does not seem to occur in relationship to any particular child.

Figure 6–1
Frequency of Aggressive Acts at School per Day at Baseline

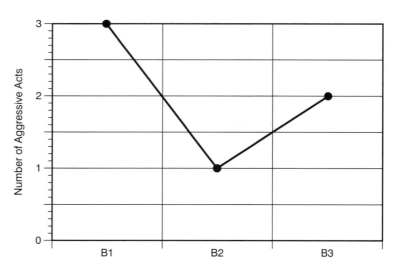

Behavior Sampled on Three Days

Team members determine that it is important to involve Aaron's mother in all of the problem-solving attempts. They appoint the school psychologist as the case manager. The case manager interviews the mother, Erica. Erica expresses great concern about Aaron's behavior and states that she would like assistance. She questions whether fatigue, hunger, or other physiological factors cause his angry reactions. At home, Aaron's aggressive behaviors occur more often before mealtime and bedtime (i.e., must turn off the TV). Aaron does not control his anger when faced with frustration or disappointment. He becomes physically and verbally out of control. He will scratch, kick, hit, punch, and bite. He will use objects to harm his mother, younger brother, and the family dog. The home incidents occur at the rate of two to three per day.

Erica described the antecedents to Aaron's behavior as follows: He does not receive something that he would like, something does not happen that he expected, there is a misunderstanding, or he is not in control of a situation. Transitions are a problem, especially bedtime. Asking him to turn off the television and go to bed results in physically aggressive behavior. Ineffective interventions during these times have been (1) verbal comments such as "Stop it, you're not going to get it" or "I know you're getting angry"; (2) trying to talk him out of it; (3) touching him; and (4) spanking him. Restraining him by holding him has worked somewhat. Erica holds him until he agrees to stop the behavior. It takes about ten minutes for him to become calm, but another outburst will usually follow. Sometimes he will display a marching walk until he is calmed down. She does not use time-out because Aaron refuses to go. When she has sent him to a time-out spot, she has resorted to holding the door shut to keep him in the time-out space.

After reading about Aaron's history, it should be clear that school interventions alone will not be sufficient to help Aaron meet classroom expectations. Based on the information provided by the teacher and the parent during interviews, Aaron's target problem was identified as following adult directions the first time given. All of his angry outbursts occur when a teacher or his mother asks him to do something that he does not want to do.

The reinforcement system was developed to provide rewards for following directions the first time given. Gloria and Erica agreed to meet with Aaron and discuss the new plan. His ideas about the plan were to be considered but the adults were not to be talked out of using appropriate consequences. Specifically, they were to discuss and role-play how to demonstrate the target behavior of following directions the first time given, how Aaron would earn and record points, how to turn points in for a reinforcer, and how to go to and return from time-out.

Erica agreed to use the reinforcement program, time-out, and an instructional program to replace angry behaviors. The school psychologist taught Erica how to use time-out appropriately. Specifically, Aaron's time would start when he was in the time-out space and quiet. That eliminated the mother having to hold the door shut while he pulled from the other side in an attempt to get out. The teacher agreed to use the same interventions at school. She was instructed to start Aaron's time when he was in the time-out space and quiet. For every minute that he dawdled, another minute was added to his time-out, both at home and school. That eliminated having to physically take him to time-out.

Aaron completed a reinforcer survey and indicated he liked these things: fishing, swimming, movies, gold necklaces, power ranger toys, candy, ice cream, stickers, computer time, play time with toys, getting a frog, time with parent, and watching TV (favorites were "Thumbelina" and cartoons). Point values for each of his reinforcers were determined by the teacher and parent.

With reinforcement, Aaron's aggressive behaviors at school began to decrease. When Aaron has a week of one or no aggressive acts, the reinforcement system can be faded. Fading in this situation would mean that he would be expected to have more good days in order to earn the same amount of points. Fading could also mean that the number of points that each item is worth is increased. Fading will be more successful when adults who give him rewards verbally emphasize the importance of his appropriate behavior rather than the value of the reward. For example, when fading the teacher could say, "Aaron, you made good choices all week and followed directions the first time given very well. Because you are showing me how good you are at following directions, I will not be marking every time you follow a direction. You won't know when I am marking so you will need to remember our rule about following directions and do it every time. Do you have any questions?" To reiterate earlier points, the structured reinforcement system is used to get Aaron's attention and quickly put a stop to harmful behaviors. At the same time, the teacher, mother, and guidance counselor continue to help Aaron develop conflict resolution skills.

Making Wisecracks and Jokes

Students who are always ready with a joke or wisecrack are usually talented, capable, and a pain in the neck. Although students are funny, they sometimes get their laughs at the expense of others Sprick (1985).

Jokesters get reinforced for their behavior by others who enjoy their cleverness and wit. Making wisecracks becomes a habit, a way of interacting. The student may be bored and so occupies himself by thinking of comebacks instead of focusing on academic tasks. If school is too easy, the bright student may use humor as a way of filling time and entertaining himself. The student may use wisecracks as a way to engage in intellectual competition with the teacher. The student may not realize that some of his comments are actually rude and cruel. Some students use humor as a way to manipulate the classroom and teacher, as a way to challenge authority, as a way to put a teacher down without punishment.

The following plan will not squelch the student but will channel the student's talent and humor into appropriate classroom behaviors. First, you determine the level and amount of work the student is expected to do in class. Adjust work if it is too easy. Give extra-credit assignments that stretch abilities or provide independent study.

The second planning consideration is to establish a mild consequence for unacceptable wisecracks. Use a mild consequence when the student has demonstrated a disregard for someone else. This indicates that the student probably needs to learn how to be sensitive to the feelings of others. An example of a mild consequence is two minutes of time owed from lunch for each unacceptable comment.

Next, hold a conference with the student at a private and neutral time. Keep in mind that the goal is not to make the student feel punished but to help the student see his behavior from someone else's perspective. Before you hold the conference, prepare a list of comments and jokes the student made. Use some examples that were funny and appropriate for class. Use other examples that were insensitive, were hurtful, or disrupted instruction. Then meet with the student and examine the difference between acceptable types of humor and unacceptable that humiliates. By this you will help the student see that humor is fine but that he sometimes places others in an untenable position.

Explain that you sometimes will make subjective evaluations and express confidence in the student's ability to make judgments. Explain the consequence that you will use for comments that you judge to be inappropriate. Tell the student that if he isn't sure whether a comment is appropriate, it might be best not to say it.

In class, be sure to interact with the student in supportive ways when the student participates appropriately in class. Calmly inform the student of the consequence when the student makes inappropriate comments. Absolutely do not lecture; instead, say "That was an unnecessary comment. You owe time after class." If the student disagrees, say "You can tell me after class." Reinforce the student for his self-control when he makes a significant improvement. Here are examples of reinforcers: sending a note from the teacher to the student or the parents, discussing his improvements privately after class, telling the student a joke when you see him in the hall, and asking the student to tell you a joke when you see him in the hall.

Obtaining Assistance from the Building-Level Problem-Solving Team

Many teachers struggle throughout their professional careers to manage student behaviors successfully. Few teachers take to managing student behaviors like ducks take to water. Do not think that everyone besides you knows exactly what to do with problem behaviors. Most of us have to study and practice and study and practice some more in order to work successfully with students who do not respond to basic classroom management plans. School counselors, school psychologists, and school social workers earn advanced degrees in human services work and they are available to assist teachers.

Although support personnel are willing to assist teachers in developing intervention plans, teachers will need to carry out most plans with students in classrooms. Students develop prosocial behaviors best in their natural environment. For example, pullout programs in social skills training are generally not supported by research. Social skills development needs to be conducted with a group of peers

Specialists on the school's problem-solving team help teachers develop intervention plans.

using esteemed peers as models, with follow-up in the natural environment of the school building, classrooms, and playgrounds. In other words, social skills is a systems-level intervention. The entire system needs to support the use of the targeted social skill across all students, not just the one you have picked out as having a problem. Asking the school psychologist or school counselor to pull a lone student in for counseling on social skills is rarely effective. A student may be able to demonstrate a skill in the counselor's office but cannot generalize the skill to the classroom, hallways, or lunchroom.

Self-Management in Education

Doyle (1986) reviewed interventions that teachers use to repair breakdowns in classroom order. He concluded that attention has shifted from having teachers implement behavior modification programs to helping students learn to self-monitor and self-control. Self-management in education consists of self-monitoring, self-reinforcing, self-evaluation, and self-instruction. Self-monitoring is described in this section. Considerable research evidence exists for the application of self-monitoring to school problems of regular education, the learning disabled, behaviorally disordered, mentally retarded, multiply handicapped, and attention deficit.

Sprick et al. (1993) offered the following rationale for self-monitoring interventions. Some students are not aware of their actions that get labeled as behavior problems. Because they are unaware of their actions, they end up seeing their problems as a reflection of who they are rather than the actions they take. For example, their actions may be impulsive but they have learned to label themselves as irresponsible, obnoxious, or bad. Many students begin to feel hopeless; self-monitoring can help them regain hope through regaining control.

Additional rationale for the use of self-monitoring in educational settings includes five major points (Lloyd, Landrum, & Hallahan, 1991). The first rationale is that instilling self-control in our youth is one of the primary goals of education. The second rationale is based on research that indicates self-monitoring may increase the effectiveness of interventions. Third, self-monitoring may decrease the demand for direct intervention by teachers, saving them time. The final two points are that self-monitoring may improve the maintenance and transfer of intervention effects.

The purpose of self-monitoring is to increase a student's awareness of a particular area in which he or she lacks self-control. Students actually observe their own behavior. In turn, this helps them take responsibility for their behavior and control what they do. The hallmarks of successful self-monitoring include the following:

1. Student learns to pay close attention to what she is or is not doing.
2. Student counts and charts improvements, enhancing intrinsic motivation.
3. Student typically needs no further reinforcement than the sense of accomplishment.

Educators can use self-monitoring when a student has some motivation to change problems associated with mild behavior problems: blurting out, complaining, all types of inappropriate comments, off-task behavior, careless work, and inappropriate interactions.

An example of a student who might benefit from self-monitoring is Sue, a gifted third grader who is very unhappy. She shows off her own accomplishments, subtly puts down peers' efforts, and uses her success to be the center of attention. Sue's peers do not want to be around her and form cliques that exclude her. Sue thinks that the other kids don't like her because she is smart. During problem solving, the teacher hypothesizes that the bragging, showing off, and criticizing of others are what peers don't like. She suggests to Sue that she is bright and can learn to be more sensitive. They decide to try a self-monitoring system to make Sue more aware of her comments.

The educator preplans by gathering relevant background information to help design the intervention. Unless you have practiced this intervention through course work or in-services, you should seek assistance (e.g., master teachers, school counselors, school psychologists) the first few times you use self-monitoring interventions.

After developing the self-monitoring plan, it is best to complete a planned discussion with the student and parent(s). Let's look at the example of Rita, a second grader who is pleasant and participates in class. Her work on in-class assignments is low-average to average. She needs directions repeated most of the time. Mrs. Brown, her teacher, has initiated planned discussions and a classwide structured reinforcement system that rewards all students for following directions. They have yielded poor results for Rita. Mrs. Brown decides to seek consultative assistance. The consultant interviews the teacher and finds out this information:

1. *Schoolwork:* Rita was a low-average student in first grade. When teachers repeat directions, she is able to do the work. Rita wanders around the room, talks to others, and moves a great deal during group time on the carpet. She has difficulty following directions in multiple settings. She likes teacher attention. Mrs. Brown thinks that she has attention deficit hyperactivity disorder (ADHD) and needs medication to help her control her behavior.
2. *Social skills:* Rita has many friends. The teacher likes her and describes her as a pleasant student.

Before referring students for an evaluation for possible ADHD, teachers need to implement structured interventions with progress monitoring to see how successful the interventions were. In the case we have been analyzing, Rita needs to self-monitor following directions the first time given. The teacher collects the frequency with which Rita follows directions the first time given for three days; days are divided into three time periods: morning, midday, and afternoon.

The consultant and teacher set up a self-monitoring system that requires Rita to circle a smiley or sad face at the end of each class. A small paper with each class listed and faces are taped to her desk. Rita circles a smiley face if she follows about four of every five directions (or most of the time) the first time given.

The system should be fairly unobtrusive. The power of this intervention is decreased when a student is embarrassed. Older students, in particular, need to have the form inside a notebook. Younger students usually like the intervention and feel special. Other students may want to self-monitor. Let them. Any student can benefit. Sprick et al. (1993) provide self-monitoring recording forms that can be duplicated for use in classrooms.

Consider these examples of ways to record behaviors:

1. Tally on-task and off-task behavior during independent work.
2. Tally positive interactions with peers during specified times.
3. Give a plus (+) for responsible behavior or a minus (–) for irresponsible behavior.
4. Circle a number each time a task is completed successfully.
5. Rate effort.
6. Use a checklist for tasks that have to be completed.

Times when the student could record behavior include these:

1. Monitor once a day at a specified time; choose the most problematic time. For example, if a student has the most difficulty paying attention during the afternoon, monitor only in the afternoon.

2. Monitor during certain activities. For example, if a student has difficulty keeping hands and feet to self when lining up or sitting together on floor, monitor behavior during those activities.
3. Monitor at specified intervals. For example, if a student has difficulty with work completion, mark the number of problems completed in a fifteen-minute period.
4. Monitor at random intervals. For example, if a student has difficulty with on-task behavior, monitor behavior at random intervals.
5. Monitor all occurrences of the behavior. For example, use for hand raising, waiting to be called on, talking respectfully to the teacher, and engaging in positive self-talk.

It is important to design a cueing system to prompt the student to record. If counting specific behaviors, the behavior is the cue. If counting on-task behavior at random intervals, teachers can use a timer or a beep tape. A beep tape has prerecorded beeps that sound as cues to students who observe and record their own behavior.

Plan to have an adult occasionally monitor the student's behavior and compare results with the student's record. In early phases, an adult should monitor frequently as the student is self-monitoring. If the two agree on the rating, commend the student. If they do not agree, hold a discussion and make sure the student is clear on what to record. Fade adult monitoring when the student develops reliable self-monitoring skills.

You must identify ways to determine whether the intervention is helping the student reach her goal. It is recommended that you use at least two separate means of measuring effectiveness (e.g., records of student and adult, subjective impressions of student and adult, grades, attendance records, office referrals). Graph and discuss student progress. Figure 6–2 shows graphs of Rita's progress. The first three data points represent her frequency of following directions prior to self-monitoring. This is referred to as her *baseline.* Note how the self-monitoring intervention increased her direction following within a week and maintained it over time. Successful interventions like this one may decrease referrals for medical treatment of suspected ADHD.

It is important to encourage students in their efforts. Remember that learning new behaviors and discarding old ones are very difficult. Students may need a lot of practice, the opportunity to make errors and adjustments, and a lot of encouragement along the way. Make periodic revisions and adjustments to the plan as necessary. When the student demonstrates consistent success, fade the intervention. Once the intervention has been faded, provide continued follow-up, support, and encouragement.

CONCLUSION

Conduct management, when integrated with the leadership functions associated with content management, creates the foundation for an orderly, task-oriented

Figure 6–2
Frequency of Following Directions
Prior to and After Self-Monitoring

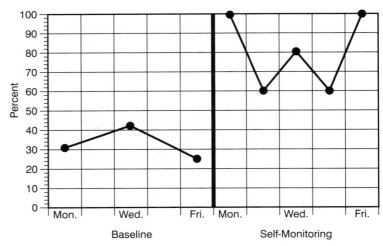

approach to teaching and learning. Conduct management serves to socialize students to the classroom culture and deserves greater attention during the early months of the school year. Effectively handled conduct functions, though more controlling than may be appealing to many teachers, gradually socialize students toward greater independence and autonomy.

SUPPLEMENTARY QUESTIONS

Now that you have studied various interventions to use for classroom behavior problems, you should be able to problem solve the following vignettes. See if you would manage them any differently after reading this chapter than you would have before this chapter.

1. You walk into your first-hour class several minutes before the bell rings and see a group of students who have arrived early. Several of them are teasing a lone student who is crying. This student has never been a problem for you. How would you solve this problem?

2. You have a student who spends a great deal of class time either joking around or debating the inherent value of your lessons and assignments. Classmates laugh at his jokes and seem to like him. Today is no exception. During the first few minutes of the lesson, he first cracks a joke about it and then remarks that it is a waste of time and has no relevance to life outside of school. How would you solve this problem?

3. You are leading the students in a review of some difficult course material. Two students seated toward the back of the room are quietly talking to each other. You asked them once already to stop talking. Now they are talking again. How would you solve this problem?

4. You are explaining the distribution of grades on the exam you have just passed back to students. You describe how this one grade fits into your grading system. One bright student begins to criticize your grading policies, saying that they are unfair. How would you solve this problem?

5. Class is over and students are exiting the room. Two students begin to argue and one pushes the other with enough force that the student falls into nearby desks. How would you solve this problem?

REFERENCES

Berne, E. (1964). *Games people play.* New York: Grove Press.

Canter, L. (1978). *Assertive discipline in the classroom.* Hollywood, CA: Media Five.

Canter, L. (1979, January). Competency-based approach to discipline—it's assertive. *Thrust for Educational Leadership 8,* 11–13.

Canter, L., & Canter, M. (1976). *Assertive discipline: A take-charge approach for today's educator.* Santa Monica, CA: Canter & Associates.

Doyle, W. (1986). Classroom organization and management. In M. C. Wittrock, (Ed.), *Handbook of research on teaching* (pp. 392–431). New York: Macmillan.

Dreikurs, R., & Cassell, P. (1972). *Discipline without tears: What to do with children who misbehave.* New York: Hawthorn Books.

Gathercoal, F. (1990). *Judicious discipline* (2nd ed.). Ann Arbor, MI: Caddo Gap.

Greenberg, H. M. (1969). *Teaching with feeling: Compassion and self-awareness in the classroom today.* Toronto: Macmillan.

Hoy, W. K., & Woolfolk, A. E. (1990). Socialization of student teachers. *American Educational Research Journal, 27,* 279–230.

Kagan, D. M. (1992). Professional growth among preservice and beginning teachers. *Review of Educational Research, 62,* 129–169.

Kohn, A. (1997). How not to teach values: A critical look at character education. *Phi Delta Kappan, 78,* 429–439.

Lloyd, J. W., Landrum, T. J., & Hallahan, D. P. (1991). Self-monitoring applications for classroom intervention. In G. Stoner, M. R. Shinn, and H. M. Walker (Eds.), *Interventions for achievement and behavior problems* (pp. 210–213). Silver Springs, MD: National Association of School Psychologists.

Mcneely, S. R., & Mertz, N. T. (1990, April). *Cognitive constructs of preservice teachers: Research on how student teachers think about teaching.* Paper presented at the Annual Meeting of the American Educational Research Association, Boston, MA.

Rich, J. M. (1988). Punishment and classroom control. *The Clearing House 61*(6), 261–264.

Rinne, C. H. (1984). *Attention: The fundamentals of classroom control.* Columbus, OH: Merrill.

Schloss, P. J. (1983). The prosocial response formation technique. *The Elementary School Journal 83*(3), 220–229.

Silberman, M., & Wheelan, S. (1980). *How to discipline without feeling guilty: Assertive relationships with children.* Champaign, IL: Research Press.

Sprick, R. S. (1985). *Discipline in the secondary classroom: A problem-by-problem survival guide.* West Nyack, NY: Center for Applied Research in Education.

Sprick, R., Sprick, M., & Garrison, M. (1993). *Interventions: Collaborative planning for students at risk.* Longmont, CO: Sopris West.

Swanson, H. L., O'Connor, J. E., & Cooney, J. B. (1990). An information processing analysis of expert and novice teachers' problem solving. *American Educational Research Journal, 27,* 533–556.

Wayson, W. W. (1980). Developing schools that teach self-discipline. Columbus, OH: Professional Development Associates.

York, P., York, D., & Wachtel, T. (1982). *Toughlove.* New York: Doubleday.

CHAPTER 7

Covenant Management: Teacher and Student Relationships

An understanding of the material in this chapter will help you do the following:

❑ Describe the dominant features of the four developmental stages in the formation of groups.

❑ Describe the purposes of role-oriented teachers and role-oriented schools.

❑ Discuss the implications of control theory for the lead-manager.

❑ Use William Glasser's eight-step problem-solving strategy with discipline problems.

❑ Describe the procedures for using class meetings, prepare a set of questions to guide a class meeting, and conduct an abbreviated version of a class meeting.

❑ Demonstrate the group leadership skills that enable a teacher to serve as a facilitator for a class.

Managing people is much more challenging than managing the organization of materials and the planning of lessons that precede the first day of classes. Throughout this chapter, there are invitations to *hypothesize* and *prescribe* (propose). Eventually, if–then propositions expressing the cause-and-effect relationships that make sense to you will be tested.

Any initial effort to understand the covenant management function should begin with a *description* and *analysis* (reflecting) of the classroom group. It is the students, as a group, who will present the teacher-leader with opportunities to perform interpersonal management functions.

THE CLASSROOM GROUP AS A SOCIAL SYSTEM

The collection of individuals in a classroom becomes a distinct group with its own character. Each person in the group has multiple functions to perform and does so within certain constraints that grow out of the expectations of group members. Even the appropriate ways to cause trouble are prescribed by teacher and peer expectations.

How this aggregate becomes a group, with dispositions to behave in certain ways, has been described and analyzed by Getzels and Thelen (1960). Figure 7–1 draws on Getzels and Thelen's terminology and processes to conceptualize how a group is formed and how it acquires distinctive ways of thinking about and doing things. Let us look at the process and at the implications for the teacher-leader.

Figure 7–1
Group and Individual Roles

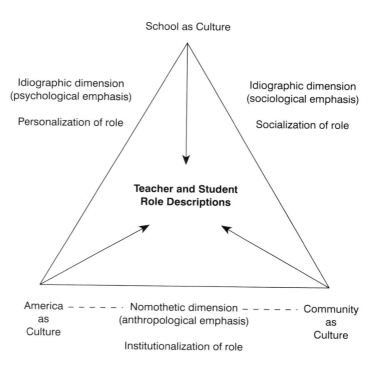

School as Culture

Idiographic dimension
(psychological emphasis)

Personalization of role

Idiographic dimension
(sociological emphasis)

Socialization of role

**Teacher and Student
Role Descriptions**

America
as
Culture – – – – – · Nomothetic dimension – – – – – · Community
(anthropological emphasis)   as
                                Culture

Institutionalization of role

Teacher and Student Roles

Like government, family, and religion, schools are institutions that have been created by society to serve certain societal functions. The school exists within a culture that determines its goals and functions. What the school is expected to do and the standards that will be used to judge its performance are referred to as the *nomothetic dimension* of the model. *Nomothetic* refers to the norms, or normal expectations, that define the roles and functions of persons who work within the institution.

The expectations for teachers—what they are to do and how they are to go about doing it—differ from those for students. Thus, one of the initial functions of the teacher-leader is to ascertain the obligations, prerogatives, and powers that circumscribe the role of teacher (Bany & Johnson, 1975). The teacher must become knowledgeable about the societal norms that define these expectations, determine the extent to which these expectations are present in the community, and become familiar with the acceptable ways to go about fulfilling these functions.

With an understanding of his or her own role expectations, the teacher is in a better position to establish expectations for the role of students. Again, society provides the limitations within which the teacher must operate, but the teacher has considerable latitude when defining role-appropriate behavior for students. Certainly, the type of culture to be transmitted by the school, how the school is to function as a purveyor of culture, and the way that the culture defines adult–child relationships are all factors that will help define the role expectations for both teachers and students.

Institutionalization of Roles

The initial job of the teacher-leader as a representative of the culture is to accomplish these goals:

❑ To make institutional goals and roles explicit.
❑ To develop measures to win support for the goals.
❑ To ensure adherence to the roles.

This process is called the *institutionalization of roles* (see Figure 7–1). The institutionalization of roles, though taking into account the social-emotional well-being of youth, is largely one of intellectual development. Schools are the culture's primary way of transmitting the accumulated wisdom of the ages. How this is done varies across school systems. Just as schools do not have similar visions about what needs to be taught, they differ as to the ways to learn what is being taught. In some schools, students are regularly involved in the decisions about what and how to learn. In others, curriculum decisions are made in the district office, teachers are expected to use prescribed text materials, and students have absolutely nothing to say about goals and methods of instruction.

Socialization of Roles

Although our culture prizes democratic principles and practices, we typically modify these principles when it comes to adult–child relationships. Because of the sheer magnitude of the task we call schooling, we are compelled to insist that individuals relinquish some freedom in the interests of order and group solidarity. The two *idiographic* (individual) *dimensions* are shown in Figure 7–1, on either side of the triangle. One we will discuss here; the other is discussed in the next section.

On one side, the *socialization of roles* refers to common expectations for roles, regardless of the roles incumbent. Herein, the individual must conform to make the situation more manageable. The socialization of roles results in the shared characteristics of the group, and conformity to these shared characteristics produces a sense of belonging. However, the school culture does support accommodations for the developmental needs of youth. In fact, many of the policies and practices that govern the day-to-day operation of schools reflect this concern. The length of the school day and of class periods and the methods for delivering the curriculum are influenced by developmental considerations. Thus, the structure for schooling affects the role expectations for students. You will see as you continue to read this chapter that the socialization of roles is also mediated by aspects of conduct and covenant management.

Personalization of Roles

On the other side of the triangle in Figure 7–1, we have the other idiographic dimension, the *personalization of roles*. This element allows for the unique characteristics of the person to be brought to bear on role expectations. Herein, students find an outlet for what gives them a sense of being worthwhile and feeling important.

In this culture, the two primary institutions for acculturation—home and school—prize individual differences. Psychology has been the medium for understanding the learner and the learning process. Thus, the curriculum for preparing teachers draws heavily from psychological principles to help teachers recognize and provide for the differences in aptitude and attitudes among students. Individual differences must, however, be weighed against institutional considerations. What constitutes role-appropriate behavior involves a constant give-and-take between institutional and individual role expectations. When properly balanced, students feel that the expectations are reasonable and find personal need fulfillment within the group activities.

Consider, for example, that we might say all students, by virtue of being cast in the role of a student, are expected to show deference to their teachers by addressing them with titles (e.g., Mr., Ms., or Dr.). On the other hand, all students are expected to take three units of social studies prior to graduation, but the specific ways to fulfill this expectation are left up to the individual. When children enter school, they must often abandon their plans and substitute the plans of their teachers. However, some teachers try to increase the meaningfulness of the school experience by engaging students in planning sessions. Other teachers offer little opportunity for students to determine the content of the curriculum.

These two illustrations show how role expectations can be narrowly and broadly defined. There must be enough held in common so that individuals can identify with the group as well as enough uniqueness so that they can serve their own identity. Cohesive groups find ways to blend teacher, group, and individual expectations.

The cumulative effect of all these decisions results in role descriptions that define the normative expectations for teachers and students. The teacher-leader not only helps establish, interpret, and negotiate these expectations but is also responsible for enforcing them. When the contribution of the nomothetic and idiographic dimensions is put together, the teacher-leader has made provisions for the intellectual, social, and emotional development of youth.

The Emergence of a Group Personality

As representatives of society, teachers are responsible for melding societal expectations with those of the young people entrusted to their care. This constant interplay between the requirements of society and the preferences of individuals produces the composite character of a classroom group. Within these limits, a group takes on the personality of its individual members, some of whom will have a more compelling impact on the group than others. As a result, groups can help or hinder the teacher's efforts. Some will be an absolute delight to the teacher, whereas others will be abrasive and resistant. This condition, and the corresponding challenges of classroom management, can be better understood by noting the power aspects of the "hidden curriculum" (Jackson, 1968, pp. 33–34) that set many of the demands of classroom life (see Table 7–1).

Breakdowns in group functioning are generally due to identity or rationality problems. Students who cannot find a significant role in the group (identity) or who persist in believing that the goals of the group make no sense (rationality) gradually withdraw from full participation. Identity problems become discipline problems when students, who lack social and academic connections to the group, feel that they do not belong. Rationality problems become discipline problems when students see no connection between the present demands of living, their aspirations for the future, and the curriculum. The group only marginally influences role and goal decisions of students who see no connection. Thus, teachers must be vigilant about students who fail to identify with the group or to believe in its goals.

The Classroom as a Unique Social Organization

A teacher can begin to understand some of the complexities and difficulties of building group identity and rationality by noting the distinctive characteristics of the classroom as a social organization. Schools—and, by extension, classrooms—are unique social organizations (see Table 7–2). They are not created by the persons who populate them. Those who populate schools, students and teachers, often have a version of reality that is quite different from those who created the social organization. Their wants and needs differ markedly from the practices of the organization. Rather than a consensus, there is often tension and conflict. The conflict is intensified by compulsory membership in the organization and mandatory participation in the program. Some refuse to pay their dues and could not care less about the well-being of the membership.

Table 7–1
Social Structure and Character of the Classroom: A Power Position Viewpoint

Structure Determinants	Role Descriptions: School Expectations	
	Teacher	Student
Institutional Aspect of Role		
Societal Expectation	Produce model citizens and good workers	Be attentive to teacher behavior- and work-expectations and learn to operate within the limits prescribed by them
Community Expectation	Evaluate a student's efforts, progress, and achievements	Be prepared to accept the criteria and the methods for judging one's motivation and performance
Idiographic Aspect of Role		
Socialization	Inculcate the shared history of the nation, state, and community to promote respect for, and loyalty to, a common set of standards for living	Learn, accept, and behave according to the strictures of virtuous conduct, or at a minimum, create favorable impressions by learning to live responsibly within the framework of restricted freedoms
Personalization	Draw upon and affirm individual and collective talents that help achieve mutually acceptable aims	Assert one's individuality in the interests of the common good

Unlike most social enterprises, the participants in schools have little recourse if dissatisfied with the program or with one another's company. Teachers and students are assigned to classes, generally with little consideration for individual preferences, and they are expected to get along with one another. Even when students elect to take certain courses, they seldom have the opportunity to choose from among a large number of teachers. When teachers have a chance to participate in the assignment of students to classes, they seldom get a class comprised of their first choices. Thus, learning to live together in a classroom, often doing things not of one's choosing, and interacting with a collection of persons one might not select as friends are often overlooked challenges of education. It is an enormous challenge particularly for the teacher leading a disenfranchised and often disillusioned collec-

Table 7–2
Unique Characteristics of the Classroom Group

Goals

1. Learning is the primary objective (rather than a secondary one).
2. Outcomes of learning and procedures for achieving them are chosen before the group is assembled.
3. There is little participation by the members of the group in the assessment and revision of goals and methods of instruction.

Participants

1. Mandatory participation by students is enforced by law.
2. Time of birth and place of residence determine school and class placements.
3. Members of the class have no control over the composition of the group.

Leadership

1. The leader is chosen without the participation or consent of the membership.
2. Law and custom, rather than group consensus taking, establish the prerogatives of the leader.
3. Freedom of expression and movement are controlled by the leader.

Relationships

1. What the class can and cannot do is often determined by those who preceded and will follow them.
2. Membership in other groups may exert strong pressures to accept or reject classroom norms.
3. Other groups often carefully scrutinize the work of students and their teachers.

Based on "The Classroom Group as a Unique Social System" by J. W. Getzels and H. A. Thelen, 1960, in *56th Yearbook: The Dynamics of Instructional Groups. Part II* (pp. 53–82). Chicago: National Society for the Study of Education. Copyright 1960 by National Society for the Study of Education. Adapted by permission.

tion of individuals. Creating a working unit from such an assortment of individuals while preserving members' individuality is an awesome responsibility.

The fact that the teacher is the designated leader of a diverse class of students (hardly a group in the sense of having well-defined and shared norms and aspirations) may possibly be the first source of friction and discontent. The teacher, who has no recourse but to serve as the leader, is expected to gain personal approval while building acceptance among members of the classroom group. Let us examine the four stages of the group formation process.

The Four Stages in Group Formation

Mauer (1985) formulated the stages of group formation as follows:

1. Forming
2. Storming
3. Norming
4. Performing

We will discuss the four stages to highlight changes in management functions throughout the school year. The emphasis will be on typical student behavior and the teacher-leader's orchestration of the psychosocial dynamics of group formation.

The Forming Stage

The *forming* stage can be characterized as the "honeymoon" period. This is the stage when students are generally on their best behavior. They tend to be task oriented and to look to the teacher for structure and direction. Because they are often uneasy about their relationships with other members of the class, they also look to the teacher to structure these relationships.

During this stage, leadership is largely a matter of engaging students in the activities of (1) linking, (2) establishing roles and procedures, and (3) information seeking. These activities generally occupy a significant portion of the school day during September and part of October.

Linking activities are designed to help students see connections between what was learned last year and what will be learned this year. Students' confidence grows as they realize that prior learning has set the stage for success. They also view the teacher positively because he or she is experienced as an encourager and enabler.

A natural outgrowth of linking activities is *establishing roles and procedures*. As students engage in academic activities that assure high levels of success, they can turn some of their attention to finding their place in the social group. As the teacher makes provisions for various types of group activities, sometimes assigning roles and other times allowing roles to emerge, students gradually get a clearer sense of what they can do and what others think they can do.

Information seeking can be carried out in a mutually advantageous way during the early weeks of school. Free of the more involved management responsibilities associated with teaching new material, the teacher can thoughtfully observe and record the distinctive characteristics of each student. Similarly, when students initially spend a large portion of their time with independent work assignments, they can seek information peculiar to their needs.

During the forming stage, conduct and covenant management begins but content management considerations are the most numerous. Teachers have long proclaimed that the best hedge against disciplinary problems is an enticing curriculum taught by an enthusiastic and well-prepared instructor. Intellectually stimulating and well-organized lessons, complemented by actively engaged students, are viewed as the best way to prevent discipline problems.

The Storming Stage

Testing the limits is a common way to characterize the *storming* stage. Students begin to create some social distance from their studies and from one another. The stability of the forming stage has provided them with a secure base of operations. They are now willing to take a few risks. A teacher not attuned to this natural dynamic, which often occurs between October and December, might overreact to this change in what has previously been such a cooperative atmosphere. Rather than becoming upset, a teacher should see this as a reasonable "setback." The opportunity to restructure and renegotiate relationships can be used to raise expectations and establish the leader's authority.

During the storming stage, the leader must pay more attention to conduct management, which substitutes reasoned and impartial judgment for some of the emotionality of this stage. Expectations are made more explicit and are consistently enforced. As a result, there is some distancing from the teacher, who becomes the focal point for group norms.

The Norming Stage

The *norming* stage, which often extends several months after the Christmas break, is dominated by *orienting* and *fueling* activities. Students begin to accept both content and conduct standards and use these standards to *orient* themselves. They can figure out what is expected by relying on an internal set of cognitive maps.

Just as students engage in more subject-orienting behavior, they also begin to acknowledge and accept the roles assigned earlier in the school year. There is less conflict between and among students as role-appropriate behavior becomes stable and predictable. Unfortunately, some assume a role that is neither personally fulfilling nor helpful to the group.

Fueling activities are designed to garner the energy to meet academic and social demands. All too often, students will compromise their aspirations because they cannot muster the strength. As students survey a task, they assess their abilities and their chances for success. They set a tentative goal based on their past performance. In some cases, they may find that they are not expending enough energy. In other instances, success that comes with a modest expenditure of energy may result in elevating expectations. It is noteworthy that the source, amount, and distribution of energy become important features of this stage of development. Teachers should not assume that tasks are left undone due to a lack of ability. All too often, unfinished work results from an inability to harness the needed energy and deploy it in an efficient and effective way.

Similarly, fueling is important in social relationships. Whereas the energy of some students is depleted by social situations, others find social interactions energizing. The former must find ways to compensate for the tendency to withdraw from relationships. Sometimes these are task-oriented students who will be rejuvenated by success in the academic realm. The latter, whose task batteries are recharged by social activities, may need more help in containing their tendency to "waste" task time. Help in fueling activities is equally important in either case because the social aspects of fueling often determine the direction of a student's academic decisions and performance.

For teachers, the norming stage is the most productive period in the school year. During this stage, the relationship between the teacher and students is grounded in mutual respect. They share common aims and aspirations, and when differences do arise, they work them out in mutually acceptable ways. Communication becomes an important element in the process of establishing norms and negotiating changes in them. They are engaged in a process that builds and depends on trust. This process results in a covenant that expresses their faith in common purposes and in one another.

At its best, the norming stage culminates in a bond based on a promise to make the most of a relationship, a relationship that orients one to academic possibilities and fuels a personal commitment. Although these are lofty aims not easily attained, this process can set the outer limits for the performing stage.

The Performing Stage

The *performing* stage is the coalescence of the three previous stages and can be very satisfying for both the teacher and the students. In the parlance of classroom management, students are now self-reliant, self-controlled, and self-disciplined. They are capable of working independently but can rely on the teacher and their classmates when they lose their sense of direction and/or need an emotional lift. This period of productivity occurs within the other three stages and reaches its zenith during the final months of the school year. The extent to which the performing stage is distributed throughout the school year depends on the eclectic management abilities of the leader.

Synthesis of the Group Process

At this point, you are likely to conclude, correctly, that effective group managers must be concerned about all three of the management functions: content, conduct, and covenant. Figure 7–2 graphically depicts this idea and illustrates the relationships among the three management functions and the stages of group formation. Content and conduct considerations form the base of the triangle. These functions set the stage for learning. Without a planned and organized program of studies and an orderly way for people to conduct themselves, little teaching and learning will occur. Both of these functions are heightened by covenant considerations. Students' receptiveness to the curriculum and their willingness to abide by the rules can be greatly increased by the communication-fostering qualities of the teacher and his or her relationship with the students. Thus, this eclectic management triangle reveals a triad of functions that affect the way a teacher views the work of teaching and suggests ways to best perform the work requirements.

The effective classroom manager must be able to perform all three functions and meld them to maximize the contribution of each. Teachers are generally more proficient in the management of content and conduct conditions; many who are not might take advantage of learning opportunities in these areas. Teachers tend to view

Figure 7–2
Eclectic Management Model

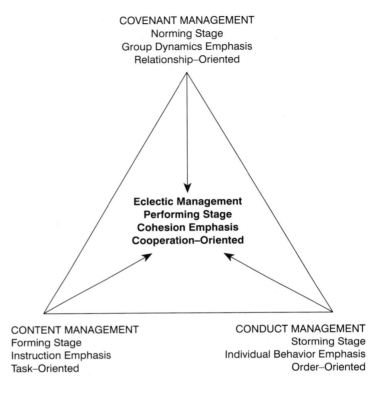

COVENANT MANAGEMENT
Norming Stage
Group Dynamics Emphasis
Relationship–Oriented

**Eclectic Management
Performing Stage
Cohesion Emphasis
Cooperation–Oriented**

CONTENT MANAGEMENT
Forming Stage
Instruction Emphasis
Task-Oriented

CONDUCT MANAGEMENT
Storming Stage
Individual Behavior Emphasis
Order–Oriented

themselves as well endowed with human relationship skills but the primary skills that remove barriers and build commitment to learning demand attitudinal underpinnings and a technical facility that one is unlikely to acquire in the normal course of life events.

Covenant considerations require respect, diplomacy, compassion, and cooperation—attitudes and skills that characterize democratic interpersonal transactions. Creating and nurturing the arrangements that bring people together in these ways require uncommon communication skills and a commitment to egalitarian principles. Most beginning teachers understand and subscribe to the principles, but they have had little experience applying them in a school setting. Teachers can acquire and refine these communication and problem-solving skills if they are more conscious of how they influence student behavior. When it becomes apparent that they are relying on "I said so" and "you ought to" communications, it is time to look for alternatives that invite agreement.

THE RELATIONSHIP BETWEEN PERSONAL RELATIONSHIPS AND ACHIEVEMENT

When students are asked to account for their motives for learning, they frequently cite their admiration and respect for a particular teacher. They express their desire to please this individual and often attribute their effort to an affinity for the teacher rather than for the subject. They report never caring much for history until they took it from Mr. Lincoln. Such students' commitments to learning are founded on a relationship that means something to them. The relationship provides both the inspiration and an incentive to learn.

In *The Identity Society,* Glasser (1972) highlights the powerful impact of personal relationships on an individual's aspirations and achievements. According to Glasser, today's society is role rather than goal oriented. In a role-oriented or identity society, people place more importance on being respected as human beings than on being valued for what they can do. They believe that one's worth should not be measured by accomplishments but by one's membership in the human family.

In the early decades of this century, life for the average U.S. citizen was marked by scarcity, and, Glasser has argued, it was imperative that every person contribute to the general welfare. People who gave their full measure not only improved their own condition but that of their neighbors as well. Hard workers were

---

Management Challenge 7–1
Role Versus Goal Conflicts

According to Glasser (1976), role-oriented students personalize everything. When Bill gets a failing grade on a math paper, he regards it as a statement about himself. His teacher insists that the grade merely indicates the quality of his work in mathematics, but Bill insists it reveals a personal shortcoming or is at least a judgment about his worth.

Many teachers claim that the majority of students, despite Glasser's observations to the contrary, are still goal oriented. These students work hard and strive to get good grades. They would like to be favorably regarded by their teachers and their peers, but their sense of self-worth is tied to accomplishment rather than acceptance.

Glasser would undoubtedly agree with this observation but with a disclaimer: These students already have a role. They see themselves as good students, a role reinforced at home and by their success in school. They go for goals because they have found a role. But what about individuals who lack the home and school support for the role of student? They need first to feel worthwhile as human beings. Then they can muster the courage to take the risks inevitably associated with learning.

1. What side of this argument makes the most sense to you? Why?
2. Can you envision an instance or cite a particular case in which a student personalized a teacher's judgments about his or her work and concluded that he or she was inadequate and unworthy of respect? How might this individual express disappointment and discouragement? Are these behaviors ordinarily treated as disciplinary problems? Should they be?
3. Assuming role precedes goal, how would you go about helping a student whose role is that of a failure and whose goal is to make you feel as miserable as he or she does?

admired. Ambition, diligence, dependability, thrift, industriousness, and tenacity were considered cardinal virtues. Personal accomplishments and public deeds contributed largely to the common perception of a person's worth.

Usher in the abundance of the 1960s and 1970s, a period that Glasser has contended placed role before goal and allowed more people the luxury to ask the fundamental role questions of "Who am I?" and "What do I want to become?" Generally, people concerned with putting food on the table and keeping a roof over their heads have less time to ask these existential questions. But when one's stomach is full and the next meal is assured, there is opportunity to ponder such issues. One's sense of significance is not defined by contributions to the community's well-being because getting the most from each member is not nearly so important when there is plenty to go around.

Implications of Role Versus Goal for the School

Role begins to emerge as a more dominant consideration in life decisions when the importance of goals is downgraded. One can be somebody without proving one's worth in the marketplace. I can insist that I have a right to respect and dignity apart from what I am able to do. As a student, I want to be treated kindly and considerately, not just because I fulfill teachers' and institutional expectations, but because every person has a right to such treatment. What I am is the true measure of my worth; what I can do, the measure of my generosity of spirit.

Glasser (1972) claimed that many students in our schools today are role oriented rather than goal oriented. They want teachers to appreciate and respect them as human beings, to draw on their interests as they make curriculum decisions, to understand their frustrations, to minimize their failures, and to elevate their accomplishments. They are not inclined to subordinate their wants and wishes for the sake of being accepted.

It is little wonder that task-oriented teachers are distressed by the "I want something for nothing" mentality that might be said to characterize many of today's youth. This attitude is repugnant to teachers who place goals before roles. They see students as spoiled and self-centered and try to counter this attitude with more explicit expectations and rewards contingent on fulfilling these expectations. They make it emphatically clear that in the absence of achievement, there will be little recognition in their classrooms.

Task-oriented teachers may be inclined to operate according to two principles that Glasser (1969) claims dominate practice in most schools: the certainty principle and the measurement principle. The *certainty principle* asserts that there is a right and wrong answer for everything. Teachers spend a good part of each day dispensing right answers, conducting recitation periods in which students demonstrate their command of the right answers, and grading worksheets that provide for the practice of right answers. Those who can consistently give the answers that teachers want are winners in school. They have proven their worth as individuals, and their goal orientation is rewarded.

The emphasis on right answers is amplified by the *measurement principle,* the second principle that, according to Glasser (1969), dominates educational practice.

Students want teachers to draw on their interests as they make curriculum decisions.

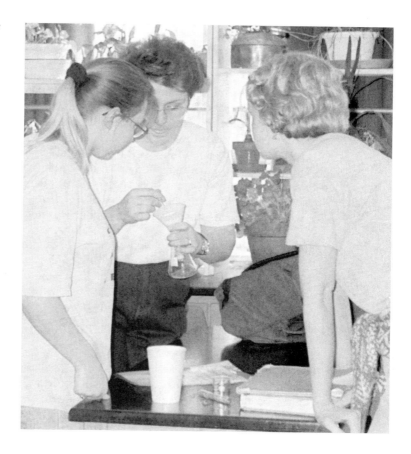

This principle asserts that what cannot be measured is of questionable value. In other words, the products of learning should lend themselves to quantification; teachers should be able to assign a number to the effects of teaching and learning. Thus, learning becomes a summative process. Students who have accumulated the most points for giving right answers are referred to as good students. They have an important role in school.

Teachers who subscribe to a role-oriented approach to student problems generally believe that teaching is first and foremost the function of a relationship (Purkey & Novak, 1984; Schmidt, 1989). This relationship fulfills a need for acceptance on the part of students and fosters a sense of social responsibility. Students who feel that they belong are more likely to become responsible members of the group and cooperate in the need-fulfillment activities of others.

Characteristics of Quality, Role-Oriented Schools

Glasser (1990) offers a rationale and structure for a role-oriented school that eliminates discipline problems by involving students in quality education. He asserts that quality education is the only answer to our school problems and explains procedures for helping teachers and administrators manage students so that a substantial majority do high-quality schoolwork. He claims that educators, because they seem to have given up on the idea of many students doing quality work, have merely increased the amount of low-quality work that they assign. This is the work students find repetitive and boring, the work that encourages them to resort to defiance and/or indifference. Teachers and administrators tend to respond to indifference with coercive measures.

The quality school Glasser has in mind is managed by people who understand the principles of control theory, which he sets out in detail in two other books (1984, 1986). In *The Quality School* (1990) he explains and applies these principles when highlighting the characteristics of a *lead-manager.*

The lead-manager in a quality school is one who accomplishes these tasks:

❑ Confers with students when deciding about the work to be done, setting up a schedule for doing it, and establishing quality standards.
❑ Models the job and seeks student input about better ways to achieve a quality product.
❑ Invites students to evaluate their own work for quality.
❑ Provides the tools and setting that promote self-confidence and congeniality among the students.

In contrast, the boss-manager does not consult students about what work needs to be done; instead, he tells students what to do and seldom asks them how things might be done better, sets the standards for quality and evaluates student work without ever involving them in the process, and relies heavily on coercion to secure compliance.

Clearly, when school personnel are lead-managers, students will feel good about school and about themselves. A quality school will be experienced in the following ways. It will be a place where (1) people cooperate to define quality work, (2) low-quality work is not acceptable to teachers or students, (3) poor grades are no longer used as a tool for coercion, (4) students are allowed varied lengths of time to master a subject, and (5) teachers are role models.

QUALITY SCHOOLS, CONTROL THEORY, AND LEAD-MANAGEMENT

Basic Concepts of Control Theory

Covenant management emphasizes a teacher's role in helping students take effective control of their lives. Glasser (1984, 1986) explains how we attempt to control our lives, particularly how we can manage our emotions and actions to live happier and more productive lives. His basic concepts of control theory provide educators with the conceptual tools for guiding students as they make behavioral choices. Figure 7–3 presents the key concepts and the dynamics of behavioral control psychology

(BCP). As you read the following sections, apply the ideas to your efforts to take charge of your life, and look for ways that you can use this understanding to help students take charge of theirs.

Basic Needs and the Internal World

Some theories assume that behavior is driven by forces within the individual (e.g., psychoanalytic thought). These forces, or needs, mobilize behavioral choices. Glasser (1986) emphasized the need for personal power. He believed that the need for power was a dominant force in people's lives. The need for power reveals itself in people's seeking to feel important and competent. Glasser contends that few students find outlets for this need in the academic program. The popularity of extracurricular activities can be partially explained by the opportunities that they provide for personal power and a sense of importance. Any effort to prevent discipline problems must begin with opportunities for students to gain power and belonging in the academic aspects of the school program.

Reference Perceptions and Behavior

Glasser (1981) visualized an internal world made up of pictures. He posited that a sensory camera is constantly taking pictures of those things in the external world that satisfy needs in the internal world. We collect these pictures, as in a photo album, and as needs arise, we search the album for a picture we believe will satisfy the need. Such a picture is described as a *reference perception*. We refer to it as we look for a corresponding picture in the external world. We begin the search because we believe that satisfying this picture will satisfy the need. We can be said to be *controlling for* a picture that has the potential for satisfying a need.

New pictures are constantly being added to the album. When the teacher is a significant person in the student's life, his or her picture is placed in the album. The teacher's expectations become need-satisfying pictures. The greater the correspondence between the pictures presented by the teacher and the school and the need-satisfying reference perceptions of students, the fewer discipline problems.

Comparing Stations

The concept of *comparing stations* comes from Glasser's book (1981) *Stations of the Mind,* in which he likened comparing stations to train depots where trains are constantly arriving and departing. Like trains, reference perceptions are also coming and going as needs change. In the comparing station, one looks for similarities and differences between the picture that one is controlling for and the picture one gets. For example, a student who feels a need to be important searches for a picture to satisfy this need. Good grades might be regarded as a sign of competence and might contribute to one's sense of importance. In this instance, an A grade may become the reference perception and the outcome from the external world that the student is controlling for.

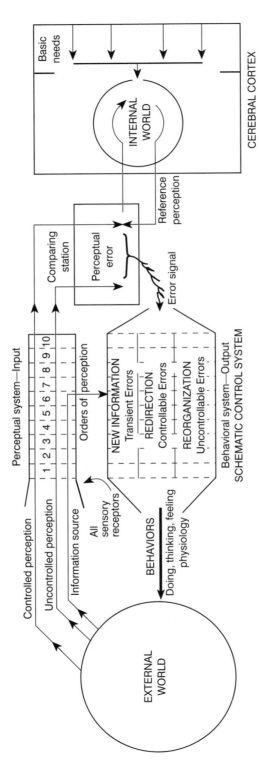

Figure 7–3

Behavior: The Control of Perception Psychology

Source: Excerpts from *Stations of the Mind* by William Glasser, MD. Copyright © 1981 by William Glasser, Inc., Joseph Paul Glasser, Alice Joan Glasser, and Martin Howard Glasser. Reprinted by permission of HarperCollins Publishers, Inc.

Management Challenge 7–2

Using Control Theory as a Diagnostic Tool

Lucius has been displaying rapid and extreme behavior changes in Mr. Arcadian's class. At times his behavior is marked by exhilaration and euphoria. He is very talkative and cooperative. A half hour later he may show signs of restlessness and irritability. Mr. Arcadian suspects that Lucius is using drugs. Before he approaches Lucius to discuss his suspicions with him, he wants to try to understand the possible appeal of drugs to this student and the possible ways to counteract this situation. He decides to use the control of perception psychology model as a diagnostic tool.

1. Work your way, step by step, through each of the concepts in the model (Figure 7–3) as you seek an explanation and understanding of Lucius's behavior.
2. What concepts did you find particularly useful as you tried to formulate a description and understanding of the dynamics of human behavior?
3. Ultimately, to help Lucius, you will have to help him either (a) change pictures to ones that he has a better chance of getting or (b) acquire better behaviors, ones that will enable him to get the picture he is now controlling for. Which approach do you think has the best chance in this situation? Why?
4. Why is it so important that Mr. Arcadian's picture be in Lucius's album if any good is to come of his efforts to help?

Controlled and Uncontrolled Perceptions

The external world can deliver two kinds of perceptions: controlled and uncontrolled. Note that in Figure 7–3 both types of perception appear as options in the comparing station as well. In our illustration, our hypothetical student is controlling for an A. If he does indeed get an A, we would say that he got a controlled perception; there is a one-to-one correspondence between what he got and what he wanted. This is a perfect state of affairs and would be accompanied by feeling important and competent. If, on the other hand, the student gets a C, an uncontrolled perception, he will feel less in control, a need will go unsatisfied, and he will either have to change the picture that will satisfy the need or find a better behavior to get the picture he wants. Teachers who know what students are controlling for and can help them get the picture they want will experience less conflict, which is often the basis for discipline problems.

Error Signals

An error signal—a feeling of pain—occurs when the individual gets an uncontrolled perception. Whenever we lack adequate control of the external environment and have to settle for a picture we find less satisfying, we experience some form of discomfort. The discomfort is a signal that the behavior we chose to get the picture we wanted did not work.

The intensity of the error signal depends on the magnitude of the difference between what we wanted and what we got. A student controlling for an A who gets an F will generally experience a more intense error signal than a person controlling for a C who gets an F. Thus, the amount of emotion that drives a subsequent behavior is often due to the distance between the controlled and the uncontrolled perception.

Students who are constantly confronted by large error signals are likely to feel defeated and discouraged. Seldom getting a picture they are controlling for and often experiencing the debilitating emotion of powerlessness, they look for other outlets to feel important.

The Behavioral System and Total Behavior

Error signals can also produce constructive behavior. The student may decide that the picture she is controlling for is worth additional effort. Rather than attributing the discrepancy between the reference perception and the uncontrolled perception to things that lie outside of her control, she seeks to gain greater control of the external world. Greater effort, represented by devoting more time getting the picture of competence (an A), may be the answer. When referring to the picture album, she finds many pictures that combine effort and success. In this instance, the student decides to emphasize the doing segment of a total behavior.

Note that a total behavior is comprised of four elements: *doing, thinking, feeling,* and *physiology* (see Figure 7–3). As you will see when we examine disciplinary procedures advocated by Glasser, the doing or action component is emphasized because an individual has the most control over this component. In fact, Glasser asserts that we have trouble assuming responsibility for our feelings. We believe that they just happen to us and that we cannot control them. However, we can change our feelings by changing our doing. Thus, we gain control of, or over, our feelings by refusing to believe they just happen to us. Helping students acquire better doing behaviors makes them less susceptible to the feelings associated with error signals, gives them greater control over the way that they handle tension and frustration, and increases the proportion of constructive over destructive solutions to problems.

The External World

The external world is filled with potentially satisfying ways to fulfill the pictures in our heads. Or, we could say, the external world is a vast resource for pictures, and we should fill our albums with lots of them. The more pictures we have available to us for need satisfaction, the greater the likelihood we will find more than one to meet a given need. There are lots of potentially desirable ways to have fun, but some people only have a few pictures in this section of their album. Fewer potential reference perceptions means one must have greater control of the environment because one must get what one wants from a small number of possibilities. The need for greater control can contribute to rigid and inflexible behavior.

Basic Propositions of Control Theory

The basic concepts of control theory can be used to generate a number of propositions to help us understand the dynamics of human behavior. Each of the following propositions highlights an important feature of control theory that will later serve as the foundation for the preventive and corrective features of covenant management.

1. The main goal of life is to stay alive and be in control of life.
2. Behavior is driven by a set of genetic instructions.
3. We develop pictures in our heads that correspond with what we believe will satisfy our built-in needs/wants.
4. We choose total behaviors to try to gain control of people or ourselves.
5. We generally have little difficulty accepting the doing and thinking components of total behavior, but the same does not apply for the feeling component.
6. Because we are less able to accept responsibility for the feeling component of a total behavior, we best express feelings in verb form rather than noun or adjective.
7. Whatever total behavior we choose, it is our best attempt to gain effective control of our lives.
8. We are capable of choosing total behaviors without actually being aware of all that we are actually choosing.
9. Changing an ineffective behavior involves changing all four components of a total behavior, but concentrating on the doing component works best.
10. Our lives are spent reducing the differences between what we want and what we have.

Implications of Control Theory in the Classroom

When trying to implement control theory effectively in the classroom, keep in mind the following points. First, *we generally have pictures in our head that cannot be satisfied in the real world*. To some extent, we all live in a fantasy world. We place pictures in our albums that are only remotely connected to realistic possibilities in our everyday lives. Television has enlarged our album with unrealistic aims and aspirations. We find ourselves disillusioned because there is an enormous difference between what we see and what we have.

Even setting aside the influence of television, differences between what we have and what we want can occur in the daily transactions of life. Most people would prefer to be better looking, better liked, and better achievers, to have more fun and more control over the circumstances of their lives. In other words, we all have needs that cannot be satisfied as long as we keep certain pictures in our heads. Some pictures have to be taken off the pages that we commonly use to select reference perceptions and be put in the appendix of the album.

We cannot always have what we want no matter how badly we want it, whether for lack of resources or lack of tenacity. The problem lies in the way that we substitute less desirable pictures for those that formerly gave purpose and point to life.

In school, all too often motivation and discipline problems are manifestations of having to accept something less than what one wants. Students give up on cooperation as an outlet for their need to belong, seek alternatives to academic achievement to fulfill their need to feel important, resist efforts to influence character development by complaining about their lack of freedom, and view fun as anything that occurs outside the school curriculum.

The pictures in students' albums and those in teachers' are so dissimilar that they create huge error signals. Both parties are constantly trying to find ways to close the gap without changing their pictures. Motivation and discipline techniques are designed to get students to accept the pictures that teachers have in their heads. Both teachers and students experience school as a place where they cannot satisfy their mental pictures. Changing the pictures so that both parties are controlling for reasonably similar pictures may be the only long-term way to resolve the problem. Methods for changing pictures and acquiring doing behaviors to control for these pictures are the subject of much of the remainder of this chapter.

Second, *many of the pictures in our heads are incompatible and even in conflict with one another*. Needs compete with one another, and so do the pictures we have to satisfy these needs. Take, for example, the case of Ms. Hofferstein. She believes that students will like her more if she can make learning more fun. She creates several game-like situations to practice and review information-oriented lessons. When students become rather rambunctious during these activities, she constantly reminds them about creating a disturbance that the principal and the teacher in the adjoining classroom will find objectionable. Despite constant reminders, students persist in being too noisy. Finally, in a moment of exasperation, Ms. Hofferstein announces, much to the students' disappointment and dismay, that the game is over and that she has no intention of using this activity in the future. Amid the groans and scowls, she feels the scorn of students whom she wanted so much to like her.

Students also have needs that compete for expression. While they want to have fun, they also want fun to be allied with freedom. In the preceding example, they wanted to be free to express their exuberance as well as their knowledge. Although the teacher felt that some constraint was essential, the students were unable to subordinate the expression of one need to the expression of the other. They lost the opportunity to satisfy fun and freedom pictures because the teacher was unable to reconcile her competing pictures of fun and restraint.

Much of the conflict in a classroom is a function of the competing needs within and across individual members of the class. Students are not controlling for the same outcomes. Yet, somehow the teacher must create a lesson that is sufficiently interesting and illuminating to capture the attention of all students and to do it in such a way that they see that one or more of their needs are satisfied in the process. There is bound to be conflict, even if not open and obvious, whenever one person's picture must be used to fulfill a need.

Third, *we resist changing the pictures in our heads, despite the problems that we encounter trying to satisfy them*. We know what we want, and we can be quite stubborn about it. Our pictures are the world we know and believe in. To relinquish this view of the world is to abandon part of ourselves. There is security in knowing who we are and what we want. Giving up this security requires strength of purpose and a personal resolve to change what has become a way of life.

We would much prefer to have others change their picture of us and/or their picture of what is good for us. We would like others to accommodate themselves to our views of the world so that we can continue to operate as though our views are correct. We are often convinced that if others were not so blind and obstinate, they would see things our way.

We expect life to have some adversity, but we are often convinced that it is due to circumstances controlled by others. Thus, we see adversity as something to overcome by a more diligent effort. Sure, there will be setbacks and disappointments, but the problem is surmounting the obstacles strewn on the path to success, not the picture that we are trying to satisfy.

Teachers do not easily relinquish their beliefs about what needs to be learned and how best to learn it. Their view of the students' role in the process is not subject to much change either. Because teachers must accommodate themselves to so many external pressures and expectations, they need to feel that there are some constants establishing the boundaries for their work. Despite the difficulties that they may encounter matching their world with the one others bring to them, they will only change the more peripheral features of their world to admit the world of their students.

Students likewise have some definite ideas about what school should be like and how teachers should behave. When a teacher does not stand up to their ideal, students do not ask what they can do to make things better; they merely withhold their cooperation. Rather than changing their picture of teaching and learning, they use noncompliance to get their way. They may have to suffer for their recalcitrance, but this does not change the thinking and feeling components of their behavior. They change the doing, but their work is often incomplete, sloppily done, or not done at all. Eventually, the teacher has to lower expectations and standards or impose more powerful punitive conditions to secure acceptable doing behaviors.

Fourth, *when we lose control, we often engage in desperate, ineffective ways to regain control.* The feeling component of the behavior generally becomes most prominent. When feelings are negative, we tend to say and do things we later regret. When we regain control and the thinking component reasserts itself, we say that our judgment was temporarily impaired. We ask for pardon and sympathy, pledging to make amends.

Students, too, become desperate as they try to influence or impose their will on teachers. They can become emotionally agitated by a teacher's persistent demands and/or lack of understanding. Passive aggression, withholding effort, active aggression, or acting-out behaviors are common outlets for frustration and intimidation.

Angry feeling behaviors are often ineffective ways to make a point. They can be dramatic, but they frequently provoke a similar response. Both parties are at loggerheads with each other. Neither gains control of the situation, and the impasse can lead to long-standing hostilities that impair the effectiveness of both parties. Breaking this emotional logjam requires conflict resolution skills that enable both parties to regain control without doing so at the expense of one or the other.

The fifth point is that *helping someone regain control involves changing pictures so that the person has a better chance of satisfying the new picture or accepting the old picture and helping the person find better behaviors to get the picture for which they are controlling.* Sometimes we labor to satisfy a picture that is totally unrealistic. Of course, we must be careful when deciding what is realistic and what is not. However, teachers' experience can help them judge the realism of student choices. When teachers have some doubts about the contents of a student's album, they can help the student look selectively at the contents and gain experiences that will enlarge the album. Without standing in judgment, the teacher can broaden the vista and sharpen the images that are influencing a student's plans and efforts to realize them.

Schooling is largely helping people find better behaviors so that they can get the pictures for which they are controlling. Schooling is also about values and character building as well. Under the best of circumstances, students would be selecting pictures that are human and humane, and their teachers would be gradually equipping them to realize these lifelong goals. Our old pictures mean a lot to us. They are not just what we are after but what we are. Take away the picture and a part of the self is taken away.

Thus, we must not be too quick to ask or help people to abandon old pictures. Looking at old pictures to discern their meaning and possibilities is a worthwhile endeavor. It is easier to give up a picture when it has outlived its usefulness. But if the picture continues to evoke strong feelings and earnest efforts, the teacher should by all means help the student acquire the behaviors, including the thinking and feeling components, to transform the picture into a reality. Persistence, with an "I can" attitude, is often the difference between giving up an old picture and becoming the possibility that the picture encompasses.

Lead-Management as a Solution to Discipline Problems

Teachers who are lead-managers recognize that goal-oriented solutions will not work in every situation (Glasser, 1990). They are not going to get anywhere with a failing student as long as they press for better work. Thus, setting aside troublesome assignments, they concentrate on regaining the trust and confidence of the student. They realize that what a student needs most is reaffirmation as a person, and so they spend time establishing a relationship that will enable the student to disclose fears and vent frustrations.

Problem Solving as a Solution to Discipline Problems

When students choose to dissociate themselves from learning, the problem is often attributed to a lack of motivation. It is reasoned that given a sufficiently interesting environment and reasonably challenging task, students will choose to participate in classroom activities. The solution is not punitive but helpful. But what about students who prefer to express their dissatisfaction or disdain by actively disrupting the class? Such students are not content to be passive; they let teachers know that they are a force with which to be reckoned. The teacher cannot dismiss such openly expressed defiance or disruptive behavior. In such instances, involvement with the student as a person is only the first step in a problem-solving process designed to help the student select more responsible behavior.

Drawing on concepts from his book *Reality Therapy* (1965), Glasser (1977) describes a problem-solving process that has produced good results with a wide variety of discipline problems. The following discussion of his ideas focuses on the psychological dynamics involved in the change process and the corresponding problem-solving techniques.

According to Glasser (1969), discipline problems are simply irresponsible choices. Their recurrence can be reduced by helping students participate in a self-development program of gradual growth toward more responsible behavior. As students assume a more responsible role, they become less of a problem to themselves and to others. How does the teacher go about helping students become personally and socially responsible individuals? What can be done when students make choices that reveal an irresponsible attitude toward themselves or others? Each step in Glasser's eight-step problem-solving conference strategy (1977), discussed here, illustrates the relationship dynamics and the transfer of responsibility techniques that make it work. Note that the process is designed to help students regain control. Thus, you need to draw on concepts from control theory when applying this process.

Step 1: Get Involved with the Student.   The teacher should become friends with the student, express concern for him or her as a person, and express the belief that things can be worked out. The teacher works at building a relationship with the student. Only when the teacher's picture is in the student's album can the teacher influence the student's internal world. Students are much more willing to insert new pictures or critically look at the pictures they are controlling for when a teacher accepts them for who they are.

Glasser has emphasized the importance of helping students get attuned to the reality of the world around them. Their pain and suffering can only be alleviated by first helping them compare the reality of what they actually do with what they say they do. They must see how they delude themselves and the price they pay for evading responsibility.

The teacher creates this readiness to face irresponsible choices by asking the student "What is it you want?" or "What is it you need?" These questions call up the pictures and reference perceptions that are guiding student choices. The teacher must show an interest in the things that matter to the student.

When teachers at North Cedar Elementary School in Cedar Falls, Iowa, asked students "What do you really want to happen at school?" the responses included the following points:

Owning my problems	Being responsible for my own actions
Being noticed	Asking for help when needed
Winning	Success
Losing respectfully	Feeling good about myself
Being a leader	Self-control
Being a follower	Confident decisions

Following rules	Self-reliance
Being worthwhile	Alternatives
Being understood	More or better friendships
Understanding others	Acceptance
Talking respectfully	

Teachers found that helping students reflect on their goals contributed to an understanding of the choices that students made, choices that sometimes produced failure or, at least, ineffectual behavior.

Step 2: Deal with the Student's Present Behavior.   Avoid being a historian who talks about how many times the student has transgressed in the past. A student who has just behaved irresponsibly needs to acknowledge the infraction before there can be any change in behavior. Reminding a student of past transgressions is more likely to produce regret and promises than responsible behavior. Adding the insult of the past to the injury of the present also increases the intensity of the error signal. When these reminders are experienced as criticism, the student is likely to be more defensive and regain control by justification rather than change.

Teachers take this second step by asking the student "What were you doing?" Why should the student give the teacher an honest answer? Step 1 laid the groundwork for honesty. Facing reality honestly is easier when you trust another and trust yourself. Under some circumstances, a student might refuse to accept responsibility for a transgression by assuming an air of silence or by hiding behind an "I don't know." In such instances, the teacher can respond with "I thought I saw you [name the behavior]" or "It was reported to me that you [name the behavior]. Unless you indicate otherwise, we will proceed as though this is how you acted."

Generally, students will not hedge when teachers ask what they were doing. The doing component of a total behavior is the easiest to accept responsibility for. However, they will hedge and make excuses if asked "Why did you do it?" Students should never get the idea that they can be irresponsible if they can produce a good justification for being so. The sooner students learn what they are choosing and that they are responsible for their choices, the better.

For example, a teacher catches Don shoving John and disciplines Don, who protests that John shoved him first. Don needs to learn that shoving back was only one way to respond to a provocation. He is responsible for the behavioral choice of shoving back. Don needs to learn other ways to deal with combative behavior at school, but he must also be prepared to accept the consequences that attend unwise choices.

Step 3: Get the Student to Make a Value Judgment About the Behavior.   Once students know what they are choosing, it is time to get them to make a judgment about their choice: "Is what you did against the rules?" When rules have been explicitly stated and are consistently enforced, students know whether they have violated a rule. Sometimes the doing behavior consists of doing little or nothing. Indifference, rather than disobedience, is the problem. "Are you doing as well as you would like?" might be the value judgment question.

Some students believe that rules are made to be broken or that rules are for others. The teacher may want to establish responsibility by asking, "Is what you did helping you?" Quite often, the student will recall the short-term benefits and respond in the affirmative. When asked, "Is what you did helpful to others?" students are not likely to be so blatantly selfish. They must acknowledge that their behavior is self-serving and that it disregards the general welfare. While self-criticism may increase the error signal, it helps the student manage his or her internal assessment of a situation. This is an important step toward removing the error signal through responsible problem solving.

Students who are called on to make a value judgment begin to see the social and long-range ramifications of their choices. They begin to realize that what seemed like a perfectly reasonable thing to do has repercussions that were not immediately apparent. They begin to sense that the power to change resides within them. Without a value judgment, students have no need to change. As long as they believe that they made the right choice, that the choice is a consistent expression of their values, there is little reason to change.

When students persist in defending their behavior or refuse to make a value judgment, the teacher might say, "I don't see how your behavior is helping" or "I am having trouble seeing how what you are doing is helping. This is the way it looks to me." Without judging or moralizing, the teacher can provide a value stance that students can examine. The teacher does not impose a value, only offers another way of looking at the behavior and its consequences. Generally, students are prepared to take the next step.

Step 4: Help the Student Develop a Plan to Change the Behavior.

The value judgment sets the stage for making things better. The student's internal dialogue might go like this: "If the behavior that got me in trouble isn't really helping me and isn't helping others, I should begin to think about other alternatives. What have I got to lose? My teacher seems to believe we can work this out together. Maybe things don't have to be the way they have been. There just might be a way to work things out."

The teacher once again translates the problem-solving process into pertinent questions, such as "What kind of plan can you make to follow our rules? What kind of plan can you make to make things better for you and for others?" Basically, the teacher is asking, "Can I help you work things out?" because this step is designed to help students regain control of their lives. The plan is a management solution that puts the student in charge. Rather than offering solutions, the teacher asks questions to help students identify and judge the effectiveness of their behavioral choices. The teacher is asking the student to come up with a better way, not a perfect way, to act. Feeling better and thinking better are by-products of the process.

Students, often preoccupied with the bad behavior, tend to focus on stopping something rather than doing something. Thus, the teacher must stress building a plan that concentrates on constructive or responsible behavior. "What will I see you doing when you are behaving responsibly?" keeps the conference targeted on positive alternatives to need satisfaction. The plan should be simple; it can be extended and expanded after the student has had some initial success. Plans that provide for increments of progress are best. Keep in mind that the need to love and be loved as well as the need to feel worthwhile must find expression in the plan.

Some students find plan building difficult and are unable to suggest ways to deal with a problem. In this case, the teacher might say, "Here are some ways I have seen other students, in similar circumstances, deal with this problem. Do you think any of these solutions might work for you?" The suggestions are not the teacher's, so the student need not feel obliged to accept any of them. The teacher just might omit an obvious option, thereby leaving an opening for the student to offer another alternative. Helping the student evaluate the options and look at advantages and disadvantages of each choice increases the chances of a suitable selection and deepens commitment to see it through. The student gains strength and confidence as one workable option emerges. This final option should not, however, depend on the cooperation of a third party, a feature that decreases the student's control and can provide an excuse for not following the plan.

Step 5: Get a Commitment from the Student to Stick to the Plan.   The plan might be considered a contractual arrangement because both parties have something at stake. Students find the contract a secure reference point; they know more precisely what needs to be done and how to go about doing it. Resolve can still be a problem, but it is easier to muster when the direction and destination are clear.

Teachers concerned with the matter of resolve might ask the student, "Do you think you have a workable plan? Are you going to be able to see it through?" These questions also give the student an opportunity to discuss any misgivings or reservations about the plan. It's a good idea to clear up second thoughts before beginning.

There are no guarantees or assurances the plan will work. Nonetheless, seal the agreement with a handshake or a signature on a written contract. The agreement is more a pledge than an obligation, but a handshake or signature may prompt a more earnest effort. The student should leave the conference feeling that this is serious business.

Having reached an agreement, the student should get started immediately. The teacher may agree to check periodically with the student to see how the plan is working. There should generally be some objectives en route and some reinforcement points in a plan that cover a period of several days or weeks.

Step 6: Do Not Accept Excuses for a Failed Plan.   Excuses are used to absolve one from blame, to find fault elsewhere. The teacher is trying to teach students that they can take control of their own destiny, that they can learn to manage their affairs by creating conditions and managing choices that increase the likelihood of attaining the picture in their heads.

Teachers are partial to excuses. We know how difficult it is to be responsible; we are well aware of our own indiscretions. "Let's get on with living, just don't let this happen again" is a convenient way to dismiss a problem and hope it will go away. It seldom does go away; it merely reappears in another form. Therefore, it is

Management Challenge 7–3
Using Glasser's Problem-Solving Process

The Institute for Research on Teaching at Michigan State University has conducted a number of major research projects aimed at improving classroom management strategies. Several studies have been based on classroom teachers' responses to vignettes depicting twelve types of student problem behavior. One vignette from each of four categories of problems is reproduced below.

Instructional Concerns: Underachiever

Joe could be a capable student, but his self-concept is so poor that he actually describes himself as stupid. He makes no serious effort to learn, shrugging off responsibility by saying that "that stuff" is too hard for him. Right now he is dawdling instead of getting started on an assignment that you know he can do. You know that if you approach him, he will begin to complain that the assignment is too hard and that he can't do it.

Aggression Problem: Hostile Aggressive

This morning several students excitedly tell you that on the way to school they saw Tom beating up Sam and taking his lunch money. Tom is the class bully and has done things like this many times.

Activity Issue: Hyperactive

Bill is an extremely active child. He seems to burst with energy, and today he is barely "keeping the lid on." This morning, the class is working on their art projects, and Bill has been in and out of his seat frequently. Suddenly, Roger lets out a yell, and you look up to see that Bill has knocked Roger's sculpture off his desk. Bill says he didn't mean to do it, he was just returning to his seat.

Peer Relation Difficulty: Rejected by Peers

Mark is not well accepted by his classmates. Today he has been trying to get some of the other boys to play a particular game with him. After much pleading, the boys decide to play the game, but exclude Mark. Mark argues, saying that he should get to play because it was his idea in the first place, but the boys start without him. Finally, Mark gives up and slinks off, rejected again.

1. Demonstrate your ability to use the first five steps in Glasser's problem-solving strategy by role-playing a solution for any one of these four problems. Use as the student a class member familiar with the problem-solving process. Then find a person who is not familiar with the strategy and role-play another of the four problems.
2. After each role-playing episode, make a record of your experience, noting the ways that the strategy worked, the difficulties you encountered, and your feelings about the technique. Be prepared to describe what you liked and did not like about this approach to solving disciplinary problems.

Source: From *Teachers' General Strategies for Dealing with Problem Students,* Research Series 87 (p. 7), by M. Rohrkemper and J. Brophy, 1980, East Lansing: Michigan State University, Institute for Research on Teaching. Copyright 1980 by College of Education. Reprinted by permission.

important to be tough-minded in step 6 and to accept nothing short of another plan better designed to achieve the original objective. The teacher's attitude should be "I am disappointed, but not discouraged. You blew it today—how about tomorrow? What kind of plan can you make to live within the rules, to make things better for you and for others?" Students should learn that in this classroom incompetent doing behaviors will not be accepted.

One other cautionary note. Just as teachers may ask "why" when students misbehave, they are also inclined to ask "why" when students fail to keep the plan. A teacher should not be concerned with why but with "what" the student is going to do and "how" she is going to go about doing it. Even valid excuses should not be considered. Instead, the focus should be on the objectionable behavior and beginning the process anew. Accepting anything less than good behavior is a disservice to the student.

Step 7: Do Not Punish or Criticize the Student for Broken Plans.   Teachers should not punish or criticize the student for failing to follow the plan, but they also should not interfere with reasonable consequences. This advice might be difficult to follow. Teachers may be inclined to be punitive when students fail to live up to their agreements and responsibilities. The plan, possibly the result of a negotiated settlement, took time to develop, and the teacher expects a good-faith response. In the absence of responsible follow-through, some teachers are likely to look for ways to seek amends or secure compliance through coercive measures. These measures, which represent a teacher's efforts to gain control, contribute to a student's feeling a loss of control. This divisive dilemma poses a problem for both parties. Particularly during adolescence, punitive controls "fuel the fires of rebellion" (Nelsen & Lott, 1990).

Some teachers have found Dreikurs, Grunwald, and Pepper's concept (1982) of logical and natural consequences to be a useful way to think about and resolve this dilemma. Natural consequences are those that occur without the intervention of a second party. The consequence is delivered impartially in accord with the setting in which the behavior occurs. A student running down the hall, in violation of a school rule, stumbles and falls headlong down a stairway. Pain and bruises are a natural consequence of the student's choice to run on a recently waxed floor. Another student might be caught taking two stairs at a time in a last-minute dash to a class. A teacher observing the rule violation politely asks the student to come back down the stairs and walk up them. The delay results in the student's being tardy for the next class and automatically receiving a time owed.

The two teachers' interventions in the latter example, one requiring the appropriate behavior and the other imposing a penalty for interrupting the class by being a late arrival, are logical consequences. They are related, respectful, and reasonable (Nelsen, 1985). In the first intervention, the student was asked to negotiate the stairs properly (related), was confronted with the violation politely (respectful), and was only asked to engage in a behavior that served the student's best interests and others on the same stairway (reasonable). Similarly, making up lost time, the second intervention, is a fair exchange of a similar commodity (time) and does not embarrass the latecomer.

When we speak of no punishment, we mean no external imposition of pain to rectify a wrong or to deter the repetition of the unacceptable behavior. Generally, punishment involves taking away something desirable (often the loss of a privilege) or imposing something unpleasant (extra work, forced labor, insulting remarks) to secure compliance with a conduct standard. Proponents of natural and logical consequences point to the detrimental by-products of these uses of aversive control (Dinkmeyer, McKay, & Dinkmeyer 1980; Dreikurs et al., 1982; Nelsen, 1987). They contend that punishment does not set easy with some students, who may choose to express their discontent through passivity (tardiness, truancy, inattention, restlessness, forgetfulness) or with aggression (impertinence, rudeness, defiance, profanity, physical attacks, and vandalism). Although these behaviors are self-defeating, they may seem reasonable to someone who has lost control and wishes to strike back at the person whom they perceive as the cause of their predicament. Building a new plan keeps the focus where it belongs—on students' irresponsible choices and how they can make more responsible ones.

Teachers who use the Glasser problem-solving method (1977) frequently use time-out as a means of implementing their management plan. Time-out does not increase the size of the error signal. Students can be taught to use the questions that comprise the problem-solving sequence; a form can be prepared to guide their thinking and/or writing. "What is it you want? What were you doing? Is what you are doing helping you and others? What kind of a plan can you make to make things better for you and others?" After looking at the plan, the teacher might ask, "Is this plan going to get you what you want? Tell me how this is going to get you what you want." Then go for the commitment: "If this is going to get you what you want, are you going to be able to do it? Are you going to be able to follow-through with this plan so that you can get what you want?"

Mutual agreement on the "terms" of the contract allows students to return to the group in good standing, but students are sent back to time-out if they renege on the contract. The teacher's attitude should be one of "We cannot accept what you are doing; let's look at your behavior and make another plan within the rules." The teacher does not criticize, because criticism focuses on failure. Building a plan that has a good chance of succeeding is a good investment in the student and in the class.

Step 8: Never Give Up—Return to Step 3 and Start Again.   Because so many well-intentioned plans fail, teachers are often tempted to give up. Problem solving can seem like an exercise in futility. Students can come up with good plans because they know what to do, but they often lack the desire or determination to follow-through. Like people who try to stop smoking, students know what they should do, but the substitutes are not equally satisfying.

Some students expect the teacher to give up. Why not? They have often given up on themselves, and other teachers and adults have given up on them. But to have a chance to succeed, students must believe that their teachers will never give up. Teachers must be viewed as persons who are not easily discouraged, though they are occasionally exasperated. They must assume the stance "If this was a good plan, let's get it done."

Summary of Problem Solving

Our attention has been devoted to the development of social responsibility and to the procedures that decrease loneliness, isolation, and failure. Students must find outlets for the needs that drive their behavior and for the pictures representing these needs. Sometimes students must change the pictures that satisfy their needs or increase the number of pictures in the school section of their album.

As a student makes value judgments, he or she is reviewing the reference perceptions being used to compare internal world needs and external world possibilities. Reference perceptions can also be changed so that there is a better match between what one wants and what one has a reasonable chance of getting. Changing the reference perception, what one values, is sometimes the best way to reduce a perceptual error and decrease the intensity of the error signal. Less intense feeling behaviors can contribute to more manageable, stable, and rational doing behaviors. The student experiences greater control and confidence, which gradually help increase his or her repertoire of doing behaviors.

Schooling is aimed at increasing the number and quality of doing behaviors. Students who have experienced failure are reluctant to take the risks necessary to acquire doing behaviors. Failure contributes to indifference, apathy, and passivity. Even pictures that once seemed like potential candidates for reference perceptions are placed in the appendix of one's album. In their place are pictures of defeat and disillusionment. Doing requires dealing with feeling and thinking components that are overwhelming. It makes more sense to choose to do nothing on behalf of an unsatisfactory picture or a meaningless reference perception.

Glasser (1969) offers another pathway to a sense of identity and an outlet for a student's need for self-worth—the class meeting. Feelings of self-worth originate in responsible involvement with significant people, and the class meeting can be a vehicle for promoting these feelings. Such meetings provide a safe setting where picture albums, reference perceptions, perceptual errors, and error signals can be discussed and examined without fear of failure.

GROUP PROBLEM SOLVING VIA CLASS MEETINGS

Class meetings offer students an opportunity to entertain issues and think about problems that defy single and simple answers. Students can pose their own questions, examine one another's answers, gain new insights, and mediate their own disputes (Koch, 1988). There is a place for everyone in a class meeting because these meetings emphasize, seek, and value involvement in matters that touch the lives of the participants. Let us look at three types of meetings and the purposes served by each.

Types of Class Meetings

Social Problem-Solving Meetings

Social problem-solving meetings serve a socialization function. They help students deal with social-emotional dilemmas and peer conflicts associated with growing up (Opotow, 1991). Friendship, honesty, success, fear, handicaps, belonging, or con-

*Social problem-solving meetings
in a quality school generated
these random acts of kindness.*

formity might serve as pivotal topics. There are also many group management problems that could serve as the basis for social problem-solving meetings. Lack of unity, nonadherence to behavioral standards and work procedures, negative reactions to individual students, class approval of misbehavior, being prone to distraction and work stoppage, low morale, resistant and aggressive reactions, and inability to adjust to environmental change are cited by Johnson and Bany (1970, pp. 304–305) as common group management problems.

Open-Ended Meetings

These class meetings are probably the cornerstone of relevant education (Glasser, 1969). Students are asked to discuss thought-provoking questions that link their lives with the curriculum. They are encouraged to ask questions that deepen their understanding of a subject and to relate the subject to their personal worlds. A social studies class studying the Civil War might consider questions that connect the contemporary experiences of a student with that historical period, as illustrated by the following examples:

"What change in the conduct of the Civil War would you have made to shorten the duration of the war, alter the outcome of a single battle, or change the outcome of the war itself?"

"What one twentieth-century instrument of warfare, other than nuclear weapons, do you think would have made a decisive difference, had it been in the possession of one side in the struggle? Why?"

"What person who has lived during your lifetime might have been able to prevent the civil strife that led to the war?"

Open-ended meetings need not be confined to questions associated with school subjects. They can also be devoted to speculative questions such as the following ones that help students develop the insights and criteria for making more effective personal decisions:

"What would you do if other students made insulting remarks about your parents or friends?"

"When something—an idea, an event, a material object, a preference for behaving—is terribly important to you, what is the best way to get your way?"

Each question sparks differences of opinion, generates varied lines of defense, and is likely to provoke multiple and divergent answers. Yet every student is better informed, is likely to have found the basis for reaching an answer, and has acquired skills for tackling similar issues.

Educational-Diagnostic Meetings

These sessions are directly related to what the class is studying or to ways to improve students' learning abilities. For instance, teachers might use these meetings to solicit student opinions about an upcoming unit of study, baffling and troublesome problems that students have encountered in learning fractions, or an alternative form of evaluating English compositions. These meetings give students an opportunity to enter into a partnership with teachers as the latter search for answers to perplexing problems. Finally, these meetings may be used to find out what students would like to study and what they already know about the topic.

Purposes and Benefits of Class Meetings

Glasser has recommended frequent use of these three forms of class meetings, which are discussed at length in his book *Schools Without Failure* (1969, pp. 143–169). He believes that twenty to thirty minutes should be allotted to class meetings every day in the elementary grades and at least one class period per week in the secondary school.

Glasser's rationale emphasizes the need for a sense of identity and the importance of making education more relevant by making it more responsive to the realities of daily living. According to Glasser, classroom meetings should do the following:

❏ Provide a stable bridge across the gap between school and life.

❑ Help students believe that they can control their own destinies and that they themselves are a vital part of the world in which they live. Keep a class together because the more and less capable students can interact.

❑ Promote involvement because students can always succeed in a meeting—no one can fail.

❑ Help motivate students to do some of the less exciting fact finding necessary to make the judgments and decisions that may evolve from the meetings.

❑ Reduce isolation and failure so that a spirit of cooperation can arise.

❑ Help students gain confidence when they state an opinion before a group, which thereby helps prepare them for the many opportunities in life to speak for themselves.

❑ Increase responsibility for learning and for the kind of learning that is fostered by and shared with the entire class.

❑ Provide for the kind of involvement, value judgments, plans, and commitments that produce changes in behavior.

Discipline problems are less likely to occur in a classroom where students are disposed toward school and toward one another. Everyone has a stake in making the classroom a good place to be.

Procedures for Conducting Class Meetings

Class meetings are more likely to succeed if certain procedures are adhered to:

1. All problems relative to the class as a group and to any individual in the class are eligible for discussion.
2. Discussion is to solve problems, not to find fault or to punish, because those actions both serve as an excuse for not solving the problem.
3. The teacher, but not the class, must be nonjudgmental. The class makes judgments and works toward positive solutions.
4. Teachers can evaluate group processes and how well the procedures are working, but not the ideas of the participants.
5. Meetings should always be conducted with the teacher and all the students seated in a tight circle, with the teacher sitting in a different place in the circle each day.
6. Meetings should be thirty to forty-five minutes in duration, although the length of the meeting is less important than its regular occurrence and the pertinence of the problem discussed.
7. Meetings should be held daily in the elementary school classroom and at a regularly scheduled time. Meeting less often than once a week in a secondary school classroom does not provide enough continuity in the discussion and/or an opportunity to build group rapport and open communication.
8. Students seem to respond best if they are given an opportunity to raise their hands.

9. It is all right for the leader to call on students who do not raise their hands, usually with a remark such as "You have been listening very carefully; I wonder if you would like to contribute something?" or "I'm sure you have an idea about this, and I would like to hear from you."

10. A teacher never interrupts students to correct an idea or challenge a position, because when students are desperately struggling to express an idea or think through a problem, such a put-down discourages further participation.

Preparation for Class Meetings

Class meetings, like any other activity that produces desirable results, require judicious planning. Students should not be given free rein and permitted to take the discussion in any direction personal whims might suggest. Class meetings should be structured, even though they may be more open-ended than class recitation periods, and sufficiently flexible to entertain an unexpected turn of events.

After a topic has been selected, the leader can best prepare for the session by writing questions that can be used to direct the discussion. The *Resource Book for Class Discussion* (undated) is an inexpensive and useful resource booklet for elementary and secondary teachers. It is a compendium of topics, each developed according to a single format, that we have found to be an easy and effective way to prepare for a classroom meeting. Basically, the procedure provides for a progressively more thoughtful and insightful development of a topic in three steps: define, personalize, and challenge. Table 7–3 presents an example of a question and its development according to this format.

Teachers who used this planning guide generally felt more confident about their leadership role and reported being able to develop effective questions without a great expenditure of time. As with all skills, practice both increased the caliber of the questions and reduced the time required to prepare them.

Facilitator Skills for Class Meetings

Class meetings require some group interaction skills that teachers do not ordinarily use in classroom recitation sessions. Class meetings cast the teacher in the role of a facilitator. The session is intended to help students identify, examine, and understand personal frames of reference and to assist them as they apply these ideas to school and nonschool aspects of living. The teacher is challenged to help students expand on their ideas, make connections between their contributions and those of another class member, and examine the implications of their views. So how does the teacher prepare for this new challenge?

Experimentation has always been an exciting way to learn anything. At the outset, teachers can tell the students of their apprehension about leading class meetings, the basis for that apprehension, and why, despite these misgivings, they have decided to proceed with this experiment. The reasons can emphasize the potential benefits of the class meetings for students. Teachers who approach the situation in this way get all kinds of help from students, largely in the form of responsible participation, which in turn helps put the teacher at ease.

Table 7–3
What Would Happen If We Did Not Have Rules?

Define

1. What is a rule?
2. What are some types of rules?
3. Where do rules come from?
4. Why do we have rules?
5. Who uses rules?
6. What are some uses for rules?
7. What is an important rule?
8. How do rules become important?
9. What does it mean when someone says "Those are the rules of the game"?
10. Does everyone have to agree before something is a rule?

Personalize

1. How do rules affect your life?
2. When are rules most important to you?
3. When do you want to make rules?
4. Have you ever seen rules broken?
5. Have you ever been harmed when rules were broken?
6. How do you feel when you break a rule?
7. Have you ever been happy after breaking a rule?
8. Have you ever heard of a person called a ruler?
9. What are the rules at your supper table?
10. Have you ever tried to get someone to break a rule?

Challenge

1. When is breaking a rule very dangerous?
2. What would happen if we didn't have rules?
3. What is the color of a good rule?
4. Is there anything that can be done to reduce the need for rules?
5. If we could make just one rule for good living, what would it be?
6. Do you have a responsibility for enforcing the rules?
7. Why do some people disobey the rules more than others?
8. What would a classroom be like if everyone obeyed the rules?
9. Are there times when rules should be broken?
10. How can we tell a good rule from a bad rule?

Much has been learned in recent years about effective group leaders and the skills that seem to characterize their approach to group problem solving. Individuals with a psychotherapeutic background, such as Glasser, have no doubt influenced the transformation of ideas from the counseling literature into classroom principles and practices. Dinkmeyer et al. (1980) have adapted the work of Dreikurs and Soltz (1964) and Gazda (1973) to create group-development training materials for classroom teachers. The teacher's handbook for their training package, *Systematic Training for Effective Teaching,* discusses the differences between democratic and autocratic leadership styles and describes the skills that democratic leaders use to maximize student involvement in their classroom.

A list of essential classroom discussion leadership skills is given in Table 7–4. Some of these skills are ones that teachers already use in conducting class discussions and can be transferred to their class meetings. Other skills will expand teachers' ability to draw students into the classroom meeting and to promote critical and divergent thinking, respectful interactions, and group cohesiveness. By practicing one or two new skills each week, a teacher can gradually acquire the entire set of skills. Each of the twelve group leadership skills is designed to help students become more reflective and to help them clarify their thoughts and feelings. Those who might find remembering and learning the twelve skills a rather imposing task may want to concentrate simply on becoming an active, or reflective, listener (see Chapter 4).

CONCLUSION

Covenant management is concerned with releasing the student from teacher supervision and encouraging individual responsibility. As the relationship becomes grounded in trust, educators and students become coparticipants in the teaching–learning process, striving to make the most of themselves and their collective experience. Glasser's work has been used to describe the characteristics and purposes of covenant management and to suggest a basis for understanding and influencing students' behavior choices. Control theory is used to explain the process that invites and helps students become self-sufficient persons.

Lack of self-acceptance and self-worth is at the root of many disciplinary problems. Students who fail at school, or whose successes do not match their reference perceptions, are most likely to harbor feelings of inadequacy. Consequently, many choose to behave irresponsibly, although such behavior can further alienate them and eventually contribute to a sense of hopelessness and despair.

To help such students, teachers must find role-oriented solutions. They must begin by realizing that students personalize everything. A low grade in mathematics, for example, means "I'm a bad person" rather than "I'm doing poorly in mathematics." Students must first be helped to see that they are worthy human beings aside from their grades in mathematics. When role precedes goal, it is imperative that students are made to feel valued as persons, even though they may not do well in a particular subject. Chances are they will do better in that subject if they do not feel their personal value hinges on succeeding in it.

Role-oriented solutions must begin with a new conception of leadership and new standards for judging a quality school. Teachers who assume the attitudes and functions of a lead-manager (Glasser, 1990) will more likely create the conditions that foster the responsible involvement of students in the educational process. Students who are involved in the important decisions that affect them tend to see themselves as capable persons. They are more likely to identify with work that they help

Table 7-4
Group Leadership Skills

Skill	Purpose	Example
Structuring	To establish purpose and limits for discussion	"What's happening in the group now?" "How is this helping us reach our goal?"
Universalizing	To help students realize that their concerns are shared	"Who else has felt that way?"
Linking	To make verbal connections between what specific students say and feel	"Bill is very angry when his brother is late. This seems similar to what Joan and Sam feel about their sisters."
Redirecting	To promote involvement of all students in the discussion and to allow teachers to step out of the role of authority figure	"What do others think about that?" "What do you think about Pete's idea?"
Goal Disclosure	To help students become more aware of the purposes of this misbehavior	"Is it possible you want us to notice you?" "Could it be you want to show us we can't make you?"
Brainstorming	To encourage students to participate unhesitatingly in generating ideas	"Let's share all our ideas about this problem. We won't react to any suggestion until we've listed them all."
Blocking	To intervene in destructive communication	"Will you explain your feelings?" "I wonder how Stanley felt when you said that."
Summarizing	To clarify what has been said and to determine what students have learned	"What did you learn from this discussion?" "What have we decided to do about this situation?"
Task Setting and Obtaining Commitments	To develop a specific commitment for action from students	"What will you do about this problem?" "What will you do this week?"
Promoting Feedback	To help students understand how others perceive them	"I get angry when you talk so long that the rest of us don't get a turn. What do others think?" "I really like the way you help us get our game started."
Promoting Direct Interaction	To get students to speak directly to each other when appropriate	"Would you tell Joan how you feel about what she said?"
Promoting Encouragement	To invite students directly and by example to increase each other's self-esteem and self-confidence	"Thank you for helping us out." "What does Carol do that you like?" "Who has noticed Jamie's improvement?"

select, procedures for getting work done that involve their participation, and evaluation of quality that includes their input. When the idea of a quality school shapes the thinking and motives of students and staff, more people are going to be satisfied with nothing less than quality work. A student's role will be that of a good student. A teacher will model this role and will bring it to fruition in others.

Class meetings, by providing all students with an opportunity to succeed, offset the damaging effects of answer- and measurement-centered approaches to education. These meetings foster student involvement in school and with one another. School becomes a good place to be; students feel good about themselves and about one another.

Class meetings will not be a preventive measure for all discipline problems. Glasser's eight-step problem-solving process teaches responsibility while solving problems. Students must face the reality of their choices and the reality that they can make other choices. Facing up to themselves and the situation helps them change their lives by substituting success for failure and involvement for indifference. The teacher can *be* the difference, for a relationship is essential to getting started.

SUPPLEMENTARY QUESTIONS

1. Consider how two teachers—one you liked and one you disliked—approached the management of the unique characteristics of groups. How have their approaches shaped your experience as a student?

2. During any one of the four developmental stages of group formation, what have you observed teachers doing or neglecting to do that had a beneficial or detrimental effect on esprit de corps?

3. Allowing children and young adults to assume increasing responsibility for their own behavior requires considerable trust from adults. (a) Why might teachers be reluctant to entrust students with the freedom to become responsible persons? (b) What are the characteristic beliefs and behaviors of adults who trust students to make responsible choices?

4. Some would criticize Glasser's problem-solving solution to correct discipline problems as impractical because it requires too much time. When used to deal with minor discipline problems, it is too mechanical; that is, using standard questions to implement steps 2, 3, 4, and 5 become repetitive. How would you answer these two charges?

5. Glasser insists that punishment not be used as a corrective solution to discipline problems. There are teachers who insist that punishment is the only thing some students understand. What would be the claims and counterclaims of those on each side of this argument?

SUPPLEMENTARY PROJECTS

1. Ask a couple of teachers to describe the personality characteristics of their classroom group. Then ask them to speculate about how the group developed this personality. Keep a record of their remarks, then list them as examples of the three role categories presented in Figure 7–1.

2. Prepare a brief description of each of the four stages a group undergoes during a school year. Ask a veteran teacher whether these stages provide a realistic way to think about management priorities during the course of a school year.

3. Most prospective and veteran teachers have had experience with some type of extracurricu-

lar activity, whether it is a club, athletic team, dramatic production, or musical program. Prepare a paper describing the way in which the developmental growth stages discussed in this chapter can help one understand the psychosocial formation of extracurricular groups.

4. Interview several teachers about "breakthrough" experiences with hard-to-reach students. Prepare a paper summarizing the sequence of events or the single episode that made a difference. Try to abstract some principles of human interaction, and use them to

make recommendations for dealing with difficult students.

5. Ask a teacher to identify a student who is a chronic behavioral problem. Assume that the student's behavior is indicative of a person trying to gain control of his or her life. Conduct an interview with this student to get some sense of the internal world that drives the behavior. Write a paper, using Figure 7–3, to describe and explain the problem and offer a solution to it. Be sure to use each of the key concepts and the dynamics of control presented in the figure.

REFERENCES

Bany, M. A., & Johnson, L. V. (1975). Leadership in the classroom setting. In *Educational social psychology* (Chap. 5). New York: Macmillan.

Dinkmeyer, D., McKay, G. D., & Dinkmeyer, D., Jr. (1980). *Systematic training for effective teaching*. Circle Pines, MN: American Guidance Service.

Dreikurs, R., Grunwald, B. B., & Pepper, F. C. (1982). *Maintaining sanity in the classroom: Classroom management techniques* (2nd ed.). New York: Harper & Row.

Dreikurs, R., & Soltz, V. (1964). *Children: The challenge*. New York: Hawthorne.

Educator Training Center. (n.d.). *Resource book for class discussion*. (Available from Educator Training Center, 100 E. Ocean Boulevard, Suite 908, Long Beach, CA 90801.)

Gazda, G. (1973). *Human relations development: A manual for educators*. Boston: Allyn & Bacon.

Getzels, J. W., & Thelen, H. A. (1960). The classroom group as a unique social system. In *56th yearbook: The dynamics of instructional groups. Part II* (pp. 53–82). Chicago: National Society for the Study of Education.

Glasser, W. (1965). *Reality therapy*. New York: Perennial Library, Harper & Row.

Glasser, W. (1969). *Schools without failure*. New York: Perennial Library, Harper & Row.

Glasser, W. (1972). *The identity society*. New York: Perennial Library, Harper & Row.

Glasser, W. (1977). Ten steps to good discipline. *Today's Education, 66*(4), 61–63.

Glasser, W. (1981). *Stations of the mind*. New York: Harper & Row.

Glasser, W. (1984). *Control theory: A new explanation of how we control our lives*. New York: Harper & Row.

Glasser, W. (1986). *Control theory in the classroom*. New York: Harper & Row.

Glasser, W. (1990). *The quality school: Managing students without coercion*. New York: Harper & Row.

Jackson, P. W. (1968). *Life in classrooms*. New York: Holt, Rinehart & Winston.

Johnson, L. V., & Bany, M. A. (1970). *Classroom management: Theory and skill training*. New York: Macmillan.

Koch, M. S. (1988). Resolving disputes: Students can do it better. *National Association of Secondary School Principals Bulletin, 72*(504), 16–18.

Nelsen, J. (1985). The three R's of logical consequences, the three R's of punishment, and the six steps for winning children over. *Individual Psychology, 41*(2), 161–165.

Nelsen, J. (1987). *Positive discipline*. New York: Ballantine Books.

Nelsen, J., & Lott, L. (1990). *I'm on your side: Resolving conflict with your teenage son or daughter* (Chap. 8). Rocklin, CA: Prima Publishing & Communications.

Opotow, S. (1991). Adolescent peer conflicts: Implications for students and for schools. *Education and Urban Society, 23*(4), 416–441.

Purkey, W. W., & Novak, J. M. (1984). *Inviting school success: A self-concept approach to teaching and learning* (2nd ed.). Belmont, CA: Wadsworth.

Schmidt, J. J. (1989). A professional stance for positive discipline promoting learning. *National Association of Secondary School Principals Bulletin, 73*(516), 14–20.

CHAPTER 8

Management Style:
Classroom Control and Power

An understanding of the material in this chapter will help you do the following:

❏ Describe various ways that teachers express their management styles to enlist students' cooperation.
❏ Distinguish between authority and power, and discuss the classroom control implications of having one without the other.
❏ Describe the characteristics of five forms of power.
❏ Discuss typical ways in which teachers acquire and use these five forms of power to prevent and correct disciplinary problems.
❏ Cite the benefits and shortcomings of using each of the five forms of power in any given situation.
❏ Discuss the drawbacks of relying on some forms of power to the exclusion of others.
❏ Describe a teacher who effectively blends the five forms of power to fulfill the three classroom management functions.
❏ Speculate about the ways in which students use the five forms of power to counteract teacher influence.

We now turn our attention away from management functions per se and begin an overview of the forms of influence that educators can use to achieve a favorable response from students. Once again, the emphasis is on theory building, on what you believe are important management considerations and how best to carry them out in the schools. This tentative and speculative stance will help you better grasp the management rationale and recommendations made in previous chapters.

In a sense, this chapter, like the previous ones, tests your ability to entertain a number of overarching ideas related to your role as a reflective educator-leader and to examine the personal and professional significance of these ideas. As you read this chapter, keep in mind the products of reflection and proposing discussed in Chapter 1. Building linkages between the two chapters will create the foundation scaffolding for your management style. This scaffolding will enable you to construct a management position and at the same time provide a means to rebuild it. You will build and rebuild as you study and work with the concepts in this book.

THE CONCEPT OF MANAGEMENT STYLE

Like any other heterogeneous collections of individuals, classroom groups are likely to harbor differences of opinion about what is worthwhile and worth doing. Educators must be prepared to make converts of some and compatriots of others. For example, teachers must give some thought to how students will react to content, conduct, and covenant decisions and to how they will increase student receptivity of these decisions. Teachers cannot assume that their decisions will go unchallenged or uncontested. On the contrary, most decisions will be viewed as objectionable or disagreeable to at least some segment of the class. How teachers choose to meet such challenges will be outwardly expressed as their management styles.

There are many ways to enlist the cooperation of students in the affairs of the classroom and the school. Some educators believe that cooperation evolves as students participate responsibly in the decisions that affect their school lives. Students are therefore given an opportunity to talk about the advantages and disadvantages of various educational arrangements and the means to test promising possibilities. In such schools and classrooms, decision making is a cooperative enterprise that reveals a respect for both individual preferences and the corporate good. The educator's democratic management style invites involvement, creates a sense of community, and culminates in practices that reflect commonly held expectations.

Other educators are more disposed to set standards and insist on fidelity to them. They believe that cooperation occurs because they can offer a plausible and convincing rationale for the decisions that affect students' educational well-being. Students' allegiance to standards of conduct is a fundamental expectation. Cooperation is not earned; it is expected. This more authoritative management style presumes that just decisions can be rendered without consultation and that the compliance of students does not depend on their participation in the original decision making.

An educator's management style can be understood as a system of values and priorities for attending to a multitude of control functions that structure educational events. Each day educators make numerous decisions to promote some things and to discourage or stop others. Subsequent decisions are based on the effects of previous decisions and actions. The educator will choose to repeat some behaviors, modify others, and abandon some altogether. In making these adaptations, a shift occurs in the forms of authority and power that the educator uses to implement a plan and attain expectations. Authority and power are what enable educators to effect changes in students' attitudes and behaviors. Let us now examine two aspects of control (i.e., authority and power) and chart some of their implications for teacher management style.

THE DISTINCTION BETWEEN AUTHORITY AND POWER

Developing and maintaining classroom control requires both authority and power (Rich, 1982; Spady & Mitchell, 1979). *Authority* might be defined as the right to make decisions that affect the choices available to people. Educators can specify what is right or acceptable in the realm of goals and can select the means for attaining them. This authority is conferred. The state education authority and a local school board delegate the responsibility for educating children and youth to educators and grant them the authority to act in accordance with this responsibility. Thus, authority can be given; it need not be earned by acting in ways that please the group over whom the authority is exercised. In other words, students have little recourse from an educator's authority.

When teachers step into the classroom on the first day of school, they often have already made most of the major decisions about what will be learned and how students will go about learning it. This is an exercise of teacher authority. This is a legitimate way to exercise the content management function—after all, who else would know what is best for students?

Students seldom object to teacher management decisions as long as they feel that the choices made on their behalf are reasonable. However, if they believe that instruction is uninteresting, requires more effort than they wish to exert, or calls for abilities that they do not have, students may express dissatisfaction with the teacher's choices. In other words, the authority of the teacher and thereby the teacher's control are in jeopardy.

When a teacher's authority is undermined by educational choices that seem to ignore expressed student needs, the situation can be corrected. One might ask, "Are there contents that would be more appealing to students, better satisfy their educational needs and preferences, and simultaneously serve the interests of society?" or "If I cannot change the content of the curriculum itself, can I at least find more palatable ways to help students learn it?" Both questions are aimed at removing an impediment to student motivation, which consequently also removes constraints to control. The teacher's authority to make choices is reaffirmed, students choose to behave in accordance with these choices, and the teacher preserves an important aspect of the management function (Hill, 1984).

Not all teachers reexamine goal and method choices when student behavior suggests that these decisions are unacceptable. Some teachers feel compelled,

sometimes with good cause, to operate within the narrow framework of a prescribed curriculum guide or a single textbook. Or they think that their authority
has been circumscribed by decisions of the board of education or more experienced
colleagues and that they must exercise their leadership within the limits set by these
groups. It might be said that they have little authority to lead. Their educational
choices are curtailed by others; thus, the choices of students are likewise con-
strained. Rather than seeking greater authority or pressing for more autonomy in
making curriculum and methodology decisions, some teachers confronted by this
dilemma may resort to the second dimension of management—power—to solve
the problem.

Whereas authority can be conferred, *power* must be earned. Although the
teacher may be given the authority to make choices, the teacher cannot be given the
power to make students comply with these choices. For example, the teacher might
employ authority to assign a page of multiplication problems, but he must use power
to get students to complete the assignment. Why should a teacher bother making all
manner of decisions if the decisions are largely ignored? Authority is of little consequence without power. On the other hand, power seldom becomes an issue when
students do not resist authority. If students are willing to accept the teacher's decisions as serving their best interests and are willing to work as though they had participated in these decisions, the need for power would be merely an academic one
(Burbules, 1986; Smith, 1977).

TYPES, ACQUISITION, AND USES OF POWER

Seldom do educators secure unquestioned obedience to their authority or unconditional commitment to the decisions they make (Reed, 1989). The most ideal state,
of course, would be one in which students willingly do as educators say because
compelling evidence proves that to do otherwise would defeat their own purposes.
Students would reason that obeying educators would be good for them now and in
the future. Of course, some educators do have a flair for creating appealing images
of the benefits of learning, thereby sustaining high levels of student involvement and
minimizing the occurrence of disciplinary problems. In these schools and classrooms students generally do not seek alternative forms of excitement. Nevertheless,
even educators who manage to come close to creating the ideal state of affairs
sometimes need to resort to the use of power.

What forms of power are available to offset the debilitating effects of limited
authority? Five types can be used to get individuals to act in ways that educators
deem appropriate (French & Raven, 1959; Raven, 1974; Shrigley, 1986):

1. Attractive (or referent) power
2. Expert power
3. Reward power
4. Coercive power
5. Legitimate power

Management Challenge 8–1
Student Power and Teacher Influence

Your students are not getting work done or getting along with you or one another. Assignments are generally late, incomplete, and sloppily done. The class is constantly complaining about the length of your assignments, the difficulty of the work, the fairness of your grading practices, and the lack of correspondence between classwork and your tests. Their surly mood contributes to dissension in the classroom. Students bicker with one another and engage in backbiting. When you intervene, they gripe and complain about the way you treat them, justifying themselves by citing favoritism. They resist your efforts to restore order by being inattentive or by creating small accidents. They avoid cooperation by being indifferent to your efforts to be friendly.

1. Identify the forms of power that the teacher is lacking in this situation.
2. How might a teacher restore order and achieve an appropriate power balance?

Attractive Power

Some educators try to influence students to behave acceptably by drawing on their *attractive power*. Attractive power is essentially relationship power, the power educators have because they are likable and know how to cultivate human relationships. They do not take the goodwill of students for granted but instead go out of their way to help students feel good about themselves. Peer relationships also flourish; there is a sense of belonging and a mutual sense of purpose. Educators and students are people, and people concerns are always high on the agenda. Simply, attractive power is earned by being personable and hospitable.

Educators with attractive power influence student behavior by appealing to the human dimension (McCafferty, 1990). Students prefer to behave in accordance with educators' expectations because of genuine regard. Accordingly, students do things to please educators. Students are willing to do what educators ask because doing otherwise would impair their relationship.

Generally, teachers begin with some attractive power because most students start the school year with a favorable disposition toward their teacher. Sometimes called the "honeymoon" period, the first two weeks of school are a time of considerable harmony and congeniality. Each party to the relationship is working hard to make the other happy. Some teachers may assume that this is just the way things ought to be and therefore do little to perpetuate this lovely situation. Others do not make the assumption that students are naturally their friends, and they purposely work to build good relationships.

For example, a third-grade teacher told us that, at the end of each school year, she studies her class roster for the upcoming year. Each student who has had a history of problems with authority is noted. Prior to the start of the upcoming school year, the teacher invites said students to accompany her to a fun activity (e.g., a children's play at the community theater, out for ice cream, or to the school to help put up bulletin boards in the classroom). The teacher reported that this attractive power plan has been successful in the initial stages of building relationships with students who are not naturally friendly with educators.

Expert Power

Some educators do not have the interpersonal skills nor the personal inclination to use attractive power as a basis for influencing student conduct. They may prefer to rely on *expert power,* the power that accrues to educators because they possess superior knowledge in one or more fields. Such educators prize their command of a subject and derive great pleasure in conveying their knowledge to students. They tend to view teaching as the transmission of information and regard their role as being the primary purveyor of cultural ideas and ideals.

Teachers who prefer to rely on expert power to influence student behavior are often characterized as having great enthusiasm for their subject, enthusiasm that is often contagious. Students feel compelled to get involved in the teacher's excitement; they want a piece of the action. Because of their admiration for the teacher, students are willing to embrace the subject. They too would like to experience the exhilaration and enjoy and the sense of competence the teacher exhibits. Thus, the teacher's power resides not only in an expertise but also in a companion capacity to unveil it.

Few effective educators lead without acquiring and drawing on both attractive and expert power. Some students may be reached through attractive power; for others, expert power will be the most potent appeal. Still others will be captivated by a bold blend of the two. By using power judiciously, teachers can actually add to their power as they expend it.

Reward Power

In some respects the third form of power, *reward power,* is like the joy that students get from a relationship or the inspiration that they get from a subject. In fact, this third form of power often depends on educators' possessing either attractive or expert power. However, the ability to dispense rewards is not solely dependent on either of those types of power. Praise from an educator who is admired certainly means more to a student than praise from an educator toward whom the student is indifferent. Praise is positive feedback that affirms the value of a student's effort. Positive feedback does matter, even when it comes from an educator whom the student might not particularly like or admire. In fact, genuine praise, specifically targeted to accomplishment, may gradually lead to a more favorable disposition toward the educator who provided the compliment.

Relationships often grow and are nourished by appreciation. Similarly, the seeds of interest in a subject may be planted by praise and nurtured by admiration. Of course, reward power is not limited to social approval.

Coercive Power

When we think of rewards as ways to influence behavior, we are often reminded of the exact opposite—punishments. The fourth form of power, *coercive power,* is the ability to mete out punishments when a student does not comply with a request or a demand. It is often used as a last resort because most educators do not like to make life miserable for students. In fact, some would regard an overreliance on punishment as questionable and regrettable. They reason that educators ought to be able to secure cooperation without resorting to such aversive tactics. They also recognize that punitive tactics often have retaliatory side effects, some active (spite, revenge, vandalism, assaults) and some passive (tardiness, truancy, inattention, restlessness). All of these defeat the very purposes of effective leadership. Punishment can actually increase resistance to educator influence and create conflict that is not easily overcome by exercising other forms of power.

Despite the drawbacks of coercive power, it is used rather extensively in schools (e.g., time-out, detention, suspension). Educators sometimes contend that this is the only kind of "treatment" some students understand. The use of coercive power, although unpleasant and often distressing to both parties, can institute a process that produces positive results. Although punishment can stop bad behavior, it does not teach the desired behavior. This point was made in Chapter 6 and guidance was provided on how to teach replacement or desired behaviors.

Legitimate Power

Finally, the educator might employ *legitimate power* to obtain cooperation with academic and behavioral requirements. Legitimate power emanates from the student's belief that the educator has a right to prescribe the requirements. Similar to authority, legitimate power permits the educator to make decisions because that is the educator's rightful role. The difference lies in the student's acknowledgment of this right; it is not just the conferral of authority by those who hired the educator. In this sense, students accept the educator as leader, even though they had no role in the individual's selection. They willingly follow educator requirements out of respect for the role incumbent. Although who happens to occupy the role does make a difference, not all educators are regarded as having legitimate power and the "right" to make claims on students' time and energy.

The term *in loco parentis* is often used to refer to the educator's legitimate power. Acting in place of the parent has long been regarded as a legitimate function of the educator. Just as child rearing is a socialization process, so too is citizen rearing. The teacher, as the representative of society and the temporal head of the classroom family, must establish rules of conduct and devise measures for exacting conformity to them. When students affirm educators' rights to make decisions, compliant behavior increases. Sanctions for noncompliance are accepted. Little strife or turmoil mars this arrangement because the superior position of one party is acknowledged by the other.

As noted earlier, it is the coalescence of several forms of power that produces the best results. One can see that legitimate power, when coupled with expert power, has a greater potential for influence. Likewise, legitimate power may be more readily accepted if the educator also possesses attractive power. Thus, various combinations or pairings of power geometrically increase the educator's influence (Fairholm & Fairholm, 1984). Imagine a triad of power: The teacher is liked by students (attractive), admired for knowledge of the subject (expert), and sought out as a source of affirmation for one's achievements (legitimate). Truly, then, the teacher is a power to be reckoned with, one whose influence pervades all aspects of the learning experience.

THE RELATIONSHIP BETWEEN MANAGEMENT FUNCTIONS AND MANAGEMENT STYLE

Having examined the characteristics of each of the five forms of power, let us now turn to the relationship between management functions and the corresponding forms of power. Figure 8–1 should help you visualize the forms of power that support the competent expression of each of the management functions. Let us look briefly at some of the premises underlying this conceptualization of management functions and power.

Figure 8–1
Management Triangle: Management as Power Analysis

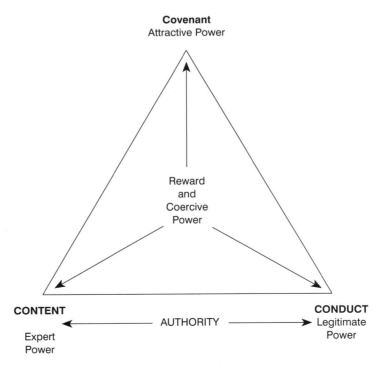

Premise 1: Eclectic Management Is Most Effective

The first premise is that the most effective classroom managers are eclectic. They borrow the best from several positions and meld them into a personal management style that transcends any single point of view (Smith, 1987). The eclectic classroom manager uses all five forms of power. Attractive, expert, and legitimate power are more likely to be earned through mutual respect and cooperation. The educator uses these as the three primary forms of power in all school settings, including the classroom. Coercive and reward power tend to be imposed and create dependent relationships; these secondary forms of power are best used to fortify the educator's leadership position.

Premise 2: Expert and Legitimate Power Form the Base

The second premise is that there is a progression of professional development in the acquisition and use of these three basic forms of power. Note in Figure 8–1 that expert and legitimate power form the base of the triangle and are connected by authority. Authority is best used to undergird expert and legitimate power. For the less effective or novice educator, conferred authority may serve as a temporary substitute. For example, teachers who have a modest command of their subject or who are less than convincing when making a case for content-oriented decisions may nonetheless claim the right to make these determinations. Similarly, an educator who meets with opposition when enforcing unstated or poorly stated rules may quell the resistance by insisting that it is an educator's prerogative to make, interpret, and enforce those rules. In each instance, invoking the authority principle may save the day. However, management is not a day-to-day proposition. Power makes for more enduring influence. Woe be it to the educator who continues to substitute authority for expert and legitimate power. For example, novice teachers who want to become expert teachers must improve their command of academic subjects in order to obtain the expert power of good classroom managers.

Because it is earned rather than conferred, power is the form of influence that students respect most. Educators know that students often resist leadership grounded in a deference for authority and an appeal to duty. Student resistance may reveal something of the character of American society: We espouse egalitarian principles and admire those who win our loyalty rather than expect it.

Premise 3: Attractive Power May Develop More Slowly

Relationships progress more slowly and gradually peak near the end of the school year. Thus, attractive power is placed at the pinnacle of the triangle in Figure 8–1.

An educator's attractive power, unlike expert and legitimate power, which can be augmented with authority, might actually be impaired if students are suspicious or scornful of authority figures. In addition, the educator's use of authority can provoke resistance and thwart amiable relationships. Thus, any impediments must be offset by admirable personal qualities expressed authentically. Individually, students must feel important in some personally fulfilling way.

Premise 4: The Educator Knows How to Use Forms of Power

The fourth premise is that the educator-leader must know how to integrate and jointly apply the five forms of power. The three primary forms of power—legitimate, expert, and attractive—are seldom sufficient to meet the daily challenges of teaching, regardless of the way teachers acquire and use them. In many instances, the teacher must resort to other measures to build support and maintain commitments. These measures can be pleasant or unpleasant; they can increase the number of behaviors that advance the aims of the organization or decrease the number of behaviors that do not. We generally refer to these pleasant and unpleasant consequences as *rewards* and *punishments*.

In Figure 8–1, the two remaining sources of power—reward and coercive—are shown inside the triangle with arrows directed toward each of its corners. These power sources should not be viewed as the impetus for any one of the central management functions but rather as ways to supplement the other three forms of power. For instance, a teacher might choose to use reward and coercive power in conjunction with legitimate power. By doing so the teacher is saying, "I have a right to decide what is best for you. If you choose to abide by the decisions I make while operating according to this principle of legitimate power, I will reward you." Thus, the teacher relies rather heavily on a "secondary" triangle of power. A secondary power triad is formed whenever one of the three primary forms of power—expert, legitimate, or attractive—is placed at the apex of the triangle, and the two secondary forms of power—reward and coercive—are placed at the base. In Figure 8–2, legitimate power is at the pinnacle of the triangle and reward and coercive power form the base. The most desirable coalescence of power is the eclectic model, represented in Figure 8–1.

Placing reward and coercive power inside the triangle also symbolizes the secondary role that they play in a management plan that makes adequate provision for content, conduct, and covenant control considerations. The skillful exercise of these forms of power establishes an intrinsic basis for good behavior. Students behave acceptably, becoming responsible partners in the educational process, because of internal controls rather than externally contrived rewards or punishments. We speak of self-reliant, self-regulated, and self-disciplined students to characterize the ultimate outcome of a well-managed classroom. However, the ideal may not be realized without some initial incentive for good behavior and some unpleasant consequences for unacceptable behavior. Thus, reward and coercive power do serve a useful purpose and gradually diminish in importance as learners are able to supply their own rewards and punishments as their behavior dictates.

How rewards and punishments are defined depends on which of the three primary forms of power an educator chooses to emphasize. An educator who uses attractive power as a primary source of social influence is more likely to use social reinforcers (verbal forms of praise or nonverbal forms of appreciation) rather than tangible reinforcers (a piece of candy or a certificate) as a way of acknowledging praiseworthy behavior. An educator who chooses to use expert power as a primary source of power and who does very little to build warm relationships with students

Figure 8–2
Legitimate Management Triangle: Secondary Power Triad

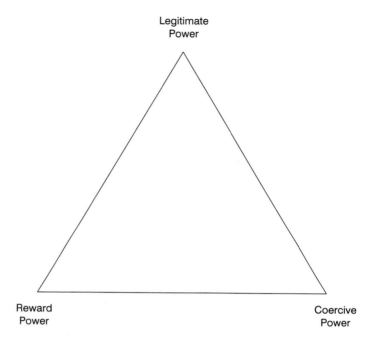

Legitimate
Power

Reward
Power

Coercive
Power

may be more inclined to use tangible reinforcers. A grade is one such tangible expression of approval or disapproval. It can be used to purchase effort, as well as achievement. Similarly, an attractive-power-oriented educator is more likely to use small doses of social isolation as a form of disapproval, whereas an expert-power-oriented educator may be more likely to exclude a student from some highly desirable activity. The point: Rewards and punishments are viewed and used differently by those who subscribe to the use of different primary forms of power. A teacher with a more balanced use of each of these primary forms is also more likely to employ a more wide-ranging and balanced approach to rewards and punishments.

THE RELATIONSHIP BETWEEN MANAGEMENT FUNCTIONS AND CLASSROOM CONTROL

Prevention, Maintenance, and Correction Programming

When discharging the three management functions, the effective manager uses three levels of supportive programming en route to student self-control (Charles, 1985; Palardy & Palardy, 1987; Stefanich & Bell, 1985): (1) prevention, (2) maintenance, and (3) correction.

Prevention programming is aimed at minimizing the onset of disciplinary problems, which the educator tries to anticipate through planning. Predicting what is likely to happen, given certain school and classroom activities, is an important element in the design and selection of preventive measures. For example, whenever a

---

Management Challenge 8–2

Teacher Power and Management Decisions

Ms. Montecino usually sets aside a portion of the lesson for independent study. During these periods, students are instructed to work individually, without conversing with each other. Despite these instructions and her efforts to maintain compliance by circulating and scanning the room while pupils work, sporadic conversations do occur. Ms. Montecino believes that these conversations disturb other members of the class and diminish the quality and quantity of work completed. She is at a loss as to what to do next. What would you recommend?

1. Use one of the three secondary power triads to suggest a solution to this problem. Offer a justification for your choice.
2. Describe the particulars of your solution, emphasizing the aspects of control that loom larger. What are some potential side effects of your choice of power? Of your solution?
3. Compare your solution with that of someone who has used one of the other secondary power triads. Discuss what you find more or less appealing about your management decision compared with your classmate's rationale and solution.
4. As a class, use the justifications cited in response to the first item to build a "defense profile" for each secondary power triad.

---

classroom activity calls for the movement of students or furniture, there is bound to be some commotion. Teachers who realize that kids will be kids try to visualize the things that could go wrong. The skillful transformation of the picture from one of confusion to one where decorum prevails is an aspect of good management.

Maintenance programming is aimed at helping students before their behavior becomes a full-fledged problem. For example, educators often stand in the vicinity of students to encourage them to behave properly. Similarly, a teacher might use a verbal or nonverbal cue to remind students to raise their hands before speaking or to remain in their seats. The cue is delivered just before such students behave contrary to the rules. The behavior prompt is a form of "first aid" to "injury-prone" students with little control over their own impulses. Without help, they easily forget the rules and slip away from the task at hand.

Correction programming focuses on the discipline of students who have not met the standards of responsible behavior. Educators use correction after students disregard prescribed rules and procedures. When the student's behavior is inappropriate and objectionable, the educator applies punitive measures or, at a minimum, a warning to redirect the behavior. The educator sometimes has to help the student regain control by making life momentarily unpleasant. When the student's behavior again falls within the acceptable range, the educator may revert to maintenance measures. Educators use incidents to identify preventive measures that will further decrease the recurrence of this behavior.

The topography of prevention, maintenance, and correction programming differs, and these three types of control are experienced differently by students. What students say to themselves after a teacher uses maintenance and correction measures will affect future behavioral choices. Although we can never be sure what students say to themselves, we can note the immediate and delayed effects of the message. An observer could readily help a colleague map the use of these three forms of control by noting the types of behavior preceding each control choice and the student's reaction to the intervention. Although the results of preventive measures are less evident, a record can be kept of the conditions that prevail when students are behaving appropriately. Such management mapping could help educators make adjustments in the types of control used to effect proper student behavior.

Management Functions and Forms of Control

Table 8–1 illustrates how a teacher might use each of the three types of programming while fulfilling each of the three management functions. For example, the effective delivery of instruction draws on content management skills and on prevention, maintenance, and correction. Teachers who use class discussions to develop and assess student understanding of a topic must know their subject, but they must also be able to manage this discussion to maximize student attentiveness, involvement, and achievement. In the first example of content management, the teacher maintains control by using silence to create an expectation, and a bit of anxiety, so that everyone feels like a potential target for the question. The same teacher might help a reticent student fulfill the expectation with encouraging remarks and a few well-chosen cues. On other occasions, the teacher might use a well-timed question to call a daydreaming or mildly disruptive student back to the task.

Table 8–1
Management Functions and Forms of Control

	Prevention	Maintenance	Correction
Content Management	Teacher asks question, pauses, and looks about the room before calling on one student.	Teacher helps student formulate an answer to a question.	Teacher asks inattentive student to react to previous student's contribution.
Conduct Management	Teacher makes explicit rules and states consequences for noncompliance.	Teacher gives warning before imposing a penalty for the next infraction of the rules.	Teacher imposes an unpleasant consequence for a transgression of a rule.
Covenant Management	Teacher helps students become acquainted with one another.	Teacher compliments several students who use the contributions of peers as building blocks for their own remarks.	Teacher works with class leaders to help them increase the acceptance of less-liked peers.

As two additional examples in Table 8–1 demonstrate, conduct and covenant management functions also lend themselves to each of the three levels of programming. Thus, as teachers engage in the conduct management function—for example, creating and sustaining an orderly classroom environment—they invariably find ways to get what they want by planning (preventive), by increasing the likelihood of securing student cooperation (maintenance), and by minimizing the recurrence of departures from what they want (corrective). Similarly, as teachers try to develop cohesive classroom groups, they look for ways to include everyone in class activities, promote respectful interactions among pupils, and remove obstacles to the acceptance of socially isolated students. A management and control analysis from the standpoint of developmental stages in the formation of groups appears as Table 8–2.

The hurdle lesson is a form of situational control designed to help a student who reaches a block in a lesson sequence (Redl & Wattenberg, 1959, p. 354). Teachers can intervene to help a student cope with some phase of the work as a preventive measure (before the frustrated student raises a hand for help), as a maintenance measure (soon after the student has raised a hand), and as a corrective measure (after the student has engaged in a social conversation with a classmate). By being creatively attentive to the various ways that each technique can be used, you will learn to apply it in situations beyond those presented in this text.

THE RELATIONSHIP BETWEEN TEACHER CONTROL AND STUDENT COUNTERCONTROLS

Students come into a classroom with their own agenda. They have ideas about what schools and teachers should be like and about their own likes and dislikes. They may not share the teacher's vision of education and the educational process. Consequently, they will attempt to shape the teacher's vision so that it is more compatible with their own.

Students can be good impression managers. They can use seduction techniques that capitalize on the teacher's preference for congenial and cooperative relationships. They can give and withhold approval to influence the teacher's conception of teaching and learning as well as the role responsibilities of students in this process. They apply their wares in much the same way as the teacher, drawing on each of the five forms of power to secure conformity to their expectations. Thus, teachers learn that *all forms of control are reciprocal.*

When teachers comment that their "class is out of control," they are really saying that the "class is in control." Because whenever a teacher relinquishes control, whether by design or default, someone or some group will fill the gap. If students do not share the teacher's vision of schooling or do not trust the teacher to maintain control, they will attempt to take charge of the situation because they want either more desirable educational arrangements or a more predictable and reasonably stable environment. Students want some control over their learning. They want to know from one day to the next what will be expected of them and how to go about meeting these expectations. This knowledge reduces the uncertainty and risks of making mistakes.

Table 8–2
Stages in Group Formation and Forms of Control

Forming Stage and Content Management	
Problem:	Anxious about academic background (linking).
Prevention:	Design assignments that allow for a wide range of reading levels and/or problem-solving skills.
Maintenance:	Devote most of class period to independent seatwork activities that permit frequent teacher program checks.
Correction:	Pair "I can" and "I can't" students to promote helpfulness and to create models of success.

Storming Stage and Conduct Management	
Problem:	Test teacher's patience and resolve (distancing).
Prevention:	Teach, practice, and review rules and routines so they become habits of civil behavior.
Maintenance:	Appreciatively recognize responsible behaviors by noting specific acts of courtesy, kindness, and consideration.
Correction:	Express disapproval and disappointment when students disregard duty and dignity.

Norming Stage and Covenant Management	
Problem:	Loss of fervor for learning (fueling).
Prevention:	Share decisions about the arrangements for learning a prescribed body of material.
Maintenance:	Build group morale by interspersing creative, novel, and playful activities among periods of intellectual intensity and academic rigor/routine.
Correction:	Provide students a form that can be used to record and graph their motivational level at teacher's designated times. After several days, meet as a class to discuss results.

However, in their efforts to exercise control, teachers may err in the way that they use power to secure compliance and/or cooperation, even if they are cognizant of student needs and wishes. Power struggles are inevitable in any group in which one person attempts to regulate the behavioral choices of others. And teachers are constantly reducing behavioral options as they make decisions about what needs to be learned and how best to learn it. Students are going to have competing opinions on both counts. They will withhold cooperation or actively resist when they are convinced that their opposition will make things better for themselves. Again, teachers learn that all forms of control are reciprocal.

Students also possess expert, legitimate, attractive, reward, and coercive power. They can use their social influence, individually and collectively, to negotiate more favorable classroom arrangements. Most often, teachers experience student power as unobtrusive pressure to make decisions that students do not find offensive. As a consequence, teachers need to know the limitations of each form of student power in terms of the manner and the extent to which it can be used to achieve control. For example, students' countercontrol limits the ways teachers can use legitimate power to regulate pupil conduct. Pushing the limits by being overzealous can create considerable resistance. When the teacher reacts with correspondingly strong enforcement of expectations, the students may wage war by attacking the very forms of power that the teacher is using to secure compliance.

As students resist punitive measures, the teacher must resort to increasingly tenacious tactics, ones that may draw other reluctant parties into the fray. The principal and parents, for instance, are often unwilling allies of the teacher. Their lack of cooperation and resolve can undermine the legitimate power of the teacher, who may be forced to seek a truce. Such a negotiated settlement generally results in compromises unacceptable to either party. Rebuilding a basis for working together will often depend on a more effective use of expert and attractive power. This process might be best facilitated by drawing on the student leadership within the class, those who lead because they possess similar forms of power.

Reflective teacher-leaders are cognizant of the need for classroom control and of the fact that students need to feel in control. Some teachers feel in control when they make and carry out most of the decisions. Others believe that good control is largely knowing how to put students in control. Most teachers try to achieve some balance between the two. They look for ways to gradually increase opportunities for students to assume responsibility for their behavior. They help students gain and use power to increase their sense of duty and personal well-being.

Reflective teacher-leaders are also aware of the wisdom of using preventive and supportive, rather than corrective, measures to secure cooperation. The student retains more control when less obtrusive measures are used. When corrective measures are used, the student not only loses control but must fight to regain it because these solutions are experienced as a criticism or a confrontation. In either case, it is natural for students to feel defensive or resistant. When such feelings pile up, the stage is set for explosive, violent behavior or for intransigence. If teachers rely on control techniques that invite cooperation, power is less likely to be an issue.

Reflective teacher-leaders do not avoid or discount the potential value of power struggles (Bolton, 1979). There is no place for timidity in the classroom. Teachers must be prepared to stand firm when maturity and reasoned judgment should prevail. They must also negotiate differences to promote progress toward self-control. At the time, the benefits of conflict may not be apparent to either party. But conflict can be a useful way to reexamine the rationale for using selected practices, consider alternative courses of action, and look for more compatible solutions to problems. Teachers and students can find ways to respectfully work out their differences and forge a partnership that serves their mutual needs and interests.

CONCLUSION

Each day the teacher will make hundreds of decisions and will rely on various forms of power to carry them out. More often than not, the skillful conjoining of these forms of influence will make the difference. A particular decision may be justified to students by drawing on legitimate power, made manifest by using expert power, and substantiated by reward power. However, over time, as decisions accumulate and produce varied results, the teacher will gradually drift toward preferred ways of getting things done. Some forms of influence seem to get better results than others or, if not better, then results with greater personal satisfaction, or perhaps just with less hassle. The business of teaching, as a matter of social influence, changes as the learning landscape changes. Thus, the cumulative effects of each day's performance become the backdrop against which the teacher makes future management decisions, and successful performances become the standard for seeking and using the forms of power that make a difference.

No teacher relies exclusively on one of the five forms of power or narrowly attends to just one of the three management functions listed in Table 8–3. A teacher might use a direct and conformity-insistent practice on one occasion and an indirect and consensus-seeking approach on another. Preventive discipline might emphasize direct adherence to a rule during a drill-and-practice session. Preventive discipline

Table 8–3
Management Goals: Attaining and Maintaining Cooperation

Forms of Power	Management Functions		
	Content	**Conduct**	**Covenant**
Expert	Teacher inspires and challenges students to excel.	Teacher monitors pupil progress and provides corrective feedback.	Teacher uses activities that foster high levels of pupil involvement.
Legitimate	Teacher offers reasons for rules.	Teacher consistently enforces rules.	Teacher permits students to participate in rule setting.
Attractive	Teacher is a model of decorum.	Teacher helps students acquire academic and social engagement skills.	Teacher promotes a sense of belonging and group cohesiveness
Reward	Teacher offers verbal commendations for academic accomplishment.	Teacher provides tangible recognition for appropriate behavior.	Teacher expresses satisfaction with pupils as persons.
Coercive	Teacher takes away a privilege.	Teacher imposes a penalty.	Teacher withdraws approval.

might be achieved with a captivating film on a day in which students have trouble concentrating. Likewise, selecting and utilizing corrective measures might depend on a combination of several types of power enlisted in the service of several management functions. Thus, teachers cannot be strictly classified according to power preferences and management priorities.

Teachers are neither democratic nor autocratic. Effective teachers are eclectic (Duke & Jones, 1984; Glickman & Wolfgang, 1979; McDaniel, 1981; Nyberg, 1981). They act so as to acquire all five forms of power, and they judiciously use power to fulfill all three management functions.

SUPPLEMENTARY QUESTIONS

1. "A Concept of Power for Education," an article by David Nyberg appearing in the Summer 1981 issue of the *Teachers College Record*, asserts that "the idea of power has lain more completely neglected in educational studies than in any other field of thought that is of fundamental social interest. Power talk is conspicuously absent from schools and from educational literature" (p. 535). Assume that Nyberg's assessment is correct. What do you believe accounts for the lack of serious attention to this topic?

2. What are some early signals that a teacher's choice or use of power may be ill advised? What might the teacher do when it becomes rather obvious a change must be made? Do you think a teacher could deliberately set out to acquire one of the five forms of power to counteract signs of a power dilemma? Justify your answer.

3. Assume that your fairy godmother could confer one form of power; in other words, you would not have to earn it. Which form of power would you choose? What would be some of the benefits and shortcomings of relying almost exclusively on this single form of power? If applying this form of power proved to be ineffective, to what would you attribute this failure? Answer without reference to the other four forms of power.

4. Describe the developmental characteristics and typical lifestyle preferences of students at the grade level at which you plan to teach. Given these descriptions, which types of power decisions are they most likely to resist? What types of countercontrols, as uses of power, are they likely to employ?

5. Teachers are sometimes heard to say that they feel powerless to change a particular situation or relationship. What do you make of this disposition? What contributes to this feeling of powerlessness? What can be done to restore a teacher's sense of possessing power and commitment to make a difference?

SUPPLEMENTARY PROJECTS

1. Prepare a philosophy of teaching statement for a teacher who believes that the acquisition and use of attractive power are essential for success. Prepare similar statements for a teacher who subscribes to legitimate power and one who advocates expert power. Compare and contrast the belief systems of these teachers, and speculate about the implications of their respective role perceptions.

2. Ask several teachers to describe their philosophy of classroom management and how they deal with some of their most common disciplinary problems. Make a list of their beliefs and practices. Then classify their statements and solutions according to each of the five forms of power. Note the alignment between the forms of power in which they believe and those they use.

3. Design a checklist of behaviors that seem indicative of each form of power. Observe a teacher working with a class for approximately thirty minutes; keep a record of the teacher's use of power. Discuss with the teacher the correspondence between his or her power preferences and your findings.

4. Interview several students to ascertain the management practices used by their most and least favorite teachers. Classify the practices of their teachers according to the five forms of power. Meet with other members of the class to discuss similarities and differences across grade levels.

5. Using the *Education Index,* select and read three articles devoted to classroom discipline/management techniques. Discuss the forms of power that support the techniques advocated in these articles.

REFERENCES

Bolton, R. (1979). *People skills* (Chap. 12). New York: Simon & Schuster.

Burbules, N. C. (1986). A theory of power in education. *Educational Theory, 36*(2), 95–114.

Charles, C. M. (1985). *Building classroom discipline: From models to practice.* New York: Longman.

Duke, D. L., & Jones, V. F. (1984). Two decades of discipline: Assessing the development of an educational specialization. *Journal of Research & Development in Education, 17,* 25–35.

Fairholm, G., & Fairholm, B. C. (1984). Sixteen power tactics principals can use to improve management effectiveness. *National Association of Secondary School Principals Bulletin, 68*(472), 68–75.

French, J. R. P., & Raven, B. H. (1959). The bases of social power. In D. Cartwright (Ed.), *Studies in social power* (pp. 150–168). Ann Arbor, MI: University of Michigan Press.

Glickman, C. D., & Wolfgang, C. H. (1979). Dealing with student misbehavior: An eclectic review. *Journal of Teacher Education, 30*(3), 132–138.

Hill, S. (1984). Motivational controls: Power, force, influence, and authority. *The Teacher Educator, 19*(4), 14–20.

McCafferty, W. D. (1990). Prosocial influences in the classroom. *The Clearing House, 63*(8), 367–369.

McDaniel, T. R. (1981). Power in the classroom. *Educational Forum, 46,* 31–44.

Nyberg, D. (1981). The concept of power for education. *Teachers College Record, 82,* 535–551.

Palardy, J. M., & Palardy, T. J. (1987). Classroom discipline: Prevention and intervention strategies. *Education, 108*(1), 87–92.

Raven, B. H. (1974). The comparative analysis of power and power preference. In J. T. Tedeschi (Ed.), *Perspectives on social power* (pp. 172–198). Chicago: Aldine.

Redl, F., & Wattenberg, W. (1959). *Mental hygiene in teaching.* New York: Harcourt, Brace, & World.

Reed, D. (1989). Student teacher problems with classroom discipline: Implications for program development. *Action in Teacher Education, 11*(3), 59–64.

Rich, J. M. (1982). *Discipline and authority in school and family.* Lexington, MA: Heath.

Shrigley, R. L. (1986). Teacher authority in the classroom: A plan for action. *National Association of Secondary School Principals Bulletin. 70*(490), 65–71.

Smith, J. (1977). The decline of teacher power in the classroom. *Peabody Journal of Education, 54,* 201–206.

Smith, R. O. (1987). Discipline in the middle school: A hierarchical model keeps things in perspective. *Middle School Journal, 18*(2), 23–25.

Spady, W. G., & Mitchell, D. E. (1979). Authority in the management of classroom activities. In D. L. Duke (Ed.), *Classroom management: The seventy-eighth yearbook of the National Society for the Study of Education* (Part II, pp. 75–115). Chicago: University of Chicago Press.

Stefanich, G. P., & Bell, L. C. (1985). A dynamic model for classroom discipline. *National Association of Secondary School Principals Bulletin, 69,* 19–25.

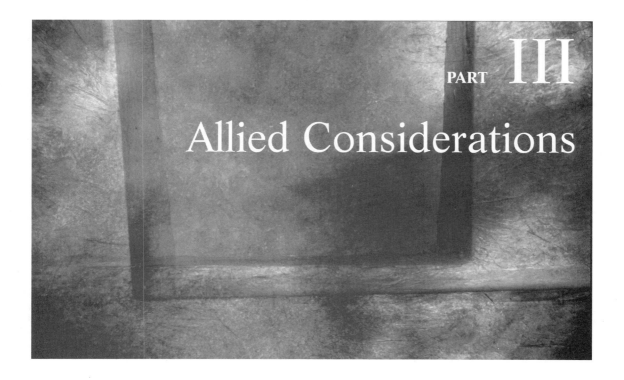

PART **III**

Allied Considerations

CHAPTER 9
Home–School Partnerships

CHAPTER 10
Legal and Ethical Aspects of Management

CHAPTER 11
Stress Management for Professionals

Home–School Partnerships

An understanding of the material in this chapter will help you do the following:

- ❑ Offer reasons for working with parents and including them in the classroom management plan.
- ❑ Compare and contrast school and home management conditions to demonstrate the unique, demanding aspects of the former.
- ❑ Identify reasons why parents might resist a teacher's efforts to include them in the classroom management plan.
- ❑ Identify ways to counteract parents' resistance or indifference to invitations to become involved in their child's education.
- ❑ Discuss personal and professional considerations that might influence a teacher's choice of parental involvement activities.
- ❑ Discuss ways to use parent volunteers, and identify the supervisory requirements and the benefits and drawbacks of parental participation.
- ❑ Describe ways to prepare for and conduct a parent–teacher conference, distinguishing between a conference devoted largely to student progress and one devoted to a disciplinary problem.
- ❑ Develop a home–school response–cost contract that combines behavioral expectations and consequences in both settings.

At the end of a psychologically demanding and physically exhausting day in the classroom, the last thing a teacher needs is a conference to discuss a behavior problem with Bobby's parents. Most parental contacts do occur at the end of a school day, and they are often scheduled to deal with problems. Thus, it is not surprising that some teachers are less than enthusiastic about including parents in their classroom management plan. Their enthusiasm may be further dimmed by thoughts of losing time to grade papers and make plans for the next day.

Sore feet, splitting headaches, and paperwork aside, teachers face genuine apprehensions about working with parents. They cannot be sure that parents will understand their point of view or appreciate the circumstances that often restrict their options when dealing with disciplinary problems. Teachers often feel that parents sit in judgment of them because they are employed by the community. This feeling is intensified when the parents' education is equal to or exceeds that of the teacher. Thus, teachers can be intimidated by parents, a situation compounded by the lack of support that many teachers receive from colleagues and administrators.

Given these impediments to school–home relations, a teacher might ask, "Why should I try to work with parents? How will the time spent working with parents benefit me and my students?" Answers to these questions, addressed in this chapter, can help teachers and future teachers assess the costs and benefits of partnering with parents in the management of classrooms.

REASONS FOR WORKING WITH PARENTS

Understanding Parental Attitudes and Home Conditions

Children who come from homes with a stable center are easier to manage in school. They expect adults to take charge, and they respect and appreciate them when they do. The lessons learned at home are readily applied at school. There will be some testing of limits because children need to know that an adult can be trusted to lead, but generally they respond positively to adults who treat them fairly and firmly.

Children who come from homes where parents are uncertain about or are frightened by their authority do not really know what to expect from an authority figure when they come to school. Thus, they are careless about how they conduct themselves. Although teachers regard them as troublemakers because they always seem to be creating confusion, they are really trying to resolve their own confusion. Only the teacher can reduce their confusion by giving them some fixed targets against which to judge their behavior.

Thus, knowing something about the home situation, particularly about how parents interpret and use authority, can help the teacher determine how to manage what Rosemond (1981) has referred to as "exercises in democracy." Teachers can and should gradually give students more opportunities to become self-governing and self-reliant. But such opportunities come earlier to children who have experienced a secure base of family living and a safe school setting. When teachers and parents provide young people with a consistent set of ethical standards and insist on behavior compatible with these standards, classroom discipline problems decrease.

Informing Parents of the Demands of Children and Schooling

Under the most ideal circumstances, all parent–teacher conferences would be scheduled the first day of school. After a summer spent hearing "When are we going to go?," "I'm bored, there's nothing to do," and "Mom, you told Brian not to but he did it anyway," parents are willing to pay a ransom to anyone who will take the kids. And teachers do take the kids—for nine months and under less favorable circumstances than parents enjoy during a three-month summer vacation.

Recall the subtle yet significant differences between conditions at home and school that were presented in Chapter 3. It should be apparent that behavior problems common to both settings may occur with greater frequency and intensity at school because of setting circumstances. Accenting these distinctions may help teachers more fully appreciate the enormity of their task and make them less apologetic when seeking home support for their endeavors.

Teachers might casually introduce these ideas into conversations and conferences with parents, not to evoke parents' sympathy but rather to help them obtain a better understanding and appreciation of a teacher's situation. Parents are less inclined to be critical of teachers with disciplinary problems and are more receptive when called on to help if they also grasp the enormity of the teacher's task.

Recall from Chapter 3 that Silberman and Wheelan (1980, pp. 172–173) offered these five observations about classroom and family differences: (1) Classrooms are crowded places, (2) classrooms present little opportunity for privacy, (3) classroom relationships are less intimate, (4) fewer means of rewards and punishments are available, and (5) teacher authority is easily undermined. Although unlikely topics for a single parent conference, they can make quite an impact whenever they are presented.

Parents' Right to Know About Their Child's Behavior and Performance

Parents are understandably upset when they learn at grade time that their child has fallen behind in schoolwork and has been penalized with a grade not indicative of the child's ability. They have reason to raise questions about the propriety of the teacher's decision to wait so long to inform them of their child's negligence. Likewise, parents want to know when their child is struggling and unsuccessful and when remedial efforts are not getting the hoped-for results. Instead of wishing that tomorrow or the next day would provide a breakthrough, the teacher would be wiser to meet with parents to explain the predicament. Often the opportunity to talk about the problem with other vitally interested people will open the door to new insights and solutions.

Naturally, parents also like to know about their child's accomplishments. Learning about them on other than standard occasions—at conference time or the end of a grading period—means so much more to them. Use children's accomplishments as opportunities to forge partnerships with parents. Make a telephone call or send a note home. We all like to be caught by surprise when it comes to good news.

Parents as Valuable Resources

Most parents believe that school will help their child make the most of life, but many do not know how to support their child's efforts in school. They may have had limited success in school themselves and may be incapable of doing anything more than telling their child to behave and mind the teacher.

Teachers can educate parents about ways to support their children. We will examine several ways to do so later in this chapter; at this point, we merely stress the importance of viewing parents as partners rather than as a pain in the neck (Henderson, Marburger, & Ooms, 1986). Some parents, though they mean well, can be perceived by busy teachers as demanding, tiresome, and exasperating. A teacher who gives them the benefit of the doubt can generally convert good intentions into appropriate interventions.

Parents' Ability to Augment a Management Plan with Home Consequences

Teachers are well advised to seek parental help when the consequences that they are using do not seem to make a difference. Parents can easily understand the relationship between their child's behavior and positive and negative consequences. They have observed the effectiveness of using various pleasant and unpleasant consequences to manage behavior at home and have no doubt made changes in their choice of consequences to get the cooperation that they want.

Given parents' considerable experience and their practical grasp of contingency management, teachers can increase the power of their management plan by

---

Management Challenge 9–1
Dealing with a Parent's Complaint

Mr. and Mrs. Samuelsen are irate because you have been using cooperative learning strategies that appear to be detrimental to their child. Alexa has complained about having to spend so much of her time helping the less able members of the class. Her parents are upset because she is being deprived of enrichment activities provided in other classes when she finishes her work. They insist that you excuse her from the cooperative group activities in the interests of her education.

1. What do you see as the problem? What do you think accounts for the problem?
2. What do you know about Alexa that might help you deal with this situation?
3. What do you know about the benefits of cooperative learning that might be pertinent in this situation?
4. How would you like this problem to be resolved? On what do you think this solution might depend?

joining forces with parents. Sometimes the solution is merely a matter of intensifying the effects of an already desirable consequence. A perfect paper or test score may mean more when it is followed by the child's favorite dessert at dinner. A weak reinforcer, such as a teacher compliment for a modest improvement, can be strengthened by making more of it at home. The price of a movie, an extension of the Saturday night curfew, or an unexpected trip to the local pizza parlor can be an incentive for additional increments of effort and progress. On other occasions parents can help by substituting reneged TV privileges for an after-school detention or the loss of recreational time with friends for a missed recess. When home and school act in concert, children are more likely to get the message and act on it.

Although most parents are congenial and cooperative, some will resist involvement or refuse to cooperate. Knowing some of the reasons for such behavior can help the teacher approach the parents and gradually draw them into a participatory role. Why do some parents, often with good intentions, resist and refuse to get involved?

WHY SOME PARENTS RESIST INVOLVEMENT

Fear of Divulging Conflicts at Home

No one likes to air their dirty linen in public. Even when problems at home are unbearable, many parents shoulder the entire burden all by themselves. Some parents, as a matter of principle, do not want teachers to intrude on their private lives. They believe that home and school are separate aspects of living and that it is best to keep it that way.

Parents may also fear revealing how conflicts are resolved at home. Some parents may be abusive to their children and have been abused as children themselves. Formerly abused adults may lack the skills to deal with difficult children or to cope with stressful events in their lives. They may feel helpless to prevent siblings from abusing one another.

Panic over Child's Possible Failure

Parents' hopes and aspirations for their children often include success in school. They sometimes have grave forebodings that their children will not succeed. Any hint that things are not going well throws them into a tizzy; their worst fears are coming true.

People consumed with fear want to protect themselves from anything that will make things worse. The teacher is often perceived as a person who will make things worse. Rather than face the situation, such parents try to deny it and thereby reduce the threat.

Guilt About Lack of Parenting Skills

Trouble at school can be taken as a personal indictment. Just as teachers often regard disciplinary problems as a sign of their own incompetence, parents feel that their child's unacceptable or ineffective behavior reflects negatively on them as parents. They have tried to be better parents, but it does not seem to make any difference. The walls just seem to come tumbling down around them.

Unfortunately, guilty parents often believe that their admission of guilt absolves them from further responsibility. They express remorse and entreat others to take over their problem, as if to say, "How can anyone expect something from people as helpless as us? Do what you must. We will agree to whatever you think best." Some guilty parents dislike, even resent, being judged or made to feel that they are lacking in some way. They are not about to stand still for such accusations. The teacher does not actually have to accuse the parents—just being told of their child's problem can make the parents think that the finger of blame is being pointed at them. They must defend themselves against the appearance of inadequacy.

Belief That the Teacher Is Trying to Shift Responsibility

Some parents are suspicious of teachers who seek their cooperation. They believe that the child is the school's responsibility during school hours. When students get out of hand, school personnel should take care of the problem. Some parents may feel that the teacher and the way in which schools are organized and managed create the problems in the first place. Their attitude is "How dare you try to make your problem our problem! Johnny never acts like that at home." These parents are not about to be talked into taking on what they perceive to be someone else's obligation.

Some parents feel that they already have all they can do to cope with life. If they are not careful, their life will be further complicated by demands made on them by school personnel. It is thus best, they think, to keep a safe distance from school and the chances of getting drawn into the fray.

Reluctance to Interfere in the Teacher's Work

There are parents who believe that they can best express their confidence in teachers by staying out of the way. They may have heard teachers complain about parents who look over their shoulders or have heard accounts of teachers who felt that their hands were tied by a disgruntled or influential parent. Rather than being accused of being pests or know-it-alls, such parents adopt a hands-off policy. When they do not see eye to eye with the teacher, they dismiss their differences as a matter of philosophy, as half-truths perpetuated by malcontents, or as a suitable and reasonable course of action if all the facts were known. Thus, they can keep their distance, hope for the best, and take some pride in their attitude of noninterference.

Belief That They Would Not Know How to Participate

Some parents may not be convinced that the teacher is doing everything possible for their child, but they do not believe that they themselves know the first thing about how to improve the situation. Others may have some ideas about how to make things better but lack the confidence to take their case to school. In both instances, the parents may be intimidated by an ingrained submissive role as student, a lack of education, or the bureaucratic attitude that contends that, when it comes right down to it, the teacher is generally right.

Teachers' invitations to parents may be expressed in such general terms that the parents cannot visualize a way to participate. They envision a conference with the teacher in which they must defend their viewpoint or try to enlighten a teacher about their perception of their child and the best way to work with him or her. Again, they may feel intimidated—after all, what do they know compared with a person educated in psychology and teaching/learning?

The foregoing discussion, devoted to parental resistance or reluctance to get involved, is not meant to demean parents or discourage teachers from seeking parental assistance. On the contrary, knowing possible reasons for parents' reluctance will help teachers remove barriers to involvement. Parents, like teachers, mean well. Yet, even well-meaning people are sometimes reluctant to get involved, particularly if they have doubts about themselves or suspicions about others. Teachers who are sensitive to the full range of parental viewpoints and uncertainties can more effectively promote home–school collaboration.

BUILDING A PARENTAL SUPPORT SYSTEM

Counteracting parents' indifference (Walde & Baker, 1990) or resistance (Moore, 1991) is vital to building a viable support system. Parental views of teachers and schools are not without foundation. The ways in which teachers conduct themselves and in which schools deal with the community can build and sustain parental suspicion, fear, guilt, and hopelessness.

Management Challenge 9–2

Appropriateness of Seeking Parental Assistance

Educators differ about the appropriateness of asking parents to help settle disciplinary problems. Some believe that if the problem originates at school, school personnel should be responsible for solving it. Others think that the school is frequently a convenient outlet for venting problems originating at home and that joint action is called for.

1. On which side of this issue do you find yourself? What is the basis for your position?
2. What circumstances might make you more favorably inclined toward the other side of this issue?
3. Do you think that parents share your convictions about this matter? Why or why not?
4. Do you think students favor your stance? Why or why not?

So what can teachers do to counteract the unfortunate consequences of parental apathy or resistance to participation in their child's education? Teachers can lay the foundation for a parental support system by doing four things:

1. Identify parents' expectations (Lindle, 1989).
2. Examine their attitudes toward those expectations.
3. Determine their own expectations and build their confidence.
4. Identify types of parent–teacher contacts

Let us take a closer look at these links to a sound parent–teacher support system.

Identifying Parents' Expectations

Both parties to a relationship can be more trusting, open, and helpful to one another if they have clear expectations about each other's contributions to the relationship. Since it is the teacher who initiates the relationship and must be most responsible for nurturing it, the teacher should try to identify the parents' expectations.

Generally speaking, parents expect teachers to do the following:

1. *Be concerned* about their child; be interested in the characteristics that define the child as a unique person
2. *Teach* their child; help their child acquire the foundations for lifelong learning, learn how to interact successfully with others, and understand and appreciate the achievements of humankind
3. *Inspire* their child to want to learn and to make the most of the opportunities the school has to offer
4. *Stimulate* their child's efforts to *celebrate* attainments and *cultivate* aspirations
5. Help their child *develop* self-control
6. *Keep them apprised* of their child's progress and of any difficulties that might require their cooperation
7. *Work diligently and earnestly* to make the most of the community's investment in education and to address parents' concerns for their child's well-being

When teachers ask themselves what they can do to demonstrate commitment to these expectations, they have taken the first step toward drawing parents into a relationship that will benefit the child. The expectations must be realistic, ones to which a teacher can honestly subscribe. They must be expectations that can be discussed with parents and can serve as the common ground for a commitment to quality education.

Examining Attitudes Toward Parental Expectations

The next step in building a parental support system is for the teacher to ask, "What are the personal and professional implications of these parental expectations? What do I think and feel I must do to honor or abide by these expectations? Can I do these

---

Management Challenge 9–3
Caught Between Dissimilar Parental Expectations

Carla is copying other students' work and has cheated on several tests. During a meeting with Mr. and Mrs. Harrelson to discuss the problem, it becomes apparent that Carla's mother and father do not share similar views of her abilities, character traits, and responsibility for creating and solving the problem. You believe that solving the problem depends on common perceptions in these three areas.

1. Why do you believe it is essential for her parents to share similar views of Carla before embarking on a solution to this problem?
2. What would you do to secure similar perceptions of Carla and the situation in question?
3. Would you work toward a common view similar to your own? Why or why not?
4. Given a common basis for working on the problem, what role would you see for these parents? How might your expectations differ because the parents did not share similar viewpoints at the outset?

---

things and demand no more of myself than I believe to be reasonable? Can I behave this way and still maintain high levels of satisfaction with my work? Will these ways of believing and behaving contribute to positive relationships with parents?"

Sometimes teachers feel that parents expect too much. They think that parents want them to *care* for their child more than is possible when there are a couple dozen other youngsters in the class. Parental expectations must be tempered by humane considerations. A teacher cannot possibly be all things to all people.

There will be times, as in any relationship, when teachers feel that they are being called on to do too much. Rather than suppressing their resentment, they should discuss their feelings with the parents. An honest and forthright discussion can clear the air, create the basis for some new beginnings, and produce results that will be more satisfying for all parties.

Determining Personal Expectations and Building Confidence

Parent–teacher conferences are often fraught with apprehension and uneasiness. Neither teachers nor parents really know what to expect from one another. Teachers are worried that they will be judged too severely, and parents are concerned that they will be viewed as being too passive or too pushy. Both fear that their perceptions of the child or the purposes of education will clash.

Under these circumstances it is not surprising that teachers feel insecure. They give a diffuse description of what the class is doing and a guarded appraisal of the child's work. This does not evoke a response from the parents that builds confidence. The teacher does not ease up and become more effusive; the parents do not warm up and become less reserved—hardly a confidence-building experience for the teacher.

The confidence of teachers grows less in proportion to what they know and more in proportion to how *convinced* they become about what they know. Teachers who succeed most may not know the most; they are just more committed to what they know. They can take a stand on an issue because they have given thoughtful consideration to alternative views and their practical implications. They can act on their position because they are not held hostage by indecision. A decisive teacher simultaneously inspires and acquires confidence.

Identifying Types of Parent–Teacher Contacts

The types of invitations that a teacher extends to parents should be consistent with the teacher's level of confidence. For example, a teacher who would be threatened to have parents visit the classroom should not invite them to do so. Encouraging parents to call whenever they are concerned about their child's response to school could be very troublesome to some teachers. It is not helpful to request parental input when the procedures through which it is secured are fraught with risks.

A list of ways in which parents can become involved in the classroom or help the teacher become more knowledgeable about their children serves several purposes (see Table 9–1). Because there are more possibilities than can ever be included in a parental partnership plan, teachers may feel relieved that they do not have to select forms of involvement with which they are uncomfortable. The list can also help teachers identify the types of demands and the forms of payoff associated with each choice. Complementary activities that may corroborate knowledge acquired in other ways and provide unique perspectives can be selected. Parental involvement activities that help all children can be balanced by activities that serve the interests of a single child.

The demands that parental involvement activities make on the teacher's time and abilities should be carefully considered. By listing these demands next to each activity, teachers can initially make selections that play to their professional strengths and personal self-assurance. Such activities will increase parents' confidence in the teacher. Gradually, activities that make parents look good can be added. Parents will normally choose from the original list according to their strengths, too. As the list is enlarged, more parents will find a place where they feel comfortable and confident.

PARENTAL PARTICIPATION PROGRAMS

The parental participation program should be aimed at helping children succeed in school (Brandt, 1989; Comer & Haynes, 1991; D'Angelo & Adler, 1991; Epstein, 1990; Kennedy, 1991; Warner, 1991). Teachers should be sure that the things parents are asked to do are not merely self-serving. Such forms of parental involvement, though they may have secondary benefits for students, can make parents suspicious

Table 9–1
Forms of Parental Involvement

Make a presentation on:
1. Interests and hobbies
2. Trip(s)
3. Occupation(s)
4. Memorable experience(s)
5. Goals and aspirations
6. A favorite book
7. Fascinating person(s)
8. Controversial issue
9. Public service project
10. Family holiday observances

Provide clerical and auxiliary services:
1. Grade papers
2. Chart pupil progress
3. Prepare bulletin boards
4. Make telephone calls
5. Arrange special activity
6. Write notes to children
7. Observe and record student behaviors
8. Type handout materials
9. Prepare art materials
10. Prepare classroom events' calendar
11. Record material on audio tape
12. Set up science lab
13. Write as child dictates
14. Prepare graphic materials
15. Check out reference materials
16. Develop parent and nonparent resource file
17. Organize and maintain class library
18. Take attendance and prepare proper forms
19. Collect money and keep records
20. Beautify classroom

Provide supervision:
1. Serve as a field trip escort
2. Chaperon parties
3. Be a playground attendant
4. Serve as a library aide
5. Assist with extracurricular event
6. Assist students with money-raising project
7. Help with learning games/ simulation exercises
8. Assist at school assemblies
9. Serve as club coordinator
10. Help student volunteers

Home-based support activities:
1. Assist with contingency management program for school behavior problems
2. Assist with homework
3. Guide use of television watching
4. Assist with creative ideas/ suggestions
5. Prepare child for special school project
6. Build inexpensive home library
7. Take child to museum
8. Converse with child about school activities
9. Provide teacher feedback on home-based activities
10. Talk to other parents about home-based support activities

Provide remedial and enrichment experiences:
1. Locate materials
2. Listen to students read
3. Tutor a student
4. Teach a skill
5. Conduct small-group discussions
6. Discuss homework assignments
7. Develop learning packages
8. Present drill work
9. Construct a learning center
10. Conduct outdoor, on-school-site activities

of the teacher's motives. When the teacher can demonstrate direct connections between parents' activities and the well-being of their children, parents are more likely to participate and do so without feeling used (*Instructor and Teacher*, 1986).

At a minimum, parental involvement can begin with the open house that often inaugurates the school year, continue through occasional notes and telephone conversations as the year progresses, and conclude with a conference that summarizes a student's accomplishments and takes a look toward the next school year. These activities might be appropriate for all parents. Other activities may address special needs or occasional problems that require a more concerted effort and sustained participation of both parents and teacher.

Parental Survey

Let us assume that the school year begins with an open house. This activity gives teachers and parents an opportunity to meet one another in a social setting. Generally, the teacher provides a brief program that includes a description of his or her teaching philosophy, the course work objectives, how the class is typically conducted, and methods of evaluating and reporting pupil progress. The session concludes with an invitation to parents to ask questions.

Parents may inquire about the teacher's general educational outlook and the practices that the teacher has found successful when dealing with certain types of learning problems. Someone will generally ask how parents can be helpful. When a parent does not introduce this topic, the teacher may conclude the session by describing ways that parents have assisted at home and school, perhaps by citing specific instances when parental involvement made a significant difference in the life

---

Management Challenge 9–4
Training a Parent Volunteer

Mrs. Luiz has volunteered to help you work with children who are falling behind in their work. She is very conscientious and is well received by students in your classroom. However, she views helping as giving answers. Students soon learn that they can rely on her when they want to get an assignment done with the least amount of time and effort.

1. How might you work with Mrs. Luiz to help her understand the basis for and the long-term consequences of her actions?
2. How might your approach to solving this problem serve as a model of what it means to help?
3. What kinds of skills will she need to learn in order to be a suitable helper? How might you help her to acquire these skills?
4. What might you do to ease the change by alerting students to her new helping role?

of a child. Using the account to highlight forms of parental involvement provides parents with specific behavioral targets.

A general introductory session might be followed by the administration of a survey instrument. Since the teacher cannot possibly meet each parent and acquire information about each child—much less remember details from such conversations—a written instrument might be used. It might employ an open-ended format, or it might be a checklist. The educational backgrounds of parents should be considered when choosing a format. Items of information that might be collected include the following:

❑ Qualities of the child that the parents believe to be particularly praiseworthy
❑ Things that the child likes to do in school or areas in which the child has been particularly successful
❑ Things that the child tries to avoid in school or areas in which the child has encountered some difficulty
❑ Impressions of the child's social acceptance at school
❑ Qualities or practices of teachers about which the child comments favorably or unfavorably
❑ Their child's reactions to selected kinds of incentives for good work and corrections for unacceptable behavior
❑ Management techniques that work best for parents
❑ Behaviors of the child that they have tried to eliminate at home without much success
❑ Disciplinary measures that the parents prefer to have the teacher use
❑ Receptiveness of parents to jointly applied home–school consequences for appropriate and inappropriate behavior

Parents generally use the informal period that normally concludes the evening to talk about items on the survey instrument. These conversations can alert the teacher to take note of areas of particular concern to individual parents. The conversations also may suggest ways to revise the instrument.

Keeping in Touch

Teachers can maintain communication with parents by sending them a letter following the open house. It can simply say, "Thanks for attending; it was a pleasure to meet you. Your responses on the survey instrument will be very helpful." Similarly, a letter expressing disappointment to those who were unable to attend and informing them of what was accomplished at the meeting is a good way to open communication. Thereafter, occasional positive notes to the home build the relationship and establish the foundation for parental cooperation. Parents are more likely to ask their child about events at school when they are periodically reminded that the teacher takes their child's work seriously.

Notes home can be brief. They may merely repeat a positive exchange that took place between the student and teacher that day or make an observation that confirms a point made on the parental survey instrument. Some schools encourage notes home by using an attractive certificate-of-achievement format, including a picture of the school emblem or mascot and space for a brief statement. For example, a principal at McKinstry Elementary School in Waterloo, Iowa, printed an attractive memo form that included spaces for the names of the parents and their phone number. He called parents, read the message from the teacher, and offered his own congratulations before giving the memo to the student to take home. Parents appreciate calls from the main office that are not a signal of trouble.

Teachers who present their management plan at the open house may want to send a letter home to introduce the plan to parents who did not attend. Teachers who use the survey instrument during the open house might indicate that parents' suggestions at previous meetings have been incorporated into the plan.

Parent–Teacher Conferences

The parent–teacher conference has been the mainstay in programs of parental cooperation (Rotter, Robinson, & Fey, 1988; Wolf & Stephens, 1989). Many schools schedule one or two pupil-progress conference days each year. The sessions are devoted to brief descriptions of a student's adaptation to the social dimensions of schooling and academic achievements.

During the course of the conference, the teacher tries to draw the parents into a discussion of the report. The teacher may lead with questions that seek the parents' input before disclosing his or her assessments. Playing off the parents' observations can keep the conference targeted to their interests and concerns. Most parents, however, feel less anxious and are often more talkative if the teacher takes the lead and they are able to react to the report. Regardless of the teacher's procedure, the successful conference requires conscientious preparation and communication skills.

A teacher might want to begin preparing for the conference by referring to the survey instrument completed at the open house. Discussing the survey information during the conference shows parents that the survey was not just an exercise and that the teacher has a genuine desire to provide for individual differences. This approach can increase the parents' willingness to share additional information about their child. If the teacher goes on to share insights about the child's attitudes and actions in school, again revealing a personal interest in their child, parents will be more accepting of and responsive to the achievement report. If the report is likely to be less favorable than the parents would like to hear, it is particularly important to use the rapport-building measures just described.

Keeping Anecdotal Records

It is beneficial to try to anticipate what parents will want to know about their child's performance in the school program. Parents experience similar anxieties and share common concerns and desires for their children. Teachers can reduce the time required to prepare for conferences if these considerations are used as the backdrop for looking at children throughout the school year. One convenient way to maintain this focus is to keep a folder of work samples, test results, and anecdotal notes for each student. Anecdotal notes, which are periodic entries summarizing significant incidents, are an invaluable tool for building rapport with parents and demonstrating an appreciation for a child's unique characteristics and activities.

Figure 9–1 provides a sample anecdotal entry for a student whose performance is being affected by the home situation. For the moment, the teacher has decided to seek a solution that can be implemented without the mother's participation. However, should the problem persist, documented by additional anecdotal entries, the teacher has the basis for initiating a parent–teacher conference. A conference at this stage is more likely to produce a jointly sponsored home–school plan because the teacher can cite specific instances of the problem and can describe the measures that have produced only modest success. Myrna's mother would surely be favorably disposed to a teacher who had taken such a personal and active interest in her daughter.

Anecdotal reports are often used to make note of the following:

❑ Marked and unexplainable changes in a student's behavior
❑ Reactions to typical classroom events such as examinations, homework assignments, and discussion periods
❑ Interactions with classmates
❑ Reactions to praise and correction
❑ Glimpses of the student in informal situations

As an observational system, the anecdotal report may serve as an account of any significant episode in the life of a student. However, it is important that these vignettes be divided into the four parts illustrated in Figure 9–1. Hence, the actions that occurred are kept separate from the interpretation and recommendation.

Anecdotal notes taken over a period of time provide a cross-section of the student's life at school and provide clues about the ways to help the student make the most of school experiences. Entries are used to report on a pupil's progress, note praiseworthy attainments, and select future goals. When it comes time to report to parents, a wealth of information will have been collected from one's daily observations. A simplified version of this record-keeping strategy has been proposed by Levin, Nolan, and Hoffman (1985, pp. 14–15).

Anticipating Problems and Arguments

Parents and teachers will not see eye to eye on all matters reported in a conference. They are less likely to agree when the conference is scheduled to deal with a series of disciplinary incidents. Even if the teacher has followed all of the foregoing suggestions, some parents may be annoyed or downright angry about being called to school. Some of their hostility may be based on the handling of the problem, but often they are upset because the child has created problems in public settings. They may not be able to separate the two sources of their anger. This condition might be

Identifying Information:

Date: <u>Friday, September 12, 1991</u>   Time: <u>9:48 a.m.</u>

Activity: <u>Prior to bell to begin class</u>

Persons Present: <u>Teacher, student, classmates</u>

Incident Observation:

Myrna entered the room and came directly to my desk. She asked if we were "still going to have the test today." I indicated that the test would be given as scheduled. As I spoke, I could see tears beginning to form in her eyes. I said, "You seem troubled." She said, "I am not ready to take the test." I said, "Sounds like we have a problem. What do you suggest?" She went on to say that she wasn't ready for the test because she had taken care of her baby brother and younger sister until her mother returned from shopping. She said after helping put the children to bed she had to help with the housework. She said she was just too tired to study after finishing household chores. I asked Myrna if she could see me after school so that we could discuss the matter further. She said she had to go home right after school so her mother could take a nap before going to work. She said she could see me during her fifth-hour study hall. I agreed to meet with her at that time. I told her to take her books to the school library and to use the time to prepare for the examination. She thanked me and left the room.

[The foregoing statement provides an objective and brief "word snapshot" of a single incident. The observations, confined to a description of the setting and the behavior of the two parties, exclude all evaluative terms.]

Interpretation:

I believe Myrna desperately wants to succeed in this class. I think she believes that acceptance by other students hinges on being an academic success. She does operate at the fringes of the group and seems to have a very tentative hold on her own sense of self-esteem. Her anxiety contributes to a tentativeness in class discussions and a reluctance to contribute unless called upon. However, her contributions are sporadic, often brief answers, so she does not draw much favorable attention to herself.

[This section includes subjective judgments. The teacher treats the situation as a social adjustment problem and begins to formulate explanations for Myrna's behavior. These tentative interpretations are used to devise an intervention that might help Myrna deal with more than the immediate problem. Another party encountering the same incident might arrive at different conclusions and other remediation procedures.]

Recommendation:

Plan some cooperative problem-solving activities in the class. Pair Myrna with Shelly G. Shelly is a mature and popular student who will be helpful while taking a personal interest in Myrna. Working with a highly visible and well-respected person may draw favorable attention to Myrna and might give her a little more self-confidence during the discussion sessions that follow small-group exercises.

[The teacher decided upon a course of action based on her interpretation of the problem. Another teacher might agree that social acceptance and self-esteem needs lie at the root of the problem but might select other means to alleviate or remediate the condition.]

Figure 9–1
Sample Anecdotal Entry

exacerbated by the ripple effects of divorce, separation, and single-parent situations (*Learning 86, 1986*).

The teacher may get the full measure of their wrath and may, as a result, adopt a nonassertive response style. Canter and Canter (1976) have noted that under these circumstances, teachers are likely to apologize for bothering the parents, downplay the problem, belittle themselves, let the parents off the hook, or downgrade the consequences of the child's behavior. In each of these instances, the teacher will probably come away from the conference feeling even more responsible for the problem and more burdened by the solutions.

A teacher well prepared for the conference and well prepared in communication skills is less likely to slip into the nonassertive response style or, worse yet, to exchange hostility with hostility. Anticipating parents' problems, feelings, and the arguments that they frequently advance can be one useful form of preparation. Dreikurs, Grunwald, and Pepper (1982) developed an exhaustive list of arguments that parents use to support their position. Gordon (1974) devised a list of problems that come up during parent–teacher conferences. These are problems that might catch teachers unprepared, leaving them stunned and helpless or defensive and hostile. Finally, a practical guide for helping parents of a misbehaving high school student can be found in Hall (1982); the guide can be readily adapted to the parent–teacher conference format.

Using the Assertive Response Style

Another useful step in preparing for the conference is provided by Canter and Canter (1976), who recommend that the teacher have a clear idea of how to present the following points:

1. *Goals for the conference.* "I need your cooperation to deal with the following problem."
2. *Objectives for the conference.* "I specifically want you to do the following things at home."
3. *Rationale for the conference.* "I am asking you to assist me because it is in your child's best interest that we work together."
4. *Consequences for the child if the parents do not cooperate.* "I am personally convinced that if you do not take steps to resolve this problem your child will fall even further behind in his work or will be even less acceptable to his peers."
5. *Documentation for your assertions.* "I have come to these conclusions after receiving about half of the homework assignments, getting test scores at the bottom of the class, and hearing his silly remarks when I confront him about my concerns" (pp. 161–162).

The statements following each of the five categories illustrate the assertive response style. The teacher can temper the authoritative role illustrated here by inviting parental reactions after presenting materials for each of the five categories. The assertive communication strategy, active receiving of a message, or Gordon's (1974) reflective listening and I-messages can also be used to change the tone of the conference while maintaining the teacher's strong stance.

Neither party should be intimidated by the other, and the child's best interests should be the primary focus of the conference. However, when a conference is required to resolve a discipline problem—whether the problem is one of having to give constant reminders to remain seated during seatwork assignments, periodic reprimands for using vulgar language, or deal with occasional acts of insubordination—it is imperative that the teacher obtain a solution with which he or she can live. In addition, parents should be included in the solution and kept apprised of the results of any interventions.

The assertive approach advocated by Canter and Canter (1976) is but one way to work with parents to solve children's difficulties. Some teachers may prefer a problem-solving approach that invites greater parental involvement in defining the problem, generating and evaluating solutions, determining how to implement the chosen solution, and helping evaluate the solution's success. These teachers can profitably use the Glasser (1977) approach described in Chapter 7. The guidelines for conducting a parent–teacher conference, summarized in Figure 9–2, may be a useful adjunct to the foregoing preparation suggestions.

Teacher–Parent–Student Contracts

Conferences at which the teacher, parents, and student are present can be an effective way to produce a behavioral improvement contract. Although opinions differ about whether children should attend conferences on pupil progress, few would argue with the importance of having the student present for a pupil management conference. Differences about the behavior problem or how to handle it ought to be discussed with the student present. As long as there are differences about what has happened, there will be differences about the need for change as well. Without a student acknowledging that a change in behavior is needed, it is futile to make a contract.

A contract should represent a genuine intent to change and include specific ways to bring about the change. A contract may include any number of provisions and may cover differing periods of time (Lehman, 1982, pp. 35–38; Welch & Tisdale, 1986, pp. 35–40). Figure 9–3 presents an example of a typical teacher–parent–student contract that lists home consequences to deal with a student's behavior in school. All of the consequences are external forms of control and are introduced in the absence of self-control. Generally, the contract will include the following (regardless of the age or grade level of the student):

- ❏ A description of the desired behaviors
- ❏ A description of the home and school situations in which these behaviors are to occur
- ❏ The time span to be covered by the contract
- ❏ The good things that will occur at home or school if the contract is honored

The situation is warmer and easier when the teacher sits away from his desk (the symbol of authority or position). Parents can also be put at ease if the meeting takes place in a small conference room rather than a classroom, if possible. If such a room is not available, the teacher could arrange chairs at the back of the room for a more informal setting.

Don't rush the interview. It will probably take time for parents to relax, tell what they are really worried about, and express their real feelings and fears.

Be willing to agree with parents whenever possible. When the answer must be no, take a long time to say it, and say it softly, without hostility. When there is agreement on a hundred small things, it is easier for both parent and teacher to state their differences frankly if a difference of opinion does exist.

Listen with enthusiasm. Parents should be encouraged to do the talking, telling, and suggestion making. Give parents a chance to "sound off," especially if they are angry or upset. After they have let off steam, you will find it easier to discuss the problem calmly. Try not to argue with them. Control your facial expressions of disapproval or anger. A wince or frown at a parent's comment or revelation may embarrass him or put him on guard.

Examine your own emotional reaction to criticism. Do you dislike people who give you new ideas or who disagree with you? If so, you may be getting this message across in subtle, unspoken ways.

Decide in advance what is to be discussed during the parent conference. Assemble a folder of the student's work, and jot down a checklist of the various problems to talk about.

Use the simplest and clearest words you can find to explain what you and their child do in school. Gear your talk to the parents' interests and avoid "pedegese" at all costs. At the same time, don't talk down to parents. They are not children, and they resent being treated as such.

Don't let comments about other children creep into the conversation. Avoid making comparisons with the student's brother and sisters or with his classmates.

Provide parents with at least one action step—one thing they can do at home to help their child overcome a particular problem you've been discussing. Help them understand that their child's success in school must be a joint project of home and school.

Begin and end the conference with a positive and encouraging comment about the child and his school activities.

Don't take notes while talking with parents. They may feel intimidated and afraid to speak up.

Don't forget the follow-up. The first step is to write down the gist of what was discussed, so you won't forget it when writing the child's next report card or when preparing for the next parent conference.

Figure 9–2
Guidelines for Conducting a Parent–Teacher Conference (Author Unknown)

Desired Behaviors

1. Be in seat and ready to work when bell rings.
2. Listen during teacher presentations.
3. Participate in class discussions.
4. Attend to task during independent study time.
5. Complete homework.

Positive Home Consequences

Step I—Trip to ice cream store when 10 squares are filled
Step II—Extra hour of TV when 20 squares are filled
Step III—Money for a movie when 40 squares are filled
Step IV—Extra hour before bedtime when 60 squares are filled
Step V—Supper at fast-food restaurant when 90 squares are filled

> Note. One square is filled for each desired behavior, each day. Five bonus squares are filled when all five desired behaviors are achieved for a given day. Start over after 90 squares. Change the positive consequences for each step.

Negative Home Consequences

Failure to demonstrate any of the desired behaviors during a given day:

1 violation—No phone calls
2 violations—No television viewing for the evening
3 violations—No outside-the-house activity after supper
4 violations—Confinement to house all day Saturday
5 violations—One week of confinement at home (no phone calls or TV)

> Note. Begin with clean slate each day.

Contract is now to cover the period between _____ and _____.
                                                 (date)   (date)

Today's date _____

Signatures _____ _____
                    (teacher)   (student)

_____
          (parent[s])

Figure 9–3
Teacher–Parent–Student Disciplinary Contract

❑ The bad things that will occur at home or school if the contract is broken
❑ The date on which the contract was written
❑ A place for the signatures of the student, the parent(s), the teacher, and (if desired) the principal

Care should be exercised when making plans that cover long time periods and a large number of behavioral changes. An agreement can be reached about the need for future contracts and their content at the outset. Always keep the ultimate objective in mind and write a series of contracts that lead to the objective. Only the first contract needs to be completed with parents present but all contracts must carry their signature.

Generally, the cumulative effects of rewards are more profound when contracts specify small behavioral changes to be accomplished in short time periods. A single contract might include progressively more powerful inducements for desired behavior as the student fulfills the daily contract requirements. Parent(s) and child can chart each day's achievements, based on a report from the teacher, and use the charting activity as the basis for a conversation about events at school.

Even though the contract illustrated in Figure 9–3 is very advantageous to the teacher, parents may be willing to cooperate for two reasons: Their child's success in school is very important to them, and they are convinced the teacher has exhausted all reasonable alternatives to secure their child's cooperation.

However, if the parents view the contract as a technique designed to transfer responsibility for the problem to them, they may resist taking part in this remedy. Rosemond (1981) offered an alternative that appeals to the self-interest of both parties. In the alternative, the home–school contract is aimed at behavioral changes in both settings. The consequences that attend acceptable and unacceptable behavior begin at school and are continued at home. Developing the home–school contract is described in Table 9–2 and entails the following points:

1. Identify the keystone problem in each setting. In school, this might be failure to follow verbal directions; at home, failure to complete assigned chores.
2. Identify target behaviors that will be the subject of disciplinary controls in both settings. If the problem in both settings is essentially disobedience, the following phrases can be used to get at the objectionable behavior:
   a. "When I tell you to *do*, you. . . . "
   b. "When I tell you to *stop doing*, you. . . . "
   c. "When I *repeatedly tell* you to do, you. . . . "
3. From the list of target behaviors, select four to six in each setting that are the most troublesome. Concentrate on the elimination of these behaviors. Remember, the plan calls for simultaneous solutions to problem behaviors at home and school.
4. Decide what home privileges will be revoked after the child has exceeded the number of allowable departures from expectations. Students are to learn that the quality of their life at home depends on good behavior at home and school. Activities permitted earlier on a noncontingent basis now depend on an appropriate response to adult expectations.

Table 9–2
Simultaneous Home–School Contract

	School	**Home**
Keystone problem	Obedience: Does not follow directions.	Obedience: Does not do chores.
Target behaviors	1. Continues working on previous assignment. 2. Does not listen when given directions. 3. Asks to have directions repeated. 4. Talks to neighbors before beginning work.	1. Leaves bed unmade. 2. Has to be reminded to take out garbage. 3. Complains when asked to pick up dirty clothes. 4. Leaves breakfast dishes on table.
Privileges to be revoked	*Elementary School:* 1. Recess. 2. Unsupervised lunch. 3. Free reading period. *Secondary School:* 1. Access to lounge 2. Dismissal at regular time. 3. Attendance at next assembly.	*Elementary School:* 1. Play with friend. 2. TV. 3. Regular bedtime. *Secondary School:* 1. Use of telephone. 2. Use of automobile. 3. Unrestricted use of house.

5. Devise a response–cost card to provide an ongoing record for target behavior and attendant consequences (see Figure 9–4). Early in the behavioral change process, the card may allow for a number of warnings (three in the case of this illustration). Consequences, the privileges noted in Table 8-2, are applied the fourth time that the student exhibits a target behavior, regardless of where the behavior occurs. In this illustration, the first three consequences are applied in the school setting. The final consequence should generally take the child out of circulation for the day. This is the ultimate denial of freedom, the cost of being irresponsible.

6. Meet with the student to explain the procedures: The student must carry the card at all times and present it to the teacher each time a target behavior is noted. The teacher will cross out one number on the card for each violation. Failure to bring the card home each evening will be dealt with as if all numbers were crossed out; that is, all privileges will be revoked. Parents take up crossing out numbers and removing privileges where the teacher left off at school. A new card is issued at school each day.

7. Implement the plan. Changes can be made in the target behaviors, the number of warnings, and the privileges as the situation dictates. If some behaviors were excluded because the original list was too long, these objectionable behaviors may be added to the list by deleting target behaviors that have been extin-

guished. The gradual turning of control over to the student is accomplished by giving fewer warnings and using less potent privileges to sustain appropriate behavior. Likewise, if the initial consequences do not give the parents sufficient control, more valued activities can be substituted for those in the original plan.

The response–cost system teaches students that most things in life are not free. Getting what one wants will often mean choosing behaviors that restrict one's freedom to do as one likes.

Parent Volunteers

Another adult in the classroom can be a powerful inducement to good behavior. When this adult is an additional source of recognition and approval, students are likely to be on their best behavior. Even students who are not especially desirous of adult approval are less likely to misbehave if they are more likely to get caught.

Without some very specific guidelines and duties, however, parent volunteers can also be a distraction. The bother of supervising them can outweigh the contri-

Figure 9–4
Examples of Response–Cost Cards

Elementary school student

1	2	3
4 Recess	5 Lunch	6 Reading
7 Friend	8 TV	9 Bedtime

Secondary school student

1	2	3
4 Lounge	5 Dismissal	6 Assembly
7 Phone	8 Car	9 House

bution they make to pupil deportment and learning. A teacher should be prepared to refuse help that is not helpful, to schedule help and accept it only during appointed time blocks, and to insist that help be provided on the teacher's terms. Although their input may be valued, volunteers are not decision makers; the teacher must provide both the substance and structure for their work.

Arrangements for using parent volunteers proceed best when the class day is visualized as a series of activities. The teacher can consider possible uses of parent volunteers when she looks at the requirements for each activity—organization, content, duration, space, type and number of students, props/resources, expected behavior from students. Assuming that the desired activity is a lecture, the teacher might have the parent arrange for an outside speaker, type assignment materials, prepare transparencies, set up the demonstration portion of the presentation, keep a record of student responses to questions during the lecture, chart the incidence of selected teacher behaviors, or assist with student independent practice exercises following the lecture. Parents can better see the possibilities when activity analyses are used to identify things that they can do.

If parent volunteers are used effectively, teachers can acquire additional time to perform instructional functions. Students will also benefit from additional adult help because teachers cannot possibly do all the things associated with planning and delivering quality instruction, much less find time to treat individual differences the way they would like. Additional suggestions and references for building home–school enterprises can be found in Haley and Berry's (1988) *Home and School as Partners: Helping Parents Help Their Children.*

Assessing Parental Contacts

Cultivating home–school contacts is likely to be confined to school-required conferences, open houses, and chronic discipline problems unless the teacher develops a plan and conducts periodic progress checks. The plan, which can simply be a list of activities and a time frame for implementing them, can easily be converted into a checklist (see Figure 9–5). This can be reviewed each month to note the variety and extent of contacts. From such an analysis the amount and emphasis of a teacher's activities can be modulated.

CONCLUSION

Learning to work with parents can make a profound difference in the quality of life in a classroom. Parents can be a particularly valuable tool in the teacher's preventive disciplinary plan. Parents are a primary influence in their child's motivation to learn, and the formative effects of their input last through the high school years and beyond (Jaynes & Wlodkowski, 1990).

Many disciplinary problems originate from a teacher's inability to fulfill the many varied, demanding tasks of teaching. Problems that do occur can be corrected with more certainty when parents and teachers present a united front. When students realize that

	Sep	Oct	Nov	Dec	Jan	Feb	Mar	Apr	May	Jun
1. Sent an information newsletter to parents										
2. Called parents to report on positive achievement of child										
3. Invited parent to spend portion of a school day in classroom										
4. Invited parent to serve as resource speaker										
5. Conversed with a parent at school event										
6. Conversed with parent in non-school setting										
7. Reported to class/colleague on conversation with parent										
8. Sent congratulatory note to parent on student's achievement										
9. Sent questionnaire to parents to solicit opinions										
10. Called parent to seek assistance and/or express concern about student										

Figure 9–5
Parental Involvement Checklist

parents and teachers are of one mind, they are more likely to live up to commitments to improve their behavior. More favorable attitudes and behavior will in turn help students produce achievements that will make them feel worthwhile to themselves and others.

SUPPLEMENTARY QUESTIONS

1. Both teachers and parents describe meetings with one another as an anxiety-provoking experience. Why are such situations stressful? Is this a desirable or undesirable state of affairs? Explain. If you regard it as undesirable, what measures might be taken to ease the emotional stress associated with such meetings?

2. Some educators claim that there has been a steady rise in disciplinary problems in schools and a corresponding increase in similar problems in the home. Assuming that this statement is an accurate assessment, what do you think are the common denominators in the school and home that might account for this situation?

3. When children are persistent troublemakers in school, some teachers are prone to place the blame on parents. What do you think accounts for this disposition? What would teachers offer in support of their contentions?

4. Teachers are often distressed because the parents who really need to attend parent–teacher conferences seldom or never do. Speculate about why these parents do not attend. Based on your speculations, what could be done to increase these parents' participation in the education of their children? Refer to the reasons these parents do not now participate as you defend your suggestions.

5. What are some common child-rearing mistakes that contribute to behavioral problems in the classroom? What compensating behaviors on the part of the teacher might reduce the impact of these parenting practices?

SUPPLEMENTARY PROJECTS

1. Interview several parents who have children in the age group that you plan to teach. Select questions that will reveal their conceptions of schooling and of the teacher's role and functions. Prepare a paper wherein you discuss the similarity and differences between their views and your own. Assuming that their children hold views similar to those of their parents, discuss the implications for your work with their children.

2. Ask permission to attend a conference where a consultative team is dealing with a chronically disruptive student. Keep a record of the words the teacher uses to describe this student, the ways in which the teacher has tried to deal with these behaviors, and why the teacher believes these interventions have failed. Place a check next to each of these items whenever someone on the team refers to these remarks of the teacher. What do you conclude from this analysis?

3. Volunteer to begin a parental resource file for a teacher. Create an instrument for collecting data from parents regarding their availability for assisting with classroom activities and their willingness to make a presentation about their job, hobbies, or travel. Develop a handy resource card for compiling the data. Secure permission from the principal to administer your instrument to a small sample of parents. Assemble the results.

4. Observe one student during a large block of the school day, both inside and outside of the classroom, and read all of the student's work submitted for teacher evaluation. Then prepare a hypothetical progress report that you could send to parents. Discuss your report with the student's teacher. How similar or dissimilar are your views?

5. Interview several parents to find out what kinds of persistent behavioral problems they think would justify the teacher seeking their assistance. As you listen to the parents describe the incidents, note what they believe precipitates such problems, the corrective measures that they would advocate, and how they view their role in dealing with chronic behavioral problems.

REFERENCES

Brandt, R. (1989). On parents and schools: A conversation with Joyce Epstein. *Educational Leadership, 47*(2), 24–27.

Canter, L., & Canter, M. (1976). *Assertive discipline: A take-charge approach for today's educator.* Los Angeles: Lee Canter and Associates.

Comer, J. P., & Haynes, N. M. (1991). Parent involvement in schools: An ecological approach. *The Elementary School Journal, 91*(3), 271–277.

D'Angelo, D. A., & Adler, C. R. (1991). Chapter 1: A catalyst for improving parental involvement. *Phi Delta Kappan, 72*(5), 350–354.

Dreikurs, R., Grunwald, B. B., & Pepper, F. C. (1982). *Maintaining sanity in the classroom:*

Classroom management techniques (2nd ed.). New York: Harper & Row.

Epstein, J. L. (1990). *School programs and teacher practices of parental involvement in inner-city elementary and middle schools.* Baltimore: Johns Hopkins University Center for Research on University and Middle Schools.

Glasser, W. (1977). Ten steps to good discipline. *Today's Education, 66*(4), 61–63.

Gordon, T. (1974). *Teacher effectiveness training.* New York: McKay.

Haley, P., & Berry, K. (1988). *Home and school as partners: Helping parents help their children.* Andover, MA: Regional Laboratory for Educational Improvement of the Northeast and Islands.

Hall, J. P. (1982). A parent guide for the misbehaving high school student. *Adolescence, 17*(66), 369–385.

Henderson, A. T., Marburger, C. L., & Ooms, T. (1986). *Beyond the bake sale: An educator's guide to working with parents.* Columbia, MD: The National Committee for Citizens in Education.

Instructor and Teacher. (1986). Parents—Your first partners. *Instructor and Teacher,* Winter(Special Issue), 12–16.

Jaynes, J. H., & Wlodkowski, R. J. (1990). *Eager to learn: Helping children become motivated and love learning.* San Francisco: Jossey-Bass.

Kennedy, C. (1991). Parent involvement: It takes P.E.P. *Principal, 70*(4), 25, 27–28.

Learning 86. (1986, January 5). Family problems: How they're affecting classrooms today: Part 1. *Learning 86,* 34–39.

Lehman, J. D. (1982). *Three approaches to classroom management: Views from a psychological perspective.* Washington, DC: University Press of America.

Levin, J., Nolan, J., & Hoffman, N. (1985). A strategy for classroom resolution of chronic discipline problems. *NASSP Bulletin, 69*(479), 11–17.

Lindle, J. C. (1989). What do parents want from principals and teachers? *Educational Leadership, 47*(2), 12–14.

Moore, E. K. (1991). Improving schools through parental involvement. *Principal, 71*(1), 17, 19–20.

Rosemond, J. (1981). *Parent power! A common-sense approach to raising your children in the eighties.* New York: Pocket Books.

Rotter, J., Robinson, E., & Fey, M. (1988). *Parent–teacher conferences* (2nd ed.). Washington, DC: National Education Association.

Silberman, M. L., & Wheelan, S. A. (1980). *How to discipline without feeling guilty.* Champaign, IL: Research Press.

Sprick, R. (1981). *The solution book.* Chicago: Science Research Associates.

Walde, A. C., & Baker, K. (1990). How teachers view the parents' role in education. *Phi Delta Kappan, 72*(4), 319–320, 322.

Warner, I. (1991). Parents in touch: District leadership for parent involvement. *Phi Delta Kappan, 72*(5), 372–375.

Welch, F. C., & Tisdale, P. C. (1986). *Between parent and teacher.* Springfield, IL: Thomas.

Wolf, J. S., & Stephens, T. M. (1989). Parent/teacher conferences: Finding common ground. *Educational Leadership, 47*(2), 28–31.

CHAPTER 10

Legal and Ethical Aspects of Management

An understanding of the material in this chapter will help you do the following:

- ❏ Understand the reasoning of the courts that contributes to the legal context for the regulation of student conduct.
- ❏ Know the discretionary powers and legal limitations that govern a teacher's efforts to maintain order and reasonable decorum in the classroom.
- ❏ Be familiar with current legal thought regarding the rights to which students are entitled when various disciplinary sanctions are imposed.
- ❏ Be aware of the legal repercussions that can follow the use of unsanctioned disciplinary practices.
- ❏ Distinguish between substantive and procedural due process and the rights and restrictions associated with each.
- ❏ Identify resources that teachers can use when trying to ascertain the legal ramifications of various management policies and practices.

BASIS OF CONTROL

In the United States, education is considered to be a function of state governments rather than of the federal government. As such, the constitutions in each of the fifty states provide for a publicly supported system of education. School districts function as agencies of the state and exist for the purpose of carrying out educational mandates of statewide concern. Thus, local school boards derive their powers from the legislature and are thereby limited by the state constitution and acts of Congress. Although the United States does not have a unified educational system, the decisions of the U.S. Supreme Court are equally applicable to schools in all states. Fortunately, the similarities in the operation of schools across the country mean that the Court's decisions seldom have a widely uneven impact on the state systems.

Throughout most of the nation's history, local school boards have been powerful bodies. They have had legislative, executive, and judicial powers and only modest interference in the exercise of these powers. To the chagrin of local authorities, however, the areas of their discretion are becoming more and more curtailed by court decisions. School authorities must be much more knowledgeable about student rights and the limits of their authority (Lehr & Haubrich, 1986; Melnick & Grosse, 1984; Ornstein, 1981; Rossow & Hininger, 1991). The increased involvement of the courts in the management of schools, particularly in reviewing conduct regulations and means of administering them, has been attributed to a multitude of sociological, psychological, philosophical, and legal forces. Haubrich and Apple (1975) have suggested several interrelated forces:

1. The changing role of the child within the family structure
2. The changing role of the school in a highly bureaucratized, industrial, technological society
3. The growing interest of the state in a redefinition of childhood and adolescence based on the increasing interest of the state in talent, achievement, and international competition
4. The growing political power of youth in America stemming in large part from the length and extent of the Vietnam war as well as the struggle for civil rights. (p. vii)

These forces have resulted in a reassessment of the relationship between schools and the public, particularly between school officials and students, and have contributed to new ways of exercising authority over children.

Scope of Control

The control that school authorities may exercise over the activities of students is circumscribed by the nature of the relationship between public schools and pupils. This relationship has been defined by common law according to the concept of *in loco parentis* (Reutter, 1975):

> This doctrine holds that school authorities stand in the place of the parent while the child is at school. As applied to discipline the inference is that school personnel may

> establish rules for the educational welfare of the child and the operation of the school and may use punishments for not following the rules. Obviously, however, a school employee legally cannot go as far as a parent can in enforcement of matters of taste, extent of punishment, or disregard of procedural due process. School rules that are contrary to expressed wishes of a parent generally will be subject to more careful judicial scrutiny than other rules. (p. 3)

The doctrine, as originally conceived, was intended to give teachers considerable discretion in disciplinary matters. It was presumed that teachers having this authority would act reasonably and with due regard to children's interests. The concept has undergone considerable change as a result of differences among adults about what constitutes appropriate discipline and also as a result of increased parental challenges to the reasonableness of disciplinary actions taken by school officials (Rossow & Hininger, 1991; Zirkel & Reichner, 1987).

The Role of the Courts

The courts are reluctant to interfere with the executive and legislative branches of government. They do so only when a litigant can show that a branch has exceeded or abused its powers.

> It must be emphasized that the question before a court is not whether the court approves the rule as one it would have made, had it been in control of the administrative or legislative situation. Nor is the question whether the rule is essential to the proper operation of the school. As noted previously, the burden of proof of improper action by school authorities is generally on the complainant. But if a rule restricts a so-called "fundamental" right—one explicitly or implicitly guaranteed by the Constitution—the burden of proof of an overriding need is placed on school authorities. (Reutter, 1975, pp. 4–5)

Thus, a complainant must show that the subject matter of a school regulation is not an appropriate one for intrusion by school officials, that the regulation violates the U.S. Constitution or a state constitution or statute, or that the regulation is unreasonable because it cannot be demonstrated to be necessary to the institution's educational mission.

As a result of court rulings in recent decades, the decisions of school authorities are now more likely to be challenged by students and parents. When these actions are believed to be arbitrary and capricious, the complainants are increasingly likely to seek relief in the courts. This increased reliance on the courts to resolve conflicts between the public and school authorities has contributed to a "we versus them" mentality in some circles and, at a minimum, to a sense of uneasiness and timidity among educators who fear becoming defendants in federal lawsuits.

Bartlett (1985), who reviewed federal court decisions issued between February 1969 and the end of 1982, concluded that because court decisions won by school officials received relatively little attention, there exists something akin to "litigation paranoia" among educators. He asserted, as have others (Underwood & Noffke,

1990), that the condition is largely unfounded because school officials do win many lawsuits and the courts have helped educators by more clearly delineating the legal responsibilities of students (p. 39).

The legal derivation of student rights has focused the court's attention on the First and Fourteenth Amendments of the U.S. Constitution. The First Amendment reads as follows:

> Congress shall make no law respecting an establishment of religion, or prohibiting the free exercise thereof; or abridging the freedom of speech, or of the press; or the right of the people peaceably to assemble and to petition the Government for a redress of grievances.

The Fourteenth Amendment (1868) states in part,

> No State shall make or enforce any law which shall abridge the privileges or immunities of citizens of the United States; nor shall any State deprive any person of life, liberty, or property, without due process of law; nor deny to any person within its jurisdiction the equal protection of the laws.

Because teachers are agents of the state, their actions are subject to constitutional scrutiny as provided by the Fourteenth Amendment. Thus, the freedoms granted in the First Amendment are made applicable to students through the Fourteenth Amendment.

The matter of due process, substantive and procedural, has been the basis for most litigation initiated by students and their parents. Thus, the remainder of this chapter is devoted to a discussion of due process and other school-related legal issues and the ramifications of court decisions for classroom teachers. Since the discussion focuses on the disciplinary situations and techniques typically associated with the instructional duties of teachers, the issues of freedom of expression—that is, guarantees of speech, symbolic expression, press, assembly, association, and matters of conscience—are not addressed.

RULES OF CONDUCT AND DUE PROCESS CONSIDERATIONS

Arguments about student rights generally occur on two levels: *substantive* and *procedural*. Substantive due process issues deal with whether an individual student's constitutional rights have been judiciously considered in the creation of regulations to manage and protect the school system and to protect the rights of other students to secure an education. The emphasis is on the fairness of the policy or the rule itself.

In determining the substantive rights of students, one should ask,

1. Will the actions of the student cause substantial disruption to the educational process and/or the normal operation of the school?

2. Will the actions of the student be an invasion of the rights of others? (Furtwengler & Konnert, 1982, p. 201)

School officials who answer in the affirmative to either of these questions must still be prepared to defend the policy and their actions. The courts have taken a dim view of actions to circumvent student misconduct based on supposition and speculation.

Procedural due process provides students accused of misconduct or slated for punishment an opportunity to defend themselves. The students' rights are secured when they know what they are accused of doing, know the basis for the accusation, and are given an opportunity to present their side of the story. Thus, officials must proceed to take actions in a defensible and reasonable way, which ensures proper form and fairness for the accused.

Student claims for due process rights have been used to test the traditional management practices of U.S. school systems and to question the legal authority of school teachers and administrators. Many of these claims begin when students question the rules themselves and the reasons given for a denial of freedoms covered by the rules. A set of well-formulated, explicitly stated rules is the first step toward reducing disputes and reconciling conflicts without legal action. After having analyzed hundreds of cases decided in federal and appellate state courts, Reutter (1975) offers the following essentials for an enforceable rule:

1. The rule must be publicized to students. Whether it is issued orally or in writing, school authorities must take reasonable steps to bring the rule to the attention of students. A major exception is where the act for which a student is to be disciplined is obviously destructive of school property or disruptive of school operation.

Management Challenge 10–1

Balancing Rights and Responsibilities

The language of the law has gradually become more prominent in discussions about disciplinary practices in the school setting. Students and parents claim that they have their rights. And they do have a constitutional right to freedom, justice, and equality. The controversy emanates from differences about what is meant by these terms when they are translated into political, legal, and educational realities by the courts.

1. What limits on freedom do you believe to be justified in a classroom or school situation? How and when would these beliefs be expressed in your classroom?
2. What provisions for due process (justice) in schools do you find defensible or indefensible? Why?
3. The proper distribution of rights and responsibilities (equality) is a perplexing problem. How might a teacher build a management plan that recognizes the delicate balance between individual liberties and civil accountability?

---

2. The rule must have a legitimate educational purpose. The rule may affect an individual student's learning situation or the rights of other students in the education setting.
3. The rule must have a rational relationship to the achievement of the stated educational purpose.
4. The meaning of the rule must be reasonably clear. Although a rule of student conduct need not meet the strict requirements of a criminal statute, it must not be so vague as to be almost completely subject to the interpretation of the school authority invoking it.
5. The rule must be sufficiently narrow in scope so as not to encompass constitutionally protected activities along with those which constitutionally may be proscribed in the school setting.
6. If the rule infringes a fundamental constitutional right of students, a compelling interest of the school (state) in the enforcement of the rule must be shown. (p. 6)

In view of the aforementioned redefinition and enlargement of student civil liberties, prudence suggests student involvement in the formulation of the rules, periodic review of the rules with student input, and the designation of responsible authorities for the implementation of the rules.[1]

CORPORAL PUNISHMENT

The term *corporal punishment* refers to any type of punishment that inflicts physical pain to modify behavior. The term is usually used to refer to paddling within a school setting. There is much disagreement among educators regarding the necessity or the desirability of using corporal punishment as a disciplinary measure, and numerous local school boards and some states have banned its use. However, it is wise to know the legal implications (Henderson, 1986) because many educators continue to believe in and use this method of discipline.

Supreme Court Decisions

Two U.S. Supreme Court decisions have established the boundaries within which teachers must operate, as discussed in the following subsections.

Ingraham v. Wright

Ingraham v. Wright (1977) deals with issues of excessive punishment and whether or not such punishment violates the cruel and unusual punishment clause of the Eighth Amendment. The case originated in Dade County, Florida, where corporal punishment is specifically authorized but explicitly limited by school board policy. Two students were allegedly subjected to a severe paddling during the 1970–1971

---

[1] I wish to express my appreciation to Dr. E. Edmund Reutter for granting permission to reprint in this chapter large narrative sections of his publication *The Courts and Student Conduct* (1975), which was commissioned by ERIC Clearinghouse on Educational Management and published by the National Organization on Legal Problems of Education.

school year. Ingraham was struck twenty times with a flat wooden paddle (fifteen times more than the school board policy permitted) because he was slow in responding to his teacher's instructions. The paddling resulted in hematoma, and the subject missed eleven days of school. The second student, Andrews, was paddled so severely on his arms that he lost full use of them for more than a week. A Florida law forbade punishment that was "degrading or unduly severe" or that took place prior to consultation with the principal or the teacher in charge of the school.

Thus, two issues were brought to the attention of the courts: (1) Was the use of corporal punishment in violation of the Eighth Amendment? and (2) Was some type of procedural due process required before a teacher or other disciplinarian could employ corporal punishment?

The Supreme Court ruled, as did the district court and the court of appeals, that the beatings, although excessive and unreasonable, did *not* violate the Eighth Amendment. The justices concluded, in a five-to-four decision, that the amendment was never intended to apply to schools but was created to control the punishment of criminals. In essence, corporal punishment is *not* cruel and unusual punishment.

With regard to the second question, the court stated, "We conclude that the Due Process Clause does not require notice and a hearing prior to the imposition of corporal punishment in the public schools, as that practice is authorized and limited by common law" (*Ingraham v. Wright,* 1977). The majority reasoned that the purpose of corporal punishment would be diluted if elaborate procedures had to be followed prior to its use.

Although these two rulings permit the use of corporal punishment without a formal due process hearing, educators are advised to investigate the facts before using this form of punishment. Students may still sue on the basis of violation of substantive due process rights, embodied in the Fourteenth Amendment, or seek remedies through an indictment for criminal assault and battery (Piele, 1978).

Baker v. Owen

The second case that helps educators understand the issues and devise procedures for the use of corporal punishment was brought by a parent who wanted to restrict the use of corporal punishment on her child by school authorities. In this instance, the high court let stand a decision by a federal district court in North Carolina in *Baker v. Owen* (1975). Although the court was sympathetic to the contention that parents have a fundamental right to select appropriate disciplinary methods for their children, it refused to support the argument that these rights extended into the school. In fact, the Court upheld the right of educators to administer corporal punishment over the objections of the parents because of the "legitimate and substantial interest" of the state "in maintaining order and discipline in the public schools." This court decision may have prompted some states (e.g., California) to pass laws that provide for prior written parental approval before a student may be spanked.

School personnel may have been given considerable latitude in the use of corporal punishment, but wisdom suggests using the minimal due process requirements

Management Challenge 10–2

Defending Due Process

Balancing the rights of the individual against the need to protect the welfare and interests of society is the essence of due process litigation. When the courts deal with alleged violations of due process, the government must demonstrate a compelling state interest that individual rights must be abridged to serve the public good. In a school situation, this means that a single student may be deprived of certain freedoms of expression in order to protect the collective rights of the student body. However, if a student is deprived of substantive rights and the actions of school officials are contested, these officials must demonstrate a compelling state interest in (1) preventing property loss or damage, (2) protecting and maintaining legitimate educational purposes/decisions designed to support student learning and achievement, (3) protecting the health and safety of students, and (4) establishing and enforcing rules that create and maintain an appropriate educational environment.

1. Secure several student handbooks. Examine the sections devoted to school-wide policies. Identify two examples of policies that illustrate each of the four areas of "compelling state interest" noted above.
2. What freedoms of choice or expression are being denied by these policies?
3. What reasoned or valid objections might students or parents offer in defense of their claim that the particular policy deprives them of some lawful right?
4. How might questionable policies be changed to make them less vulnerable to substantive due process objections?

---

that were an outgrowth of the *Baker v. Owen* decision. A simplified rendering of the *Baker v. Owen* case provides the following procedural safeguards:

1. Generally, corporal punishment should not be used to correct first-offense behaviors.
2. Students should know what misbehaviors could lead to corporal punishment.
3. An adult witness should be present when the student is given reasons for the punishment and during the administration of the punishment.
4. On request, the disciplinarian should provide the student's parents with an explanation for the punishment.

Compliance with these guidelines will permit the educator to operate within the framework of the Eighth Amendment.

Civil Liability Considerations

What constitutes excessive use of corporal punishment? Although there is no exact way to ascertain the reasonableness of using corporal punishment or what constitutes moderation in its application, the disciplinarian would be well advised to consider

> the age, sex, and size of the pupil; his apparent physical strength and structure; that the type of instrument should be one suitable and proper for the purposes; and that punishment should be proportioned to the offense, the apparent motive and disposition of the offender, and the influence of his example and conduct on others. (Drury & Ray, 1967, p. 44)

Court opinions devoted to this issue have also provided some clues about what constitutes reasonable use of corporal punishment (O'Reilly & Green, 1983):

1. *It is consistent with the existing statutes.* Where corporal punishment is authorized by the statutes, and where boards of education have policies that are in compliance with the statute, or where corporal punishment is allowed by the statutes, the courts will—as a general rule—hold in favor of the board of education and its employees.
2. *It is a corrective remedy for undesirable behavior.* Occasionally, the teacher, like the parent, will need to resort to corporal punishment as the last means of correcting a child's errant behavior.
3. *It is neither cruel nor excessive.* The courts will weigh the evidence to determine if, in the face of the facts, the punishment was excessive—not reasonably believed at the time to be necessary for the child's discipline or training. If it is found to be excessive, the school authorities who inflicted it may be held liable in damages to the child and, if malice is shown, they may be subject to criminal penalties.
4. *There is no permanent or lasting injury.* The implication here is that there may be a temporary injury that is insufficient to bring a finding against the school official.
5. *Malice is not present.* It is a standard rule of thumb that no punishment should be administered in a fit of anger on the part of the teacher or principal. Revenge is not a valid reason for administering corporal punishment.
6. *The punishment is suitable for the age and sex of the child.* The standard to be applied here is one of reasonableness.
7. *An appropriate instrument is used.* The courts will consider the appropriateness of the instrument when given the evidence in the case. Among the various types of instruments that have been considered to be reasonable are a wooden paddle and a twelve-inch ruler. The questionable factor is not the instrument used so much as the portion of the anatomy that is struck, the degree to which the instrument is used, and the end result of the corporal punishment. (pp. 144–145)[2]

These guidelines should not be regarded as unquestionable standards. Whether a punishment is unreasonable or excessive raises questions of fact that may have to be settled by a civil lawsuit.

---

[2] Reprinted by permission of Greenwood Publishing Group, Inc., Westport, CT, from *School Law for the Practitioner* (pp. 144–145) by Robert C. O'Reilly and Edward T. Green. Copyright by Roger C. O'Reilly and Edward T. Green and published in 1983 by Greenwood Press.

ASSAULT AND BATTERY

When school personnel are charged with assault and battery, these charges usually arise from the administration of corporal punishment. The cases generally involve a person who is not authorized to administer corporal punishment or an authorized person who uses excessive punishment. In these instances, individuals may be required to defend themselves in criminal action against the charges of assault and battery.

Nolte (1980) defines *assault* as

> an illegal attempt or offer (without actual contact) to beat or touch another person in such a way as to cause that person to apprehend immediate peril. Thus, the attempt must be coupled with the ability or what the person believes to be the ability to execute the threat. (p. 114)

Battery is described as

> the willful touching of another person by the aggressor or by some substance put in motion by him; or as it is sometimes expressed, a battery is the consummation of the assault. (pp. 114–115)

Thus, assault is essentially a mental rather than physical interference, whereas battery is physical damage to a person.

Assault and battery cases are generally decided by a jury with instructions from a judge. Because most civil suits do involve an alleged abuse of corporal punishment, the jury has to decide whether the teacher, acting *in loco parentis,* has behaved according to a standard of care that the average and normally prudent parent would have applied in the same or similar circumstances. Criteria used by the courts to identify excessive punishment, discussed earlier with regard to corporal punishment, are used to ascertain criminal wrongdoing.

Generally, the reasoning in such cases involves the application of tort law, which is beyond the scope of this book. Suffice it to say that tort law provides a remedy for persons who believe a particular instance of corporal punishment exceeds the considerable latitude given educators and the forms of punishment that might be condoned by the Eighth Amendment.

NEGLIGENCE

Tort law, defined as a legal wrong or injury (not involving a breach of contract) for which a civil suit can be brought, is frequently used to collect damages from teachers charged with negligence. Although teachers have enjoyed a limited, or conditional, immunity from civil suits due to negligence, largely on the grounds that they stand *in loco parentis* to the child, legal protection on this basis has been declining. Because teachers participate in many aspects of the classroom and schoolwide management system, they are liable for wrong acts, whether intentionally or carelessly caused.

> A teacher can be held liable for damages to an injured student if, and only if, the student proves four things: (1) the teacher had a duty to be careful not to injure the student and protect him from being injured; (2) the teacher failed to use due care; (3) the teacher's carelessness caused the injury; and (4) the student sustained provable damages. (Fischer, Schimmel, & Kelly, 1981, p. 68)

In other words, in cases of tort liability, the courts generally discuss two issues: (1) Was any duty of supervision owed? and (2) Was an owed duty satisfied? When students do sustain an injury, it is generally not very difficult to prove that the teacher had a duty to be careful toward those being supervised and that the injuries warrant monetary damages. Exactly what caused the injury is sometimes difficult to prove. The critical consideration becomes the teacher's duty to be careful and therefore not negligent.

Potter (1983), following a review of teacher liability lawsuits, offers the following guidelines for reducing liability:

1. *Precaution 1:* Teachers should closely supervise activities that are inherently dangerous or that require training and skill to be performed properly.
2. *Precaution 2:* Teachers should make certain that any requests for help from a student are not beyond the physical and mental capabilities of the student.
3. *Precaution 3:* The teacher in charge of a group of students on a field trip should be able to demonstrate that reasonable and cautious plans were made and carried out to assure a safe trip.
4. *Precaution 4:* A teacher should be cautious not to mismatch or "overmatch" students when supervising extracurricular athletic or intramural activities.
5. *Precaution 5:* When a child is seriously injured, a teacher should summon competent medical help rather than attempt to administer first aid directly, unless it appears necessary to save his life. (p. 12)

SUSPENSION

Although teachers have a legal right to suspend a student, pending board action, most teachers are reluctant to use suspension to secure compliance with classroom rules or to preserve the rights of other class members. Teachers do not like to deny students access to the educational benefits of schooling, nor do they want to deprive them of the social interaction that is such an integral part of classroom living. Yet some students, despite a concerted effort to secure their cooperation, do not obey the rules. Suspension is an effort to convey the serious nature of their actions and to muster a greater resolve on the part of all parties to the dispute.

Educators who propose to include suspension in their schoolwide management plan should understand the distinctions between short- and long-term suspensions. The opinion issued by the U.S. Supreme Court in *Goss v. Lopez* (1975) established distinctions between these two types of suspensions and set guidelines for their proper administration.

Short-Term Suspension

A short-term suspension is an involuntary absence on the part of the student from school for a period of ten days or less. Prior to *Goss v. Lopez,* there was considerable uncertainty about the length of time a student could be suspended without a hearing. Lopez brought the issue to a head by claiming that he was an innocent bystander in a school lunchroom disturbance, that he was never told what he was accused of doing, and that no evidence was presented against him. Thus, he was suspended without ever having a chance to tell his side of the story. Similar allegations were made by other students who were also suspended for up to ten days for allegedly disruptive or disobedient conduct.

The Supreme Court examined the complaint as a procedural due process issue; that is, the Court viewed the educational process as a property right and a right not to be taken lightly. Thus, the due process provisions of the Fourteenth Amendment were applicable. The Court ruled in a five-to-four decision that at the very minimum, therefore, students facing suspension and the consequent interference with a protected property interest must be given *some* kind of notice and afforded *some* kind of hearing (Court's italics) (Connors, 1979, p. 15).

The Court proceeded to describe the type of minimal due process hearing procedure that should be followed, even when a suspension is for a single day:

> Students facing temporary suspension have interest qualifying for protection of the due process clause, and due process requires, in connection with a suspension of ten days or less, that the student be given oral or written notice of the charges against him and, if he denies them, an explanation of the evidence the authorities have and an opportunity to present his side of the story. The clause requires at least these rudimentary precautions against unfair or mistaken findings of misconduct and arbitrary exclusion from school. (Connors, 1979, pp. 15–16)

These procedures were viewed by the Court as "rudimentary precautions against unfair or mistaken findings of misconduct and arbitrary expulsion from school" (*Goss v. Lopez,* 1975). The justices saw no need for a delay between the time that notice is given and the time of the hearing. In emergencies, when lives and property are endangered, prior notice and a hearing can occur "as soon as practicable." Thus, the hearing may be informal and conducted with dispatch. The fulfillment of due process standards was not intended to jeopardize the school's disciplinary authority.

Schools can adhere to the spirit and the substance of this ruling by following simple guidelines. Rules governing the hearings should be formulated by the faculty and student government representatives and should be published. The procedures should adhere to the following due process considerations (Connors, 1979):

1. The disciplinarian should inform the student as to what rule he or she broke.

2. The disciplinarian should tell the student how he or she became aware of the fact that the student broke the rule.

3. The disciplinarian should give the student an opportunity to tell his or her side of the story.

4. If there are contradicting facts, the disciplinarian should at least make a rudimentary check on the facts before imposing a suspension.

5. A student should not be suspended for more than ten days. (p. 16)

These procedures are so simple and require so little time that they should not deter a teacher or administrator from using short-term suspension as a disciplinary measure. Educators should know that this is a lawfully constituted method.

Suspension of Students with Disabilities

The Individuals with Disabilities Education Act (IDEA) does not specifically address the suspension or expulsion of students with disabilities (Maloney, 1994b). In matters of school discipline, these students were initially treated no differently than regular education students. The late 1970 and early 1980 federal court decisions in cases involving students with disabilities shaped new directions for school discipline policies.

In addition to *Goss v. Lopez* (1975), described earlier, a second landmark Supreme Court case had significant effects on current discipline procedures and practices for students with disabilities. In *Honig v. Doe* (1988) school officials were prevented from unilaterally removing students with disabilities from classrooms when their dangerous behavior was related to their disability. The district court ruled that indefinite suspensions deprived students of their right to a free and appropriate public education under the then Education of the Handicapped Act. The court ruled that (1) the school district may only use two- and five-day suspensions against any student whose behavior rises from their disability, (2) the district may not make any change in educational placement without parental consent during due process proceedings, (3) the state may not authorize districts to make unilateral placement changes, (4) the state must develop a compliance-monitoring system for districts, and (5) the state must provide educational services directly to students when a school district does not.

It now appears clear that a ten-day rule exists under IDEA; it is less clear under Section 504 of the Americans with Disabilities Act. Recent Office of Civil Rights (OCR) rulings on cumulative suspensions in excess of ten days have found those suspensions to illegally constitute a significant change in placement (San Juan, CA, School District, 1993; Cobb County, GA, School District, 1993; Bay County, FL, School District, 1993) and to not do so (Ponca City, OK, School District, 1993). Other recent cases of suspension beyond ten days have been faulted for not invoking a reevaluation of the student (San Juan, CA, School District, 1993; Montebello, CA, United School District, 1993). When counting suspension days, districts should not forget to count in-school suspensions or extended time-outs. In-school suspensions can deprive a student of a free and appropriate education as much as an out-of-school suspension (Lincoln, 1994). When students have been denied a free and appropriate education, courts have awarded compensatory education and reasonable attorneys' fees to parents. An exception to a prohibition on a school district's unilateral removal of a student with a disability from their official program occurs when that student brings a gun or a bomb to school. This is described later in the section on gun-free schools legislation.

Long-Term Suspension

A long-term suspension is an involuntary absence from school for a specified period of time, generally for periods in excess of ten days. Drury and Ray (1967) wrote:

> It has been judicially held that a child may be suspended or expelled for disrespect toward school authorities; for immorality; for drinking; for smoking; the use of cosmetics contrary to school regulations; irregular or tardy attendance at school; refusal to write a composition; refusal to follow proper orders; refusal to obey when told to read from a schoolbook; refusal to submit to the examination of the school physician on the grounds of conscientious objections; refusal to give the name of a pupil who has been guilty of a breach of rules when he knows the name of the pupil; making a speech in a school meeting criticizing the board of education; being drunk on Christmas Day; publishing in a newspaper a satirical poem reflecting on school policy; failure to maintain a required scholastic standing, although there is substantial authority to the contrary; failure to pay for school property willfully or maliciously destroyed; and for general failure to obey the school rules or orders reasonably issued by any teacher or administrator. (p. 46)

The authors later pointed out:

> It has been held that a child cannot be suspended or expelled merely because of marriage, unless the married person's conduct is detrimental to the good order and discipline of the school; or the pupil is difficult to teach; or he refuses by direction of his parents to follow a particular branch of study; or he is involved in the loss of school property because of mere negligence. (p. 47)

The courts are less clear about the appropriate length and administration of long-term suspensions. However, since the student is deprived of a property interest for an extended period, the courts have generally enforced more stringent hearing requirements.

Some civil liberty lawyers contend that suspensions that last longer than a few days should be treated as disciplinary reprisals by school authorities and preceded by notice and hearings. Thus, serious breaches of discipline or an accumulation of minor offenses must be handled with due process to ensure that charges are true and actions appropriate.

When the school disciplinarian deems a long-term suspension to be an appropriate remedy for a problem, the following procedure should be taken (Connors, 1979):

1. The student and parents should be given written notice of the charges against him.

2. A hearing date should be scheduled giving the student enough time to prepare a defense—but not too far in advance to damage his property interest. It is suggested that this hearing be scheduled within two weeks of the date of the infraction (unless the student requests otherwise).
3. At the hearing, the student has the right to be represented by legal counsel.
4. At the hearing, the student has the right to face his accusers.
5. At the hearing, the student has the right to cross-examine witnesses.
6. At the hearing, the student has the right to present a defense. This includes calling witnesses and presenting evidence.
7. The student has the right to an impartial tribunal at the hearing. This requirement has been the subject of much litigation in the last ten years. While some courts hold that the school principal is an "impartial" judge, it is recommended that some adult(s) totally unfamiliar with the incident be used for the tribunal. Citizen advisory groups are especially valuable for this purpose.
8. The decision of the tribunal must be based solely on the facts presented at the hearing. A student cannot be suspended for something that is unrelated to the infraction that instigated the hearing. (pp. 17–18)

School personnel are well advised to be represented by legal counsel if the student is so represented. Attorneys should review both procedural and substantive issues before the hearing. The courts do not look on school personnel kindly if due process rights have been violated or if the actions appear to be predicated on malice or to serve as a defense for earlier unreasonable actions.

Extracurricular Activity Suspensions

Depriving students of extracurricular activities has become a popular disciplinary measure. In the past, this practice was only infrequently challenged because such participation was regarded as a privilege. However, recent court decisions have upheld participation in extracurricular activities as a property right and have applied suspension standards to these activities.

> A student may not be prohibited from participation because of his dress or appearance unless it impairs his ability to perform or constitutes a danger to his health or safety or that of others. Marriage, pregnancy, or parenthood may not be used (in and of themselves) as a reason for exclusion from extracurricular activities or from regular classroom activities. (Furtwengler & Konnert, 1982, p. 203)

These provisions in law are consistent with educator claims that such activities are actually cocurricular and an integral part of the educational program. Thus, to suspend a student from such activity requires the same procedural due process rights. The informal and formal hearing procedures prescribed for short- and long-term suspensions should be applied to corresponding periods of involuntary absence from an extracurricular activity. Teachers who want to enforce a conduct rule or an academic requirement by suspending a student from an extracurricular activity need not fear legal reprisal if they follow the aforementioned suspension procedures.

Expulsion

Two federal court decisions, *Doe v. Koger* (1979) and *Stuart v. Nappi* (1985), held that students with disabilities could not be expelled for reasons that were related to their disabilities. Two other decisions prohibited schools from discontinuing educational services to disabled students when they were expelled for reasons not related to their disability (*S-1 v. Turlington,* 1981; *Kaeline v. Grubbs,* 1982).

A significant change took place in 1994 when the Elementary and Secondary Education Act of 1965 (ESEA) was amended to include the Gun-Free School Act. The act states that in order to continue to receive federal funds under ESEA, a school district must have a policy in effect that requires the expulsion from school for a period of not less than one year any student who brings a weapon to school. Weapons have been carefully defined as those described in Section 921 of Title 18 in the United States Code. They can basically be any firearm that can expel a projectile by the action of an explosive or any other destructive device (e.g., bombs, grenades, rockets, missiles, mines, or any similar device). Even after the Gun-Free Schools Act was enacted, special education students were required, in most circumstances, to be returned to their original placement (e.g., "stay put") after ten days of suspension.

Under the 1994 Jeffords Amendment to the IDEA, students with disabilities who bring weapons to school may be placed in an "interim alternative educational setting" for not more than forty-five days. After forty-five days or less, the multidisciplinary team must have a more permanent educational placement determined for the student. If a qualified multidisciplinary team determines that the incident was unrelated to the student's disability, the student may be expelled to an alternative educational placement (Maloney, 1994a). On the other hand, if the incident was related to the student's disability, the student may not be expelled from school for bringing the weapon.

DETENTION

In view of the serious nature and consequences of using corporal punishment and suspension to correct breaches of conduct, teachers frequently use detention or time owed. Students are detained during periods when they would usually be free, such as recess, lunchtime, and before and after school, as a form of punishment. The action is predicated on students' desire to avoid the loss of social contacts and fun-time activities that occur outside of the classroom. Teachers may impose detention for reasonable periods of time and for clearly punishable offenses with no legal question of authority. The practice has been tested in the courts, and school authorities' actions have been upheld (Peterson, Rossmiller, & Volz, 1978, p. 354). Remember that detention or time-owed consequences used with special education students contribute to their maximum allowable suspension days.

GRADE REDUCTION AS AN ACADEMIC SANCTION

The courts have consistently held that school authorities have the right to impose academic sanctions for poor academic performance. There has been less agreement regarding the use of grade reductions as punishment for student misconduct or absences. The use of academic penalties for nonacademic reasons raises complex legal issues. The practice also raises serious educational issues.

> Grades are very specialized criteria in education. They are supposed to denote a student's accomplishment in a particular subject. They are an indication of student understanding of concepts, facts, and skills. They are not indicators of attendance, although grades may reflect low accomplishment due to poor attendance. They are not indicators of deportment. They are not indicators of whether or not the teacher's personality meshes well with the student's personality. Grades, then, are purely objective, *measurable* indicators of a student's mastery of the material in a given subject area. It is when a grade attempts to become more than this that the issue becomes a legal one. (Connors, 1979, pp. 49–50)

Thus, both the legal and educational issues remain open to challenges. In the case of the legal issues, challenges may proceed through the Family Educational Rights and Privacy Act (FERPA, 1974), which affords parents the right to challenge inaccurate or misleading information in student records (McCarthy & Cambron, 1981, p. 298).

The practice of lowering grades as an automatic penalty, such as "each day missed is a zero," is suspect. The courts would be sympathetic to extenuating circumstances, which the student is entitled to tell the teacher. "Blanket" policies for lowering grades, regardless of the reasons, are also open to court challenge (Nolte, 1980, p. 71). Generally, the courts have held that teachers have considerable discretion when evaluating student work. The courts will intervene in this process only if a student can show that a grade was lowered for nonacademic reasons or can verify that the teacher acted maliciously or arbitrarily. The burden of proof for such claims resides with the student. Such contentions are difficult to prove. I have been unable to find any court-reported challenges to grades received by students in elementary and secondary schools.

The use of grade reductions as a disciplinary measure is quite prevalent among teachers. Although the courts are reluctant to enter such disputes and generally refuse to substitute their judgment for that of the teacher, those who use this penalty should be sure that it is reasonable and related to legitimate educational objectives. A separate evaluation for conduct or citizenship would be a better practice. Official notification through a student handbook, where the practice is used schoolwide, or through a course syllabus is also a prudent legal protection.

SEARCH AND SEIZURE

A considerable amount of litigation associated with the public school setting has involved the "unreasonable search and seizure" phrase of the Fourth Amendment (Lincoln, 1986). Generally, lawsuits have been aimed at school personnel who have searched students or their school lockers. The courts have generally held that searches based on a "reasonable suspicion" that the student possessed some form of contraband in violation of the law could be conducted without the student's consent and without a valid warrant. Searches conducted when a student is believed to have stolen property that is sought as evidence in a non-school-related crime have also been sanctioned by the courts. Court decisions, for the most part, have supported these search practices by referring to the doctrine of *in loco parentis* or by finding that the search did not meet the standard of unreasonableness prohibited by the Fourteenth Amendment.

Teachers should be wary of using the *in loco parentis* doctrine to legitimize a search of a student's locker or desk or to justify asking a student to remove items from pockets, purses, or book bags. Although the school building is not a privileged sanctuary from the law, neither is it a place where students relinquish their due process rights. Teachers would do better to act as wise parents, intent on protecting the child's interests, rather than as state agents seeking evidence on which to convict the student.

The susceptibility of children and teenagers to the use of drugs has placed teachers in a special relationship to the problem. Parents who surrender their children to the school for large parts of each day expect school personnel to provide reasonable safeguards against young people's inexperience and lack of mature judgment. Thus, when judging the actions of school personnel, the courts weigh the constitutional safeguards of other individuals and the methods that school personnel use to maintain discipline. Random or arbitrary searches, even if announced in advance, are discouraged. McCarthy and Cambron (1981) have suggested that school personnel protect themselves from litigation by adhering to the following guidelines:

1. If police officials are conducting a search in the school, either with or without the school's involvement, school authorities should ensure that a search warrant is obtained.
2. Students and parents should be informed at the beginning of the school term of the procedures for conducting locker searches and personal searches.
3. Before school personnel conduct a search, the student should be asked to turn over the contraband, as such voluntary submission of material can eliminate the necessity for a search.
4. The authorized person conducting a search should have another staff member present who can verify the procedures used in the search.
5. School personnel should refrain from using strip searches or mass searches of groups of students.
6. Any search should be based on at least "reasonable belief" or "suspicion" that the student is in possession of contraband that may be disruptive to the educational process. (pp. 307–308)

The courts have issued more stringent standards when the privacy of one's person is invaded. In this regard, compulsory drug testing for all students, specifically urinalysis, has been looked on with disfavor by the courts. This procedure, which has been compared to a strip search, involves students' Fourth Amendment rights (Rossow & Hininger, 1991).

The judgment in *Odenheim v. Carlstadt–East Rutherford Regional School District* (1985) was based on principles of search, wherein the school official must have reasonable grounds for suspecting that the search will reveal evidence that a rule or law has been violated. In this instance, it would be highly unlikely that every student in a school would give officials a "clear indication" that they were breaking a school rule concerning drug usage. When standards of reasonableness cannot be met, it is improper for school officials to try to regulate the behavior of an entire student body.

Thus, "reasonable suspicion" may be sufficient to search a locker, but "probable cause," the standard used by law enforcement officials, is generally applied to body or strip searches. This means the school official must have evidence from highly reliable sources that a particular student is using or hiding illegal or dangerous materials. These more stringent standards are applied to protect the privacy of students and to prevent psychological damage to sensitive children.

AWAY-FROM-SCHOOL INJURIES: FIELD TRIPS

Field trips represent one category of away-from-school situations in which disciplinary problems may culminate in injuries. Similarly, pupil conduct problems may result in a student's being injured en route to and from school. Injuries may also occur on, near, or because of school buses. Schools have used the *in loco parentis* doctrine to claim disciplinary control over children in all of these situations. This claim has been challenged by parents to justify bringing civil suits for children's

---

Management Challenge 10–3
Ethical Considerations

Ethical practices manifest the conscience of a profession and constitute acceptable standards of conduct. Often, professional ethics are referred to as "beginning where the law stops" (Gathercoal, 1990, p. 119). There are many legally acceptable but unethical ways for teachers to conduct the business of the classroom. A teacher can publicly make disparaging remarks about a student's characteristics or humiliate a student by displaying poor work. A teacher can accept another teacher's unfavorable assessment of a student and treat the student accordingly. Ethically speaking, the teacher cannot do any of these things because all of these social interactions are demeaning to the student and undermine the ability of the student to learn.

1. What professional attitudes and values would typify a teacher who sees ethics as beginning where the law stops?
2. What operational ethical principles might be abstracted from the foregoing attitudes and values?
3. Which specific management practices would be favored and which frowned on?

---

injuries sustained in these activities. The review here is confined to field trips, since they represent a more direct supervision responsibility for classroom teachers.

Field trips are high-liability events because of the high probability of someone sustaining an injury. Parents should be asked to sign a "liability release" form, even though these forms do not relieve the teacher from claims of negligence.

Educators can lessen the likelihood of an injury through judicious planning and responsible supervision. Consideration should be given to the type of facility or program to be visited, the number and age of the pupils, and the general composition of the student body. A teacher can better foresee the potential dangers by inspecting the sites to be visited. Problems can also be reduced by instructing students about these hazards and by providing sufficient supervision to secure adherence to precautionary measures. Finally, be sure that the transportation is adequate, that is, that it is fully insured and that a safe driver is provided. Prudence in these matters provides reasonable protection for students and a controlling factor in the recovery of damages in a civil suit.

CONCLUSION

Maintaining an environment conducive to learning is a primary responsibility of the classroom teacher. Classroom management policies are formulated to communicate these expectations, and disciplinary practices are sometimes used to enforce these expectations. Teachers have been granted broad powers in the administration of these policies and practices. Community sentiment and standards generally favor an educator's prudent use of authority to manage individual and group behavior. Similarly, the courts are unlikely to substitute their judgment for that of educators as long as there are no blatant violations of a student's constitutional rights (McCarthy, 1990).

However, because civil rights have been explicitly extended to the educational setting and because the denial of fundamental liberties is increasingly being challenged in the courts, educators must be more knowledgeable about student legal guarantees and the ways to translate them into practice. They must move to preserve these guarantees reasonably and equitably and must also carefully document their attempts to do so.

SUPPLEMENTARY QUESTIONS

1. What disciplinary practices have you observed or been subjected to that might have been contested in the courts? What do you believe would have been the central issues in the proceedings?

2. You have read the due process requirements for several common disciplinary measures. Imagine a situation in which a disciplinary action

you have taken is challenged because the student insists that he or she has been denied due process. Explain what usual procedures you would follow to ensure due process.

3. Some would assert that providing full procedural safeguards in the case of suspension discourages teachers and administrators from using this conduct management method.

Would you agree or disagree with this assertion? Why?

4. The courts have given teachers considerable latitude as disciplinarians because they stand *in loco parentis* before the law. Do you think this doctrine is as defensible today, when teachers are less regulated by the mores of the community, as it was when teachers' lives were expected to be beyond reproach?

5. Assume you are a judge. What factors would weigh heavily in any disciplinary case brought to your courtroom? What arguments could you muster to support your reliance on these factors?

SUPPLEMENTARY PROJECTS

1. Ask several teachers what they view as the effects of the courts' involvement in matters of school discipline. Also ask them if, and how, the fear of a civil lawsuit has curtailed their choice of disciplinary techniques or influenced their relationship with parents. Report your findings to the class.

2. Interview a person who has served several terms on a local school board. Inquire about the legal issues that have been discussed during the official's tenure on the board. Also ask the board member how teachers view their job or discharge management functions that make them vulnerable to lawsuits.

3. Pair off with another person and role-play the two sides of a civil case that has influenced school disciplinary practices. Make explicit the salient aspects of the conflict and the principles of law brought to bear on the resolution of the conflict.

4. Chapters 2 through 6 and 8 are devoted to a discussion of common schoolwide and classroom management functions, ways to secure student cooperation through preventive management techniques, and procedures for dealing with disciplinary problems. Review the contents of these chapters for suggestions and recommendations that would reduce the likelihood of a teacher being involved in a lawsuit. Write a paper devoted to the legal principles that are well served by following these suggestions/recommendations.

REFERENCES

Baker v. Owen, 395 F. Supp. 294 (M.D.N.C., 1975), *aff'd,* 423 U.S. 907.

Bartlett, L. (1985). Legal responsibilities of students: Study shows school officials also win court decisions. *NASSP Bulletin, 69*(479), 39–47.

Bay County, FL, School District, 20 IDELR 920 (1993).

Cobb County, GA, School District, 20 KDELR 1171 (1993).

Connors, E. T. (1979). *Student discipline and the law.* Bloomington, IN: Phi Delta Kappa.

Doe v. Koger, 480 F. Supp. 225 (N.D. Ind. 1979).

Drury, R. L., & Ray, K. C. (1967). *Essentials in school law.* New York: Appleton-Century-Crofts.

Family Educational Rights and Privacy Act, 20 U.S.C. 1232g (1974).

Fischer, L., Schimmel, D., & Kelly, C. (1981). *Teachers and the law.* New York: Longman.

Furtwengler, W. J., & Konnert, W. (1982). *Improving school discipline: An administrator's guide.* Boston: Allyn & Bacon.

Gathercoal, F. (1990). *Judicious discipline* (2nd ed.). Ann Arbor, MI: Caddo Gap.

Goss v. Lopez, 419 U.S. 565, 729 (1975).

Haubrich, V. F., & Apple, M. W. (Eds.). (1975). *Schooling and the rights of children.* Berkeley, CA: McCutchan.

Henderson, D. J. (1986). Constitutional implications of involving use of corporal punishment in the public schools: A comprehensive review. *Journal of Law & Education, 15,* 255–269.

Honig v. Doe, 108 S. Ct. 592 (1988).

Ingraham v. Wright, 430 U.S. 651 (1977).

Kaeline v. Grubbs, 682 F.2d. 595 (6th Cir. 1982).

Lehr, D., & Haubrich, P. (1986). Legal precedents for students with severe handicaps. *Exceptional Children, 52,* 358–365.

Lincoln, E. A. (1986). Searches and seizures: The U.S. Supreme Court's decision on the Fourth Amendment. *Urban Education, 21,* 255–263.

Lincoln, E. A. (1994, May). In-school suspension: Is the child deprived of FAPE? Seminar presented at the 15th National Institute on Legal Issues of Educating Individuals with Disabilities, San Francisco, CA.

Maloney, M. (1994a). A flowchart for disciplining gun-toting students with disabilities. *Individuals with Disabilities Education Law Report, 21,* 75–76.

Maloney, M. (1994b). Introduction. In *Disciplining violent or disruptive students with disabilities.* Danvers, MA: LRP Publications.

McCarthy, M. M. (1990). The courts as educational policy makers: Recent trends and future prospects. *Educational Horizons, 69*(1), 4–9.

McCarthy, M. M., & Cambron, N. H. (1981). *Public school law: Teachers' and students' rights.* Boston: Allyn & Bacon.

Melnick, N., & Grosse, W. J. (1984). Rights of students: A review. *Educational Horizons,* Summer, 145–149.

Montebello, CA, Unified School District, 20 IDELR 388 (1994).

Nolte, M. C. (1980). *How to survive in teaching: The legal dimension.* Chicago: Teach 'em.

Odenheim v. Carlstadt–East Rutherford Regional School District, 510A, 2d 709 (N.J. Saper. Ch. 1985).

O'Reilly, R. C., & Green, E. T. (1983). *School law for the practitioner.* Westport, CT: Greenwood.

Ornstein, A. C. (1981). Student rights for secondary students: An overview. *Contemporary Education, 52,* 214–218.

Peterson, L. J., Rossmiller, R. A., & Volz, M. M. (1978). *The law and public school operation* (2nd ed.). New York: Harper and Row.

Piele, P. K. (1978). Neither corporal punishment nor due process due: The United States Supreme Court's decision in *Ingraham v. Wright. Journal of Law & Education, 7,* 1–19.

Ponca City, OK, School District, 20 IDELR 549 (1993).

Potter, C. A. (1983). Teachers and the law. *School and Community, 69*(5), 10–12.

Reutter, E. E. (1975). *The courts and student conduct.* Topeka, KS: National Organization on Legal Problems of Education.

Rossow, L. F., & Hininger, J. A. (1991). *Students and the law.* Bloomington, IN: Phi Delta Kappa Educational Foundation.

S-1 v. Turlington, 635 F.2d 342 (5th Cir. 1981).

San Juan, CA, School District, 20 IDELR 549 (1993).

Stuart v. Nappi, EHLR 557:101 (D. Conn. 1985).

Underwood, J. K., & Noffke, J. (1990). Good news: The litigation scales are tilting in your favor. *The Executive Educator, 12*(3), 16–20.

Zirkel, P. A., & Reichner, H. F. (1987). Is *in loco parentis* dead? *Phi Delta Kappan, 68*(6), 466–469.

CHAPTER 11

Stress Management
for Professionals

An understanding of the material in this chapter will help you do the following:

❑ Recognize ways in which stress is experienced by educators.
❑ Identify some of the sources of occupational stress for educators.
❑ Identify some of the harmful consequences of stress for educators and those with whom they work.
❑ Identify techniques that can be used to assess levels of stress.
❑ Develop ways to monitor and decrease levels of stress.
❑ Identify the sources and manifestations of student stress and suggest ways to remove the causes of stress.

The teacher's lounge is often a sanctuary, the only place that teachers can go to get away from the constant and persistent demands of their job. The conversations frequently turn to job-related frustrations and tensions. Listen to one such conversation and see what you can make of it.

Mr. Anders enters the room, pours a cup of coffee, and joins Mrs. Carson and Mr. Bell, who are talking about a student who has been a constant source of disruption in both of their classes. Mr. Bell is describing his latest confrontation with Bill Brown.

Mr. Bell: Bill came into the classroom today listening to a transistor radio with an earplug. Before he sat down, I caught his eye and motioned to him to remove the earplug and put the radio in his desk. He nodded yes while pointing to the clock and holding up one finger, telling me he had one minute before the bell. Just like him, never complies on request—always finds a way to press his claim to do as he pleases for just a little longer. Last week it was finishing a conversation in the doorway of the classroom after the bell had rung. Yesterday he wanted to return to his locker to get his homework assignment.

Mrs. Carson: I know exactly what you mean! I often have to wait to begin class because he is out of his seat when the bell rings or he's visiting with his neighbor. He is not aggressively defiant, but he always wants to have things his way. When you reprimand him, he is always offended, acts as though you are totally unreasonable. Yesterday, after I waited for him to finish his conversation with another student, I sarcastically thanked him for letting us begin the class. He responded with "Excuuuuuse me." The class laughed— I was torn between humiliation and committing an act of violence on his person.

Mr. Bell: He does have a way of turning a situation to his advantage. Being one of the more popular members of the class doesn't help. Other students condone, even admire, his acts of defiance. In fact, they make him even more popular.

Mr. Anders: I can't resist saying something about this situation. Bill came into my class last year with that same cocksure attitude and proceeded to see what he could get away with. After a few verbal confrontations, I sent him to the principal's office. To make a long story short, Mr. Shorter told me to handle these problems myself. He didn't want to have to deal with such minor incidents. So I called Bill's parents. Again, to be brief, they couldn't understand my being so upset about such minor infractions of the rules.

Mr. Bell: Just as I suspected—a pampered brat! He can't do anything wrong. An admission by the parents that Bill might be at fault would require something from them.

Mrs. Carson: Or it would be an admission that they aren't quite the perfect parents they think they are.

Mr. Anders: You've got it exactly! This kid is accustomed to running over all adults, and there isn't much we can do about it.

Mr. Bell: Do you mean to say I'm going to have to put up with this behavior all year?

After having read this book, you should know how to respond to Mr. Bell's question. You should also be able to see self-defeating assumptions and conclusions in the thinking and attitudes of the parties to the conversation. Several ways to correct the disciplinary and motivational problems should suggest themselves to you. So what is the point?

These teachers probably spend eight hours each day on the job and an average of two hours each evening performing job-related tasks. Over half of their waking hours, five days each week, are devoted to their jobs. Stressful situations like the one described here can be deleterious to physical and mental health when so much of one's time is spent on the job. And this scene is not confined to the faculty lounge or to schools with a large number of recalcitrant students. Variations of this conversation occur in classrooms before and after school, in hallways, rest rooms, and school parking lots.

These conversations serve a cathartic function; seldom do they culminate in solutions to the problems. Thus, the frustrations are merely vented, only to be reignited by objectionable student behavior the next day. The frustration mounts so that the teacher becomes increasingly disenchanted with teaching and increasingly disgruntled with students. The professional literature abounds with accounts of this phenomenon, which has become popularly known in educational circles as *burnout* (Cunningham, 1983; Farber & Miller, 1981; Freudenberger, 1974; Iwanicki, 1983; Kyriacou, 1987; Schwab, Jackson, & Schuler, 1986).

THE NATURE OF STRESS AND THE ORIGINS OF BURNOUT

Let us acknowledge at the outset that stress can both elevate or diminish achievement. Selye (1976), one of the leaders in stress research, has referred to two types of stress. *Eustress* is essential to living and actually enables the individual to adapt successfully to change, whereas *distress* causes damage while serving as a stimulus to activity. Without some stress, people might be quite content doing little, if anything. Without stress, mankind might have had to do without some of its most notable achievements. Miller (1979) captures this viewpoint as follows:

> Behind every human accomplishment lies worry, frustration, and discontent. If one were totally satisfied and free of stress, one would have little motivation to do anything. There must be a level of dissatisfaction to cause action. Avoidance of stress is not the goal. Rather a productive life needs appropriate levels of dissatisfaction, stress, or tension to get us to get the job done, but stress should not be so intense that it endangers or impairs our physical health. (p. 7)

He also points out that it is *excessive* stress that really creates the problem for educators:

> Our society, our modern manner of living, and the climate in many of our schools have created a stress epidemic. Surplus stress burdens teachers and administrators with fatigue, headaches, indigestion, and a host of other ailments. Educators under the ten-

Management Challenge 11–1
Selecting Stress Prevention and Relief Strategies

A colleague comes to your classroom after school and complains of being completely exhausted and describes the constant annoyances and aggravations that drain a teacher's energy level. The colleague mentions students who verbally harass and put down other members of the class and speaks of unrelenting efforts to control the noise level, cope with the inattention of students, and deal with persistent challenges to authority. The symptoms sound similar to combat fatigue.

1. Lazarus (1976) conceptualizes stress-reducing strategies in two categories: problem solving and emotion focused. Problem-solving methods emphasize changing the situations or events that are viewed as stressful. Emotion-focused approaches involve tension release and relaxation techniques. Given the aforementioned description of the colleague's dilemma, which type of strategy would you recommend? Why?
2. What specific problem-solving and emotion-focused strategies might be useful in this situation?
3. What other stress-prevention-and-relief actions might your colleague try that are not directly associated with work with students?

sions generated by the demands of today's classrooms and schools find it difficult to accomplish tasks in a way that meets their own personal standards. Thus, in addition to the anxiety created by the often unreasonable demands of the job, the individual's dissatisfaction with self adds to the upset. (p. 7)

We are concerned here with the sources of surplus stress and how it affects teachers' perceptions of themselves, their work, and those with whom they work (Albertson & Kagan, 1987; Humphrey & Humphrey, 1986). The intention is not to present teaching as a less enticing career or to be critical of the profession, its people, or its conditions of employment. You are merely given an opportunity to survey thoughtfully and objectively some occupation-related, stress-evoking conditions and to consider the personal and professional ramifications. Educators who are actively aware of these conditions are less likely to succumb to the problems and are more likely to notice the symptoms of distress in themselves and colleagues. Let us examine some of the conditions that induce stress and some of the common manifestations of distress in a school setting.

SOURCES AND CONSEQUENCES OF STRESS

Societal Sources of Stress

A poor public image of teachers and educators is a major source of teacher stress (Iwanicki, 1983). Stringent funding for education reinforces the image and adds to the stress. Inadequate teacher salaries create social and economic barriers for teachers. They cannot afford the cultivated tastes of a liberal education, nor can they give their families many of the advantages of "the good life." Cost-cutting measures that have increased class sizes, reduced expenditures for books and materials, and decreased spending for building maintenance and repair also can undermine teachers' job effectiveness and satisfaction.

Educators often try to counteract the criticisms of education by trying to be all things to all people (Sparks, 1979). Combatting criticism is doubly difficult when educators are uncertain about what their job should entail. For example, Duke (1984) states, "The proliferation of pedagogical panaceas has served to undermine traditional conceptualizations of the job of teaching without replacing them with any clear-cut, universally accepted notion of what teachers should be doing instead" (p. 37). When educators are confronted by relentless criticism and bandwagon panaceas and there is no consensus about goals, they are bound to behave irrationally. Their behavior then validates the claims of groups with a vested interest in change and another round of criticism begins. According to Bloch (1977):

> This steady stream of criticism, particularly in the wake of deteriorating working conditions, is bound to be demoralizing to educators, lessening their self-esteem and contributing to resentment toward the public that expects more of educators and contributes less to support their work. (p. 58)

A surplus of teachers in many teaching fields and many parts of the country during the past ten years has contributed to less job mobility among teachers. School boards, particularly those with limited resources, prefer to hire beginners who start at the bottom of the salary schedule. In addition to harboring ordinary concerns about the wide differences in the cost of living and real estate prices from city to city, teachers considering a job move must also take into account great variations in educational opportunity and quality. Thus, teachers cannot easily register their disappointment and displeasure with a system by simply relocating. They must often continue to endure an unsatisfactory situation in the interests of holding a job.

Teachers who feel compelled to remain in a school system because the employment prospects are slim elsewhere often feel vulnerable and yield grudgingly to administrative edicts and community criticism. Although one can argue that continuing contracts and tenure laws provide substantial job protection, teachers have little to say about job placement and instructional assignments. Cichon and Koff (1980) have found that for Chicago teachers, involuntary transfer ranked first among thirty-six stress-related events. In other words, teachers may not fear for a job, but the job they have may be less stress inducing than the one to which they could be assigned. Compliance may reduce the magnitude of stress but at an emotional cost to the teacher. When jobs are in jeopardy, teachers are not likely to advocate change and seek redress for grievances. A sense of resignation, helplessness, and despair can be an outgrowth of having to capitulate to the system as a form of self-preservation.

Self-doubts can be another outgrowth of the compromises that one makes when opportunities for employment are scarce. Young persons who enter teaching

Management Challenge 11–2
Dealing with Anger and Fear

Four students in your class are the primary instruments of stress in your life. As such, you are more likely to single them out for some form of discipline. Your disciplinary actions are met with accusations of unfairness and resistance in the form of incomplete work. Your efforts to justify your actions and to meet their resistance with understanding are met with indifference by the students. Their reaction only intensifies your anger. You are fearful that you may soon do something you will regret.

1. Use the work of Glasser (1986) to size up this situation. What would he suggest as the origins or causes of this problem?
2. What would he suggest as a plausible solution to the problem? What would he offer as a defense for his solution?
3. Do you favor his reasoning and solution? Why or why not?

are idealists; they believe that they can make a difference and are determined to do so. If they must sacrifice their ideals in order to keep their jobs, they are inclined to raise questions about their calling and their fitness for teaching. They cannot help but wonder if they would not be better off, and their students also, if they left the profession as a form of protest (Bardo, 1979). Some do leave; most remain. They swallow their pride and make the most of things as they are. The stress may be transformed into energy that is used productively or into regrets and guilt.

Clearly, societal and organizational sources of stress are interrelated. The bureaucratic structure of a large school system, like that in Chicago, may make teachers more vulnerable to arbitrary job transfer decisions. Some may argue that teachers in smaller urban and rural communities would be less subject to this form of harassment. But my experience indicates that there is a widespread feeling among teachers that job assignments are used to reward those who support the system and penalize those who do not. Thus, job assignments can be used to create pressures that control the behavior of teachers, but not without some detrimental psychological side effects.

Organizational Sources of Stress

A number of researchers have investigated organizationally based stress by looking at the effects of human and environmental interactions. A modified version of French and Caplan's (1972) P-E Fit categorical scheme has been used by Milstein, Golaszewski, and Duquette (1984) to describe five environmental categories that exist within any organization:

1. Relationships at work
2. Organizational structure and climate

3. Factors intrinsic to the job
4. Role in the organization
5. Career development

These categories are used here to describe and examine the stress inducers in the work environment of teachers and the debilitating effects of these stressful conditions.

Relationships at Work

Lipsky (1980) refers to teachers as "street level bureaucrats who work in situations which tend to maximize the likelihood of debilitating job stress" (p. 32). The teacher's day often begins by monitoring hallways or supervising the playground. The first order of business in the classroom generally involves taking attendance, reading announcements, collecting fees, selling tickets, and attending to other clerical, low-level management functions. All of these bureaucratic functions elevate stress associated with the goal- and achievement-oriented preferences of teachers and their increasingly accountability-minded publics. The dilemma is one that creates much tension for teachers and eventually contributes to considerable friction between teachers and administrators, whom teachers often view as either the perpetrators of the bureaucratic minutiae or as unsympathetic bystanders.

Teachers frequently complain about having little time to interact with one another. Most of their time during the day is spent with students. So-called "free" periods are often used to work with individual students, read papers, and prepare lessons. Coaching and supervision of extracurricular activities occupy the after-school hours of a large segment of the staff. Thus, teachers have few opportunities to engage in prolonged professional conversations. Their views of one another are often based on hearsay remarks of parents and students, infrequent and casual observations of a colleague's classroom, conduct in faculty meetings, and brief exchanges in the faculty room.

It is difficult to develop collegiality—a sense of confidence, loyalty, and trust—when there are so few occasions to interact with one another. Teachers thus tend to be anxious about how they are perceived by their colleagues, uncertain about their colleagues' views on many important aspects of the job, and reluctant to depart from perceived professional norms. The anxiety, uncertainty, and reticence induce stress and result in a tentativeness and cautiousness that rob teachers of the resourcefulness and imagination that renew their enthusiasm and replenish their stamina.

Organizational Structure and Climate

Teachers frequently complain about the autocratic and bureaucratic way in which schools are run. Administrators, particularly those opposed to collective bargaining practices, are likely to distrust the motives of teachers and to fear the changes that would come about if they had a larger role in school governance. Thus, teachers are seldom consulted about the things that really matter to them. Curriculum decisions and resource allocation decisions are generally made by the board of education and the superintendent. Staff assignments, evaluation procedures, and faculty development decisions are often the prerogative of the principal. Class schedules and pupil assignments are done by counselors. Faculty meetings are generally confined to the dissemination of mundane information or are used to respond to administrative mandates. Seldom are these meetings used to examine educational goals and priorities, evaluate the effectiveness of the school's organizational structure, and systematically plan better ways to carry out the school's educational mission.

The accountability movement in education, partially a response to collective bargaining and public disaffection with the quality of education, sometimes has sharpened the distinctions between teaching and administration. Principals devote more of their time to supervisory and evaluative activities; classroom visits and performance conferences are more common. These activities create new tensions because there are differences of opinion about the criteria for judging good teaching, the evidence of effective teaching, and the qualifications of principals to make these judgments. Teachers accustomed to considerable job autonomy must now undergo evaluation by people who are not teaching, who may never have taught in their area, and who may rely heavily on personal biases about curriculum goals and instructional methodology. Teachers often feel that they have little to say about the substantive and procedural matters associated with the evaluation process and the use of the results. Thus, the process becomes a source of anxiety, and how the results are used becomes a source of friction.

Factors Intrinsic to the Job

The sheer volume of work, accentuated by daily deadlines, contributes to pressure-packed performances. Very few teachers can leave their jobs when they leave the building. Because most of the day is spent performing instructional and allied instructional duties, teachers must work evenings and weekends to check the effectiveness of their teaching and provide supportive and corrective feedback to students. The pressure to disseminate more and more information and to assist students during independent study and guided practice sessions eliminates the use of class time to read homework assignments and grade examinations. Preparations for the next day's lessons must also be done outside of school hours. The quantity of work and the lack of time to do it create pressures that even the best-organized and most efficient teachers find burdensome and sometimes overwhelming (Raschke, Dedrick, Strathe, & Hawkes, 1985).

With such time constraints, the quality of a teacher's work is bound to suffer. Teachers speak regretfully of all the ways that they could do things better if there were only more hours in the day. Although teacher-educators speak of better ways to prepare teachers to teach, few teachers are able to teach as well as they already know how to teach. Much discontentment is the result of seeing the potential in children never realized and seeing the possibilities in materials and methods go unexplored. These experiences are a drag on teachers' resourcefulness and vitality. Much early fervor for teaching is lost because dreams are smothered by paperwork and excessive demands within the classroom day.

Management Challenge 11–3

Laughter as Stress Reduction

In his book *Control Theory in the Classroom* (1986), Glasser postulates a need for fun and suggests that we put experiences of fun in our picture albums. In *Anatomy of an Illness as Perceived by the Patient* (1979), Cousins attributes a remarkable improvement in health to watching a lot of funny movies. We all need fun and laughter in our lives because it is good for us and for the people around us.

1. What makes you laugh? Who are the people who make you laugh?
2. How prominent are these sources of laughter in your life? What can you do to make them more so?
3. What is therapeutic about laughter?
4. What can you do to bring more laughter into the lives of others? What do you visualize as the secondary benefits for you?
5. What do people mean when they say that someone has a good sense of humor? What can you do to cultivate this quality? How can this quality act as a stress reducer?

Role in the Organization

Many of the problems addressed in this book, when unresolved, contribute to inter-personal distress. Disciplinary and motivational problems head the list (Swick & Hanley, 1980). But teachers also face the problems of developing challenging and creative instructional programs and materials, devising suitable ways to work with students with special needs, securing time-effective ways to upgrade professional preparation and refine instructional skills, and garnering time to cultivate positive relationships with coworkers and parents. Without the time and support to engage in these activities, teachers lose their zest for teaching. They feel resigned to do what they did last year and to do it in spite of knowing the limitations for students and the lost opportunity for intrinsic job satisfaction.

Teachers try to recover the time lost to bureaucratic minutiae by introducing more economical methods of information dissemination. Material is covered with lectures rather than with problem-solving activities; students are given less guided practice and independent study time. This problem has been accentuated by recent efforts to mainstream handicapped and other special-needs students (Bensky et al., 1980). As a consequence, many students possess a very limited grasp of the material and do not do as well as expected on teacher-made tests and standardized examinations. The stress associated with using compensatory methods and with getting disappointing results contributes to a sense of hopelessness and despair. Some teachers escape by calling in sick. Some just try to hang on until the next vacation.

The effects of self-destructive forms of escape are not confined to teachers. When teachers cannot surmount organizational obstacles, the consequences can undermine their relationships with students as well. Teachers may lose a sense of proportion. A teacher can become short-tempered and lash out at students for minor disturbances. Students, noting the disproportionate response, attribute the problem to a personality deficiency and respond by being less cooperative. They become less tolerant of teachers' mistakes, more resistant to teacher requests, and more critical of and antagonistic toward one another. Their lack of cooperation becomes disagreeable and distressing to the teacher, and this furthers the rift that started with unresolved frustrations. Stress can create vicious cycles of claims and counterclaims that cannot be resolved as the two parties drift further apart.

Career Development

There is little opportunity for advancement in the teaching profession. Because administrators are generally more respected than teachers, many good teachers take this avenue to achieve status and recognition in the education profession. Although there have been occasional discussions about career ladders and recent experiments to recognize competency and preparation levels, teachers are often the most vocal critics of these ways of differentiating assignments and recognizing exemplary professional achievement. Most of the criticism is aimed at the criteria and procedures for identifying individuals, at the meager remuneration given the talented performer, and at the disagreeable job assignments given those who are judged to be less proficient.

Some claim that in the absence of salary incentives and promotions to positions of greater leadership, there is insufficient competition among teachers to do their best. Without such incentives, they contend, there is a leveling of aspirations and attainments. Teachers argue that, on the contrary, competition contributes to dissension and distrust. School morale suffers, and the learning environment is adversely affected. They contend that teachers must be encouraged to cooperate and share their knowledge and skills and that they must be given time to do so. Time is a valued commodity, and sharing produces much intrinsic satisfaction; both, many argue, would be sufficient incentives to raise the aspirations and the performance of the teaching force.

Many teachers also argue that substantial increases in the base salary and in salary schedule increments should precede merit salary incentives. Experienced teachers contend that their families are already denied many of the material comforts and opportunities for leisure-time pursuits afforded members of other professions. Living without the marks and opportunities of professional status can be disheartening. To augment their teaching salaries, some teachers take second jobs; but holding down two jobs cannot help but reduce their commitment to students and teaching. Job security is a stress reduction factor in teaching. Yet job security and summer vacations are often cited by critics to counter the demands of teacher unions for higher salaries and improved fringe benefits.

Citizens are also critical of the profession's unwillingness or inability to police its membership. Parents can point to persons who should have been dismissed long ago. Teachers are often sympathetic to their concerns, but they also recognize their own vulnerability to the capricious claims and fickle preferences of a few influential people or a vocal minority. Research still has not provided valid criteria and irrefutable techniques for measuring and judging effective teaching. This ambiguity, and the argument of critics citing instances of teacher inadequacies and incompetence to strengthen their case, are bound to be stressful for many conscientious and capable teachers.

COUNTERACTING INSTITUTIONAL SOURCES OF STRESS

Reducing Societal Sources of Stress

People working in public service occupations are often the targets of criticism. Educators are particularly vulnerable because most have an earnest desire to serve—so much so that they are quick to jump on the latest bandwagon and march to the current tune of public sentiment. The school curriculum is in a constant state of flux as educators try to compensate for and be responsive to changes in the composition of the school population, the disorganization of the nuclear family, the dangers of drug and alcohol abuse, the ramifications of a liberal sexual morality, and the impact of technology on the work world. Initially the educator's receptiveness is heralded with widespread support, at times acclaim, only to be the subject of criticism when the pendulum swings back to another set of priorities. As the mood or the priorities of the country change, education is often a scapegoat and the target for reform.

The cycles of public opinion that create pressures for change lie outside of the control of educators. Educators would be better off focusing their attention on those organizational conditions and professional or personal performance variables that they can influence. Teachers can be responsive to stable community values and can increase the intrinsic satisfaction of teaching by doing as Truch (1980) has suggested:

1. Seek to improve your own teaching skills. Since, for the most part, teachers who feel burned out also feel they are no longer making a difference with their students, then it is urgent that you see that *you* must make the changes yourself. It is vital that you see that you *do* make a difference in children's lives and that you *can* control or improve on this in yourself and in your classroom.
2. Learn to become open and to share feelings with students and colleagues. You may be quite surprised at how receptive others will be when dealt with in this way.
3. Extend the freedom you enjoy in making curriculum choices. Develop themes and lessons based on them. If you do not enjoy freedom of choice in curriculum areas, seek positive ways of changing this.
4. Change your classroom conditions. Sometimes just rearranging the furniture helps.
5. Create ways of teaching the "basics" but if you are always changing things, take a rest and evaluate the effectiveness of what you are doing.
6. Work toward expanding your professional growth. (pp. 77–78)

These practices will contribute to a sense of self-assurance and self-fulfillment. Self-assured, fulfilled teachers will be able to withstand assaults on their work. They also will be sufficiently secure to examine the merits of any criticisms and to respond to promising suggestions for change.

Reducing Organizational Sources of Stress

Not all stress in an organization is due to external forces. As pointed out earlier, much stress originates from bureaucratic structures and outmoded practices. We help create the stress with which we must contend.

Research findings on the characteristics of healthy organizations (Payne & Pugh, 1971) and the ways to create such organizations can be a useful start for looking at ways to reduce this type of stress. Gardell (1971) asserted that healthy work environments exist when individuals have an opportunity to

1. influence if not control their work situation,
2. be engaged in meaningful and socially important activities,
3. feel a sense of belonging to their work groups, and
4. satisfy their needs for self-esteem. (pp. 151–152)

One way to determine how the school organization helps and hinders professional development in these areas is provided by Wayson et al. (1981). His instrument can be used by school personnel to identify, describe, and analyze school trouble spots. Trouble spots are typically instances where administrative and instructional practices have been adopted without sufficient attention to the many and varied consequences. Practices instituted to solve one problem may well create others. The ensuing problems may become the impetus for disruptive behavior in the school and classroom.

The eight categories in Wayson's instrument, described in Figure 11–1, isolate organizational aspects of schooling that contribute to the pervasive and often subtle attitudes and practices that affect school morale and productivity. These organizational factors, and the concomitant attitudes and practices, warrant scrutiny because they determine what is important and unimportant, what is done and what is left undone. The entire instrument is not reproduced here, but the category descriptions in Figure 11–1 do provide a sufficient basis for pinpointing possible areas of tension or friction, identifying the stress inducing consequences, and suggesting promising solutions. For example, a faculty member might ask what is being done or what might be done to promote the desirable state of affairs represented by each category description. This process may well suggest the need to promote a greater sense of community among students and staff. Categories 3, 4, and 8 might become the basis for a norm-developing discussion and, still later, for ways to make these norms the basis for a schoolwide management plan, a plan that results in stress reduction by promoting more harmonious and productive relationships.

The entire school staff must make a concerted effort to remove the bureaucratic barriers to the responsible expression of professional interests and talents.

Reducing Role-Related Stress

Dealing with role-related stress is crucial to the mental health of educators and those with whom they work. The advice in this area is as plentiful as the sources of

Introduction: This inventory is neither a "score card" nor an objective test. It is a working guide for use by school personnel, students, and parents to analyze programs and to identify problem areas on which they wish to work, to reduce disruption, and to improve discipline in their schools.

1. *The way people work together for problem solving and decision making.* Generally, more open and widespread participation is related to fewer disruptive behaviors and greater feelings of responsibility among teachers and students.

2. *The distribution of authority and status.* Generally, when there are fewer barriers to communication, more involvement in exercising authority, and fewer status differences, the result is a more widespread sense of responsibility and a greater commitment among staff and students.

3. *Student belongingness.* Students feel that the school serves their needs, is a safe and happy place to be, treats them as valued individuals, and provides ways in which student concerns are treated fairly. When students feel supported and are involved in the life of the school, fewer disruptions or irresponsible behaviors will occur.

4. *Procedures for developing and implementing rules.* Generally, when rules are made by the people involved and when expectations are clearly understood, there are fewer transgressions. The more nearly rules are derived from principles of learning and of normal human behavior, the more effective they are. The more the school operates like a community, as opposed to a prison or army, the fewer the problems.

5. *Curriculum and instructional practices.* A curriculum that emphasizes learning that is appropriate for the students served and that provides a greater variety of materials and activities tends to reduce discipline problems.

6. *Processes for dealing with personal problems.* Generally, practices that help people cope with their lives outside the school and with problems that are not directly related to school matters stimulate greater commitment to participate fully in the work of the school.

7. *Relationships with parents and other community members.* Generally, more open relationships with parents and other community members result in better achievement and behavior in the school. Close home and community contacts also enhance the students' sense of belonging.

8. *Physical environment.* Generally, environments that are pleasant for adults and students to work in and that reflect the interests, culture, and values of students encourage good behavior. The more the school environment looks like a workshop, a library, a restaurant, or a conference center and less like a prison or institution, the fewer the problems.

Figure 11–1
The Discipline Context Inventory

Source: From *Handbook for Developing Schools with Good Discipline* (pp. 92–99) by W. W. Wayson et al., 1981, Bloomington, IN: Phi Delta Kappa. Copyright © 1979 by W. W. Wayson. Reprinted by permission.

stress that it is designed to counteract (Dedrick & Raschke, 1990; Gold, 1988; Martinez, 1989; Saville, 1988; Slife, 1988). The choice of techniques will depend on the source of the stress, the specific ways in which the stress is experienced, and the personality of the role incumbent.

For example, the same stress reduction strategies will not necessarily yield equal benefits for teachers and administrators who have been told that their instructional materials and supplies budget will be drastically cut. Some techniques will be chosen for the short-term effects, others to attain long-term results. Similarly, teachers who have large numbers of pupils "at risk" in their classes will deal differently with the strain of selecting suitable methods and materials. Educators also vary greatly in their responsiveness to pupils with varied background and abilities.

Pressure to conform to a narrowly defined picture of the "perfect" teacher lies at the root of much role-related stress. Instead, teachers must begin to respect and encourage diversity. They must seek ways to assess and capitalize on their strengths and those of their colleagues. There are many different ways to conceptualize and execute the teaching task (see Joyce & Weil, 1980). Lortie (1975, p. 236) offers teachers and others interested in a "greater lateral organization of teaching" a number of ways to blend creatively the individualistic predispositions of beginning teachers with the needs of the profession and the organization for collegial responsibility. The coalescence of these ideas can foster an invigorating pluralism while simultaneously encouraging a shared responsibility for the educational enterprise.

COUNTERACTING PERSONAL SOURCES OF STRESS
Dispelling Faulty Self-Perceptions

What we think of ourselves has a great deal of influence on how we behave. When we have distorted perceptions of ourselves and these perceptions are used to structure our world of experience, we are likely to make errors in judgment. As a consequence, our behavioral choices do not fit the situation, and we come away feeling less capable and confident about our ability to manage our affairs. Cedoline (1982) has pinpointed the following typical examples of faulty perceptions that undermine our sense of well-being and eventually contribute to distress:

1. Evaluating yourself as less worthy because you have fallen short of another's expectation.
2. Believing that others really don't care and that you're not very important.
3. Regarding yourself as inferior.
4. Feeling you are incapable of handling an extremely stressful situation.
5. Stereotyping others as bad because of isolated behaviors, or feeling you are the judge of how others must act.
6. Believing that worry is necessary in anticipating each future event. (p. 111)

According to Ellis (1973), such maladaptive thinking patterns can be overcome with positive self-talk. His rational emotive therapy is aimed at using inner talk to change thoughts and feelings that undermine effective behavior. This approach is consistent with the findings of Beck (1970), who has concluded that people suffering from severe stress could be characterized by the faulty beliefs that they expressed in self-verbalizations. He categorizes the faulty beliefs into four areas:

1. Arbitrary inference, dividing everything into opposites or extremes—"All of the other teachers dislike me."
2. Overgeneralization, making far-reaching generalizations—"My principal let me down. I'll never confide in him again."
3. Magnification, viewing things in an exaggerated way, usually as catastrophic—"Why even try to help her, it won't do any good, she's a hopeless case."
4. Cognitive deficiency, drawing conclusions without evidence, often in a self-deprecating way—"I messed up again; I just can't do anything right." (pp. 190–191)

Teachers can reduce the distress associated with negative self-talk by being sensitive to the ways that faulty beliefs distort self-perceptions, aware that negative self-talk drives some of their behavior, and cognizant of how to replace negative thought patterns with self-confident and self-trusting interior monologues. Several writers refer to this process as *stress inoculation*.

Meichenbaum (1977), as well as Forman (1982) and Kalker (1984), have recommended stress inoculation as a method of reducing the stress in a situation. The success of this cognitive-behavioral technique depends on achieving a conceptual understanding of a situation's reality and then recognizing the accompanying subjective stress. Seeing this connection can eventually help the individual manage the stress by using the cognition to control the affect. Realizing that the problem is situational in nature decreases the guilt, shame, and helplessness that often contribute to maladaptive solutions.

Educators who become proficient in the use of stress inoculation are better able to cognitively restructure their job circumstances and monitor their own self-statements. They are less likely to engage in negative self-talk or dwell on the intransigence of their situation. By gradually making more self-reinforcing statements and reducing unreasonable self-demands, the individual forestalls feelings of hopelessness and helplessness.

Forming Social Support Groups

Burnout is less prevalent among helping professionals who have access to some sort of social–professional support system (Dunham, 1977; Holt, Fine, & Tollefson, 1987; Jenkins & Calhoun, 1991; Maslach & Pines, 1977). Unfortunately, most educators are so isolated from one another, with little opportunity to emotionally support one another and common time to share experiences, that they are highly susceptible to stress and stress-related illness (Farber & Miller, 1981; Lortie, 1975).

It is always consoling to know that other people have encountered similar problems and have struggled to find suitable solutions. Knowing of their successes and failures is also reassuring. Frequently persons in trouble think that they are the only ones who have the problem or are coping so inadequately. Recurring problems tend to restrict perspectives and result in a preoccupation with the negative aspects of self and the work situation. Help can come only to those who are convinced of the need to share common concerns, but there must also be persons capable of creating the safe climate that encourages people to divulge these concerns. Forming a group whose members share these qualities is no small accomplishment because burnout victims often develop cynical, excessively pessimistic, callous, and contemptuous attitudes about their work and their colleagues.

A support group can be an uplifting experience for individuals who are down on themselves. Initially, the group can help participants become more sensitive to the causes and symptoms of occupational stress. Support groups thrive on positive self-indulgence. They supplant negative self-talk with encouragement; they heighten one's sense of self-importance. Persons who desperately struggle to see through the morass of negative thoughts need colleagues who can help them realize the good that they are doing and capitalize on their potential for enlarging on that good. Participants can be helped to see how they contribute to their problems and to reflect on the effects of coping strategies.

Support groups can also help individuals review their reasons for entering the profession and reaffirm their original commitment. Dwelling on the terrible and terrifying aspects of work or the shortcomings of colleagues is not an uncommon reaction to stress. But a preoccupation with failed techniques and working conditions that cannot be changed can be debilitating and demoralizing. In desperation, the person asks the group, "Where have I gone wrong? What can I possibly do that I haven't already tried? I just don't seem to be accomplishing anything." The group can pose alternative questions: "What do you believe about yourself? About children? About teaching and learning? How do these beliefs contribute to the problems you have and to the solutions you have tried?"

Sometimes individuals need to discriminate clearly between the actual demands of the job and the demands that they place on themselves. A teacher's sense of idealism and dedication may result in unreasonable and unattainable expectations. A support group can help the individual realize that working harder at solutions to problems is not always the most productive strategy. So often the individual's assumptions about a problem drive behavior in unproductive directions; seeing differently enables a person to behave differently.

Better honed communication skills, another useful means of reducing stress, are often a by-product of participation in support groups or human relations training programs (Gazda, 1973; Johnson, 1972). To a great extent, teaching depends on good relationships and strong interpersonal communication skills, but few provisions are made for the acquisition and refinement of these skills in a teacher's preservice preparation program. Individuals who possess self-expressive and supportive communication skills can derive, as well as provide, greater satisfaction from human relationships.

Finally, support group sessions undoubtedly lead to a greater realization and appreciation of the unique abilities and talents that reside in the group. Individuals can be asked to offer workshops devoted to examining new materials or techniques. Some teachers will demonstrate a talent for working with students with special needs or with those who pose certain types of disciplinary or motivational problems. Programs that capitalize on individuals' areas of expertise can become esteem-building sessions that help prevent and alleviate stress for all participants.

Benefiting from Relaxation, Exercise, and Diet

Despite accusations of producing a youth-worshiping culture, the health and fitness movements have undeniably achieved one important goal: raising the health consciousness of most individuals. And being more attuned to our physiological and psychological selves has a definite advantage: We can more easily pinpoint the causes of stress and its physical effects. This heightened sense of awareness can be a useful deterrent to the mounting stress that eventually leads to burnout.

Numerous techniques are available for both preventing and alleviating the physical consequences of stress. Truch (1980) has advocated a stress management program (READ) that integrates four essential ingredients:

❑ Deep *relaxation*
❑ Regular *exercise*
❑ *Attitude* and *awareness*
❑ *Diet*

Simple breathing exercises, which can be done for brief moments during the school day, can be used to relax body and mind. Relaxation exercises and meditation produce similar positive effects, but these techniques take more time and require a form of solitude seldom found in a school setting. Self-hypnosis, emotive imagery, yoga, prayer, biofeedback, and autogenic training are also used as relaxation responses to stress (Warshaw, 1979; Woolfolk & Richardson, 1978). Some teachers rely exclusively on one approach, others combine approaches, and still others link techniques with selected physiological responses to stress. Numerous self-help books, providing step-by-step directions, can be used to become acquainted with the limits and benefits of various techniques.

While relaxation training can be used to control the physiological accompaniments of stress, physical exercise programs can also facilitate good health and a sense of well-being. Regular exercise, rather than any specific form of exercise, and sound nutrition with limited intakes of caffeine, nicotine, salt, and sugar are the key ingredients of a good health plan.

Too often, however, educators ignore such basic elements. They are prone to skip breakfast or lunch to cut calories, drink coffee to pick them up, and excuse themselves from a regular exercise program because of fatigue. Ironically, the exhaustion at the end of the school day is often due to poor nutritional habits, over-reliance on stimulants, and too little vigorous exercise.

Creating Work Incentives

Teachers can get together and create a varied and effective reinforcement system, one that compares favorably with the more expensive and highly regulated reinforcement system that businesses use to spur people to greater accomplishment. Teachers tend to be more highly motivated by personal forms of approval and uniquely tangible forms of recognition anyway.

One school in Waterloo, Iowa, boosts teacher morale with a secret admirer's club. At the beginning of each year, all staff members' names are placed in a hat. Each teacher draws a slip with another teacher's name on it, thus becoming that person's secret admirer. Twice each month the admirers exchange thoughtful, inexpensive gifts: a bouquet of flowers or a bag of fresh assorted vegetables from someone's garden, a solicited appreciative note from a parent, an invitation from a student to share a specially packed box lunch, a ticket to a special theater production or sporting event, or a note describing a particularly praiseworthy characteristic of the individual. It is the thought that counts.

What a morale booster! Because few days go by without at least one such demonstration of affection—and curiosity about who is the thoughtful party—there is constant conversation about the form of kindness and how well it suits a particular individual. The staff becomes aware of sides of people that had been hidden because no one had bothered to search for the special, and often unappreciated, gifts that individuals bring to teaching.

This particular activity is illustrative because it has the potential for combining tangible and social reinforcers as a stress prevention and reduction strategy. However, in this instance, secrecy adds an element of excitement and intrigue that comes to a climax when the identities of the secret admirers are revealed at the end-of-the-year school picnic.

ORIGINS AND DIMENSIONS OF STUDENT STRESS

For teachers and students to deal effectively with stress, they must understand the three dimensions of time, space, and relationships. These three dimensions provide the context in which all stress-inducing events occur (Swick, 1987, p. 10). Each of these constructs is neutral with respect to stress. How these conditions are perceived and managed makes them potentially stressful features of the school and classroom setting, because stress is a subjective response to a particular situation or series of events (Goldberger & Breznitz, 1982). Understanding the messages that each conveys to the participants and how they handle these messages help persons deal with the positive and negative perceptions of stress.

Time as a Stressor

Time becomes stress inducing when one feels controlled by it. When students feel that there is never enough time to do what is required, they may become frustrated and annoyed. They may feel that regardless of how they allocate and spend their time, they will be left with work undone or with too little time for leisure pursuits. The perils of work overload and job dissatisfaction in the marketplace have counterparts in the classroom. Any efficiencies that students gain through self-management skills will not be sufficient to the task. Thus, they often feel overwhelmed by the sheer magnitude of the teacher's expectations.

Time can also become a stressor for students when the pace of instruction leaves them behind, when they are unable to keep up with the other members of the class. It is not just a matter of being given too much to do but being able to handle the teacher's delivery of the material. The student never quite catches on to an idea or process before the teacher moves on. The struggle to keep up creates anxiety, which further impedes the ability to comprehend. Continuing to fall further behind, the student finally throws in the towel.

Time also can trigger stress when too much of it is allocated to some activities. Boredom is an outgrowth of involvement with activities that have long lost their appeal or whose potential has been exhausted. Weariness is an outcome of activities that have wrung out the energy and endurance of a student. In either instance, the student who is under the sustained stress of paying attention often seeks outlets in the novelty and excitement of creating disturbances. Release of the tensions often results in preventable disciplinary problems.

Time can be a stressor when schedules disrupt one's usual life pattern. When children enter a school setting, they must adapt to time structures that might not fit their background or disposition. Having to adapt to another's contrary and capricious interpretations and use of time can be stressful. Being out of synch with the timing of one's own biological clock or cultural heritage can be disconcerting.

Space as a Stressor

Space—physical, psychological, and social—can influence the teaching–learning process. The aesthetic appeal of the school and classroom can affect stress. Students experience stress when they are faced with classroom settings that are the product of years of neglect and damage. They must fight the inclination to be negative and resentful when they enter a building that reveals a lack of commitment to them.

Space is a void that can be filled with happiness or sorrow. The space in a school building may be physically drab and uninviting, but when it is filled with friendship and fun, the surroundings matter less. On the other hand, a building designed to evoke excitement may be experienced as an empty hull if students find no one there who cares for or about them. The space that exists between and among people can be more important than the structure where they come together. Students who have to cope with the emotional distress of loneliness and powerlessness are ill equipped to focus their efforts on productive pursuits.

Relationships as a Stressor

Human relationships, too, can be stress evoking or stress reducing. How people interact with one another can encourage or impede healthy views of self and others. Students who experience teachers as positive and help-oriented are more likely to experience themselves as worthy and capable persons. They reason that people enjoy them and care about them because there is something inherently good about them. That belief encourages acts of civil and cooperative behavior, which further reinforce students. There is a melding of who they are with what they can do—a unifying theme that gives purpose and point to their life.

Most educators can recount stories that illustrate the connections between stress and school performance. They can also pinpoint instances when the source of negative stress originated in human relationships. Teachers, parents, and peers can create pressures when they withhold approval to impose their performance expectations.

Students feel psychologically harassed by the need to be affirmed and to chase a goal of someone else's choosing. Stress is also possible when students remain involved in a mentally unhealthy program or activity because they do not want to disappoint an important person in their life. Students may also experience stress when they are lonely and alienated, when they are not connected to others in any significant way.

COMBATTING STUDENT STRESS

Removing Time-Induced Stressors

Helplessness is a stressful feeling. One tends to feel helpless when one has no control over a situation. Gaining control over time may be as simple as giving students an opportunity to participate in the scheduling of activities. Teachers might establish the time limits for a given activity (or several activities) and invite students to isolate time segments within (or across) the activity. As students participate in this exercise, they are evaluating their emotional wherewithal to make good use of various units of time and are psychologically preparing themselves for the activity itself. Students feel more in control when they are allowed to make decisions about the use of time.

Not all of the time that students spend in school is devoted to academic activity. There are many administrative tasks: attendance must be taken, money collected, announcements made, and materials distributed. Some activities are designed to build school pride and loyalty: school assemblies, pep rallies, program rehearsals, and early dismissals for athletic trips. Others are created to serve special-need populations: remedial pullout programs, gifted and talented curricula, and enrichment programs. These ways of using and structuring time often become rituals that can undermine the mental health of students. Periodic examination of these school rituals can help remove outmoded practices and revitalize the basic mission of the organization.

Institutions also gravitate toward standardized ways of carrying out their mission. Often these methods evolve from certain public expectations about how the institutional mission should be implemented and evaluated. Schools are expected to socialize students and disseminate information. Educators have responded to these expectations by creating assessment and reporting tools, but tests and grades can be a source of much stress for students. Some students may have to deal with excessive pressure to succeed. The pressure can contribute to a heightened need to escape through drugs, suicide, or an intense dislike for anything and everything associated with schooling. In the latter case, students may continue to excel, but at the expense of attitudes that support lifelong learning.

Removing Space-Induced Stressors

There are many ways to make school and classroom space attractive. Often attitudes make more of a difference than money. Even an old, battered building can be kept clean. When people pledge themselves to such a common endeavor, the results can be invigorating and fulfilling. Neatness is often an inducement for people to add their own personal touch, to share their artistic talents or their material possessions. Artistic talents can transform a wall or bulletin board into a colorful display. Material possessions can change the teacher's desk, tables, bookcases, shelves, and floor space into interesting activity zones.

The psychological space that separates people can be bridged by teachers who give small gifts of attention. Everyone likes to be noticed, to be singled out for some form of favorable attention. Another person's approval can remove the distress of self-doubt. Cooperative learning can also create bridges and teach students how to get along with one another. Lessons that include social skills can provide the building blocks that some students do not acquire at home. Students lacking such skills often fill the vacuum with misguided efforts to win acceptance. The stress associated with rejection can be devastating at a time in life when self-acceptance depends so much on affirmation from others.

Removing Human Relationship Stressors

The teacher sets the tone and establishes the dynamics for interpersonal relationships in the classroom. When students observe a teacher who respects the dignity and prizes the contributions of each class member, they are more likely to imitate the teacher's attitudes and behavior. There is something infectious about people who make us feel good about ourselves and about others; we welcome the chance to reciprocate. Much of the stress associated with our uncertainty about how to favorably present ourselves to others and how to maintain friendships can be eased by a teacher who can embrace diversity.

Schools that use extracurricular activities as a tool for building human relationships will see that the benefits carry over to the classroom as well. Extracurricular activities provide students not only an outlet for their talents but also opportunities to win and enjoy the approval of their contemporaries. Moreover, there is generally considerable latitude for self-expression, a variety of ways to make a contribution, and a distribution of responsibility to achieve success. A student can have a minor role in a dramatic production, join a club, work behind the scenes as a member of student government committees, be one of several tenors in the chorus, and still be regarded as "one of us." The amount of stress can be regulated by the individual's decision on how much of a leadership role to take. A teacher or coach can also be instrumental in regulating stress by keeping the socialization and personal growth values of the activity foremost in their minds.

Some students need help in developing positive interpersonal relationships. Many of the skills described in this book, particularly the covenant-oriented skills described in Chapter 8, can be acquired as part of a leader-manager's classroom. According to Cartledge and Milburn (1978), in recent years some schools have inte-

---

Management Challenge 11–4

A Stress Management Program for Students

You are convinced that disruptive behaviors in your classroom are due to student stress. You want to check out your hunch by developing and implementing a stress management program in your classroom.

1. How would you go about identifying the stressors in students' lives?
2. What strategies for stress prevention and reduction would you consider in devising your program?
3. How would you match the causes of stress and the strategies for dealing with stress?
4. How would you incorporate these strategies into your classroom program?
5. What would you accept as evidence of program success?

---

grated social-skill training programs into their curricula. Generally presented in problem-solving formats, these skills are practiced by the entire class as a group. Students are then encouraged to use the skills in daily classroom interactions. These life management skills can become proactive and stress-alleviating instruments for teaching social skills in the classroom.

CONCLUSION

Much can be done to make teaching and contacts with colleagues more pleasant and satisfying. One may not be able to eliminate or even moderate many of the most disagreeable and debilitating sources of stress. Many situational factors are almost givens, and there is no point in fretting about them. Of course, professional organizations should continue to press the claims of their constituents; classroom teachers can help by working to remove organizational constraints to the effectiveness of these groups. Even here wisdom suggests selective attention to less entrenched policies and practices or to ones that can clearly and persuasively be shown to be detrimental to teachers' well-being and contrary to the purposes of education. And having selected points of contention and created an agenda for change, educators need to talk less and act more.

Teachers can accomplish the most, and do it most assuredly, with the role-related sources of stress. We do altogether too little to take care of our own. We are just as likely to join the criticism of a colleague as we are to turn the conversation to that person's strengths. We too often see where we can help but excuse ourselves by not wanting to interfere, not wanting to seem superior, or just not wanting to take the time.

Stress in the classroom is not confined to teachers. Some disciplinary problems may well be symptomatic of the stress that students encounter as they go about their work. Students who take school seriously are more likely to experience the pressures of time and the multiple demands of the school experience. Students who view school as an unfortunate necessity may be unduly influenced by the space and human relationship factors. Already alienated and disenfranchised by their attitudes and performance, they are more attentive to affective cues. A dismal setting and unfulfilling relationship will fuel their disenchantment. For these students, stress is experienced as a sense of helplessness and hopelessness.

Teachers can be stress-reducing agents. How they help students manage time, how they structure the setting for learning, and how they foster positive self-concepts can help students deal with stress. Teachers can also help students acquire stress reduction self-management skills, provide guidance in the use of these skills, and offer feedback that validates proactive behavioral patterns. Students can reach their potential when teachers create contexts that minimize frustration, anxiety, feelings of rejection, conflict, and excessive expectations (Elkind, 1980).

When concerns are consolidated and efforts solidified, much can be done to understand the sources and effects of stress, ameliorate the causes of stress, alleviate some of the adverse effects, and help one another rebound from stress-induced aspects of the job. Rewards will come in the form of more enjoyable relationships with colleagues, a greater commitment to work, more productive and satisfying relationships with students, and a school system that enjoys the respect of an appreciative public.

SUPPLEMENTARY QUESTIONS

1. Some people seem to need more stress in their lives; others seem to need less. Some people seem to be able to manage large amounts of stress; others are overcome by only modest amounts. What do you believe accounts for individual differences in the amount of stress that people need and can handle?

2. Knowing what you do about yourself and about teaching, what combination of personal qualities and occupational conditions is likely to interact to make certain aspects of teaching stressful for you?

3. This chapter identifies numerous sources of personal and occupational stress, some of which are more readily managed than others. What makes teachers more and less susceptible to various types of stress? What can be done to make them less vulnerable to the stressors that are most debilitating?

4. The three general ways in which a person can deal with stress are to face it squarely and cope with it, fight against it, or flee from it. What are some of the advantages and disadvantages of each approach?

5. H. Greenberg (cited in S. Greenberg, 1984, p. 14), in his perceptive and poignant treatise on the subjective dimensions of teaching, referred to certain myths that make unrealistic demands on teachers. The myths state that the teacher must do the following:

- Remain calm at all times.
- Assume a philosophy of moderation in all things.
- Place all students' feelings above his or her own.
- Love all students.
- Remain consistent.
- Be permissive.
- Hide his or her true feelings.
- Have no prejudices.
- Have no favorites.
- Know all of the answers.
- Make learning take place without confusion and uncertainty.
- Cope with life without stress, anxiety, or conflict.
- Teach students to cope with life without stress, anxiety, or conflict.
- Protect students from negative feelings and situations.

What do you believe accounts for these myths? How do they contribute to stress and to the choice of stress reduction strategies?

SUPPLEMENTARY PROJECTS

1. Form a four-member panel and debate this proposition: Burnout is highly unlikely among people who ardently believe in what they are doing and derive great satisfactions from doing it.
2. Identify three coping strategies that seem to have promise for you. Employ these three strategies, one each day, alternating over a fifteen-day period. Compare and contrast the effectiveness of each technique by discussing its positive results.
3. Keep a diary of your activities for one week. Set the diary accounts aside for one week, and then reread them. Use the entries for the days that you believe were the most and the least stressful to reflect on differences in the quality-of-life experiences for those two days. Prepare a summary of your observations.
4. Dunham (1984, p. 109) administered a checklist to teachers in three British comprehensive schools to ascertain the most frequently used coping strategies. The ten most frequently used strategies were as follows:
   - Setting aside a certain amount of time during the evenings and at weekends when I refuse to do anything connected with school.
   - Trying to come to terms with each individual situation.
   - Talking over stressful situations with my husband/wife/family.
   - Involving myself with my family and my own circle of friends when I am not working.
   - Trying to say "No" to unnecessary demands.
   - Switching off.
   - Trying to bring my feelings and opinions into the open.
   - Admitting my limits more easily than when I first became a teacher.
   - Accepting the problem.
   - Talking about it, usually with colleagues at school.

   Ask several teachers to rank these ten items according to the frequency with which they use these techniques. Present your findings and analysis to the class.
5. Observe students at several different grade levels and in a number of different situations to ascertain how children and youth try to control one another at various stages of development. That is, students have to learn to manage one another if they are to get what they need and want. Make a list of the stress-inducing characteristics associated with these forms of social influence and suggest stress reduction strategies.

REFERENCES

Albertson, C. M., & Kagan, D. M. (1987). Occupational stress among teachers. *Journal of Research and Development in Education, 21*(1), 69–75.

Bardo, P. (1979). The pain of teacher burnout: A case history. *Phi Delta Kappan, 61*(4) 252–254.

Beck, A. (1970). Cognitive therapy: Nature and relations to behavior therapy. *Behavior Therapy, 1,* 184–200.

Bensky, J. M., Shaw, S. F., Gouse, A., Bates, H., Dixon, B., & Beane, W. (1980). Public Law 94-142 and stress: A problem for educators. *Exceptional Children, 47,* 24–29.

Bloch, A. M. (1977). The battered teacher. *Today's Education, 66*(March–April), 58–62.

Cartledge, G., & Milburn, J. (1978). The case for teaching social skills in the classroom: A review. *Review of Educational Research, 48,* 133–156.

Cedoline, A. J. (1982). *Job burnout in public education: Symptoms, causes, and survival skills.* New York: Teachers College, Columbia University.

Cichon, D. J., & Koff, R. H. (1980). Stress and teaching. *NASSP Bulletin, 64*(34), 91–104.

Cousins, N. (1979). *Anatomy of an illness as perceived by the patient: Reflections on healing and regeneration.* New York: Norton.

Cunningham, W. G. (1983). Teacher burnout— Solutions for the 1980s: A review of the literature. *The Urban Review, 15,* 37–51.

Dedrick, C. V. L., & Raschke, D. B. (1990). *The special educator and job stress*. Washington, DC: National Education Association.

Duke, D. L. (1984). *Teaching: The imperiled profession*. New York: State University of New York Press.

Dunham, J. (1977). Tasks and skills in interprofessional communication and cooperation. *British Journal of Mental Subnormality, 23*(2) 45, 61–69.

Dunham, J. (1984). *Stress in teaching*. New York: Nichols.

Elkind, D. (1980). *The hurried child: Growing up too fast, too soon*. Reading, MA: Addison-Wesley.

Ellis, A. (1973). *Humanistic psychotherapy: The rational emotive approach*. New York: Julian.

Farber, B. A., & Miller, J. (1981). Teacher burnout: A psychoeducational perspective. *Teachers College Record, 83*(2), 235–243.

Forman, S. G. (1982). Stress management for teachers: A cognitive–behavioral program. *Journal of School Psychology, 20*, 180–186.

French, J. R. P., & Caplan, R. D. (1972). Organizational stress and individual strain. In A. J. Marrow (Ed.), *The failure of success* (pp. 30–66). New York: Amacom.

Freudenberger, H. J. (1974). Staff burnout. *Journal of Social Issues, 1*, 159–164.

Gardell, B. (1971). Alienation and mental health in the modern industrial environment. In L. Levi (Ed.), *Society, stress and disease* (pp. 148–180). Oxford: Oxford University Press.

Gazda, G. (1973). *Human relations development: A manual for educators*. Boston: Allyn & Bacon.

Glasser, W. (1986). *Control theory in the classroom*. New York: Harper & Row.

Gold, Y. (1988). Recognizing and coping with academic burnout. *Contemporary Education, 59*(3), 142–145.

Goldberger, L., & Breznitz, S. (1982). *Handbook of stress: Theoretical and clinical aspects*. New York: Free Press.

Greenberg, S. F. (1984). *Stress and the teaching profession*. Baltimore: Paul H. Brooks.

Holt, P., Fine, M. J., & Tollefson, N. (1987). Mediating stress: Survival of the hardy. *Psychology in the Schools, 24*, 51–58.

Humphrey, J. M., & Humphrey, J. H. (1986). *Coping with stress in teaching*. New York: AMS.

Iwanicki, E. F. (1983). Toward understanding and alleviating teacher burnout. *Theory into Practice, 22*(1), 27–32.

Jenkins, S., & Calhoun, J. F. (1991). Teacher stress: Issues and intervention. *Psychology in the Schools, 28*(1), 60–70.

Johnson, D. W. (1972). *Reaching out*. Upper Saddle River, NJ: Prentice-Hall.

Joyce, B., & Weil, M. (1980). *Models of teaching* (2nd ed.). Upper Saddle River, NJ: Prentice-Hall.

Kalker, P. (1984). Teacher stress and burnout: Causes and coping strategies. *Contemporary Education, 56*(1), 16–19.

Kyriacou, C. (1987). Teacher stress and burnout: An international review. *Educational Research, 29*, 146–150.

Lazarus, R. S. (1976). *Patterns of adjustment*. New York: McGraw-Hill.

Lipsky, M. (1980). *Street level bureaucracy: Dilemmas of the individual in public services*. New York: Russel Sage Foundation.

Lortie, D. C. (1975). *Schoolteacher: A sociological study*. Chicago: University of Chicago Press.

Martinez, J. G. R. (1989). Cooling off before burning out. *Academic Therapy, 24*(3), 271–284.

Maslach, C., & Pines, A. (1977). The burn-out syndrome in the day care setting. *Child Care Quarterly, 6*, 100–113.

Meichenbaum, D. H. (1977). *Cognitive–behavior modifications: An integrative approach*. New York: Plenum.

Miller, C. (1979). *Dealing with stress: A challenge for educators*. Bloomington, IN: Phi Delta Kappa.

Milstein, M. M., Golaszewski, T. J., & Duquette, R. D. (1984). Organizationally based stress: What bothers teachers. *Journal of Educational Research, 77*(5), 293–297.

Payne, R. L., & Pugh, D. S. (1971). Organizations as psychological environments. In P. H. Warr

(Ed.), *Psychology at work* (pp. 347–402). Harmondsworth, England: Penguin.

Raschke, D. B., Dedrick, C. V., Strathe, M. I., & Hawkes, R. R. (1985). Teacher stress: The elementary teacher's perspective. *The Elementary School Journal, 85*(4), 559–564.

Saville, A. (1988). Stress squashers. *National Association of Secondary School Principals Bulletin, 72*(510), 71.

Schwab, R. L., Jackson, S. E., & Schuler, R. S. (1986). Educator burnout: Sources and consequences. *Educational Research Quarterly, 10,* 14–30.

Selye, H. (1976). *The stress of life.* New York: McGraw-Hill.

Slife, B. D. (1988). Coping strategies for teachers. *Academic Therapy, 24*(1), 9–19.

Sparks, D. C. (1979). A biased look at teacher job satisfaction. *The Clearinghouse, 52,* 447–449.

Swick, K. J. (1987). *Student stress: A classroom management system.* Washington, DC: National Education Association.

Swick, K. J., & Hanley, P. E. (1980). *Stress and the classroom teacher.* Washington, DC: National Education Association.

Truch, S. (1980). *Teacher burnout and what to do about it.* Novato, CA: Academic Therapy Publications.

Warshaw, L. J. (1979). *Managing stress.* Reading, MA: Addison-Wesley.

Wayson, W., et al. [Phi Delta Kappa Commission]. (1981). *Handbook for developing schools with good discipline.* Bloomington, IN: Phi Delta Kappa.

Woolfolk, R. L., & Richardson, F. C. (1978). *Stress, sanity, and survival.* New York: Signet by New American Library.

Observation Checklists for Three Management Functions

CONTENT MANAGEMENT

Observation of Content Management

_____   _____
(Observer)   (Time)

_____   _____
(Class)   (Date)

_____   _____
(Teacher)   (Grade Level)

_____
(Schoolwide discipline plan)

_____
(Rules taught, posted, consequences)

_____
(Description of lesson: Activities and size of group, transitions)

Seating arrangement appropriate
____Yes ____No   Circle(s), semi-circles, rows and columns, rectangles

Movement Management

___Yes ___No   1. Thrusts (bursts into activity without warning and gives directions for another activity)
                        If yes, describe any management problems that arose _____

___Yes ___No   2. Dangles (leaves one activity dangling in midair, begins another, returns to the first)
                        If yes, describe any management problems that arose _____

___Yes ___No   3. Truncations (leaves one activity, goes to another, never returns to the first)
                        If yes, describe any management problems that arose _____

___Yes ___No   4. Flip flop (terminates an activity, begins a second, surprises with a flashback
                        to the first)
                        If yes, describe any management problems that arose _____

___Yes ___No   5. Overdwelling (spending too much time on directions, explanations, details to
                        the exclusion of the main idea, prolonged discourse expressing displeasure)
                        If yes, describe any management problems that arose _____

___Yes ___No   6. Fragmentation (breaking down into an infinite number of parts an activity that
                        does not require such discrete units)
                        If yes, describe any management problems that arose _____

Group focus

___Yes ___No   7. Group format (everyone shares knowledge and skills/teacher expectations)
                        If yes, describe any management problems that arose _____

___Yes ___No   8. Degree of accountability (creates a sense that everyone is responsible for
                        what happens in the group)
                        If yes, describe any management problems that arose _____

Avoidance of Satiation

___Yes ___No   9. Progress (restructure the program to promote movement forward)
If yes, describe any management problems that arose _____

___Yes ___No 10. Variety (when interest is waning)
If yes, describe any management problems that arose _____

___Yes ___No 11. Challenge (appropriate to each student)
If yes, describe any management problems that arose _____

___Yes ___No 12. Communicating expectations
___lesson objectives
___be on time and have materials ready
___standards for performance
___equal opportunity to participate

Teacher Expectations
(Ysseldyke & Christenson, 1993–1994)

___Yes ___No   1. Goal of lesson was clear to all students and all were told what was to be learned (not what was to be done).
Evidence _____

___Yes ___No   2. Teacher provided opportunities for all students to respond actively.
Evidence _____

___Yes ___No   3. Teacher provided equal opportunities for all students to respond.
Evidence _____

___Yes ___No   4. Teacher provided prompts and cues for all students to respond successfully.
Evidence _____

___Yes ___No   5. Student knows she/he is held accountable for work.
Evidence _____

___Yes ___No   6. Amount of work to be done is clearly communicated to all students.
Evidence _____

___Yes ___No   7. Accuracy of work to be done is clearly communicated to all students.
Evidence _____

___Yes ___No   8. Expectations are realistic and high for amount and accuracy of work (evidence that expectations are based on students' current level of performance)
Evidence _____

___Yes ___No   9. Teacher checked students' understanding of expectations for work to be completed.
Evidence _____

___Yes ___No 10. Teacher checked students' understanding of how mastery will be demonstrated.
Evidence _____

*Ysseldyke, J., & Christenson, S. (1993–1994). *The instructional environment system—II: A system to identify a student's instructional needs.* Longmont, CO: Sopris West.

___Yes   ___No   11. Students know the consequences of not achieving expected standards of performance.
                  Evidence _____

___Yes   ___No   12. Expectations for use of time in the classroom are clear.
                  Evidence _____

Teaching Structure

___Yes   ___No   1. Daily Review
                  If yes, describe any management problems that arose _____

___Yes   ___No   2. Presentation
                  If yes, describe any management problems that arose _____

___Yes   ___No   3. Seatwork
                  If yes, describe any management problems that arose _____

___Yes   ___No   4. Homework
                  If yes, describe any management problems that arose _____

___Yes   ___No   5. Special Review
                  If yes, describe any management problems that arose _____

___Yes   ___No   6. Discussion
                  If yes, describe any management problems that arose _____

___Yes   ___No   7. Projects
                  If yes, describe any management problems that arose _____

Problem Solving

___Yes   ___No   1. Off task
                  If yes, describe any management problems that arose _____

___Yes   ___No   2. Talking without permission (during lectures, during class, failing to raise hand)
                  If yes, describe any management problems that arose _____

___Yes   ___No   3. Poor listening and not following directions
                  If yes, describe any management problems that arose _____

___Yes   ___No   4. Not bringing materials to class
                  If yes, describe any management problems that arose _____

___Yes   ___No   5. Late or incomplete assignments
                  If yes, describe any management problems that arose _____

___Yes   ___No   6. Tardiness
                  If yes, describe any management problems that arose _____

___Yes   ___No   7. Failure to be motivated
                  If yes, describe any management problems that arose _____

___Yes   ___No   8. Cheating
                  If yes, describe any management problems that arose _____

___Yes   ___No   9. Test anxiety
                  If yes, describe any management problems that arose _____

CONDUCT MANAGEMENT

Statement of the Rules

1. Rules are stated as desired behaviors or actions.
2. Classroom rules are confined to five or six and are taught and modeled by the teacher.
3. Special activity procedures, as differentiated from rules, are clearly specified, demonstrated, and practiced.
4. Rules are publicly displayed for easy reference.
5. Rules are periodically reviewed, and appropriate behaviors are practiced.

Application of the Rules

6. Appropriate and inappropriate behavior can be easily detected and dealt with immediately.
7. Techniques for discipline are applied consistently to all students.
8. Application of the stated rules minimized distractions or disruptions that interfere with student academic progress.
9. Students do not disobey the rules simply to get attention.
10. The frequency and duration of disciplinary incidents are well within teacher expectations.
11. Classroom rules are consistent with or identical to the code of conduct for the building.
12. Disciplinary practices are clearly linked to the student's inappropriate behavior.

Consequences for Appropriate and Inappropriate Behavior

13. Appropriate student behavior is rewarded in a variety of ways and in ways that are appealing to students.
14. Occasional checks are made to be sure rewards continue to be attractive incentives.
15. Negative consequences are explicitly stated and consistently applied.
16. Warnings and threats are not substituted for the administration of logical and/or negative consequences.
17. Occasional checks are made to ascertain the deterrent value of penalties.
18. Administration of the reward and penalty system does not take an inordinate amount of time.
19. A severe clause is used to deal with extreme and persistent disciplinary incidents.

Provisions for Cooperation

20. Students are developmentally equipped to meet the standards of conduct.
21. Students are knowledgeable about rewards for desired behavior and know what to do to get them.

22. Parents are provided a written copy of the rules and the consequences for lack of adherence to them.
23. Parents are periodically informed about their child's citizenship/character development.
24. The principal has been given an opportunity to review and suggest revisions of the classroom management plan.
25. The principal has agreed to participate in the use of predetermined positive and negative consequences.
26. Colleagues who are directly affected by the management plan have been apprised of the particulars and have been given an opportunity to suggest changes.
27. Colleagues who have been asked to participate in the administration of selected consequences approve of these procedures and their professional involvement.

COVENANT MANAGEMENT

Climate Characteristics

1. Class members are invited to participate in goal setting.
2. Freedoms are expressed within explicitly stated and consistently enforced limits.
3. Students choose from a wide variety of activities to achieve common goals.
4. Students progress, as much as possible, according to individual interests and abilities.
5. Group cohesiveness and cooperation are stressed over competition.
6. Democratic practices are used to maintain order and secure compliance with reasonable limits.

Relationship Qualities

7. Teacher and students can be direct and honest with one another.
8. All members of the group feel they are valued by the other members.
9. There is a sense of interdependence; common bonds define group expectations.
10. Each person is encouraged to make the most of unique talents and interests.
11. No one individual's needs are met without regard for the needs of others.
12. Faith and trust are built from a sense of community and shared purpose.

Communication Characteristics

13. Conversations are positive, constructive, and aimed at understanding one another's point of view.
14. Blame-free messages, I-messages, are used to convey a teacher's emotional reactions to a student's objectionable behavior.

15. Corrective measures are not accompanied by sarcasm and ridicule.
16. Disciplinary actions are aimed at the situation, not at the student's personality or character.
17. Communications safeguard self-esteem, convey respect, and encourage students to take charge of their lives.
18. Appreciation is expressed as descriptive rather than evaluative praise.
19. Diagnostic and prognostic statements that classify and categorize students are avoided.
20. Economical messages, verbal and nonverbal, are used to deal with minor incidents.

Forms of Assistance

21. "Why?" questions, which evoke defensiveness and deceit, are avoided.
22. The temptation to reassure students or offer them solutions to their problems is resisted.
23. Problem-solving methods are used to place power in the hands of students and increase their sense of self-efficacy.
24. Reflective listening is substituted for giving advice so students can formulate solutions to their problems.
25. Class meetings are used to provide students an opportunity to examine the ideas and feelings that influence value judgments and decisions as well as the ways chosen to fulfill them.
26. Building confidence and fostering involvement are viewed as primary and enabling objectives.
27. Lesson content and activities help students link school and life outside of school.
28. Duties and responsibilities are delegated in such a way that all students succeed and become fully functioning members of the class.

Building a Classroom Management Plan

AN AUTHORITATIVE ORIENTATION

Step 1: State beliefs and expectations by using Canter's four commitments, Rosemond's voice of authority, York's ten beliefs, and Dobson's teaching respect and responsibility.

_____

_____

_____

_____

Step 2: Make a list of:

Non-Assertive Behaviors (to avoid)	Hostile Behaviors (to avoid)	Assertive Behaviors (to cultivate)
_____	_____	_____
_____	_____	_____
_____	_____	_____

Step 3: State rules that govern responsible conduct; that is, conduct that enables us to get work done and get along with one another.

1._____

_____

(Note: Use this format for each additional rule)

Specify behavior expectations covered by this rule.

1. _____
1.1 _____
1.2 _____
1.3 _____
1.4 _____

Step 4: State unacceptable requests that you find it difficult to refuse:

1._____
2._____
3._____
4._____

State the assertive way you will handle each of these requests.

1._____
2._____
3._____
4._____

Step 5: Identify key activities/methods used to deliver instruction and specify the directions students need to follow when participating responsibly in these activities.

Activity

1._____

_____

(Note: Use this format for each additional activity)

Directions

1.1 _____
1.2 _____
1.3 _____
1.4 _____

Step 6: Select several low-profile techniques you will use to prevent problems.

_____

_____

_____

_____

Identify situations where these techniques may be most appropriate.

_____

_____

_____

_____

Step 7: Select a hierarchy of consequences that will be applied when students disobey the rules.

Least Severe _____

_____

_____

_____

_____

Most Severe _____

Select severe consequences that will be used when a student's behavior is absolutely intolerable and/or is not well-managed by the regular plan.

Consequences that can be administered without cooperation of others:

_____

_____

Consequences that require assistance:

_____

_____

Step 8: Identify common side tracking tactics students use to avoid negative consequences or obedience.

_____

_____

_____

Identify assertive communication techniques to counteract these student tactics.

_____

_____

_____

_____

Step 9: Select consequences that will be used to support good behavior; that is, to reinforce behavior that helps us get work done and get along well with one another.

Social (Verbal/Nonverbal)	Written/Spoken	Public/Private
_____	_____	_____
_____	_____	_____
_____	_____	_____
Activities and Privileges	Individual	Classwide
_____	_____	_____
_____	_____	_____
_____	_____	_____
Tangible (if any)	Individual	Classwide
_____	_____	_____
_____	_____	_____
_____	_____	_____
Token (if any)	Individual	Classwide
_____	_____	_____
_____	_____	_____
_____	_____	_____

Step 10: Select non-contingent (quality-of-life) reinforcers that will be made contingent.

_____   _____
_____   _____
_____   _____

Step 11: Identify people and roles essential to the implementation of your plan.

Person _____   Role _____
Person _____   Role _____
Person _____   Role _____

Step 12: Identify ways to document behavior to evaluate the effectiveness of your plan.

_____   _____
_____   _____
_____   _____

Resources

Canter, L., & Canter, M. (1976). *Assertive discipline: A take-charge approach for today's educator* (Chaps. 1 and 2). Los Angeles: Lee Canter & Associates.

Dobson, J. (1970). *Dare to discipline* (Chap. 1). Wheaton, IL: Tyndale House.

Rosemond, J. (1989). *Six-point plan for raising happy, healthy children* (Point 2). Kansas City, MO: Andrews & McMeel.

York, P., York, D., & Wachtel, T. (1982). *Toughlove* (Part 2). New York: Doubleday.

A DEMOCRATIC ORIENTATION

Step 1: State beliefs and expectations by drawing upon Dreikurs's "Ground Rules for a Democratic Classroom" and "Effective Disciplinary Procedures," or Glenn and Nelsen's "Guidelines for Developing Self-Reliance."

_____

_____

_____

_____

Step 2: Make a list of your management behaviors (use Nelsen's behavior categories to identify examples).

Object: Done to (excessive control) behaviors (e.g., demanding, punishing, lecturing)	Recipient: Done for behaviors (excessive pressure) (e.g., rescuing, indulging, overprotecting)	Asset: Done with behaviors (firmness with dignity and respect) (e.g., involving, inviting, encouraging)
1. _____	1. _____	1. _____
2. _____	2. _____	2. _____
3. _____	3. _____	3. _____

Step 3: Engage students in a discussion to identify the conditions that make school a good place to be.

Identify the behaviors of teachers and students that contribute to these conditions, and formulate rules to state these as behavior expectations.

1. _____   1._____

2. _____   1.1 _____

3. _____   1.2 _____

4. _____   1.3 _____

5. _____   1.4 _____

(NOTE: Use this format for each additional rule)   Rule_____

_____

Step 4: State unacceptable requests you find it difficult to refuse.

State the I-messages you will use to handle these requests.

1. _____   1._____

2. _____   2._____

3. _____   3._____

4. _____   4._____

Step 5: Identify key activities/methods used to deliver instruction, and specify the directions students need to follow when participating responsibly in these activities.

Activity

1. _____

_____

(NOTE: Use this format for each additional activity)

Directions

1.1 _____

1.2 _____

1.3 _____

1.4 _____

Step 6: Select several low-profile techniques you will use to prevent problems.

1. _____
2. _____
3. _____
4. _____

Identify situations where these techniques may be most appropriate.

1. _____
2. _____
3. _____
4. _____

Step 7: Select a behavior manifestation for each of the four mistaken goals (Dreikurs) that would be most troublesome for you.

1. _____
2. _____
3. _____
4. _____

Identify natural and/or logical consequences (use Nelsen's "Three R's for Logical Consequences") for each mistaken goal.

1. _____
2. _____
3. _____
4. _____

Step 8: Identify specific teacher behaviors that undermine the development of responsible children (use Glenn and Nelsen's "Five Barriers").

1. _____
2. _____
3. _____
4. _____
5. _____

Identify specific teacher behaviors that affirm and validate responsible behaviors (use Glenn and Nelsen's "Five Builders").

1. _____
2. _____
3. _____
4. _____
5. _____

Step 9: Identify ways to win cooperation through encouragement (use Gordon's active/reflective listening; Nelsen's "Four Steps for Winning Cooperation" and "The Three R's of Recovery," or Dinkmeyer and Losoncy's, "Differences Between Praise and Encouragement."

_____

_____

_____

_____

Step 10: Demonstrate the way to use a class meeting to improve the quality of life and decision-making in the classroom. (Employ the "define, personalize, and challenge" format for applying Glasser's group arrangement and process guidelines, and the Dinkmeyer and Losoncy's, group leadership skills for facilitating these meetings.)

_____

_____

_____

_____

Step 11: Identify people and roles/functions essential to the implementation of your plan.

Person_____   Role/Functions _____

Person_____   _____

                                 Role/Functions _____

                                 _____

Step 12: Identify ways to evaluate the effectiveness of your plan.

_____

_____

_____

_____

Resources

Dinkmeyer, D., & Losoncy, L. E. (1980). *The encouragement book: Becoming a positive person.* Upper Saddle River, NJ: Prentice-Hall.

Dreikurs, R., Grunwald, B. B., & Pepper, F. C. (1982). *Maintaining sanity in the classroom: Classroom management techniques* (2nd ed.). New York: Harper & Row.

Glasser, W. (1969). *Schools without failure* (Chaps. 10–12). New York: Harper & Row.

Glenn, H. S., & Nelsen, J. (1989). *Raising self-reliant children in a self-indulgent world.* Rocklin, CA: Prima Publishing & Communications.

Gordon, T. (1974). *Teacher effectiveness training.* New York: McKay.

Nelsen, J. (1987). *Positive discipline.* New York: Ballantine Books.

Model Solutions to Three Prototypic Disciplinary Problems

REFLECTING ON CONDUCT MANAGEMENT

Problem

Bill and Mark are inseparable inside and outside of school. Ms. Wenzel is not surprised when they ask for permission to be seated next to one another. Although another teacher who has both boys in class has expressed her consternation about their outrageous behavior, Ms. Wenzel, not wishing to be unduly influenced by her colleague, agrees to give them a chance to prove that they can be responsible while seated in adjoining desks. The boys prove worthy of her trust for several days. But following a period of exemplary behavior, they begin to whisper back and forth and persist in this behavior after being asked to be quiet on numerous occasions. On this particular day, Ms. Wenzel loses her patience and angrily tells the boys to shut up or get out. Bill stands up at his desk, glaring belligerently at the teacher, and storms across the room. He deposits his textbook in the wastebasket as he exits through the back door. Mark remains at his desk and stares out the window for the remainder of the class period. What should Ms. Wenzel do now?

Solution

This problem originated in the ineffective use of legitimate power and should be dealt with as a conduct management problem. Ms. Wenzel does have the right to determine where students are seated in the classroom, a right to which Bill and Mark acceded when they sought her permission to take adjoining seats. She also has the responsibility to set standards for social and work relationships in the classroom. Unfortunately, Ms. Wenzel acted as though the boys could be trusted to behave properly, despite information to the contrary, and permitted them to sit next to one another on a noncontingent basis. We do not have a clue to her motives, but her behavior might be traced to a nonassertive response style.

Had Ms. Wenzel been assertive, a leadership stance that is suggested by the circumstances, she would have at a minimum instituted several preventive management measures. She would have told Bill and Mark that they could sit next to one another if they agreed to certain terms. The terms would have been expressed as specific behaviors: "You may sit next to one another on two conditions. First, you begin work promptly and continue without reminders during independent study time, and second, you confine your socializing with one another to the period before class begins and after the bell rings." An affirmative response to these two conditions would have served as a contractual agreement.

Ms. Wenzel would have used supportive management techniques to help the two boys honor their agreement. At first, these would have consisted of proximity control and generous use of positive reinforcement for on-task behavior. She would not have assumed that they could responsibly manage their behavior; without some external forms of support, the temptations to socialize are too great for such close friends. She could have created incentives to behave appropriately to counterbalance tendencies to disregard the rules and engage in inappropriate behavior.

Finally, Ms. Wenzel would not have tolerated unacceptable behavior to the point of becoming angry. Her hostile response followed a series of requests for appropriate behavior, requests that were not accompanied by a statement of the consequences for failure to comply with the rules. Had Ms. Wenzel stated what would happen if the boys persisted in misbehaving, her corrective management decisions might have saved the day. Prompt and decisive action might have reinstated the conditions of the original contract, taught the boys the importance of honoring contractual obligations, and preserved the good feelings that accompanied the initial decision to allow them to sit together.

But what should Ms. Wenzel do now? At a minimum, she should send a student to the office to notify the principal of the incident. School personnel are responsible for knowing the whereabouts of students during school hours. Mark would be a good candidate for this errand because he would most likely want to extricate himself from the present situation. Going to the office to report Bill's absence from the class would also be a small mark of cooperation. Since it is quite likely that Bill is just down the hall, not really knowing what to do or where to go, Mark is also a prime candidate for securing his cooperation. Mark should be told that in the event he sees Bill, he should tell Bill to go to the office and remain there until he has spoken with the principal. Mark should be instructed to return after notifying the principal or seeing to it that Bill does so, because Ms. Wenzel needs to know what has transpired.

In a well-managed school, the principal will have a procedure for handling teacher–student flare-ups. In this instance, the principal might convene the parties after school and withdraw if the parties believe that they can settle the matter. The principal may remain to arbitrate a solution, if that is deemed necessary.

If Bill cannot be found in the building or on the grounds, his parents should be notified. They should be asked to call the school or a home number of a school official when Bill does arrive at home. Bill's parents should be told to have Bill report to the principal's office before going to classes the next day. Ms. Wenzel and the principal will have had a chance to discuss next steps.

We see in this episode how a teacher lost an opportunity to teach two young men respect for authority and respect for themselves. They did not learn that a privilege is accompanied by responsibility. The boys' and the teacher's failure to act responsibly led to behaviors that discredited all parties. The teacher can hardly be respected for her part in maintaining control of the class and for her hostile behavior. The boys can hardly respect themselves for violating a trust and provoking the teacher's angry outburst. This disciplinary problem might have been inevitable; however, the final dramatic scene would not have been played out had the teacher used legitimate power and the principles and practices associated with the conduct management function.

REFLECTING ON COVENANT MANAGEMENT

Problem

Marsha is a loner. Each day she enters Ms. Halster's classroom by herself and goes directly to her desk. Social conversations take place all around her, but she is never included. Although she seems to be unobtrusively attentive, she never makes an effort to join these conversations. When assigned to small-group projects, Marsha occasionally shares an idea or an experience, but her contributions are frequently unrelated to the topic and are seldom acknowledged by other group members. Despite the indifference of her peers and her modest success in class, Marsha does not appear to bear any ill will toward her peers, but she does show signs of becoming more and more disinterested in the class. She often daydreams during independent study, frequently seems distant when spoken to, and appears to be content to get by with a minimum amount of work. What should Ms. Halster do now?

Solution

We do not know why Marsha is a loner, but we do know that loneliness is a relationship problem. We also know that relationship problems are best solved with a covenant management model. This choice of models suggests the use of the principles and practices advocated by Glasser, Gordon, Dreikurs, and Nelsen. Glasser believes that some students are alienated and lonely because they do not fare well in a school system that operates according to certainty and measurement principles. Marsha's growing disinterest in school might be attributed to a lack of encouragement for her modest contributions and what appears to be a total disregard for her social and belonging needs. Dreikurs tells us about the faulty logic that drives the behavior of students who cannot find a place for themselves. Marsha's display of inadequacy can be explained by her discouragement.

Marsha needs to experience the encouragement of a person who cares. She needs a role-before-goal teacher who starts by helping her feel like a worthwhile human being. Marsha's discouragement can be ameliorated by giving her a chance to succeed at some small but publicly visible tasks. Every teacher who has attractive power has ways of conferring status on students by giving them responsible roles in the classroom and then making something of their contributions. Preventing Marsha from sinking deeper into discouragement can be achieved through carefully orchestrated success experiences, particularly ones that draw her into the classroom group and give her a sense of social significance.

Marsha may make halting progress; she may even resist doing some things because they draw too much attention to her. But Ms. Halster should not become discouraged. Reflective listening skills can be used to help Marsha achieve insights and become self-directing. Encouragement is another supportive management technique that can be used to help Marsha appreciate her accomplishments and see herself as a lovable, worthwhile human being.

Glasser's problem-solving strategy could be used as a corrective management solution. Making friends with Marsha, using the previously mentioned preventive and supportive management techniques, would be a good starting point. Recall that a role-oriented student personalizes everything. Marsha must feel differently about herself before she can begin to act differently; behavior starts inside. Having made friends with Marsha and having lessened her sense of discouragement and distrust, Ms. Halster can ask her, "Marsha, what is it you want to happen at school?" or "Marsha, how could things be better for you at school?" And later, "Is what you are doing getting you what you want?" If not, "Are there some better ways?" The questions guide a process that helps Marsha use her full powers for making a difference in her life. She can begin to use Ms. Halster's friendship and encouragement as sources of strength, the personal insights as the tools for changing behavior, and the plans as a means to acquire the knowledge and skills that lead to a more personally fulfilling life.

Marsha provides Ms. Halster a chance to use the personal ideals that drew her to teaching and the opportunity to employ interpersonal relationship skills that enrich the lives of children. All three management approaches—preventive, supportive, and corrective—can be used to forge a plan that can make a profound difference in the lives of students who only want what Glasser has said all students want: to be worthwhile to themselves and to others.

REFLECTING ON CONTENT MANAGEMENT
Problem

Roberta is a very academically able and socially popular student. She is able to complete assigned work in about half the allotted time and is disposed to use the remaining time to socialize with students who have not completed their work. Mr. Anderson decides to control this disposition by giving Roberta additional questions to answer or problems to solve. Initially, Roberta views the additional work as a competitive challenge. She tries to finish her work before other members of the class complete the common assignment, but generally she is not able to do so. After several weeks of this more academically rigorous regimen, Roberta lodges a protest about the extra work by slamming her book to the floor and angrily complaining about the unfair treatment. After all, she asserts, "Why should I have to do more work than everyone else just because I get busy and do the work quickly?" What should Mr. Anderson do now?

Solution

Some preventive management techniques do not work because the teacher does not involve the student in choosing the method or because the teacher neglects to offer the student a convincing rationale for a particular decision. Mr. Anderson obviously viewed the problem from a content management perspective, but he used legitimate power to curtail Roberta's gregarious tendencies. Had he relied on expert power, he might have worked with Roberta to find mutually agreeable outlets for her academic interests and talents.

Additional practice with similar materials might be a suitable alternative in some areas of the curriculum; enrichment materials that go well beyond common class assignments might be the arrangement in other areas of the school program. Or, Roberta might be given some tutorial responsibilities or an opportunity to undertake an independent project. Complete and accurate assignments would be rewarded with time to tutor or to pursue the independent project.

Mr. Anderson might have salvaged his legitimate power–based decision had his preventive management technique been accompanied by some supportive management measures. Had he introduced some ways to recognize Roberta's accomplishments—an occasional report to the class, a special note to her parents, or a specially arranged time to share her learnings with him—she may have been less likely to feel put upon for being a good worker.

Roberta's academic aptitude and esteemed status in the class increase the corrective management options. Beyond planning concrete proposals, such as tutoring and independent projects, Mr. Anderson should be looking for ways to help Roberta maximize her talents while becoming increasingly less dependent on the teacher and peers for task-sustaining supports. Here is a student who should be helped to find intrinsically satisfying ways to express her interests and abilities. She should be given greater latitude to manage her own affairs.

Correcting the problem should be aimed at relinquishing controls and giving Roberta more freedom to be a responsible decision maker. Expert power should be used to create enough structure, in the way of materials, activities, and supervision, to help Roberta select goals, devise ways to achieve these goals, develop self-monitoring progress procedures, and choose ways to report her results. The tangible products of her work and the pride that accompanies accomplishment will be proximate sources of motivation. The ability to think and work independently and to achieve a broad-gauged, meaningful grasp of ideas will be ultimate sources of motivation. Such intrinsically motivated students are seldom disciplinary problems.

Name Index

Abrahams, R. D., 93
Achenbach, T. M., 166
Adler, C. R., 292
Aiello, J. R., 94
Aitken, J. L., 8
Albert, L., 62
Albertson, C. M., 335
Alleman-Brooks, J., 153, 154
Anderson, L., 100, 153, 154
Apple, M. W., 311

Baker, K., 289
Bandura, A., 49
Bany, M. A., 222, 251
Bardo, P., 337
Barnhart, C. L., 32
Baron, R. M., 92
Bartlett, L., 312
Bates, H., 340
Batsche, G. M., 6, 7, 33, 35, 41, 42
Beane, W., 340
Beck, A., 346

Becker, W. C., 63
Bell, L. C., 271
Bennett, N., 49
Bensky, J. M., 340
Bernard, M. E., 93
Berne, E., 188
Berry, K., 306
Black, A., 49
Bloch, A. M., 336
Bloom, B. S., 159
Blundell, D., 49
Bolton, R., 276
Brandt, R., 292
Brantlinger, E., 75
Brattesani, K. A., 135
Breznitz, S., 349
Bridges, E., 5
Brophy, J. E., 5, 134, 135
Brown, S. D., 91
Brubaker, N., 153, 154
Bruner, J., 139
Burbules, N. C., 264

Subject Index